ORTHODOXY ON THE LINE

NORTH AMERICAN RELIGIONS

Series Editors: Tracy Fessenden (Arizona State University), Laura Levitt (Temple University), and David Harrington Watt (Haverford College).

Since its inception, the North American Religions book series has steadily disseminated gracefully written, pathbreaking explorations of religion in North America. Books in the series move among the discourses of ethnographic, textual, and historical analysis and across a range of topics, including sound, story, food, nature, healing, crime, and pilgrimage. In so doing they bring religion into view as a style and form of belonging, a set of tools for living with and in relations of power, a mode of cultural production and reproduction, and a vast repertory of the imagination. Whatever their focus, books in the series remain attentive to the shifting and contingent ways in which religious phenomena are named, organized, and contested. They bring fluency in the best of contemporary theoretical and historical scholarship to bear on the study of religion in North America. The series focuses primarily, but not exclusively, on religion in the United States in the twentieth and twenty-first centuries.

Books in the series

The Notorious Elizabeth Tuttle: Marriage, Murder, and Madness in the Family of Jonathan Edwards
Ava Chamberlain

Crossing the Water and Keeping the Faith: Haitian Religion in Miami
Terry Rey and Alex Stepick

Religion Out Loud: Religious Sound, Public Space, and American Pluralism
Isaac Weiner

Walking Where Jesus Walked: American Christians and Holy Land Pilgrimage
Hillary Kaell

Border Medicine: A Transcultural History of Mexican American Curanderismo
Brett Hendrickson

Suffer the Little Children: Uses of the Past in Jewish and African American Children's Literature
Jodi Eichler-Levine

Playing for God: Evangelical Women and the Unintended Consequences of Sports Ministry
Annie Blazer

Religion in the Kitchen: Cooking, Talking, and the Making of Black Atlantic Traditions
Elizabeth Pérez

Spirituality and the State: Managing Nature and Experience in America's National Parks
Kerry Mitchell

The Production of American Religious Freedom
Finbarr Curtis

Ralph Ellison's Invisible Theology
M. Cooper Harriss

Shout to the Lord: Making Worship Music in Evangelical America
Ari Y. Kelman

Religion, Law, USA
Edited by Joshua Dubler and Isaac Weiner

Jews on the Frontier: Religion and Mobility in Nineteenth-Century America
Shari Rabin

Lifeblood of the Parish: Men and Catholic Devotion in Williamsburg, Brooklyn
Alyssa Maldonado-Estrada

When the Medium Was the Mission: The Atlantic Telegraph and the Religious Origins of Network Culture
Jenna Supp-Montgomerie

The Course of God's Providence: Religion, Health, and the Body in Early America
Philippa Koch

Religion and US Empire: Critical New Histories
Edited by Tisa Wenger and Sylvester A. Johnson

Fear in Our Hearts: What Islamophobia Tells Us about America
Caleb Iyer Elfenbein

Beyond the Synagogue: Jewish Nostalgia as Religious Practice
Rachel B. Gross

Old Canaan in a New World: Native Americans and the Lost Tribes of Israel
Elizabeth Fenton

Vernacular Religion: Collected Essays of Leonard Primiano
Edited by Deborah Dash Moore

Muslims on the Margins: Creating Queer Religious Community in North America
Katrina Daly Thompson

The Church of the Dead: The Epidemic of 1576 and the Birth of Christianity in the Americas
Jennifer Scheper Hughes

Jewish Sunday Schools: Teaching Religion in Nineteenth-Century America
Laura Yares

From Dust They Came: Government Camps and the Religion of Reform in New Deal California
Jonathan H. Ebel

Christian Imperial Feminism: White Protestant Women and The Consecration of Empire
Gale L. Kenny

Without a Prayer: Religion and Race in New York City Public Schools
Leslie Beth Ribovich

Falling in Love with Nature: The Values of Latinx Catholic Environmentalism
Amanda J. Baugh

The Church of Stop Shopping and Religious Activism: Combatting Consumerism and Climate Change through Performance
George González

Martyrs and Migrants: Coptic Christians and the Persecution Politics of US Empire
Candace Lukasik

Orthodoxy on the Line: Russian Orthodox Christians and Labor Migration in the Progressive Era
Aram G. Sarkisian

Orthodoxy on the Line

Russian Orthodox Christians and
Labor Migration in the Progressive Era

Aram G. Sarkisian

NEW YORK UNIVERSITY PRESS
New York

NEW YORK UNIVERSITY PRESS
New York
www.nyupress.org

© 2025 by New York University
All rights reserved

Please contact the Library of Congress for Cataloging-in-Publication data.

ISBN: 9781479833153 (hardback)
ISBN: 9781479833184 (library ebook)
ISBN: 9781479833177 (consumer ebook)

This book is printed on acid-free paper, and its binding materials are chosen for strength and durability. We strive to use environmentally responsible suppliers and materials to the greatest extent possible in publishing our books.

The manufacturer's authorized representative in the EU for product safety is Mare Nostrum Group B.V., Mauritskade 21D, 1091 GC Amsterdam, The Netherlands. Email: gpsr@mare-nostrum.co.uk.

Manufactured in the United States of America

10 9 8 7 6 5 4 3 2 1

Also available as an ebook

For Jeko and Grandma

Archpriest Ioann E. Sviridov (1910–2004)

Matushka Melanya Sviridov (1914–2015)

Love never ends. But as for prophecies, they will come to an end; as for tongues, they will cease; as for knowledge, it will come to an end. For we know only in part, and we prophesy only in part; but when the complete comes, the partial will come to an end.

—1 Corinthians 13:8–10

CONTENTS

Nomenclature	xiii
Introduction: Stories of Remembering	1
PART I: THE VINEYARD	
1. "This Babylon": The Russian Orthodox Immigration Society and Labor Migration	21
2. "My Sadness Is Boundless": The Intimate Worlds of Church Work	52
3. "The Holy Church Is Their Mother": The Aid and Education of Orthodox Youth	83
4. "Let All America See": The Russian-American Army in the Great War	111
PART II: THE TOIL	
5. "Waves of Anarchy": Making Meaning of 1917	137
6. "Under the Cloak of Religion": Heretics, False Priests, and the Making of Independent Orthodox Parishes	161
7. "We Go Fearlessly into the Maw of Death": Mutual Aid and the Influenza Epidemic of 1918	190
8. "These Radicals": Litigating Orthodox Ecclesiology in Red Scare Detroit	213
Epilogue: Stories of Knowing	243
Acknowledgments	257
Notes	263
Index	307
About the Author	317

NOMENCLATURE

All dates have been adjusted to the Gregorian ("new") calendar, which was in civil use in the United States during the period covered in this book. Russia utilized the Julian ("old") calendar until 1918, though the Russian Orthodox Church retained its use, both in Russia and abroad. The difference between the calendars was twelve days until 1901, then thirteen days thereafter. In North America, church correspondence and directives usually included both dates, as did the mastheads of Orthodox periodicals, notated with the Gregorian date listed first (e.g., May 29/16, 1910). For consistency, only the Gregorian date is cited for all documents and publications.

Orthodox Christian clerical ranks include the minor orders of reader and subdeacon, the major orders of deacon and priest (either married or unmarried), and the celibate episcopate. In Russian practice, the episcopal ranks (in ascending order) are bishop, archbishop, metropolitan, and patriarch. All clerical ranks are held by men. Orthodox clerical names follow unique conventions. Monastics receive new names when they are tonsured (the rite of becoming a monastic, which Orthodox teachings consider to be a second baptism) and abandon use of their surnames. In print, monastic names include clerical title and first name and the surname rendered in parentheses. For example, Metropolitan Platon (Rozhdestvensky) was the monastic name of Porfiry Rozhdestvensky. Holding to this convention, I refer to monastics at first mention in each chapter with capitalized ecclesiastical title, monastic name, and parenthetical surname and thereafter refer to them by their first name alone; for example, Bishop Alexander (Nemolovsky) is thereafter Alexander. In contrast, married deacons and priests require no separate naming conventions and are rendered with lower-case ecclesiastical title and their full name, for example, priest Leonid Turkevich.

Financial conversions were rendered using the purchasing power calculator of the MeasuringWorth Foundation. Transliterations utilize

xiii

the Library of Congress system. Most diacritics, however, are omitted. Names are rendered accordingly unless individuals themselves favored particular English spellings (e.g., Alexandrof instead of Alexandrov, Alexander Hotovitzky rather than Aleksandr Khotovitskii). Early twentieth-century transliteration of Slavic languages often rendered *v* sounds as *w* and are retained for consistency when in common use (e.g., Baikowsky instead of Baikovsky, Piotrowsky rather than Piotrovsky). All quoted misspellings and transliteration variances are retained from their original sources, with clarifications as required. Unless specified, all translations are my own.

Introduction

Stories of Remembering

But Zion said, "The LORD has forsaken me,
my Lord has forgotten me."
Can a woman forget her nursing child,
or show no compassion for the child of her womb?
Even these may forget,
yet I will not forget you.
See, I have inscribed you on the palms of my hands;
your walls are continually before me.
—Isaiah 49:14–16

One Sunday in early 1917, a boy took his father's hand and walked the five blocks separating their Southwest Detroit home from Saints Peter and Paul Russian Orthodox Church. Like so many other immigrants from the Carpathian Mountains, Wasil, the boy's father, was drawn to Detroit by the high wages on Henry Ford's assembly line. Vladimir was the eldest of Wasil's four children and his only son. Reaching the church door, where services were under way, Vladimir slipped from Wasil's grasp and passed through the congregation. To their astonishment, Vladimir walked through the royal doors of the icon screen (iconostasis), an entry into the altar reserved for priests and bishops alone, and stood at the altar next to the priest. When Vladimir and his father arrived at home, the boy complained of a stomachache. Two days later, his appendix burst. Vladimir died on Thursday, aged seven years, six months, and twenty-nine days.

Wasil and Anna, his wife, buried their son in a cemetery not far away. His flat gravestone was etched with a three-barred Russian cross and the inscription "Dear Son." He was buried not as Vladimir but as Walter, his "American" name. Vladimir's grave became his presence in their family's life, a symbol of their hopes for an Orthodox boy who never grew up and the American man they never knew. Each Memorial Day, Anna planted flowers. Wasil pushed an American flag into the grass, so certain his son would have donned a uniform. From the grave, they could see the Ford plant where Wasil worked. As the foundries and assembly lines belched smoke over the Rouge River, they prayed for their boy. In time, Wasil and Anna were buried in plots nearby.

Ninety years after Vladimir died, my grandmother still worried about her brother. She was a toddler when he fell ill and had only fleeting, perhaps received memories of his place at the supper table. Now the last from their family, she fretted that Vladimir rested alone and that he would be forgotten. She even considered having him reinterred with their parents. Each spring, she called the cemetery to have his marker raised from beneath the soggy grass and then called her priest to arrange an excursion to bless the grave. As my mother planted the flowers, my grandmother would quietly recall her brother's death: his burst appendix, how young he was, their parents' grief. And then we would plant Vladimir's American flag and pray for his eternal memory.

On one such visit, a scorching summer day when I was home from college, I kept my grandmother company in the air-conditioned car as my mother knelt in the grass with trowel in hand. After a few silent moments, my grandmother turned and asked me if I knew how Vladimir died. I responded that I did. "No," she said, "did I tell you what really happened?" She recalled his final walk to church and his unusual behavior there, details she never mentioned to me before. She described the confusion of the congregation as they watched Vladimir enter the sacred space of the altar as if someone beckoned him inside. She told of their parents' fears when Vladimir's stomachache worsened and how finally they summoned a doctor. "And when the doctor came, do you know what he said to my mother and father?" She glanced at me across the backseat and offered an unusual and angry sigh. "He said that if it had been his son, he would have called a doctor days ago." My grandmother grew quiet and stared out the car window toward her brother's grave, her knees jittering as they did only in frustrating moments. "Can you imagine saying something like that?"

As a scholar of religion, I consider how my grandmother told Vladimir's story. His sudden illness was a small crisis in a young immigrant family that compounded into horrible tragedy. In describing this, she drew from a full century of lived experience as an Orthodox Christian, a life spent living and working within a ten-mile radius of the church where she was baptized. And she took for granted that even as I am not a practicing Eastern Orthodox Christian, hers was a world that I know well, and that I too had internalized the same religious interpretations of his final days, imbued with notions of sacred space and divine judgment that spoke to the very real presence of the Orthodox Church in their community. To her last, my grandmother could walk its cramped streetscapes in her mind, recalling the families, children, and pets who lived in each house, the petty jealousies and antagonisms harbored between neighbors and kin. She described a close-knit world crisscrossed by interconnected networks of friendship and kinship, of schoolyards and alleyways, and of assembly lines and machine shops. These networks included their priest and his family, blurring the sharp contrast between clergy and laity found, say, at the Roman Catholic parish around the corner. Most people there knew Vladimir and their family, seeing them at church when they gathered to worship amid an invisible cloud of witnesses, venerating icons, lighting candles, singing hymns, and keeping a faith carried from rural Russia and Transcarpathia. And because of the internalized orders and hierarchies afforded the sacred space of their wood-framed church, they recognized at once the strangeness of Vladimir striding through the iconostasis. Did someone reach out to catch his arm? Did they whisper among themselves? What did it mean that that they had seen Vladimir enter the holiest of holies on Sunday, and by Thursday he was gone?

And there is what happened as Vladimir lay dying in the wood-framed house a few blocks away, with its framed lithograph icons of Christ and the *Theotokos*, Mary, the Mother and Bearer of God. The doctor's cold doubts of how Anna and Wasil attended to Vladimir's worsening illness reflected prejudices about class, education, and national origin common in Detroit at the dawn of the automotive age. Wasil knew the prickling sense of being watched at a time when his employer, Henry Ford, sent agents from his company's Sociological Department to homes like theirs to gauge the habits, cleanliness, and trustworthiness of foreign-born workers. And when the doctor impugned their care for their son, Wasil and Anna too felt the sting of

4 | INTRODUCTION

cruel assumptions about their intelligence, character, and capacity to be caring parents in a country whose ways, the doctor hinted, they were incapable of understanding. To endure a sudden tragedy meant confronting these dark insecurities about perception, perhaps even to wish to have done more to smooth out one's "unassimilable" edges. When should one ask for help? Should vulnerability and tragedy be laid bare?

This book contains stories of people like Wasil and Anna, labor migrants from the borderlands of the Russian and Austro-Hungarian Empires, and children like Vladimir and my grandmother, those they raised in America. Living within the world's most modern industrial society and working in a labor economy reliant on the immediate availability and replaceability of immigrant workers, people like them needed a dense network of social, spiritual, and material aid to establish themselves in places like Southwest Detroit. Through their small parish in one corner of the growing automotive metropolis, Wasil, Anna, and their family were part of a transnational religious continuum that connected them to other Orthodox parishes throughout the United States and Canada, overseen by an archdiocese that was based on the Upper East Side of Manhattan and that itself held allegiance to the Most Holy Synod of the Russian Orthodox Church in St. Petersburg. Over time, clergy and other church workers also called it "our mission" (*nasha missiia*), the American Church (*amerikanskaia tserkov'*), or American Rus' (*amerikanskaia rus'*), With an influx of migration after the Russian Revolution of 1905, however, many came to call it American Orthodox Rus' (*amerikanskaia pravoslavnaia rus'*), an idealized diasporic community that encouraged people like Wasil and Anna to keep one foot in Holy Orthodox Rus' as they planted the other in the United States. Their religious worlds transcended oceans and borders and included everyone from their fellow congregants to their parish priest and diocesan bishop to Tsar Nicholas II himself. The Russian Orthodox Archdiocese of North America endeavored to provide them aid and support. In its idealized form, however, American Orthodox Rus' was a world established *for* and *by* immigrant Orthodox Christians, clergy and lay, for the benefit of people like Wasil, Anna, and their children, which could be relied on in times of plenty just as much as those of vulnerability, crisis, or tragedy. Yet the church could not be everything to every worker or family. In time, the archdiocese would struggle to maintain the many institutions and endeavors established to support its immigrant flock.

This book came out of a typical historian's curiosity, though also a personal desire to situate families like mine within scholarly narratives from which they long have been absent. In the 1950s, the sociologist Will Herberg established what became a lasting framework for the study of North American religions, that of a "tri-faith" America dominated by Protestants, Catholics, and Jews. Orthodox Christians are neither Catholic nor Protestant, and while often confused with Orthodox Judaism, nor are they Jewish. Herberg himself dismissed Orthodox appeals for inclusion, retorting that one such critic "takes the American scheme of the 'three great faiths' for granted, and merely wants to add his own as fourth."[1] The exclusionary narrowness of this perspective has served to obscure Orthodox Christians in North America beneath clouds of incense, ignoring the unique and critical perspectives they offer across the spectrum of methodological fields and disciplines. I counter that Orthodox Christians have been a people set apart on these shores for historically conditioned, socially significant reasons, and they were in turn overlooked in the academic study of North American religions.

In this book, I place Russian Orthodox Christians like Wasil and Anna in their contexts within the Progressive-era United States—as transnational migrants, workers, family members, and social and political actors. As a project of excavation, this book asserts that their lives have much to tell us about a variety of historical narratives, including those of immigration, labor, and political culture. And it emphasizes that Orthodox Christians on these shores constituted an outsider religious community that aspired for acceptance on its own terms, only for geopolitical circumstance and nativist fervor to thrust them into national debates on immigrant assimilation and national security. They trod a narrow path between the Old World and the New, constructing over time an immigrant church that was as much an imagination of an idealized Russian past as a changing expression of its believers' evolving understandings of their American present and that mitigated anxieties about their futures. What emerges is a reading of Orthodox history in the twentieth-century United States that is both sacred and profane, both structured and chaotic, often contested and sometimes contradictory, and no longer marginalized or overlooked.

Figure 1.1. Masthead, *Russian Orthodox American Messenger*, September 15, 1896.

In 1896, the masthead atop the first issue of the *Russian Orthodox American Messenger* illustrated the missionary ambitions of the Russian Orthodox Church in North America as the twentieth century dawned (fig. 1.1). It depicts two women. One is a young maiden in traditional Slavic dress. The other is Columbia, the female personification of US national identity common to nineteenth-century patriotic imagery. Columbia rests her left hand on a shield with the stars and stripes of the American flag and with her right shakes hands with her Slavic counterpart. With tentative smiles, they gaze into each other's eyes. In the background are symbols of Holy Orthodox Rus': a cupolaed church, a large church bell. From the corner of the frame, Lady Liberty looks on, her crown and torch eclipsing the radiant sun. All suggested that as a new century beckoned, the Russian Orthodox Church envisioned its North American mission as a bridge between working-class immigrant communities and their adopted country.

The Russian Church arrived in North America during the eighteenth century through eastward missionary outreach to the indigenous peoples of Siberia. Carried across the Bering Strait to "Russian America," this mission adapted to serve Russian colonial and commercial interests in its resource-driven fur trade. The Russian Church established a formal Alaskan Mission in 1794. For nearly a century, almost every Orthodox parish in North America was under its ecclesiastical administration and located along the Pacific coast. After the sale of Alaska to the United States in 1867, the mission relocated its administrative center, its consistory, to San Francisco.[2] By the close of the century, the missionary diocese of North America and the Aleutians was becoming something far different from an arm of Russian colonial enterprise. With signs of growth in the Northeast and the shifting of missionary resources in kind, it was evolving into an identity of its own—even as it remained financially and ecclesiastically dependent on Russia. In 1905, the consistory relocated once again to New York City, a demonstration that church leaders perceived future growth in their ministry as coming from transatlantic labor migrants and not tending remnants of Russian mercantile colonialism along the Pacific Rim. In 1907, the Holy Synod raised the missionary diocese to the status of an archdiocese, affording it greater standing and resources.[3]

These developments occurred as the Russian Church was experiencing significant transformations. The 1721 reforms of Tsar Peter the Great eliminated the office of patriarch in favor of the Most Holy Synod, a group of bishops who ruled in concert with a lay Chief Procurator (*ober-prokuror*) appointed by the monarch. After more than 150 years of synodal rule, the Russian Church was changing from the ground up. Increased literacy and the popularization of religious pilgrimage manifested a whirlwind of lay spiritual renewal, with increased emphases on the importance of relics and patronal relationships with saints like the newly glorified monastic hermit Seraphim of Sarov. Monasteries flourished. The charismatic Father John of Kronstadt sparked new expressions of everyday religious devotions based on repentance and deep spirituality. And changing models of lay administration and the revitalization of rural parishes transformed the role of the church in adherents' lives, and vice versa.

Yet there was also increasing clerical upheaval, the result of mounting and uneven power dynamics between the monastic ("black") and married ("white") clergy. This was a problem further complicated by the

8 | INTRODUCTION

dense layers of state bureaucracy that bounded church life in the Russian Empire. Within the tiered rankings of social estates (*soslovie*), the clerical estate kept ecclesiastical power within the same networks of clerical families. And mounting social and political unrest throughout Russia—the growing influence of the antisemitic "Black Hundreds" and violent pogroms, haphazard pushes for industrialization, disregarded calls for democratization, the marginalization and persecution of political dissent, and the paternalistic façade of tsarist benevolence—seeped into church life as well. Many clergy and laity called for a national church council, the last of which had been called in the late seventeenth century, which they hoped would bring reform and renewal to a Russian Church whose policies and administrative structures felt increasingly out of step with contemporary conditions. Proposals included conciliar governance (*sobornost*), the liturgical use of vernacular Russian (rather than the archaic Church Slavonic), greater roles for women and laymen in church governance and activities, and perhaps even the restoration of the patriarchate.[4]

Clergy and laity in North America were not isolated from ideological shifts and debates within the late imperial Russian Church. And as a missionary diocese ruled by a bishop appointed by the Most Holy Synod and funded by an annual stipend from Russia, nor were they immune from the influence and resources of imperial bureaucracies that blurred the boundaries between the Russian Church and the tsarist state. Tensions inherent to this arrangement increased in proportion to the growth of the North American Archdiocese after the turn of the twentieth century. The sole Orthodox ecclesiastical body in the United States until 1921, the archdiocese was a complex and diverse institution.[5] The Alaskan Mission remained as an autonomous geographic vicariate led by mostly Alaskan-born clergy. The parishes scattered across the prairies of Canada operated with similar autonomy. There were three nongeographical vicariates for Syro-Arabs (today called Antiochians), Albanians, and Serbians, each with their own bishop or administrator, and also a mostly dormant missionary department for English-speaking converts.

The vast majority of the archdiocese, and the focus of this book, were the more than one hundred "Russian" parishes that spanned the continental United States, though most concentrated in Pennsylvania and the Northeast. These core "Russian" parishes served two predominant and distinct ethnic demographics. One was rural migrants from the agricultural regions of the Russian Empire, what are today Ukraine, Belarus, and western Russia. The second, and far more numerous, were Carpatho-Rusyn migrants from the Austro-Hungarian Empire, a linguistically unique Slavic ethnic group originating in the Carpathian Mountains and portions of what is today Ukraine, Poland, Slovakia, Hungary, and Romania. First arriving in the United States in great numbers during the 1880s, a minority of Carpatho-Rusyn migrants were already Orthodox Christians. Far more were Greek Catholics (sometimes called Eastern Rite or Byzantine Rite Catholics, or the pejorative "uniates"), descendants of those Orthodox Christians who aligned with the Roman Catholic Church during the sixteenth and seventeenth centuries for political and strategic reasons. Greek Catholics retained many liturgical, aesthetic, and spiritual practices of the Eastern Church, including the married priesthood. Upon arriving in America, however, they endured the blunt derision of Roman Catholic leaders suspicious of their Byzantine rite and Slavic aesthetics and particularly of their married priests. In 1891, the St. Mary's parish of Minneapolis became the first of many Greek Catholic congregations to convert to Orthodoxy in North America. Parishioners of St. Mary's, which was founded in 1887 in allegiance to Rome, later deemed their church the "American Kyiv," being for North America what Kyiv was for the tenth-century baptism of Holy Orthodox Rus'. From their conversion and the tireless missionary work of their priest, Father Alexis Toth, came a lasting stronghold of Orthodox parishes throughout the coal, steel, and factory towns of Pennsylvania and the Upper Midwest.[6]

These conversions came through the aggressive missionary efforts of Orthodox clergy and church workers, efforts that sometimes became acrimonious (even violent) and that too depended on heavy-handed measures of Russification. Orthodox missionaries encouraged former Greek Catholics to eliminate "Latinizations" in their liturgical services, church aesthetics, and devotional practices. Russian clergy emphasized the use of Russian, rather than their ancestral Rusyn tongue, and personal identifications with Russian history and culture. This was part of a larger strategy of establishing what church leaders called American Orthodox Rus' (pronounced "roos"), a wide-reaching religious, historical, social, and cultural space that tethered Russian-speaking Orthodox believers in North America to an idealized vision of Holy Orthodox Rus'.

American Orthodox Rus' was understood to encompass the ecclesiastical reach of the Russian Archdiocese, the collective ties of its parishes, and the broad array of archdiocesan and parachurch institutions established to help working-class believers and their families mitigate the hazards and inequities of the industrial United States. After the Russian Revolution of 1905, long-standing restrictions against Orthodox emigration from the Russian Empire gradually lifted, and what barriers remained were more often ignored, leading to increased numbers of adherents with roots in imperial Russia yet whose material needs were much the same. For ethnic Carpatho-Rusyns and Russians alike, paths into the US workforce led to factories, foundries, mills, farms, or mines. Drawn by industrial wages that might improve their lives at home, most intended to remain in the United States only long enough to earn funds sufficient to purchase more farmland, better livestock, or new agricultural implements. The increasing ease and speed of transoceanic passage even made it possible to travel to the United States for seasonal labor. They were a people on the move, traveling about the country in search of better or higher-paying work until they could set out across the ocean with pockets full of dollars.

Up to the First World War, the arrival of more and more peasant migrants brought heightened church-driven endeavors to address immigrant believers' social, educational, and material needs, all efforts undertaken under the triumphalist banner of American Orthodox Rus'. Archdiocesan leaders did not view industrial modernity as hostile to the faith but rather as a new way of living and being made better through a solid grounding in Orthodox praxis. What made this approach distinctive was its contrasts to other faith communities that are more familiar to scholars of North American religion. For instance, the Russian Orthodox Church did not replicate the far-reaching social and educational bureaucracies of the Roman Catholic Church. The Russian Archdiocese did not have the numerous women religious and celibate clergy who undergirded American Catholic primary, secondary, and postsecondary schools and colleges. Most importantly, archdiocesan leaders did not believe that an Orthodox education should replace US public schools. This spoke to their more general ideal that to remain an Orthodox Christian, a pluralistic United States did not necessitate a retreat into rigid traditionalism but rather intentional and beneficial engagement. Rather, one could remain true to oneself—family, faith, nation, language, religion, and culture—while also engaging fully with US politics, popular culture, and public life. Church leaders asserted that do so was not inimical to being a good American, for being a good American also made one a better Orthodox Christian.

Long before the events of 1917, American Orthodox Rus' was a rich and dynamic world with an evolving identity of its own. Religious practice in its communities was deeply experiential, sited within the tenements and boardinghouses of cities and factory towns as much as in churches, chapels, and cemeteries. United in the same faith, local contexts widely varied, from airy, ornate cathedrals with well-trained, polyphonic choirs to cramped clapboard churches echoing only with the solo voice of a lay *psalomshchik* (psalm singer) or perhaps the priest's wife and children. Sometimes, congregants sang together common chant known by heart. Thick, sweet clouds of incense clashed against the pervasive smoke and soot from the foundries and mines, the pungent earthiness of work clothes, and passing wafts of tobacco, alcohol, and strong, dark tea. Fathers adjusted the mutual-aid society membership ribbons pinned to their lapels. Altar boys in cassocks fidgeted with candlesticks. Mothers retied head scarves for their young daughters. Young people noticed one another for the first time. Hardened hands dropped coins into collection plates and candle stands, hoping to fill another blank panel in the brand-new iconostasis with a holy image.

Behind this opaque barrier and its closed central (or "royal") doors, congregants knew that their priest stood alone at the broad, flat altar table, his voice heard but his elaborate vestments unseen. Frequently, congregations did not like their priest and angled to replace him. Sometimes the feeling was mutual. On the other side of the iconostasis, an open space ordinarily (though not always) devoid of pews or chairs, congregations were bound by ethnic, familial, social, and workplace ties. What few people approached the chalice (for it would be decades before frequent communion was common to North America) felt on their tongues the dissolving softness of the body of Christ and the sweetness of his blood, then washed it down with sips of wine from a metal *zapivka* cup and a chewy lump of unconsecrated communion bread (*antidoron*).[7]

American Orthodox Rus' comprised complex sacred spaces defined by the social dynamics of eucharistic community and the multisensory richness of Orthodox worship, buoyed by adherents' successes, tarnished by their failures and disagreements, and always enmeshed with the difficulties and privations of the profane world of the industrial United States. Over the past four decades, scholars of North American religions have utilized the methodology of lived religion to think about these kinds of experiences. Building on European methodologies of "popular religion," lived religion, the religious studies scholar Robert Orsi explains, situates "religious practice and imagination in ongoing, dynamic relation with the realities and structures of everyday life in particular times and places." Treating religious adherence as malleable, even messy, lived religion attends to the wide range of things individuals do to connect themselves with their conceptions of the holy and the sacred and considers the various spaces and contexts in which they do so. And it moves past top-down ecclesiastical narratives dominated by clergy to instead foreground how people sort out practices of belief within the warp and weft of everyday life. "Rethinking religion as a way of cultural work," Orsi continues, "the study of lived religion directs attention to institutions *and* persons, texts *and* rituals, practice *and* theology, things *and* ideas—all as media of making and unmaking worlds."[8]

The most formative works in the study of North American lived religion concern Western Christian traditions, particularly Roman Catholicism, emphasizing personal devotions, individual connections to the holy, and the role of the clergy as they are perceived in Western terms. This focus offers several obstacles for its methodological application to Eastern Christians, especially in that scholars often compare Orthodoxy to Catholicism and sometimes even conflate them as one and the same. This may appear logical. Sharing roots in the early Christian Church, both are hierarchical, liturgical, and patriarchal traditions with strong doses of the mystical. They rely on iconography and hymnography to express their teachings. Both encourage deep devotional relationships with the saints, with cultures of relics, pilgrimage, and iconography. Yet their paths diverge at a most critical point: celibacy. From the walled-off domains of parish rectories and cloistered convents, preconciliar Roman Catholic priests and women religious practiced their vocations in public contexts where their presumed celibacy was exceptional. In contrast, though the opaque wall of the iconostasis separated priests from their parishioners in American Orthodox Rus', their lives outside the church intertwined at far greater degrees. The vast majority of parish clergy were married, and most had children. Clerical marriage meant that anxieties over wages and conditions of employment came not from priests' individual needs or the financial concerns of the church but rather from the responsibilities of supporting a family. Blurring the material and social differences between clergy and laity, Orthodox Christians suggest a very different picture of lived religious experience within hierarchical traditions in North America, encompassing richly experiential religious worlds in which clergy and lay believers prayed, worked, and existed together in cohesive eucharistic communities with far different dynamics of the everyday.

The historian Vera Shevzov situates Orthodox practice and community interaction in the late Russian Empire within the framework of *tserkovnost'*, or "churchness," a complex synthesis by which Orthodox Christians reoriented themselves to modernity and fostered new engagements with ritual and devotional practices. Whether at home or at work, in streets and shops and saloons or in church, *tserkovnost'* places individual Orthodox practice within the ecclesiastical, sacramental, and liturgical totality of the church. Contestations over changing individual devotions occurred within wider discussions of modernity and debates over how the Russian Church would confront the realities of a changing world. "The very meaning of church, the conceptualization of its character and life, and the internal principles by which it should be ordered," Shevzov argues, "these were the fundamental issues being radically questioned and reexamined."[9]

Shevzov's reading of Russian *tserkovnost'* widens the methodological scope to include the lived religious experiences of clergy, for whom the experience of American Orthodox Rus' was no less transnational or driven by material need. Bishops, priests, and (less commonly) deacons maintained their own ethnic, religious, and linguistic connections with Russia and kept abreast of theological discussions and debates over church reforms. They knew that missionary tenure and success could earn them ecclesiastical awards (*tserkovnye nagrady*), which included the bestowing of higher ecclesiastical ranks or the right to wear different or additional vestments, clerical headwear, and pectoral crosses, as well as medals, honorary certificates, and other items. Yet for those who yearned for Russia, worthy labors could also bring incentives like a periodic sabbatical (*otpusk*) or even permanent return into a more prestigious assignment. Just as lay adherents adapted their religious worlds to the strange and demanding world of the American industrial workplace, clergy themselves reoriented their own beliefs and vocations within the insecurities and anxieties of a distant and multiconfessional missionary setting.

Accounting for the religious lives of clergy is not to say that the story of American Orthodox Rus' remains a clerical story alone, though it is rather easy to perceive it in that way. Though the voices of working-class laity are vital for understanding the breadth of lived religious experience in American Orthodox Rus', they are not always so easy to excavate. These adherents were what the historian Richard Callahan observes as "those ordinary believers who did not write theological tomes, did not contribute to elite doctrinal debates, and did not often record their own histories."[10] As a result, we must accept that often their stories were told by their priests and bishops. American Orthodox Rus' incubated a vibrant culture of clerical writing. Clergy wrote, edited, and published an array of Orthodox newspapers in which they described the missionary life, complementing a broader Russian-language press in North America that was not always accepting of the church. Additionally, both in Russia and in North America, the looming influence of tsarist bureaucracy over the late imperial Russian Church manifested a complex paper trail of reports, logs, and internal correspondence, which themselves offer rich and candid insight into missionary life. I rely on these sources not to privilege the voices of priests or bishops but rather for the insight they provide into the lives of everyday congregants and communities.

Here we encounter a problem of historical perception. In *The Making of the English Working Class*, the social historian E. P. Thompson expressed his intention to "rescue" his historical subjects "from the enormous condescension of posterity." Thompson sought to return nuance, relevance, and agency to people of obsolete crafts and antiquated thinking, workers cast aside both in their own time and by generations of historians for their disparate turns from industrialization and social change. "Their aspirations were valid in terms of their own experience," he wrote, "and, if they were casualties of history, they remain, condemned in their own lives, as casualties."[11] This book tells the stories of people similarly cast aside by church historiography: clergy and laity who chafed against ecclesiastical hierarchies; those who sought to blend Orthodoxy with revolutionary politics; clergy and laity who collaborated with government actors and agents whose interests lay in the investigation, even persecution, of other Orthodox Christians from their own congregations and communities.

We will also trace the origins of Orthodox jurisdictional fragmentation in North America, often along ethnic lines and sometimes yet again within ethnic groups themselves. For decades, the problem of "pan-Orthodox" unity has loomed over Orthodox historiography on this continent, leading to a church-produced literature that has smoothed the rougher edges of political and ecclesiological dissent, glossed over discord, idealized interethnic cooperation, and cast aside outspoken critics as schismatics or contemptible malcontents. I assert that the people of American Orthodox Rus', clergy and lay, acted out of desires and agencies intended to mitigate the dominant problems of their own lives: immigration, assimilation, industrial labor, war, revolution, illness, and transnational political change, among others. They sought solutions that made sense to them, even as they faced scorn, marginalization, and even defrocking or excommunication for doing so. Thompson argues that these kinds of historical actors must be taken seriously for the actions and choices they made in the face of their own experiences, for "they lived through these times of acute social disturbance, and we did not."[12]

To grasp the fullness of American Orthodox Rus' requires such radical empathy for the messiness of history. This must extend to politics as well. Church historiography and historical memory alike usually draw a distinct line between Orthodox adherence and leftist politics. Writing in the 1960s, the priest and church historian Dimitry Grigorieff stressed that "actually there was very little contact between church people and [leftist political] organizations. Immigrants who organized Russian Orthodox parishes were not interested in Marxist ideologies," and "people who belonged to leftist political organizations were disposed against religion and the church."[13] While many people within American Orthodox Rus' could be considered conservative, they were not found on the right of the political spectrum alone. Clergy and laity participated in labor actions, voiced critiques of industrial capitalism, and joined

16 | INTRODUCTION

socialist, communist, and anarchist groups. They felt that doing so was not incongruent with their Orthodox beliefs, forming social and political worldviews that were as much informed by their church as they were by the magnetic pull of the Progressive-era working-class Left. In time, some even contemplated whether they should offer prayers for Lenin and the Bolsheviks, just as they once did for the tsar and the imperial house. To be clear, not everyone was a Wobbly or a communist, though some were. Bringing them into the story—people who have been cast aside by both church and secular historians alike—helps us to understand that American Orthodox Rus' was politically dynamic and ideologically fluid.

This book tells the story of American Orthodox Rus' in two, generally chronological parts that together describe the crises and vulnerabilities that determined how the immigrant clergy and laity of American Orthodox Rus' navigated a changing, industrializing, and modernizing world. Part 1 shows how from the 1890s until the First World War, the Russian Church built the groundwork for a working-class religious institution that could be a source of aid and intervention for its immigrant flock. Part 2 reveals how political changes in Russia during 1917 strained the transnational dynamics of American Orthodox Rus'. First, the February Revolution led to the abdication of Tsar Nicholas II and the fall of the Romanov dynasty. Then the October Revolution brought Bolshevik rule and the Russian Civil War. Each of these developments had substantial implications for the Russian Church—for its ability to maintain its influence in Russia and also to sustain its missionary commitments abroad. As the Bolshevik age concretized, struggles that were once felt individually widened to include the existential survival of the Russian Church itself. By 1924, financial crisis and administrative uncertainty challenged the North American Archdiocese's place within the transnational Russian Church to the point that the very survival of the mission itself became an open question.

In describing these transformations, I describe the shifting conditions of possibility that defined the lives of people whose memories I hold dear. As a rather bookish child, I would pore through the shelves of libraries and bookstores of metropolitan Detroit and look for index entries of people like me, like my grandparents, like their friends. I never found them. Sometimes I wondered if the stories they told ever happened. Maybe they did not, or perhaps they were not important enough that others would care. This book came out of a need to know and the desire to explain the traces of discomfort and anguish I sensed when those who had grown up in American Orthodox Rus' described their upbringings. Even as a child, I felt the need to preserve something of their lives, for it seemed no one else would. I wanted to understand what was lost for Russian and Carpatho-Rusyn people like them who lost or shed so much of their identities in the Cold War rush to conformity, when to call oneself "Russian" meant risking the perception of being "Red." And as I grew from a curious child into a professional scholar, I set out to locate their lives (or, more accurately, those of their parents and grandparents) within the messy ambiguities of history and to better understand them within the analytical frameworks employed by scholars of North American religions.

With this said, I wish to be clear about my place in this work. Though I share history and kinship with many of the subjects in these pages, this book is intentionally and decidedly *not* my family's story. Nor is it a comprehensive history of the Russian Archdiocese as an ecclesiastical institution or an all-encompassing narrative of Russian Orthodox Christianity in North America. Rather, I use here the tools and rigor of academic social history to explore how thousands of Russian and Carpatho-Rusyn people like Wasil and Anna and their children built social, religious, and working worlds in the United States, only to see those worlds challenged by geopolitical events beyond their control. And while the stories I heard as a child brought me to this project, they reflected only a general, if cursory, view of what I found in archival boxes, microfilm reels, and parish anniversary books. I came to see that elders like my grandmother omitted crucial details and smoothed out unsightly wrinkles when describing their lives. And I found that their accounts often complemented the gaping holes in how the church recorded and wrote this same history, making working people passive actors in top-down accounts of the ecclesiastical institutions that so defined their Orthodox identities.

What follows here are accounts of struggle and resilience that center the experiences of working-class people—children and adults, women and men, clergy and lay—who cared deeply about their church even as the world around them changed in unpredictable, even tragic ways.

Their stories underscore the deep ties that bound together the clergy and laity of American Orthodox Rus' and emphasize the palpable feelings of uncertainty, even terror, they felt when those bonds were challenged. American Orthodox Rus' was part of a transnational continuum of Russian religiosity that flowered at the cusp of the First World War, only for those blooms to swiftly and unexpectedly wilt. As a story of rapid decline, then reinvention and reclamation, this book demonstrates that for the clergy and laity of American Orthodox Rus', establishing a missionary church for working people was a great struggle of spiritual importance, what Russian Orthodox Christians call a *podvig*. They were only human, and their stories do not always have happy endings. Yet American Orthodox Rus' was for them a pearl of great price, worthy of their help when after 1917, the Russian Orthodox Church could no longer protect itself.

PART I

The Vineyard

1

"This Babylon"

The Russian Orthodox Immigration Society and Labor Migration

Then the king will say to those at his right hand, "Come, you
that are blessed by my Father, inherit the kingdom prepared
for you from the foundation of the world; for I was hungry
and you gave me food, I was thirsty and you gave me something to drink, I was a stranger and you welcomed me, I was
naked and you gave me clothing, I was sick and you took
care of me, I was in prison and you visited me."
—Matthew 25:34–36

Beginning in 1907, workers toiled beneath the ground in Valhalla, New
York, to build the Catskill Aqueduct, a series of massive tunnels to
carry water from the Catskills to Yonkers. Project administrators and
underwriters claimed to have taken great pains to create a humane,
safe, and socially uplifting environment for their workers, including
schools, recreational and children's programs, medical care, and libraries. Some workers lived in company-built towns of one-story houses,
with churches, stores, lit and paved streets, and other idyllic elements
of small-town America. These were segregated spaces, however, as
"the negroes, Italians, and other white employees were separated into
different quarters." Most were tent villages with fewer and cruder comforts. Even so, it was claimed, "the same humanitarian spirit pervaded
all." Management saw workers' happiness, cleanliness, and morality as
crucial for the project's success. And they felt the amenities of company towns and tent villages were vital for productivity, because "if the
men's time were properly employed during their recreation hours they
would pay closer attention to their work during their eight hours of
labor." On completion, project boosters compared their grand achieve-
ment to the Roman Aqueducts, though with one key difference. "The

Roman workmen were slaves," they explained. "The Catskill aqueduct workmen were freemen in the fullest sense of the word."[1]

Beneath the façade of condescending company paternalism, scientifically managed productivity, and social uplift rhetoric, however, was the grim reality that tunnel workers—called "sandhogs"—earned very little for grimy, hazardous, even unbearable toil. In the warm summer months, tunnel work was grueling and muddy. During the winter, the ground hardened, the mud froze, and fingers grew stiff. The mostly southern and eastern European sandhogs received around $1.50 per day (around $50 today). And it was dangerous work. By one estimate, 10 percent of workers were killed or injured in the tunnels, though no one knew for sure. Management considered worksite accidents so common and inconsequential that they did not bother to keep an accurate tally. "Owing to the labor being so inconspicuous," a period journalist observed, "the death by accident of one or more of them attracts no public attention."[2]

In 1911, the Russian Orthodox Immigration Society, a church-affiliated aid group founded three years before, learned of a group of Orthodox sandhogs in Valhalla, mostly Russian men who were segregated into its crude tent villages. Orthodox clergy knew somewhat of these workers, as a few attended area parishes on feast days. Yet for the most part, the missionary priest Alexander Hotovitzky observed, "the majority did not know about our church." The heiress and philanthropist Anne Morgan, daughter of the multimillionaire banker J. P. Morgan, knew of them as well, having drawn from her immense family fortune to establish a school for Valhalla's sandhogs. She held particular concern for its growing "Russian colony," men living in isolation with little leisure time and scant connections to their church. At her invitation, an Immigration Society priest began going to Valhalla that autumn to pray with a group of enthusiastic workers who, it was said, "formed a respectable choir."[3] Encouraged by the inroads the society made in Valhalla, and at Anne Morgan's enthusiastic invitation, the ruling archbishop of the Russian Archdiocese went there himself in early December. The sandhogs were energized by meeting with the archbishop and anticipated another visit from a priest for Nativity celebrations in early January. They hoped even to stage a *yolka*, a traditional festive Christmas pageant.

Yet this was not to be. On January 4, 1912, three days before they were to celebrate the birth of Christ, a dynamite explosion in the tunnels killed one of the most well-regarded Orthodox sandhogs. Two other Orthodox workers were maimed for life. A priest traveled to Valhalla for Christmas, but Alexander Hotovitzky came to bury the deceased sandhog. "It was difficult to conduct the funeral of a young man, so suddenly departed to another life," Hotovitzky recalled. He recounted with horror that the undertaker "flatly refused" to open the man's casket, as is customary for an Orthodox burial service, for "in the head's place lay a shapeless mass." The man's brother, himself a sandhog, wept near the casket, shedding tears both for himself and for their parents. "Ah, Russian life," Hotovitzky mused, "you are cheap in America!"[4]

The tragedies in Valhalla reinforced for Hotovitzky his lingering misgivings over how working-class Orthodox Christians were faring in the industrial United States. Hotovitzky realized that the breadth of work taken by Russian migrants and their difficult experiences as invisible and replaceable immigrant labor represented a missionary challenge. The needs of an Orthodox miner in Coaldale, Pennsylvania, differed from those of a textile worker in Lawrence, Massachusetts, as did those of a meatpacker in Chicago from a rural farmer in Clayton, Wisconsin. Yet American Orthodox Rus' and its Russian Orthodox Immigration Society needed to be concerned for them all, Hotovitzky argued, even if industrialists, bosses, foremen, and policy makers did not reciprocate. In Valhalla, sandhogs had formed a community of support and mutual protection. They gathered to pray. They sang. They placed hope in one another, supported their own, dreamed of their futures, and thought of those they left behind. All the while, they toiled in the tunnels for little pay. They endured the work camps. They buried their dead. "This Babylon hid many of them away in its workshops, in stifling places," Hotovitzky wrote with clear disdain, "planted behind looms, behind tailor's benches, at sewing machines, strewn on the docks, thrown about along the tunnels, along the mills"[5]

The period from the turn of the twentieth century until the outbreak of the First World War were boom years for Orthodox immigration to the United States, coming at the tail end of what was then the most significant period of immigration in the nation's history. Nearly nine million people crossed over its borders between 1905 and 1915, a figure not surpassed until the 1990s. From 1901 to 1907, the number of migrants from the Russian Empire ballooned from around 1,500 per year to nearly 10,000.[6] From Austria-Hungary, migrants classified as either Russian or Ruthenian (including both Orthodox or Greek Catholics) expanded from almost 1,400 in 1899 to over 27,000 in 1910, totaling more than 144,000.[7] As a 1909 editorial in the *Russian Orthodox American Messenger* proclaimed, "more and more Americans are beginning to discover that the Russian people in America are not some paltry handful, but thousands; [and] that, consequently, they will soon have to reckon with them."[8]

This chapter concerns one of the primary institutions established within the Russian Archdiocese to meet the needs of newly arrived immigrants, the Russian Orthodox Immigration Society, founded in New York in 1908. Situating Orthodox migrants within the larger picture of immigration and immigration discourse in the United States, it traces three complementary aspects of the society's endeavors. First are the society's efforts to inform potential migrants about the hazards of crossing the Atlantic and then to help those who needed assistance to clear immigration control at Ellis Island. Second, we turn to Lower Manhattan and the Russian Immigrant Home, where the society offered newly arrived migrants assistance and community during their first, anxious days in the United States. And finally, we explore how the society connected migrants with job opportunities elsewhere in the United States, entrusting them to the care of the many Orthodox parishes emerging alongside the path of the US industrial economy. Taken in total, the Russian Orthodox Immigration Society entrusted the endeavor of immigrant aid to clergy and lay workers, ensuring that Orthodox migrants passed safely into the United States and providing material support to ease their transitions into the US workforce. Above all, they offered migrants spiritual aid wherever their paths took them, intending that workers remained grounded as Orthodox Christians in a strange land that cared more about the sweat of their brow than it did for their physical or emotional well-being.

The "Immigrant Question" and American Orthodox Rus'

The immigrant institutions and relief agencies of the Russian Archdiocese of North America sought to counteract the melting pot stirred at virtually every level of US government and society. It was the age of mechanization and innovation, when "civilization" was a term synonymous with industrial might. The US economy relied on foreign-born laborers who were trainable, replaceable, and more willing to accept lower wages and poor living conditions. Progressive-era politicians, academics, clergymen, and social reformers, however, feared that these immigrants were not properly assimilating into American life. For them, transforming "rude" and "uncivilized" immigrants into "Americans" depended on careful observation. Among those who were considering these questions were academic researchers, whose perspectives ranged from the pseudoscience of eugenics to nascent methodologies in the social sciences. Others were ecumenically minded Protestant clergymen, who took interest in the "foreign-born" out of charitable impulses or evangelistic opportunism. There were the findings and opinions of journalists and well-to-do elites whose interests inclined them to "slumming." These kinds of authors engaged in what one historian calls "exploration writing," a sort of "specimen hunting" for readers with a taste for the exotic, "reveal[ing] with breathtaking clarity the dangers of degeneration that lurked in the dark places."[9] And there were the staffs of settlement houses, prisons, hospitals, vocational agencies, and aid groups. In general, the gazes of external observers sought unifying principles of character and predisposition by which immigrant groups could be classified, and in turn assimilated, and often were oriented less by objective truth than by religious, personal, or professional self-interests. Within such assessments were basal assumptions of Anglo-Saxon Protestant superiority as a defining factor in US national identity. As the economist Emily Greene Balch argued, "the character of the continent and the character of immigration have determined and are determining the quality of the civilization of this country, perhaps the greatest seat of the white race."[10]

Russian Church immigrant relief work harnessed the American Progressive impulse for immigration control and reform in order to create different opportunities for its foreign-born flock. Immigrant clergy recognized with urgency that their congregations—composed mostly of poor and uneducated men who migrated from eastern Europe without their families—were now in a socioreligious landscape far more diverse than what they left behind. The city and industrial workplace alike brought Orthodox migrants into contact with myriad peoples, creeds, ideas, and opportunities. Eastern European migrants like those who composed American Orthodox Rus' often took industrial jobs in the cramped quarters of factories and mines, workplaces packed with laborers from a variety of racial, ethnic, and national backgrounds, speaking dozens of languages and expressing virtually every permutation of belief and unbelief alike. While their religious worlds comprised those who looked, spoke, and prayed as they did, much of the rest of their time—at work and play—was spent in the company of a much wider variety of people and influences. "Emigration took these people out of traditional, accustomed environments and replanted them in strange ground, among strangers, where strange manners prevailed," the immigration historian Oscar Handlin observed. "The customary modes of behavior were no longer adequate, for the problems of life were new and different."[11] Church officials feared, with good reason, that migrants who had been devout, practicing Orthodox Christians at home might be easily swayed in the US, lured by dollars, dancing, and drink, drawn to wanderlust, and enticed by rampant consumerism and fast-paced popular culture. Without incentives or opportunities to remain connected to their religious traditions—and indeed their "people" (narod)—clergy feared that these believers might stray for good.

Archdiocesan leaders came to recognize the need to undertake immigrant aid on Orthodox terms. They noticed how other national groups found success with institutionalized outreach to new arrivals, as one clergyman recalled, having "saved immigrants not only from the exploitation of various entrepreneurs, but supported their connection to the people of their old countries."[12] They recognized that American progressive efforts in social aid, imbued by nativist prejudices and othering gazes, would do little to ensure that Orthodox workers would remain in the church. And they saw that in the absence of specifically Orthodox responses to the immigration question, other religious organizations were beating them to the punch—and stealing from their flock. They especially feared the St. Joseph Immigrant Home, a Roman Catholic institution in New York City for Slavic migrants. Once vulnerable Orthodox faithful were exposed to "the fanatic propaganda of the Polish Catholic priests and 'nuns,'" church leaders feared that the hand of Catholic charity might sway them to Catholicism. What was more, aid from Catholic charities might strengthen Greek Catholic immigrants' subordination to the Vatican, thereby weakening the Orthodox Archdiocese's position in North America as it strove to encourage Orthodox conversions from the so-called *unia*.[13]

In 1908, the Russian Archdiocese helped to establish the Russian Orthodox Immigration Society. With the hard work of lay employees charged to operate its various endeavors, the Immigration Society helped thousands of Orthodox workers transition into the US industrial economy. Initially overseen by priest Alexander Hotovitzky and an honorary committee that included Russia's ambassador to the United States, Baron Roman Rosen, and Tikhon (Bellavin), the former archbishop of North America, within a year the society's membership numbered nearly fifty. Though its work was slowed and then halted by the outbreak of the First World War, the Immigration Society formed a critical connection between the church and the bustling business of transatlantic migration, leading to the church's intervention in the passage and successful settling of thousands of migrants from Russia, Galicia, and elsewhere across eastern and central Europe. The society made immigrant aid a specifically Orthodox project and one that relied on the growth of the Russian Archdiocese across the United States at the turn of the twentieth century.

Russkii emigrant and American Orthodox Rus' as a Transnational Ideological Network

The work of the Russian Orthodox Immigration Society was documented and explained in a weekly Russian-language newspaper, *Russkii emigrant* (titled in English *The Russian Immigrant*). Though not an official arm of the Immigration Society, the paper was founded in 1912 under the patronage of the Russian Archdiocese and maintained a close relationship to archdiocesan clergy and laity involved in the operations and activities of the society. Published in New York, it was also distributed in Russia and Europe, with subscription rates set in both dollars and rubles. Aimed at a semiliterate readership, *Russkii emigrant* anthologized current events, published short fiction from authors like Jack London and Leo Tolstoy, described events in Russian-speaking communities around the world, advertised Russian-speaking businesses in the United States, and provided information on the activities of both the Russian Orthodox

Immigration Society and the Russian Archdiocese. *Russkii emigrant* was published in New York City, where two other newspapers dominated the Russian-speaking press: the progressive *Russkii golos* (*Russian Voice*, later *Russkoe slovo*, or *Russian Word*); and the socialist and more militant *Novyi mir* (*New World*). In comparison to these papers, *Russkii emigrant* was the most sympathetic to the church, even encouraging its readers that the content in other papers—particularly *Russkoe slovo*—was in fact inimical to their well-being in the US.

One element of *Russkii emigrant* merits careful and particular attention: its open and explicit antisemitism. This was particularly evident in the paper's first year of publication, under the editorship of Bishop Alexander (Nemolovsky). Before the founding of *Russkii emigrant*, Alexander published equally inflammatory material as the editor of *Svit* (*The Light*), the newspaper of the Russian Orthodox Catholic Mutual Aid Society. Under his editorship, as one scholar observes, *Russkii emigrant* "contained a peculiar blend of anti-Semitism, anti-socialism and, at times, anti-Americanism, coupled with an unshakable faith in the Russian tsar, Orthodoxy and all that was subsumed under these national symbols."[14] News articles, editorials, and crude jokes in the paper amplified stereotypes and conspiracies about Jews, often using the pejorative slur *zhid* (yid). In American Orthodox Rus', many clergy and laity from the Russian Empire (as opposed to Carpatho-Rusyns from Austria-Hungary) came from regions with significant Jewish populations, including places within or adjacent to the Pale of Settlement. They were part of a larger pattern of antisemitism that was not limited to the Russian Church alone, indeed spanning virtually all of Europe. Many migrants brought their prejudices to American Orthodox Rus', finding sermons, church newspapers, and everyday discourse that only served to reinforced their views. Living and working in US cities with large Russian Jewish populations, Orthodox migrants, clergy and lay, continued to encounter Jews at work, in the shop, or in the street. Their interactions were marked by mutual discomfort and antagonisms rooted in centuries of inherited experiences, prejudices, and traumas that Jewish and Orthodox Christian migrants alike carried with them across continents and oceans.

The antisemitic thrust of *Russkii emigrant* ebbed in 1913, after Alexander ceded editorship. Even so, its frequent publication of such rhetoric reflected ideas widely held within late imperial Russia, including the Orthodox Church and its clerical caste. This was especially true of the conservative priests and bishops from the so-called Black Hundreds (*chornaia sotnia*), hard-line monarchists who internalized decades-old tsarist rhetorics of "Orthodoxy, Autocracy, and Nationality" that privileged Orthodox Christians while further subjugating Jews. These ideas undergirded deadly pogroms and other acts of antisemitic state violence in the Pale of Jewish Settlement (what is today Ukraine and Belarus). Such incidents ebbed and flowed with changing sociopolitical dynamics in the late Russian Empire but became more frequent after the turn of the century and would escalate yet again during the Second World War.[15]

The global scope of *Russkii emigrant* served two purposes. First, it made subscribers in Russia aware of how their compatriots abroad were faring. Second, it helped immigrants in North America place themselves within a larger community that spanned western Europe, China, Japan, South America, Australia, and all points in between. The newspaper offered a bridge between Russia and scattered Russian "colonies" around the world and encouraged readers on both sides of the Atlantic to identify with a global, Russian-speaking diaspora. The newspaper imparted to its readers that American Orthodox Rus' was a transnational community linked by the common bonds of Holy Orthodox Rus' and the protection of its God-fearing tsar. This was the guiding ideological framework for its greater, arguably fundamental mission: encouraging Russian emigration to the United States and in turn lessening the burden of the Russian Orthodox Immigration Society for immediate relief. It offered useful advice for those who wished to migrate to the United States and guidance for those who were already in the US who hoped to help friends and relatives to join them, saving them from the pitfalls that would create more work for Immigration Society agents and officials. American Orthodox Rus' and its church-organized network of immigrant relief were but one portion of a global Russian diaspora knitted together by the ecclesiastical structures and institutional resources of the Russian Orthodox Church. Helping labor migrants reach the United States and thrive there meant building a religious community that could address the dangers, exploitations, and fast pace of the industrial city. Through *Russkii emigrant*, the Immigration Society recognized that this work began before a migrant departed eastern Europe.

Leaving for America

When the laborer and Orthodox Christian Frank Bondarenko was asked why he left the western Russian Empire, he bluntly stated, "It was no good there, so I left.... It was misery and poverty." He traveled to the US in the steerage compartment of the SS *Kursk*, disembarking in 1910 at the age of twenty-five. After a short time in Brooklyn, Bondarenko worked in a South Carolina saw mill and then as a laborer in West Virginia. He settled in Detroit in 1912.[16] Migrants like Frank Bondarenko were not just leaving their homes and families. They were also moving away from a monolithic imperial state that controlled their lives and economic potentials, as well as most domestic and international travel. Those who left the Austro-Hungarian Empire could pass rather freely. In the Russian Empire, by contrast, state control over residence and mobility was a means of maintaining and reinforcing the connection between peasants and the state, as well as reinforcing differences in social caste. The empire's stringent passport system restricted movement both domestically and abroad, though it became less strict as Russia's social and political environment changed during the latter half of the nineteenth century. The 1861 emancipation of the serfs, violent pogroms against Jewish populations, urbanization, and industrialization all came alongside reforms that selectively opened Russia's borders and eased the strictest regulations of both domestic and international travel. Slowly implemented measures toward industrialization and social reform following the 1905 Russian Revolution introduced identification documents and eased internal mobility restrictions, helping rural workers to more easily relocate into cities and take up factory positions. By 1908, the state acceded to migration from the European provinces of Russia into Siberia, hoping to ease overpopulation in agrarian areas by peopling the sparse, environmentally harsh territories of the far east—though, of course, many of the nearly three quarters of a million who moved eastward did not do so voluntary.[17]

And while domestic migration became easier, permission for foreign travel remained difficult to obtain, even before considering the prohibitive cost. The tsarist regime prioritized Orthodox Christians as important cogs for nationalist policies and was reluctant to allow them easy or open passage across the sprawling empire's borders. A passport for foreign travel cost fifteen rubles (around $500 today), a fee unaffordable for most people traveling alone and particularly so for an entire family. At the same time, the tsarist state acknowledged that migrants might return bearing newly acquired skills in technologically advanced industries, a critical need for the industrialization and urbanization of the Russian workforce. Though it remained more difficult for Orthodox subjects to leave Russia, even such limited labor migration opened greater possibilities than existed before.[18]

To counter the costs and cumbersome bureaucracies required to leave the Russian Empire, many potential migrants circumvented the process by hiring immigration agents who would help them to "steal the border" (krast' granitsu) and depart without proper documentation. A guide for travelers warned that while such crossings might seem advantageous in the short term, "in practice it turns out considerably more expensive, since the agent robs the peasant blind. Indeed, it is not safe, since a guard stands at the border."[19] These warnings were continuously emphasized to prospective migrants throughout Russia in a variety of venues, but with mixed success. "Every year scores of emigrants fall under the bullets of the frontier guard," one official wrote, "and still the clandestine traffic goes on as usual."[20] One such migrant who disregarded these admonitions recalled that he heard from men who returned from the US that he could "earn lots of money over there."[21] Lacking the required papers, he left home in secret, "in [the] company of an agent who smuggled [him] out of Russia without a passport." He boarded a train steaming through the German countryside, then walked through the night to reach another train bound for Rotterdam, and at last secured passage on a ship bound for the US.[22]

While the US industrial economy portended endless economic potential, and even as potential migrants may have been dissatisfied with their lives at home, many did not see migration to the United States as a one-way proposition, arriving with the full expectation of returning as soon as they were able. This mentality challenges the myth of the United States as a "land of opportunity" where immigrants intended to remain. In truth, immigrants held mixed ideas about transatlantic mobility. In a call for historians to focus on remigration, Dirk Hoerder categorizes immigration into three categories: "permanent immigrants, temporary immigrants who postponed departure as to finally end their lives in the

32 | "THIS BABYLON"

U.S., and immigrants who returned after a limited period, sometimes crossing the ocean several times in both directions."[23]

Russian immigrants were found in each of these categories, though the distribution significantly changed over time. Those who came from agrarian areas widely perceived emigration to the US as a pragmatic solution to acquire land—not in the United States but at home. In 1911, around seventy-five hundred Russians remigrated through the port at Liepāja (in modern-day Latvia), countered against thirty-five thousand heading for the US. That number more than doubled by 1913, when nearly eighteen thousand crossed back across the Atlantic in contrast to the seventy thousand heading westward.[24] Writing in 1912, priest Alexander Hotovitzky observed that Russian workers "do not have an aversion to farm, factory, nor coal mining work," but the meager wages they earned in physically demanding, often unsafe workplaces only went so far. "If there is money to spend, they send it to family at home," Hotovitzky observed. "And after that [it is] to escape to the homeland. It is such that in America they already see the location of their grave, but the majority want to go to die in Russia."[25]

Clergy like Hotovitzky also fixated on how Orthodox migrants crossed the Atlantic. Prior to a trip to Russia in 1911, missionary priest John Slunin was instructed by his bishop to obtain a copy of the miracle-working Kursk-Root Icon of the Mother of God and have it blessed in front of the original, thirteenth-century icon, held at Znamenskii Monastery in Kursk. Slunin was then to carry the blessed copy aboard the SS *Kursk*, the new flagship of the Russian-East Asian Line, on which he would return to the US. In the presence of officials from the steamship company and the city and port of Liepāja, Slunin offered a prayer service on the deck before the icon, bestowing blessings on one of the largest ships carrying Orthodox immigrants to the United States. "During the service," Slunin recalled, "I spoke of the concern of our *vladyka* [bishop] for Russian emigrants in America, about the Immigrant Home, and of the love with which His Most Eminence welcomes and prayerfully blesses all those who contribute to and help the noble sons and daughters of our Great Motherland who are emigrating to America." Moving inside to escape a raging storm, the assembled sang the liturgical ode for the Icon of Our Lady of the Sign ("You are an impregnable wall and a source of miracles") and hung the icon in the first-class passenger dining room. The gift of an icon—especially a copy blessed before a well-known icon associated with miracles—expressed that the church saw the transoceanic passage of Russian immigrants to the United States as a sacred undertaking. The protection and intercession of the Mother of God would safeguard migrants on the ocean and into the welcoming arms of the Russian Orthodox Immigration Society upon their arrival in North America.[26]

On the "Island of Tears"

The Russian Orthodox Immigration Society endeavored to help Russian-speaking migrants circumvent policies that might slow or prevent their migration to the United States. Ellis Island opened in 1892 to process passengers from ships like the *Kursk*, forming an integral part of a US immigration control infrastructure that evolved hand in hand with federal immigration policies. Immigration control was long a matter of barring those who were ill, had criminal records, were feared to become a "public charge," or had disabilities that would impede their ability to work. As time passed and immigration patterns shifted, however, restriction policies transformed the United States into what the historian Erika Lee calls a "gatekeeper nation." Stricter border-control practices reflected evolving constructions of racial and ethnic difference, even as immigrant groups found ways to circumvent the system. "By the 1920s," Lee observes, "a hierarchy of admissible and excludable immigrants had been codified into law, reinforcing ideas of 'fitness' that were measured by an immigrant's race, ethnicity, class, and gender."[27] Others have described how scientific racism and eugenics inscribed and reinscribed the racial hierarchies legislated into state policy, if not broader public consciousness, what the historian Mae Ngai calls "hierarchies of difference."[28] Maintaining a massive, foreign-born industrial workforce meant management and control, ensuring dominance for certain sectors of society—native-born or assimilated workers and elites coded as white—in the face of increasing markers of difference.

The first friendly face that many Russian-speaking migrants encountered on Ellis Island was a "special representative" from the Immigration Society, a man employed to prop open the golden door for the most vulnerable and hopeless of cases. One of these representatives was Arcady Piotrowsky, an Orthodox layman who came to the United States in 1906. Six years later, working at the Port of New York as a landing agent for the Baltic-American Line, Piotrowsky received a job offer from the Immigration Society. Laboring mostly alone, Piotrowsky took on the immense job of advocating for Russian immigrants facing deportation. As one of these migrants later remembered, many among this "mass of immigrants arrived on the American continent literally without a single kopek, having sold all their belongings in Russia and thus cutting themselves off from returning to the homeland." They were "destitute, humiliated, sick, without documents, helpless, in a new country knowing no one and nothing!"[29] And they had boarded ships, some of them "stealing the border" along the way, hoping to find work in the United States, often without knowing how to do so. On Ellis Island, Piotrowsky addressed crises they experienced on arrival, referring migrants to church-operated, tsarist state-funded relief efforts to ease them into life in the US.

With the numbers of needy immigrants growing each year, Piotrowsky soon realized the unceasing demands of his position. Between 1912 and late 1913, he intervened in "thousands and thousands" of such cases.[30] In 1913, the Russian Orthodox Immigration Society aided more than thirty-two hundred immigrants at Ellis Island and the Russian Immigrant Home, nearly nine new cases each day. More than three-quarters were men. The vast majority of cases were Orthodox Christians from the Russian Empire, what is today Belarus, Ukraine, and the southern and western regions of Russia. There were comparatively fewer Carpatho-Rusyn migrants from Austria-Hungary, perhaps less than 10 percent. There were others as well, not all of whom were Eastern Orthodox, including handfuls of Armenians and Poles, Tatars and Serbs, Russian Germans, and even a few from Syria.

Piotrowsky spent much of his time on Ellis Island handling paperwork that would help potential deportees remain in the United States and also marshaling funds for deportation appeals, often amounting to hundreds of dollars. He appeared at deportation hearings to pledge that a detainee would not be a burden if allowed to enter the United States, for the Russian Orthodox Immigration Society would ensure they were housed, fed, clothed, and given the tools to find work and achieve self-sufficiency. Piotrowsky described this work in regular articles for *Russkii emigrant.* In one column, he described a typical day in immigration court as "stuffy, crowded, and unbelievably boring," helping immigrant after immigrant overcome routine, fairly straightforward issues.[31] Usually, hearings addressed problems like insufficient funds and incorrect addresses for relatives or friends already in the US. Other cases hinged on poor health, prior criminal records, or prearranged labor contracts. Occasionally, there were questions of mental capacity or physical strength. Rarer, but telling of the gendered aspects of immigration policy, were cases of prearranged marriages, immorality, and pregnancies out of wedlock. In general, Piotrowsky's office was rather successful in passing these workers through immigration control. Between January and September 1913, only around 150 of the nearly 2,500 people the Immigration Society aided were deported.[32]

Many of the problems that Piotrowsky addressed stemmed from word-of-mouth advice circulating among potential migrants. Meant to ease their journeys and experiences at immigration control, instead such advice landed migrants in immigration court. During the spring of 1913, Piotrowsky encountered a newly arrived Russian couple. They were detained in temporary holding, having "categorically" told the immigration inspector that they had no money. After a night spent "among a crowd of other unfortunate ones," they spilled the truth. The couple had been "frightened by the advice of 'kind people'" and had protected themselves from predation by presenting themselves as paupers. It had worked so well that now they were "doomed to be returned to the homeland [*rodina*]." The husband opened his vest, revealing ten hundred-ruble notes sewn into its lining. Their ruse exposed, Piotrowsky was able to intervene and secure their admission into the United States.[33]

The couple's self-preserving deception, though innocently conceived, exemplified the practices and pitfalls that *Russkii emigrant* discouraged for its readership abroad. The final page in many issues printed a sidebar with detailed instructions on how passage to the US could be arranged. This primer offered grim warnings of practices like "stealing the border," which might make their passage more hazardous or expensive, even ensure their deportation. It also described the types and prices of tickets, the best months for transoceanic travel, and the procedure for obtaining a passport at a port police station. It specified the port of departure (Liepāja) and passenger carrier (the Russian East-Asian Line) that a Russian speaker ought to choose to avoid exploitation and linguistic barriers said to be common on German-operated ocean liners. The primer also advised how to avoid tipping off US border agents, who were constantly looking for migrants trying to sidestep prohibitions on "contract work" and prearranged labor positions.[34]

While many of the cases the society addressed on Ellis Island were bureaucratic, others reflected tragic situations. One such example was that of Elizabeth L., whose awful story of abuse, abandonment, violence, and despair spoke to darker aspects of labor migration. Elizabeth married her older husband in the Grodno province when she fifteen, over the resentment of his parents for her lack of a dowry. She entered "the difficult lot of a peasant wife" and soon bore two children. Their lives and labors were hard, and "her treatment from her husband's relatives was far from soft." When crop failure and a fire thrust the family into poverty, her husband set out to find work in Odesa. In his absence, and with the indifference, even sanction, of her in-laws, her husband's eldest brother repeatedly raped Elizabeth, despite her "having beaten him back with all her strength." Her husband returned three years later to find Elizabeth nursing a baby, what Piotrowsky called the result of her having "committed a sin." To Elizabeth's horror, her husband instantly reconciled with his brother over a bottle of vodka. She prepared dinner for the brothers and their parents, trembling in anticipation of a brutal beating, which indeed came. Her husband's parents drunkenly urged him on, calling out that Elizabeth should know who she was "dealing with."[35]

The family's poverty recurred, and Elizabeth's husband left once again, this time for the US. And again, Piotrowsky lamented, the "old story" repeated itself. This time it was her husband's youngest brother, who quickly "pestered her with sinful intentions" as her mother-in-law "scolded her for inaccessibility [*nedostupnost'*]." And so there came another unwanted pregnancy. Across the ocean, Elizabeth's husband adopted the habits of an "American," shaving his beard and dressing himself in fancy clothes. Soon he sent for his father and eldest brother. Later, he wrote Elizabeth that on the farm they had purchased, they were living "like gentlemen [*po panski*]." He enclosed no money or passenger tickets. For two years, Elizabeth struggled to feed five children in a small "hovel"—her father-in-law having sold the horse, cow, and much of their farmland before his departure. Finally, she could take no more.

Elizabeth retrieved a "pittance" hidden away in the barn "for a rainy day," sold off what remained of the homestead, and hired a border agent to shepherd her and the children to the US.[36]

Piotrowsky met Elizabeth and the children on Ellis Island, where they had spent two humiliating weeks waiting for her husband to answer her telegram, as they were not permitted to leave the island without his escort. The man finally arrived, adorned in "a starched collar, yellow shoes, and a gold watch," though he declared that he would take Elizabeth and only three of the children—those he identified as his own. When asked what should happen to the others, he told a horrified immigration agent, "you can drown them if you like, as you would mangy pups." Piotrowsky reported that the immigration commissioners hearing the case, accustomed as they were to the uglier sides of humanity, "cringed in repugnance." His account of Elizabeth's story ends on an uncertain note; while her husband eventually agreed to take the entire family, one of the children contracted measles. They remained on the island, "awaiting the recovery of the stricken child and the court's final decision."[37]

It is clear from Piotrowsky's retelling that he sympathized with Elizabeth and the children and was derisive of her husband and his kin— their story was subtitled "People Are Animals." Yet Piotrowsky did not intercede to protect Elizabeth and the children from the wicked relatives who had caused their abuse and neglect. Rather, Piotrowsky's role was to ensure that Elizabeth and the children endured "the island of tears" unscathed, shepherding them through immigration control and reuniting their family. Piotrowsky did not hide his contempt for the assimilation embodied by Elizabeth's husband, the clean-shaven, coiffed former peasant who happily tilled his fields in the US while Elizabeth endured the miseries of the farm and family he left behind. Still, Piotrowsky felt that circumstances had molded their difficult lives, first as peasants in Grodno and now as souls cast astray in their pursuit of US dollars. He accepted that immigration control agents would entrust Elizabeth and her children to a demonstrably malevolent father and husband whose inherent faults and cruelties were not created but rather exacerbated by his experiences in an imperfect and corrupting United States.

Piotrowsky's condescension was a response to the husband's boorish behavior but also the perception that the man's apparent assimilation

38 | "THIS BABYLON"

said something more about his crassness. Tactless as his appearance seemed, Elizabeth's husband was following guidance for what a migrant should do when interacting with US immigration agents. New arrivals passed through Ellis Island in their finest clothes, no matter the weather. During the peak travel season of spring and summer, the heaviness of their clothing, weighed down by the cold sweat of nervous anticipation, made passing through immigration control a hot, uncomfortable, and smelly crucible. Yet it was necessary, *Russkii emigrant* warned, as immigration agents were the human faces of a sprawling bureaucracy and could be satisfied if a migrant demonstrated careful, informed preparation and proper comportment. They were instructed to gloss over illnesses or domestic problems and say little about what they knew concerning job prospects in the US. Instead, they were to state, "I place hope in my strength and think that I can find a job." Family or friends who retrieved them "should have a proper appearance" and be prepared to display their bank records and citizenship papers. A migrant who foresaw problems at Ellis Island was encouraged to pass first through Canada or enter instead at the southern port of Galveston, Texas, "where the officials are less picky."[38]

Piotrowsky's observations about Elizabeth's husband reflected concerns about assimilation and comportment that were widely held by clergy and church relief workers. In a 1911 short story, the missionary priest Theofan Buketoff mused on how immigrants looked and acted differently after some time in the US. "You can always recognize a Russian man in America," Buketoff wrote:

> If he is dressed in mismatched, threadbare, and dirty Russian garb and walks as if struck dead, slightly bent and frowning about, know that he has only recently arrived from the Old Country and is not yet working, and for now lives on account of the relatives or friends who sent for him. If he is in a new and fashionable suit and shiny, gutta-percha collar fastened with a brightly-colored tie, in a bowler hat and watchchain, yet still walks unsteadily as if the new clothes constrain him, know that his countrymen already have found him a place in some plant or factory and he is working. If he got drunk and bawled in the evening in his backyard, or if while traveling by train he carelessly collapsed into a soft, velvety seat and lit up a nasty cigar, bowler hat jauntily askew, know that he is no longer a

"greenhorn," but already has a couple years in America, knowing a bit of its language and ways. But most importantly, he has money, and can pay off the police with it if necessary.[39]

The observations of Buketoff and Piotrowsky both underscore that appearance and comportment were important for how Progressive-era popular culture, dominated by an impulse toward social reform, perceived immigrant otherness. The language used to refer to immigrant communities and neighborhoods—the ethnic "colonies" dotting the US urban landscape—reflected a sense of insular otherness within US industrial capitalism. In political discourse, the media, and even the US academy, reformers and state actors favored the wholesale social and cultural transformation of the "other," believing that assimilation into a more respectable "American" came through aesthetic changes like clothing, shoes, haircuts, and grooming. In a telling example from Abraham Cahan's 1917 novel *The Rise of David Levinsky*, the titular protagonist, an Orthodox Jewish migrant from Russia, does not cease to be a "greenhorn" until he cuts his side locks and beard and purchases a fashionable suit. To be an "American" meant to *look* like one. "Not that you are a bad-looking fellow as it is," a wealthy man tells Levinsky after they meet in a New York synagogue, "but then one must be presentable in America."[40]

The Russian Immigrant Home

Other cases that Arcady Piotrowsky addressed on Ellis Island were comparatively less heartrending but no less memorable. One Thursday morning, Piotrowsky was doing his morning rounds in the temporary detention cells when a teenage boy stopped him, asking if he was "the Russian agent." Piotrowsky assumed that Fyodor Zhuk was a recent arrival, only to learn that the young man had been sitting in his cell for nearly two weeks, far longer than any temporary internee Piotrowsky had encountered. Piotrowsky determined from immigration commissioners that though briefly detained on arrival, Zhuk had been cleared for entry. Rather than boarding the ferry to New York City, however, Zhuk inexplicably had wandered back to temporary holding and calmly waited unnoticed in the dark corner of a cell ever since. Piotrowsky was able to unravel Zhuk's setback almost immediately. "In an hour," he wrote, "[Zhuk] was traveling with his protector in the carriage of an electric trolley straight to the hospitable and cordial shelter of the Russian Immigrant Home." It was the morning of the Feast of the Dormition of the Holy Virgin, the patronal feast of the Immigrant Home chapel, and a festal liturgy was taking place. Piotrowsky reported that the young man, having gone from an Ellis Island holding cell to an Orthodox chapel in Manhattan in only a matter of minutes, was so moved by his stroke of luck that he "gave thanks to the Merciful Creator with tearful joy for successful deliverance into freedom." Piotrowsky thought it divinely ordained. "Not all among us old immigrants," he wrote, "can brag that his first steps in a foreign land were so happy!"[41]

Fyodor Zhuk's path from the care of the Ellis Island agent to the Russian Immigrant Home was not uncommon. Of the thirty-seven hundred immigrants who passed through the Immigrant Home during its first year, just over five hundred—86 percent of whom were men—required the assistance of the special representative at Ellis Island. The rest, it seems, found their way through advertisements or word of mouth. Situated at 347 East Fourteenth Street, the frenetic heart of Lower Manhattan, the Immigrant Home was meant to be a warm and welcoming way station replete with the comforts and atmospheres of home. It included dormitory spaces, an industrial kitchen and dining room, and the Orthodox chapel that had welcomed Fyodor Zhuk. For fifty cents a day, a migrant like Zhuk received a bed and three "very tasty and nutritious" daily meals. They could stay for up to a week as they secured work, housing, and transportation elsewhere in the United States, a short reprieve from the strains of their journey before confronting the uncertainties of life in the US.[42]

Writing in 1912, priest Alexander Hotovitzky described a winter's evening visit to the home with Archbishop Platon (Rozhdestvensky). Walking through the door in a cassock dusted with snow, the imposing archbishop looked around and declared, "Rus', here is Rus'!" Evening vespers were under way in the chapel, "alight with the joy of prayer of simple Russian people." On the second floor, Platon examined the tidy dormitory for women and children, taking note of its hot and cold running water. Dinnertime approached, and "the smell of food wafting through the corridors teased the appetites of the Russians present, a rich

Figure 1.1. "RUSSIAN PEOPLE! Why go to strangers?!," announces this 1912 advertisement for the Russian Immigrant Home, showing the exterior of the building, its staff, and some of those migrants who utilized its services. "Hurry to your own people—to your own native Russian home. Here there is an Orth[odox] church. A corner of home. A bit of bread. A heartfelt welcome. A tender word. You will feel at home. Here you can receive advice on how to get started in America. Through the Russian Imm[igrant] Home, you can easily get a job." (*Russian Orthodox American Messenger*, August 14, 1912)

soup broth already poured onto the plates." The archbishop led a recitation of the Lord's Prayer and blessed the table, then all tucked into a sumptuous meal of soup and homemade Russian bread. Reflecting later on a cold winter's night warmed by the welcoming Immigrant Home, Hotovitzky praised the institution for "relieving the burdens that fall out of the blue onto the heads of poor emigrants at the very first moment of arrival to a strange country." To Hotovitzky, the Immigrant Home was "our pride! Our glory! . . . O Lord! This is a blessed, great cause!"[43]

Statistical reports generated by the Russian Immigrant Home offer small yet representative cross-sections of Orthodox Christian migration to North America, as well as insight into its regional and cyclical patterns. For example, the Russian East-Asian Line, the passenger service recommended by the Immigration Society, ferried seventy thousand people across the Atlantic in 1913. That year, slightly more than three thousand migrants passed through the Russian Immigrant Home.[44] Granting that only some of those passengers were Orthodox and that the Russian East-Asian Line was one of several major carriers serving New York Harbor, it is clear that only a small fraction utilized services like the Immigrant Home. Most chose to fend for themselves, had connections that made immigrant aid unnecessary, had already been to the US and were accustomed to its ways, or did not know that help was available.

Those who did seek help predominantly came from rural, agrarian places. Statistics for 1913 show that nearly a quarter came from Minsk, almost 15 percent each from Grodno and Volyn, and about 8 percent from Galicia. While a handful of migrants traveled from as far away as Central Asia and the Caucasus (and a single migrant from the Tomsk region of Siberia), most who came that year hailed from southern Russia and modern-day Ukraine and Belarus. Only four came from Moscow, and none from St. Petersburg.[45] Of the more than nine hundred people who passed through the Immigrant Home from January to April 1913, more than five hundred had the addresses of family or kin. More than four hundred, however, required vocational placement. More than a quarter were connected with agricultural labor, and nearly a fifth each were placed in domestic work and steel foundries. The rest scattered anywhere from timber camps and fishing boats to restaurants and railroads. In yet another example of the gendered aspects of immigration control, bound by legislated, moralizing notions of gender, sex, pregnancy, and unwed motherhood, five female migrants were "married by order of the Ellis Island administration."[46]

As demonstrated by the Immigrant Home's outreach to the Valhalla sandhogs, it was a hub for social aid throughout the New York area. In 1911 and 1912, the society director and priest Peter Popoff celebrated the Christmas holiday with Orthodox immigrants detained at Ellis Island. He set up an altar in a large room at the detention center and prayed with Russians, Greeks, Syrians, and others. Government immigration officials were so impressed as to invite a combined choir from the Russian cathedral in Manhattan and the Immigrant Home chapel to appear at a holiday concert alongside German and Italian choirs, where they sang yuletide songs for detainees and federal immigration officials.[47] Immigrant Home outreach efforts also reached immigrants incarcerated for crimes committed after arrival. The week after Easter in 1916, the Immigrant Home priest Michael Lakhno visited Sing Sing Prison in Ossining, New York, where a dozen Russian prisoners were serving terms of between five and twenty years. Bearing sweet Easter bread (*paskha*) and hardboiled eggs, dyed to a deep red with boiled onion skins, Lakhno heard the prisoners' confessions and celebrated an early-morning liturgy in the prison's Roman Catholic chapel. He left the men with Bibles, icons, and spiritual books and arranged for them to receive a church-published newspaper, *Russkaia zemlia* (*Russian Land*). Though they lived under difficult conditions and earned only pennies for harsh labor in prison workshops, Lakhno conveyed that "the poor [prisoners] are so thankful that their lot is eased by their brothers living in freedom."[48]

From the Russian Orthodox Immigration Society's agent at Ellis Island to the staff of the Immigrant Home to its collaboration with clergy and church workers from the Russian Archdiocese, the society sought to ease paths to self-sufficiency for Orthodox migrants. Situated at a primary entry point for new arrivals to the US, the society existed within a New York metropolitan area that offered a wide array of newspapers, businesses, and professional services for eastern European migrants, though it was also only a temporary way station. Beyond the Hudson were Orthodox parishes in factory towns and industrial metropolises where job opportunities—and the fast-paced patterns of life in the US—beckoned.

The World of Work

For migrants with limited English-language skills and few contacts, finding work in the US could prove both daunting and demoralizing. In 1909, Archbishop Platon noted that "it is a tragic situation for people, desiring to work, searching for jobs and not finding one, driving them to despair."[49] US immigration control thought little about how an immigrant had left their home country, but it cared a great deal about their fitness to live and work independently in the United States once they arrived. To Platon and others in the archdiocesan administration, the church needed to respond in kind. US industry rode on the backs of "greenhorns," overworked immigrant laborers who were cheap, available, desperate, and infinitely replaceable. Archdiocesan leaders recognized readily that US industry demanded much from these workers. A typical industrial work week was six days and upward of forty-eight hours, leaving little time or energy for regular church attendance, much less parachurch activities. "I was only there when I had time," one Detroit worker admitted of his parish, "because I work every Sunday."[50]

No matter hopeful Russian immigrants' skills or intellect, whether their past was professional success or peasant drudgery, sources like *Russkii emigrant* informed them that for most—agrarian, rural people for whom linguistic barriers could stunt further their industrial labor potential—entry into the US workforce probably meant a factory, farm, or mine. The primer in each issue of *Russkii emigrant* candidly and bluntly warned that "only the most completely physically able and healthy person" should bother making the journey—and, even then, with tempered expectations of what they would find on arrival. "Let all the intelligent be reminded," it advised, "that they must undertake the most difficult, physical work, as in America there is no firm where those unfamiliar with the English language may find such an i[ntelligent] job." Even those of higher social stations in Russia were not spared. "Officers [and] engineers do not come to America for happiness," the paper warned, "for here they will not find it, but suffer sorrows in abundance."[51]

Material conditions in US immigrant enclaves were such that fears of an early grave were not unwarranted. The sociologist and social reformer Jerome P. Davis observed that Russians received wages slightly lower than the average for foreign-born workers and endured comparatively poorer living conditions that further strained what dollars they earned. As renters and boarders, their housing costs were disproportionately higher, especially in larger cities. So was their grocery bills. Neighborhood groceries had less selection and higher prices, pushing many workers to take their meals in restaurants or saloons. Some pooled with others for sumptuous weekend suppers. Luckier still were those who found a room with a reasonable boarding fee that included cooked meals. More commonly, however, bars became both dining room and gathering space, often the only place offering passable food.[52] Compounding their food and diet insecurities, most workers did not have personal physicians, a significant issue in that their living and working conditions threatened greater exposure to physical injury, not to mention respiratory conditions like tuberculosis and black lung. "Americans build holes which are not fit for pigs to live in and rent them out to Russians," a Ukrainian doctor in Pennsylvania told Davis. "People say the Russians live badly because they live that way in Russia, but there they were compelled to live that way, here they should have a chance to improve their way of living."[53]

Investigators for the congressional Dillingham Commission visited typical areas where Slavic Orthodox workers lived, recording their findings as part of a forty-one-volume report published in 1911. Established in 1907, the commission used statistics, social science research, and ingrained ideologies of nativism, xenophobia, antisemitism, and the scientific racism of eugenics to forward policy recommendations that collectively argued for greater restrictions on migration into the United States. The historian Katherine Benton-Cohen argues against reducing the commission's work and published findings to prejudice alone, however, asserting that in fact it reflected "the collision of unprecedented numbers of immigrants with the emergence of new ideas about the federal government's capacity and social scientists' ability to find solutions to problems." Nearly all the solutions recommended by the commission—including the literacy test, greater bureaucratization and regulation of federal immigration infrastructures, restrictive national quotas, and broadening the reach of the 1882 Chinese Exclusion Act—would become law.[54]

In the coal towns of Pennsylvania, commission investigators found smoky neighborhoods caked with dust and soot, waste water, and trash filling the streets. Workers carried possessions in ratty suitcases and moved quickly. Some lived in substandard employer-owned spaces in company towns, others in crowded tenements and overfilled boarding-houses with rooms separated by curtains or sheets, often without indoor plumbing or electricity. Families rented out extra bedrooms or cordoned off space in common rooms, bringing itinerant strangers into their everyday lives. Workers routinely shared beds or alternated with others who worked opposite shifts. Some living spaces were little more than large rooms crammed wall to wall with cots.[55] A priest whom Jerome Davis spoke with in Cleveland reported ministering to a family who lived in a retrofitted boxcar, where he performed a baptism service for their newborn child. Theirs was a world that seemed entirely removed from the shiny exterior of US industrial modernity. "My people don't live in America," a Greek Catholic priest in Pennsylvania told Davis, describing Carpatho-Rusyn communities indistinguishable from their Orthodox counterparts. "They live underneath America. America goes on over their heads."[56]

A dominant industry for these migrants was coal mining. The coal fields of Pennsylvania would prove the most heavily concentrated Orthodox region in the United States for decades, emerging first in the anthracite regions in the eastern side of the commonwealth and later throughout the bituminous fields to the west. In coal towns like Mayfield and Frackville, work meant dirty and perilously dangerous toil deep beneath the ground. In the neighborhoods above, everyday life occurred beneath fears of unexpected blares from colliery whistles and frantic checks of safety boards at the mouth of the mines. Dillingham Commission investigators reported that mining company officials felt that "the existing conditions result from the fact that the foreigner is too dirty for the town to be other than what it is, but whether this is true or not, it seems that very little effort is made to improve the living conditions."[57] Mine work was so central to Orthodoxy in Pennsylvania that when Archbishop Platon consecrated a church in Coaldale in 1914, the congregation gifted him a gold cross inset with dark shards of anthracite.[58]

These coal congregations thrived with the success of the industry, but their churches faltered when the mines failed. Around 1902, a parish was contemplated in Wehrum, a western Pennsylvania mining town named for the chairman of the Lackawanna Coal and Coke Company. Workers raised money for a church but first bought a small plot of land for a cemetery. That an Orthodox cemetery was required so soon—before a church could even be built—was an ominous indication that illness, accidents, and death were real and present realities in a town with notoriously unstable mines prone to blowouts. Two years later, a deadly explosion temporarily halted mining operations. When more accidents followed, the town was abandoned. The archdiocesan directory continued to list Wehrum as a parish as late as 1911. By then, however, most of the community had followed mining jobs along Blacklick Creek to neighboring Vintondale, where they built a church in 1907. Soon the only trace of Wehrum was its overgrown Russian cemetery.[59]

Archdiocesan leaders fretted about labor conditions in places like Wehrum and Vintondale. Growing tensions between laborers and industrialists throughout the country prompted new questions about the responsibility of the church for ensuring the safety and well-being of Orthodox workers, even as they catalyzed the rapid expansion of the archdiocese throughout the Northeast and Upper Midwest. In 1902, Bishop Tikhon (Bellavin) offered public support for striking coal workers in Pennsylvania. "Without a doubt, in the future, life will become more expensive," Tikhon wrote; "supplies and goods will increase in price, while wages will remain the same and be insufficient." He feared that strikes would only increase, as an agreement "between the group of capitalists and the representatives of the workers" would only bring "temporary calm and satisfaction." Tikhon felt that Orthodox workers in other industries should demonstrate solidarity with those on picket lines. "It would be sinful not to remember the needy and suffering in the well-to-do times!" he wrote, suggesting that the Russian Orthodox Catholic Mutual Aid Society oversee a general strike fund for Russian workers. Tikhon sent the first hundred dollars himself.[60]

In contrast, other bishops and missionary clergy who served in American Orthodox Rus' perceived the North American Archdiocese as a sort of nation within a nation that could support its own in the face of exploitative working conditions, without the need for labor solidarity or self-advocacy. Most clergy opposed socialism on instinct and associated organized labor with its worst, even exaggerated traits. This is not to say that they were universally supportive of capitalism, however, especially when paired with state violence. These dynamics were tested in 1912 when in northeastern Siberia, a mass strike of gold miners led to the Lena Massacre. Tsarist soldiers arrested strike leaders, then marched on 2,500 demonstrators; 270 strikers were injured, another 250 killed.[61] In the *Russian American Orthodox Messenger*, the archdiocesan organ, Archbishop Platon responded to the massacre with a long treatise on labor and police violence in the United States, where the historic "Bread and Roses" strike in Lawrence, Massachusetts, had recently ended. "The labor question is as much a question of economics as it is, if not more so, of ethics," he wrote, though he regretted that "the antagonism between industrialists and workers has reached such a degree that the most madcap designs of the socialists find sympathy among the workers." Noting that his archdiocese predominantly served working people, Platon said that his travels through places like the industrial towns of western Pennsylvania had made him acutely aware of the motivations for Orthodox workers to participate in labor actions. "I state categorically that in no other country throughout the world can the condition of the unemployed be as terrible as in these most wealthy United States," he argued. For Platon, one contributing factor was easy to identify. "We are in need of a law that firmly asserts a worker's rights. The rights you have often are defended with the policeman's stick. Yet pardon me for saying that I cannot bring myself to wish this stick would acquire as important a role in [Russia] as it has here."[62]

Despite questions of labor conditions, worker safety, and state violence, *Russkii emigrant* published articles and advertisements announcing potentially exploitative labor opportunities. One posting from an employment agency in Chicago sought two hundred workers for "factory, foundry, and railroad work" and "children for light labor" along the shores of Lake Michigan. The agency promised free transportation once migrants reached Chicago and that there would be "steady work."[63] As the offer of transportation implies, major industrial metropolises like Chicago were catalysts for labor opportunities in surrounding areas and in turn for the emergence of new Orthodox communities in smaller or more remote places. Someone who responded to the call for workers in *Russkii emigrant* might have gone to Chicago, only to be sent west to Joliet, north to Kenosha, or southeast along the coast of Lake Michigan to Gary, Indiana. Once there, the Russian Archdiocese wanted them to find a robust Orthodox community prepared to support their spiritual and material needs.

"THIS BABYLON" | 49

Founded in 1906 by the United States Steel Corporation and named for its chairman, Judge Elbert Gary, the foundry town of Gary typified what an Orthodox migrant might have found once they ventured past New York. From its earliest days, Gary attracted thousands of Slavic immigrants with lofty promises of foundry work. By 1910, nearly half of the city's sixteen thousand residents were classified as "foreign-born whites." The first Orthodox parishes there were founded for Romanians and Serbs. The third, St. Mary's Russian Orthodox Church, was established in 1911. One of fourteen Christian churches in the city, St. Mary's was located in the south-side neighborhood known as "the Patch," a diverse neighborhood of immigrants and Black workers separated from the lakefront mills by the tracks of the Wabash Railroad. Described by one historian as a place "in which the greed of the speculator replaced the dominance of the Steel Company," the Patch was a lively, multiethnic, and multiracial enclave with crowded blocks of substandard housing. That the St. Mary's parish emerged there was the result of the draw and influence of Gary's dominant employer, the social fabric of the factory town, and the importance of religion as a focal point of community organization and support.[64]

The nucleus of the parish was Carpatho-Rusyn immigrants who constituted a local brotherhood chapter (*bratstvo*) of the Russian Orthodox Catholic Mutual Aid Society (ROCMAS). They promised archdiocesan leaders that "if there will be a Cross" in Gary, "there will be an organization" to support a church. Their congregation worshiped at first in a makeshift storefront, borrowing liturgical fixtures and vessels from the Holy Trinity parish in Chicago. The altar stood on a low platform behind an improvised iconostasis (icon screen) of wooden staves covered with cheap white linen and paper icons. An upstairs apartment served as the parish rectory. In late 1911, realizing the space would require a great deal of coal to heat during the winter, the congregation moved their "prayer house" to the home of their *starosta* (elder), the lay administrator of the community. Services occurred there in a nine-by-twenty-foot room for nine months, spanning their inaugural celebrations of Christmas and Easter. The permanent church was completed in August 1912. While much larger and more amenable for regular worship, the church retained elements of its makeshift predecessor. For three years, its altar table stood behind a low, temporary iconostasis of five framed icons affixed to white boards. The permanent iconostasis was installed in December 1915, a tall and ornate wall topped with wooden cupolas and crosses nearly reaching the ceiling. Donations large and small underwrote the project, bolstered by a $400 donation from ROCMAS. The church had been electrified earlier that year, so lines and arcs of lighted bulbs were fixed around the icons, deacon's doors, and the central royal door. Still, there was only enough money to purchase and paint half the icons. The final blank space would not be filled until October 1917.[65]

The growth of the St. Mary's parish and its quick success in raising funds for a church both reflected dominant forces common to a hardscrabble company town like Gary. The construction project was funded in part by substantial donations from U.S. Steel and Judge Gary himself, who gave the parish some $4,500 from its founding up until his death in 1927. The largest patron was a local Russian who owned one of the more than two hundred saloons found in the Patch.[66] That a primary underwriter made his money from a tavern was a minor transgression, as U.S. Steel management stressed strict temperance in the city. As it was, outsiders already perceived the St. Mary's congregation through a clash between the Bible and the bottle. An account by the editor of *Russkii emigrant* suggested that one line of demarcation was which newspapers one read. He observed that in Gary, *Russkii emigrant* was "a welcomed guest" in workers' homes and that throughout the city, "the center of life . . . is the Orthodox Church." As a result, there were no "progressive-hooligan organizations" there, and those who once read the leftist, anti-tsarist newspaper *Russkoe slovo* were now "beginning to visit church more often and go to the bar and get drunk less."[67]

In the tunnels of Valhalla, the foundries of Gary, the mines of Wehrum, and other places in American Orthodox Rus' at the dawn of a new century, the Russian Orthodox Church was a primary source of social and material aid for its working-class flock. Church immigrant relief efforts hoped to steer those migrants with evident needs from the transoceanic liner to the doors of a church-operated Immigrant Home and then on to work in a town or city where an Orthodox parish could support them. Helping workers to demonstrate their self-sufficiency, the archdiocese entrusted its parishes to take up this work in industrial cities, mining boomtowns, and agricultural regions where jobs were found. As we will see, church-affiliated schools, orphanages, benevolence societies, vocational training programs, social clubs, musical ensembles, and reading rooms supported personal improvement and spiritual growth, providing Orthodox Christians familiar touchstones in an unfamiliar world.

Most of the clergy and church workers at the parish level were immigrants themselves. When Arcady Piotrowsky left the Russian Orthodox Immigration Society in November 1913 for a position with a transatlantic shipping line, *Russkii emigrant* published testimonials to his work on Ellis Island. Priest Joseph Fedoronko had recently immigrated to the United States with his family. They were detained at Ellis Island for eighteen days, until Piotrowsky secured their release. Fedoronko noted that through the Immigration Society's "great, Christian-patriotic goal" of relief, it saved his family from calamity. "Our Russian agent is a true angel-comforter for all Russian immigrants," Fedoronko wrote. "May the Lord reward him for all the labor he had to endure out of concern for our liberation and must undertake daily in order to render help to other Russian immigrants."[68] We now turn to immigrant clergy, church workers, and their families, all of whom had parts in the task of ministering to others who also crossed oceans and continents to reach American Orthodox Rus'.

2

"My Sadness Is Boundless"

The Intimate Worlds of Church Work

He unrolled the scroll and found the place where it was written: "The Spirit of the Lord is upon me because he has anointed me to bring good news to the poor. He has sent me to proclaim release to the captives and recovery of sight to the blind, to let the oppressed go free, to proclaim the year of the Lord's favor." And he rolled up the scroll, gave it back to the attendant, and sat down. The eyes of all in the synagogue were fixed on him.

—Luke 4:17–20

In October 1915, a banquet was held in Berlin, New Hampshire, marking the consecration of Holy Resurrection Russian Orthodox Church. Guests dined on New England clam chowder, shrimp, and boiled lobster. A parishioner served his homemade cheese. At the end of the meal, parish priest Arcady Piotrowsky rose with tears in his eyes. Ordained a priest after departing the Russian Orthodox Immigration Society, Piotrowsky came to Berlin that spring knowing that his predecessor had spent two weeks in the remote paper-mill town before returning to New York and reporting that it was simply impossible to build a church there. Piotrowsky felt otherwise. After just six months, the fruits of his labors—and the benevolence of the sympathetic industrialists who owned the mills—was an understated yet elegant church whose six onion-dome cupolas shone atop one of the highest points in town, a crag at the foot of Mount Forist, which would come to be called Russian Hill. In his remarks, Piotrowsky criticized the social conditions of the immigrant workers he had steered through the crucibles of Ellis Island, arguing, "if the ruling class of America more attentively looked after the spiritual needs of emigrants, then there would probably be less crime and criminals among the immigrants and their children." Yet he felt that the industrialists of Berlin were different, seeing their Russian workers as "living souls," not "hired hands." Piotrowsky argued that the Orthodox Church was an instrument for reducing criminality, exploitation, and social degradation among the foreign-born. If the church addressed their needs, it in turn would be "preparing for the country a healthy and morally-intact second generation, born here." Piotrowsky felt that missionary clergy had a critical role in helping immigrants preserve their religious identities. "Give the immigrants their school and their church," Piotrowsky said. "As much as possible, lighten the load of their pastor-missionaries, and you will see how easy it is to solve the so seemingly terrible, proverbial 'immigrant question.'"[1]

This chapter explores how missionaries like Arcady Piotrowsky contributed to the many ways that the Russian Archdiocese addressed the "immigrant question." To explore the complex dynamics of missionary work in American Orthodox Rus', it focuses on four aspects and contexts of the clerical vocation. First, it explores the vocation itself, looking at the ecclesiastical structures in which clerical work occurred, and the complicated conventions of the clerical vocation in the late imperial Russian Orthodox Church. Second, it traces the institutional networks that brought missionaries to American Orthodox Rus' and the links of kinship and friendship that sustained clergy and church workers through the emotional strains of the missionary field. Third, it describes the critical yet often overlooked place of the clerical family in American Orthodox Rus', notably the expectations imposed on clerical wives. Finally, it broaches the everyday labors of building and maintaining missionary parishes. Taken together, the lived experiences of clergy, church workers, and clerical families in American Orthodox Rus' were bound by labors both prescribed and informal, explicitly outlined or silently expected, and rooted in the impulse to be helpers and protectors to vulnerable immigrant believers.

The clergy of American Orthodox Rus' stood out in the US ecclesiastical landscape, their beards and black cassocks clashing with the dominant image of a clean-shaven minister in clerical collar and suit. Most of the clergy who served American Orthodox Rus' held the ecclesiastical rank of presbyter, or priest (*sviashchennik*). They operated within a transnational, hierarchical church that was distinctly patriarchal and whose clerical ranks were solely held by men. What was more, they served parishes that significantly, if not mostly, consisted of young, working-class men. These structures, relationships, and contexts stood in stark relief against the different and far more informal, even subordinate roles held by women in the church. "Masculinity does not exist only in a contrary and opposite relationship to femininity," the Catholic studies scholars Alyssa Maldonado-Estrada and Katherine Dugan have observed; "rather, it is often constructed and achieved in relationships between men."[2] The missionary enterprise was defined by such relationships, including the ecclesiastical ranks that placed men in positions of authority over others, networks of vocational bonds and personal friendships, and in a number of cases, men whose brothers were missionaries, too.

In American Orthodox Rus', clerical work was just that: work. Clergy struggled with the conditions of their labor, navigating complex relationships at the parochial level that were simultaneously pastoral, social, and material. They lived in constant dependence on both the national church and their local congregation, whose spiritual protection was their charge. Nadieszda Kizenko asserts that in the late imperial-era Russian Orthodox Church, "the priest had two bodies to care for: a body private—his own salvation and holiness—and a body public—the souls and fates of his parishioners."[3] The demands of missionary labors in a distant and foreign American Orthodox Rus' amplified the stresses placed on each of these bodies. Just as the laity reframed their religious worlds within the disorientation of the factory town and the harsh demands of the industrial workplace, clergy themselves reoriented their own beliefs and vocations within the insecurities and anxieties that defined their own toil in the US. Far from home and awash in a sea of culture, politics, and social norms most unlike the Russian spaces they had left behind, clergy and church workers adapted and readapted alongside their immigrant congregations.

Though Progressive-era US society generally afforded clerics social cachet and an air of respectability, Orthodox clergy struggled with the pressures of assimilation and Americanization, just as their lay congregants did. And priests were similarly not predisposed or inclined to remain in North America, weighing pangs of nostalgia and the desire to return home against the tantalizing promise of prosperity abroad. At first, priests and church workers from Russia often thought of missionary service in the US a temporary errand for vocational advancement, biding their time until they could return home to a more advantageous post. All the same, many maintained a healthy curiosity about life in the US, making robust ecumenical relationships and forging ties with academic and social elites who could further the Orthodox mission to North America. Others grappled with homesickness and the inadequate feelings of being an outsider in a non-Orthodox culture. Some isolated themselves within their communities, harboring heavy skepticism of American mass culture and perceived decadence, even sharing their parishioners' cynical opinions toward a capitalist economy that exploited migrants' labor and broke down their bodies.

Missionary clergy and church workers labored at a time when religion was a catalyst in the refashioning of American masculinity around new ideals of emotional toughness and physical strength. This was embodied most prominently by President Theodore Roosevelt, whose public personality loomed atop his boastful exploits as a naturalist, outdoorsman, and unabashed imperialist.[4] For immigrant communities, demonstrating respectability in Roosevelt's America meant transcending assumptions about the foreign-born body rooted in eugenics and scientific racism.[5] Constructed hierarchies of race, ethnicity, class, and religion challenged dominant American Protestantism. Though coded as white Europeans, immigrant workers in American Orthodox Rus' encountered the negative stereotypes of physical weakness, mental deficiency, and limited work potential that public discourse afforded immigrants from eastern and southern Europe. In the words of the prominent eugenicist and lawyer Prescott Farnsworth Hall, migrants from these regions had "an entirely different mental make-up," standing before America's gates as "the most illiterate and the most depraved people" Europe had to offer.[6] Orthodox Christians in the United States were religious minorities whose church was often viewed through a similar lens of Orientalized immigrant otherness. Foreign-born Orthodox men from southern and eastern Europe needed to define themselves within American hierarchies of whiteness by exemplifying the strength, toughness, and respectability expected of the modern man. This began with the clergy, the most visible example of masculinity in American Orthodox Rus', and was mitigated through the lives, vocations, and relationships they fostered in the missionary field.

The Structures and Strains of the Clerical Vocation

Exploring clerical experiences in American Orthodox Rus' requires first an understanding of the ecclesiastical structures that governed their vocations. After relocating its consistory from San Francisco to New York in 1905, the Russian Archdiocese entered a period of exponential growth and bureaucratic reorganization. A new and comprehensive archdiocesan statute, issued in 1909, formalized many of the administrative structures and practical necessary to govern the expanding mission. The administrator of the archdiocese was a ruling bishop subordinate to the Holy Synod of the Russian Orthodox Church. From his see at St. Nicholas Cathedral in Manhattan, the bishop helmed the North American Ecclesiastical Consistory, a small group of clergy and laymen responsible for national church administration. The consistory also held nominal purview over diocesan institutions like its seminary, as well as charitable endeavors, fraternal organizations, and monastic communities.

Beneath the consistory, the archdiocese was organized into several substructures. There were separate vicariates for Syro-Arabs (Antiochians), Albanians, and Serbians, as well as a dedicated, albeit dormant, "department" for English-speaking converts.[7] The parishes of Alaska and Canada operated in relative autonomy, each with its own vicar bishop. The remaining parishes in the continental United States were overseen by the "Russian clergy" and constituted the core of the archdiocese. These communities were separated into regional deaneries (*blagochinie*), each with a territorial dean (*blagochinnyi*), usually an experienced priest. A typical parish (*prikhod*) was served by a parish priest (*nastoiatel'*). Sometimes he was assisted by a male psalm singer (*psalomshchik*), who might also teach in parish schools or direct the choir. While these were sometimes assigned by the archdiocese, priests and parishes could hire them, too, sometimes posting advertisements in the Russian press for open positions.[8] Lay parish leaders often included a churchwarden (*starosta*) entrusted with various administrative or functional duties. Sometimes there was a parish council or board of trustees, which managed parish funds and assets and vied for control over community life. Lay congregants could also assume roles otherwise performed by formal church workers. "In nearly every parish in America, there are always zealous church members, passionate and knowledgeable about church singing, who fulfill the duties of the *psalomshchik* for free," one priest wrote. "Without their help, it would be impossible for less affluent parishes to conduct the Divine Services."[9]

Parishes were established either at local request or at the initiative of the consistory. Beyond geographical considerations, to plant a parish required demonstrated interest and sufficient financial resources. The 1909 archdiocesan statute specified that a parish was "an ecclesiastical institution subordinate to the local Archbishop or Bishop appointed by the Supreme Church Hierarchy of Russia" and "may be of two kinds: independent [*samostoiatel'nyi*] and dependent [*pripisanyi*]."[10] An "independent" parish was self-sufficient in both resources and clerical leadership, while a "dependent" parish relied on the resources and clergy of other communities until it could amass enough members and resources to build (or buy) a church building and support a full-time pastor. In 1906, one year after the Ecclesiastical Consistory relocated to New York City, the Russian portion of the diocese had eighty-one parishes, more than thirty of which were in Alaska or Canada. Of the remaining fifty, twenty were in Pennsylvania. Within five years, the number of parishes in the continental United States had doubled, numbering nearly ninety. By 1917, excepting the ethnic vicariates for Serbs, Albanians, and Syro-Arabs, the Russian Archdiocese comprised thirty-one deaneries spanning thirty-two U.S. states and territories and six Canadian provinces, over three hundred parishes and church institutions, and more than 250 clergy.[11]

The catalysts for this growth were major parishes in a handful of major US cities, self-sustaining congregations that also served greater purposes for external perception and ecumenical outreach. Their large showpiece churches blended time-honored Russian architectural styles with the modernism of the US metropolis, drawing awareness and building social cachet for a religion generally perceived as foreign and obscure. St. Nicholas Cathedral (1902) fit seamlessly into a residential block on Manhattan's Upper East Side. Chicago's Holy Trinity Cathedral (1903), designed by the famed modernist architect Louis Sullivan, was a provincial Russian temple seen through the design aesthetics of the Prairie School. The large church built for the St. Mary parish in Northeast Minneapolis (1906) attested to the Russification of the first

Carpatho-Rusyn Greek Catholic congregation to convert to Orthodoxy in North America. In Cleveland, the thirteen gilded cupolas of the St. Theodosius church (1911) rose in the Tremont neighborhood to rival neighboring edifices for German and Slovak Roman Catholics. These and other cornerstone parishes helped upstart communities in neighboring cities and towns become strong parishes of their own and sparked chain reactions of missionary expansion. In this way, Minneapolis begat Chicago, Chicago begat Gary, and Gary begat East Hammond, a pattern that repeated again and again throughout American Orthodox Rus'.

The immigrant clergy who most drove this growth arrived in the mid-1890s, the product of demonstrated efforts to draw talented and committed missionaries to North America. During the summer of 1893, Bishop Nicholas (Ziorov) traveled from his cathedral in San Francisco to spend the summer in Chicago and the "White City" of the World's Columbian Exposition. On weekdays, Nicholas frequented the Russian pavilion in the Manufactures and Liberal Arts building, offering services three days each week in a fully outfitted model church. On Sundays, he worshiped on the city's west side with a growing congregation of Russians and Greeks. What Nicholas saw that summer inspired him to consider the potential to expand his mission farther into the Upper Midwest and Northeast, where increasing numbers of Greek Catholic congregations were entering the Russian Church en masse. In 1894, Nicholas took a sabbatical and returned to Russia, hoping to tap his own ecclesiastical connections to attract church workers who were undeterred by the prospects of working in a remote, perhaps less prestigious missionary diocese.[12]

The fruit of Nicholas's sojourn was a group of energetic, dynamic men eager for the challenges of serving in the rugged frontier of Alaska, dusty Pennsylvania mining towns, and the fast-paced bustle of New York City. The US piqued their curiosities, offering an opportunity for adventure and growth. "The challenge of laboring in a new field of church work and dealing with people in vastly different circumstances seemed to serve as a magnet to many," it was later recalled of these men.[13] The former rector of the Vologda Ecclesiastical School, Nicholas knew of a few promising recent graduates and several others then completing their educations there. He successfully recruited fourteen of them, including a set of three brothers.[14] Though Nicholas left the US in 1897, his legacy came in those whom he brought across the ocean and the doors they opened for more who arrived over the next two decades. These missionaries formed a nucleus of clergy and church workers who served in North America as teachers and professors, deacons and priests, monastery abbots and diocesan bishops, into the late 1960s. "What Metropolitan Innocent of Moscow was for Alaska," one of them later considered, "Archbishop Nicholas . . . was for the States."[15]

The men Nicholas recruited ranged in age from their early twenties to late thirties. Nearly all came from the Russian clerical caste, a peculiar product of post-Petrine reforms by which the tsarist regime ranked clergy within its tiered "social estates." The so-called *soslovie* system isolated the clergy caste into perpetual self-sustenance. The son of a deacon or priest (a so-called *popovich*) would be streamlined into a theological academy or seminary so as to follow his father into the clerical life. The daughters from these families often married clerical sons. This kept church work within generation after generation of intertwined clerical families. North American missionary activity emerged at a time when the *soslovie* system was changing and the *popovichi* studying in Russian seminaries and theological academies were becoming more radical, chafing against the personal and professional limitations inherent to the clerical estate. Even so, patterns of migration that brought church workers to American Orthodox Rus' reflected distinct traces of the clerical caste.[16]

A few among this initial group of missionaries came to North America as deacons or priests. Others were lay graduates of Russian theological academics and clerical schools who were contemplating, if not awaiting, ordination. They were to serve first as a *psalomshchik* (psalm singer), a clerical assistant whose duties included teaching in parochial schools, assisting priests with sacraments and pastoral work, and reading, chanting, and singing in church. These responsibilities required intricate and experiential knowledge of liturgical texts, tones, and melodies. While not exclusively a path to the diaconate or priesthood, a *psalomshchik* was educated and prepared as if he were to be ordained. In the US, those who were not married and who did not wish to be ordained into the celibate ranks often married women from the parishes. Some returned to Russia for courtship and marriage.

In 1904, Constantin Buketoff was working as a teacher in Oleshky, near Kherson in what is today Ukraine, when he received a letter from his older brother. Priest Theofan Buketoff needed a *psalomshchik* for his parish in Ansonia, Connecticut, and thought his brother perfect for the job. The following year, Constantin informed their parents of his decision to travel to the US, then set off across the ocean to join his brother. Theofan and Constantin Buketoff became one of several sets of brothers serving as missionaries in American Orthodox Rus'. In Connecticut, Constantin took quickly to the labors of a *psalomshchik* and soon petitioned to be ordained a priest. Bishop Tikhon (Bellavin) granted him three months' leave to travel home and marry before returning to New York for his ordination. Constantin succeeded, wedding the daughter of a provincial priest (and cousin to his sister-in-law) and was ordained in 1907. His first parish was a tiny church on a hill in New Britain, Connecticut, where the altar became so cold during the harsh New England winters that when preparing and consuming the eucharist, the young priest's lips froze to the chalice. His duties demanded frequent travel, often by foot or train, to visit priestless communities and isolated believers across Connecticut, Massachusetts, and New Hampshire. "I recall many anguished moments when Father was called for final rites with minutes to take the only train to get there," his granddaughter remembered.[17]

For missionary clergy, being a spiritual father for their parish clashed against the domestic demands of being both a husband and a parent. This is described by priest Theofan Buketoff, the elder of the Buketoff brothers, in "Christmas in a Foreign Land," one of the many autobiographical stories he published in church newspapers. Buketoff describes waking early on Christmas Eve, January 6, 1913, to the smells of his wife, Antonina, preparing rich, festive foods in the rectory kitchen. The long-awaited breaking of the Nativity fast was at hand. Yet the Christmas holidays heightened their anxieties that their daughter and son lived in two different worlds. Born in the US, they were exposed to its diverse peoples and cultures. At home and in church, they were immersed in what Buketoff calls his "native land." Neither child had seen Russia, but it loomed over their everyday lives, especially at times like the Nativity feast. Theofan and Antonina tried to temper their children's excitement during the thirteen long days separating "American" from "Russian" holiday commemorations, imparting that they "lived in the belief that for the world there is only one Christmas and it will be tomorrow, and that there is only one Santa Claus, who will be delivering toys on reindeer tonight."[18]

Father Theofan fretted over the long hours of Nativity services on January 6 and 7, a Monday and Tuesday in 1913. The church stood at the corner of a busy city block. It was recently purchased from a Methodist congregation, and its walls remained bare, the new iconostasis housed only a few icons, and rows of pews awaited removal, a common practice when retrofitting existing churches for Orthodox worship, as pews can be an impediment for prostrations and other typical movements of church prayer. Late Monday evening, after a sparsely attended vespers service, the exhausted priest descended to the basement of his apartment building to retrieve the family Christmas tree (*yolka*). Buketoff purchased it at discount after Americans shifted their focus to New Year's and hoped that none of his neighbors would laugh at the sight of a priest wrangling the tree up the stairs in January. The next day, after an exhausting Christmas liturgy, Buketoff sat with his son at the windowsill in the flickering light of the *yolka*. He explained that while this day was among the most important of their year, for everyone else it was "simply a mundane working day." This contrast, he said, was "why we are lonely in our great joy, and that's why it is endlessly difficult for us to maintain [that joy] within ourselves." Outside, the factory whistles blared. Bleary-eyed workers streamed in and out of the tavern across the street. All afternoon, knocks at the door had interrupted the family's Christmas dinner: a pushy wine salesman, a debt collector, the landlady. But in Russia, Buketoff told his son, the ornate churches were full, and workaday cares disappeared. There, "literally all of life came to a standstill in awe of the greatness of the moment." As their holiday celebrations drew to a close, another knock at the door came with a rent bill to be paid. "That is why the roses of bygone experiences wither away," Buketoff reflects. "Such is my fate, and indeed of every Russian soul in a foreign land." All the while he holds out hope for his children. "Under my protection, may they at least experience a portion of what I once did on the day of the great feast, the memory of which has always warmed and nourished my soul," he writes. "May their young souls be adorned with the rosy and fragrant flowers of life."[19]

Realities of Missionary Work

For some young men in late imperial Russia, missionary service in North America was an opportunity for reinvention. As a young seminarian in Vologda in 1907, Benjamin Kedrovsky was caught up in the wave of student protests then sweeping Russian seminaries and theological schools. Expelled for refusing to name other students involved in the protests, Kedrovsky was in a bind. Barred from ordination or even service as a lay *psalomshchik* in Russia and also banned from civil employment, Kedrovsky decided to join his three older brothers, all Vologda seminary graduates and priests who had followed Bishop Nicholas to North America in the 1890s. His barriers to church work removed, Kedrovsky found employment as a *psalomshchik* in Pennsylvania, where he met his wife. Ordained a priest in 1911, Kedrovsky set out the next day for a parish assignment in Gary, Indiana, where he would serve for nearly sixty years.[20]

The celibate priest Pavel Beskishkin came to North America in 1910, though not by choice. Educated at the seminary in Kholm, his then-bishop, Evlogy (Georgievsky), later recalled him as "a handsome boy with a wonderful voice" who had endured bullying and ridicule from classmates so severe as to have led him to attempt suicide. During his early twenties, an elderly superior dispatched Beskishkin, now a monastic priest, to visit a soldier awaiting execution for murder. His visits with the doomed man made Beskishkin convinced of his innocence. The young priest witnessed the soldier's execution, a grim pastoral task that would not leave his mind. Beskishkin's mental condition worsened, and he grew angry and defiant toward his superiors. Evlogy admitted in his memoirs to have "saddled Metropolitan Platon with [Beskishkin] in America," for monastic obedience obligated acceptance of even the most remote assignment. Evlogy recalled with regret a visit from Beskishkin before his departure and the gift of a "cheap *panagia*" from a young, distressed priest whose only wish was for his former bishop "to keep remembering" him.[21]

Separated from homes, families, and familiar habits, many missionaries found North America a mental, emotional, and spiritual struggle. It could bring material hardship as well. Clerical salaries in parish work averaged less than $800 per year in 1916 (around $23,000 today).[22] Even though these wages were relatively low, especially for those supporting a family, they were often commensurate to, if not greater than, those of working-class parishioners. In Pennsylvania that year, anthracite coal miners earned around $586, while those in the bituminous deposits earned about a hundred dollars more.[23] The average steel foundry worker earned upward of $700 per year, a male textile weaver around $650.[24] When Henry Ford introduced the five-dollar day in 1914, the average automotive worker made around $800 per year.[25] These comparisons did not usually apply, however, in smaller or rural parishes. Priest Nikita Gress served in Clayton, Wisconsin, a rural dairy-farming village. He could not support his family on his thirty-dollar monthly salary (less than $900 today) and depended on supplemental funds from the archdiocese. He could earn a bit more from *trebi*, small honorariums for services like baptisms, weddings, funerals, grave blessings, memorial prayers, and house blessings. *Trebi* fees ranged from a coin or two to upward of twenty-five or even fifty dollars and were meaningful supplements to low monthly incomes.[26]

Archdiocesan leaders recognized the material hardships of clerical work, though constant funding issues made it difficult to address them. "One may say with confidence that the work of the clergy of the Mission is more intense than the labor of the clergy in Russia," Archbishop Evdokim wrote in 1917, "since here in America one has to preach Christianity from the beginning, as it were; to organize the people into communities; to buy land for a church and rectory; to maintain everything with one's own funds; to find money to pay the priest." Evdokim felt that greater attention to clerical pay was necessary, alongside commitments to other benefits like pensions that would bring American missionaries into equity with their counterparts in Russia. Prevailing local conditions, however, shifted responsibility to the archdiocese—and it was able to offer supplementary aid to only a quarter of its clergy. "Hundreds of priests with families look to the future without hope," he wrote, "even though they are laboring more than their fellow priests in Russia."[27]

Job security for clergy in American Orthodox Rus' commonly depended on often-acrimonious relationships with lay parish leaders. Priests clashed with parish trustees over administrative decisions, liturgical practices, sermon content, community activities, and salaries. Embattled clergy frequently solicited reassignment, sometimes after only a matter of weeks, an inconvenience their families came to expect. They packed lightly when moving from one rectory to another, as parishes usually supplied the furniture, appliances, and fixtures, often even the curtains on the windows and the silverware in the kitchen drawers. Certain parishes earned reputations for their revolving-door progressions of clergy. The Ss. Peter and Paul parish in Detroit, founded in 1907, had eleven pastors over its first sixteen years. Across the Detroit River in the Ontario company town of Ford City, the St. John the Divine parish, founded in 1916, burned through eighteen in a decade, some holding as many as three, noncontiguous tenures.[28]

Layered atop the acute stresses and uncertainties of parish work were lingering and existential challenges like homesickness, longing, and despair. Another of priest Theofan Buketoff's stories begins with the priest and his wife roused from sleep in their rectory bedroom by a strange sound in the adjacent church. Buketoff is sitting half awake on the edge of the bed listening for the sound, a tolling bell, when the sight of a flickering candle in their bedroom icon corner transports his mind elsewhere. "A quiet and sacred joy filled my soul," Buketoff writes. "It felt as if I had awoken as a small boy at the dawn of a great feast, and as if this tolling was calling me to matins." In his mind's eye, Buketoff is standing "on the quiet and dark streets of [his] home town," where "already the silent, dark silhouettes of people in fur coats, caps, and headscarves are plodding by themselves in the quiet and dark streets, and all plod in the same direction, straight to church. Flinching from the nighttime chill, [he] stroll[ed] behind them." He sees himself entering the church, "white and lofty and shining in the dark night with a radiant holiness." Lit by crystal chandeliers shining brightly through incense smoke, the church is filled with "a sea of people and a sea of silent, sacred joy." But then the sound of the bell echoes once again, "and the sweet illusion disappears."[29]

The Bureaucracy of Church Work

The North American Archdiocese was a missionary enterprise structured as a transcontinental corporation, managed from New York within a larger ecclesiastical structure originating from the Holy Synod in St. Petersburg. The bureaucratization of clerical work meant the institutionalization of labor conditions, including the structuring of vacation time. Priests experiencing burnout or with pressing family crises could receive a sabbatical (*otpusk*) of sufficient time for transatlantic travel. An *otpusk* could also be a clerical award (*nagrada*) for long or meritorious missionary service. Priests and bishops used these rare opportunities to visit families and friends, to take pilgrimages to monasteries and other holy sites, or even to explore other interests outside the church. Missionaries were eligible for *otpusk* after three years and again every three to five years after that, though for most it was not a regular or repeated experience.

An *otpusk* was one way for the archdiocese to keep a disaffected or homesick priest in American Orthodox Rus', easing the strains of missionary work that some priests found lacking, if a bit provincial. Born in 1869 and educated in Kursk, priest John Slunin served as a priest for sixteen years before he sailed for the US in 1907 with his wife and two daughters. Assigned to the Holy Trinity parish in Chicago, Slunin replaced the popular priest John Kochurov, who had returned to Russia. Slunin could not conceal his disdain for the Windy City, finding his parishioners lackadaisical, even unrefined. "Merciful God," he wrote in his diary, "I've been away only two months and my heart is still so heavy, a deep unexplained sorrow. I left voluntarily to serve in a foreign land, yet my sadness is boundless, especially today." After a sparsely attended vespers service, Slunin lamented that in Russia that same evening, large crowds of worshipers packed into churches and well-trained choirs sang masterworks of Russian liturgical music, while in Chicago, "so sad, so primitive, such emptiness in this church." For the priest, the situation engendered self-reflective despair. "What is going to happen to me on Christmas and Pascha [Easter]?" Slunin soon left Chicago for New York and a position in archdiocesan administration.[30] Even after leaving Chicago for cosmopolitan Manhattan, Slunin's discomfort with US missionary work remained. "I have been in America four years already," he wrote, "which is not a long time." Even so, he admitted, "these four years were an eternity." Unlike clerical colleagues who had warmed to the US, Slunin struggled to adapt. "Life in America, no matter how long you've lived there, is life in a foreign land all the same," he wrote, "and America will never become a motherland [*rodina*] for the Russian heart, it will not replace Russia."[31]

66 | "MY SADNESS IS BOUNDLESS"

Slunin was granted his *otpusk* in 1911. His departure was scheduled immediately following Great Lent, Holy Week, and Easter, the most demanding periods of the church calendar for a priest. He sent his wife and daughters in May, with an anticipated return at summer's end. During their four-month journey, the family planned visits with friends and relatives in Kursk and Volyn and tours of some of the largest cities of the western Russian Empire. Archbishop Platon (Rozhdestvensky) assigned Slunin another task, asking the priest to use his trip to recruit monastics for missionary work in North America. Slunin scheduled a visit to the seminary in Kursk, his alma mater, and arranged meetings with important ecclesiastical figures, including members of the Holy Synod and its lay chief procurator (*ober-prokuror*).[32] Afforded greater importance were his visits to prominent monasteries. As critical fulcrums of Russian spirituality in late imperial Russia, monasteries fostered cultures of pilgrimage, helped to democratize and popularize religious literature, and transformed practices of confession and spiritual guidance.[33] Platon wanted the same for North America, asking Slunin to find men who could raise the profile of monasticism and promote similar religious and spiritual transformations in American Orthodox Rus'. Recruiting monastics was pragmatic as well, for supporting a monk cost less than a missionary with a wife and children.[34]

Slunin met with bishops, abbots, monks, and novices at two of the most important monasteries in the late imperial Russian Church: the Kyiv-Pechersk Lavra in Kyiv and the St. Alexander Nevsky Lavra in St. Petersburg. Yet it seems Slunin did not make an enticing or compelling pitch. When speaking with the metropolitan of Kyiv, Slunin recalled describing "how difficult our missionary work is and the kinds of attacks we have to endure, with our *Vladyka* [Platon] at the helm, from all sorts of non-Christians, from the Jesuits, and especially from the Jews—those people who hate all Christians, and especially Russian Orthodoxy." Slunin made a similar appeal to the monks. To his dismay, he reported that "the priestmonks would not come, for the hardships and *podvigs* [spiritual struggles] that are all of our lot, including our bishops, appeared too difficult to them." Slunin attracted only three novices from Kyiv. In St. Petersburg, he failed to persuade even a single monk.[35]

Slunin was comforted throughout his journey by the opportunity for respite and felt reluctant to return to the US. As the end of his trip neared, however, Slunin found himself yearning to depart. He reflected that it was hard to leave Russia, but, he said, "the habit of American life pulled me to the Ocean, to sail across its blue waters far, far to the west, for I wanted to see my kind *Vladika* [Platon], [and] my dear brothers, with whom I am already more connected and have more in common with than those remaining at home." Slunin disembarked in New York in late September. It was a city still strange and unfamiliar, though it remained his family's home for another four years.[36]

The Bonds of Clerical Friendship

Father John Slunin's self-reflections speak to the ways that the friendship and collegiality of other clergy and clerical families made easier the hardships of missionary work. As Slunin did, missionaries described these relationships through a vibrant culture of clerical writing in Orthodox periodicals like the *Russian Orthodox American Messenger* (titled in Russian *Amerikanskyi pravoslavnyi vyestnik*, or *American Orthodox Messenger*), the official archdiocesan organ, and *Svit* (*The Light*), the biweekly newspaper of the Russian Orthodox Catholic Mutual Aid Society. Their poems, essays, journal essays, and semiautobiographical short stories often served as odes or elegies for missionary colleagues, especially on occasions like ordination anniversaries and patronal saints' days and also at times of mourning or leave-taking. Editors of these publications—men like priests Alexander Hotovitzky, Peter Kohanik, Alexander Nemolovsky, and brothers Leonid and Benedict Turkevich—wrote, solicited, and published such materials in most editions, offering candid insight into the lives and friendships of missionaries at the turn of the century.

The late 1890s were formative for Orthodoxy in New York City. Deacon Ilia Zotikov came to Manhattan in April 1895 as the *psalomshchik* for the St. Nicholas parish, then the only Orthodox church in the city.[37] Born in Finland in 1869, Zotikov was a typical *popovich*, the son, grandson, and brother of priests. He entered St. Petersburg Theological Academy to pursue his expected vocation in the church. Zotikov met his wife, Maria, through her father, a deacon at the St. Petersburg parish where Zotikov served after his graduation.[38] In May 1895, shortly after he arrived in New York, Zotikov was ordained to the priesthood to serve as an assistant to priest Evtikhy Balanovich. Zotikov's ordination

Figure 2.1. This studio portrait probably commemorates priests Evtikhy Balanovich and Ilia Zotikov welcoming to New York five young missionaries who disembarked together at Ellis Island on October 14, 1895. Standing (*left to right*): Lay psalm singers (*psalomshchiki*) Paul Kazansky, Alexander Hotovitzky, and Jason Kappanadze. Seated (*left to right*): Priests John Kochurov, Evtikhy Balanovich, and Ilia Zotikov and priestmonk Anatole Kamensky. (Michael Z. Vinokouroff Photograph Collection, P243-5-174, Alaska State Library)

occurred during the first visit of a bishop to the St. Nicholas parish and probably was the first Orthodox ordination conducted east of the Mississippi River.[39] Around the same time, another recent graduate of the St Petersburg Theological Academy, twenty-three-year-old Alexander Hotovitzky, arrived at St. Nicholas to serve as its secondary *psalomshchik*. In 1896, Hotovitzky was ordained to the priesthood. When Balanovich elected to return to Russia later that year, the newly ordained Hotovitzky—not the older and more experienced Zotikov—was assigned as his replacement.

Along with their wives, both named Maria, Zotikov and Hotovitzky resided in the three-story townhouse that constituted the parish complex. The sanctuary took up much of the first floor. The second and third floors had apartments for each couple (neither had children) and rooms for two domestic helpers. The two young priests worked in these cramped quarters, with Hotovitzky as the parish rector and Zotikov as sacristan (*kliuchar'*). Over the next decade, St. Nicholas transformed from this small townhouse church that served more or less as an arm of the local Russian consulate into a glittering cathedral and hub for missionary work across the Northeast. Alexander Hotovitzky became one of the most dynamic and visible priests in American Orthodox Rus', recognized as a gifted orator, skilled administrator, and major figure for ecumenical relations. Shortly after his ordination in 1896, Hotovitzky founded the *Russian Orthodox American Messenger*, for which he wrote voluminously for nearly twenty years. "Your special decency and good manners, your grateful idealism, at once compelled me and disposed me to you," Bishop Nicholas told Hotovitzky, describing their first meetings in mid-1895, when the bishop was on a recruiting visit to the St. Petersburg Theological Academy. "I saw that you possess that Divine spark that makes every ministry truly the work of God and without which any calling becomes a soulless and deadening occupation."[40]

For many in the archdiocese, Zotikov was no less synonymous with the St. Nicholas parish than Hotovitzky was. On the tenth anniversary of Zotikov's ordination, Bishop Tikhon noted that that day in 1895 had "begat both parish and pastor."[41] Yet Zotikov avoided attention and seemed less comfortable with more visible pastoral tasks. As Hotovitzky's assistant priest, he tended to the sanctuary and ensured the order and organization of sacraments and services. In Hotovitzky's absence, Zotikov paid bills and attended to other financial tasks, being the only other person Hotovitzky authorized to handle parish funds.[42] His was an unglamorous and understated, albeit essential, role, freeing the younger and more charismatic Hotovitzky from everyday tasks. Intimates remembered that Zotikov's kind and warm demeanor shined most in the quiet moments of his workaday ministry. Recalling their first meeting in 1895, priest Peter Kohanik, then a student passing through New York on his way to study in Russia, recalled Zotikov gleefully downing ten cups of tea over breakfast. Even after fifty years, Kohanik "could not recall Russian tea drunk with such zeal."[43]

In the absence of a significant Russian-speaking Orthodox community in New York City, which would not concretize for some time, the early St. Nicholas parish was polyglot, drawing from a number of ethnic groups and constituencies around the city. The parish was also a critical bridge between the church and tsarist diplomacy in the United States. This was exemplified in a weekday liturgy in 1896 commemorating the coronation of Tsar Nicholas II, a service that priests were expected to carry out to honor the imperial house. Hotovitzky, Zotikov, and a Syrian reader used both Church Slavonic and English. A visiting priest prayed in Greek. The spirit of the day, however, teemed with the symbols and rhetoric of imperial Russia. Addressing a large congregation of tsarist officials and diplomats, local dignitaries, and workaday parishioners, Hotovitzky remarked, "Wherever a Slav may be, he can always look lovingly to Moscow, where our emperor has now been crowned. And do we not love him well, when those of us who must earn their bread by hard toil have laid all aside on this working day to come hither and pray for him?"[44]

Such moments of public fealty to the sovereign were expected of missionary clergy like Hotovitzky and Zotikov and underscored the broader transnational imperative of building an American Orthodox Rus' that reflected an idealized image of its mother church. As the mission grew, clergy and laity alike were encouraged to forge paternalistic identifications with the imperial house. Congregants heard petitions for the tsar at every liturgy. Their churches bore tangible reminders of his personal benevolence, from donations for building projects to icons and gospel books gifted in his name. Clergy wore pectoral crosses inscribed with his monogram and were expected to conduct services of thanksgiving in honor of his majesty. Writing in the *Russian Orthodox American Messenger* in March 1913 after the commemoration in New York of the three hundredth anniversary of the House of Romanov, Hotovitzky extolled the tsar as "a man of strength, mighty in Orthodoxy, rich in mercy, a mighty protector of the weak, a formidable advocate of truth, a faithful servant to the throne of the Tsar, a true son of the fatherland." Leading clergy like Hotovitzky afforded great importance to this lofty, romanticized image of an Orthodox sovereign, not just to maintain loyalty among people from the Russian Empire but also to engender those ideals within Carpatho-Rusyn migrants from Austria-Hungary, whose Russification was a fundamental missionary imperative. American Orthodox Rus' was an inseparable part of Holy Orthodox Rus'. "The ocean did not remove the branch from the trunk," Hotovitzky wrote of Russia and its tsar, to whom he exclaimed, "your joys are our joys!"[45]

The early reign of Nicholas II was a formative moment of transition in the Russian Empire. Beset by mounting political dissent, labor unrest, and calls for reform, the state embraced industrialization and global economic development and bolstered trade and diplomatic relations with the West. The ties that bound the St. Nicholas parish in Manhattan to these transnational ambitions were most evident in its campaign to construct a new and more elaborate church. In February 1900, on the eve of Hotovitzky's departure for a fundraising trip to Russia, Zotikov blessed the journey with a service of thanksgiving at St. Nicholas townhouse church. While Zotikov tended the parish in Manhattan, Hotovitzky traveled across the empire soliciting donations. The first 5,000 rubles came from the tsar himself. Two special collections were taken in each parish of the Russian Empire. The popular and charismatic priest John of Kronstadt gave 200 rubles and inscribed Hotovitzky's donation book with a blessing, a key endorsement far weightier and more meaningful than the revered priest's token donation. A new church for the most prominent city in the United States was considered important, even though most every person who offered Hotovitzky a donation would never see it themselves. He returned to New York with around 70 percent of the projected budget, calculated at around 114,000 rubles.[46]

In 1901, a cornerstone was blessed on East Ninety-Seventh Street between Fifth and Madison Avenues, less than a block from Central Park. Hotovitzky was conspicuous among the clergy circling the stone that was placed at the bottom of the large hole cleared for the church complex. At street level, speaking to the ties between the parish and the Russian state, Zotikov was somewhat out of sight among the crowd at street level, conducting a choir he had arranged for the occasion composed of officers and personnel from the Russian battleship *Retvizan*, then completing its acceptance trials at a shipyard in Philadelphia.[47] A year later, the new showpiece church was consecrated. Local historical memory and church history alike long associated its construction with the dynamic personality of Alexander Hotovitzky. Upon his departure from the US in 1914, the parish brotherhood installed a memorial plaque at the rear of the sanctuary, which they hoped would "remind all those who come to pray at the Cathedral, not only now, but unto generations of generations, who was the builder of this wonderful cathedral, whose voice resounded within its walls in fiery and inspired words of prayers and instruction, whose voice warmed our hearts."[48]

In 1905, the diocesan consistory moved from San Francisco to the Manhattan cathedral. A number of factors contributed to the decision. Diocesan leaders were convinced that the Alaskan vicariate had sufficient resources and cohesion to operate on its own. Outside of Alaska, they felt that going forward, their most fruitful missionary field would not be the relatively static handful of parishes along the continental Pacific Coast but rather the increasing number of communities in the industrializing Northeast. There were already upward of twenty parishes there, surrounded by yet more Greek Catholic congregations with imminent potential for conversion. And where once the New York parish constituted a small, rented townhouse in lower Manhattan, now there was a larger, more amenable complex on the Upper East Side. Finally, there was a practical justification in that international mail service with Petrograd was five days faster in New York than in San Francisco.[49] "Your city is second in the world, and first in this country," Bishop Tikhon (Bellavin) declared upon arriving in New York. "It is likewise fitting that a Russian hierarch resides in this parish, which of all the parishes is the most Russian."[50]

The presence of a bishop and his consistory altered clerical duties at St. Nicholas. Hotovitzky became the cathedral dean while also taking on administrative tasks within the consistory. Zotikov's supporting role became all the more important. A resident bishop meant managing more complex services and added new responsibilities for his busy schedule of parish visitations. And a growing parish community also meant more weddings, baptisms, and funerals. Working within an expanding administration, Zotikov assumed many of these tasks as the cathedral sacristan.

As the fifteenth anniversary of Zotikov's ordination neared in 1910, he begged off the customary celebration. Other priests insisted that he receive the recognition they felt was deserved, a sentiment reinforced by hundreds of congratulatory telegrams. A jubilee banquet was held, complete with speeches and gifts. Some of the most effusive praise came from Hotovitzky, who was apparently so overwhelmed that he saved his formal remarks for the next edition of the *Russian Orthodox American Messenger*. Hotovitzky and others knew that Zotikov was preparing to return home, long having yearned to do so. (While on *otpusk* in 1898, Zotikov even asked for permission to remain in Russia.)[51] Writing of his remarks that day, which were comparatively shorter than those of other clergy and archdiocesan figures, Hotovitzky expressed modest regret, as he "was not able to express everything that filled [his] soul, as [Zotikov's] spiritual son, his concelebrant for all fifteen years of shared residence and service in New York," but he wished to reiterate to Zotikov a heartfelt wish: "that God may honor you a hundredfold, dear, unforgettable, loyal friend and comrade, for your kind heart, counsel, and constant moral assistance!"[52]

Several weeks later, Hotovitzky described another heartfelt scene at New York Harbor, where "Fr. Ilia Zotikov and dear little *matushka*" stood on the docks with a crowd of friends and well-wishers, including local clergy, laity, and representatives from the Russian consulate. "Certainly, there was not one person amid this not touched by the sincerity of the entire experience. Simplicity and kindness have always been inherent to dear Fr. Ilia, and now this simply encircled his person with radiance," Hotovitzky recalled. He mourned the departure of a humble priest who "was not of the powers-that-be [*sil'nye mira sego*]" yet whose constant presence eased the many labors and sorrows of making New York the burgeoning epicenter of American Orthodox Rus'. "As a personal friend of Fr. Ilia, having lived with him in perfect harmony for all these fifteen years, I might be suspected of being excessively bright in my narrative color," he wrote, "but then I refer to these eyes, swollen with tears." Hotovitzky and the others remained for some time to watch Ilia and Maria Zotikov disappear over the horizon.[53]

The Clerical Family

While there was a small number of monastic clergy serving in archdiocesan parishes, by 1911, the majority of priests and deacons—upward of 80 to 90 percent—were married.[54] Unlike the celibate Roman Catholic clergy, who forsake family ties for their clerical vocations, the wives and children of Orthodox priests, deacons, and church workers made

74 | "MY SADNESS IS BOUNDLESS"

for different and complex bonds between clergy and parish. The historian Vera Shevzov notes that "in acting as administrator, the priest found himself not so much at the top of a hierarchical system as in the middle of a complicated web of relationships."[55] The clerical family was a dominant force within this complexity. The priest and his wife were the most visible members of both their kinship families and the congregations they served. The affectionate honorifics parishioners used for them—*batiushka* and *matushka*, beloved father and mother—placed the couple in a kind of parental role over the congregation. In turn, the children in their kinship families linked the priest and his wife to others in the parish. Front-porch friendships and classroom crushes, petty jealousies and deep dependencies—all were social ties not exclusive to comings and goings in the church or rectory. "For better or worse, in joy and sorrow," observes the theologian and Orthodox deacon Nicholas Denysenko, who himself comes from a clerical family, "the priest's wife and family close the separation between the priest and the parish community: The family is a part of that community, and thus lives within it, not outside of it."[56]

The clerical family provides significant insight into the role of women in American Orthodox Rus'. In general, women did not hold positions of authority in the Russian Archdiocese. They did not serve as delegates to church councils, rarely appeared on parish boards, and were canonically barred from clerical ordination. And unlike the Roman Catholic Church, where women religious were ubiquitous in their visible public vocations in established networks of schools, hospitals, and orphanages, archdiocesan institutions were far less developed and female monasticism virtually unknown. In general, women who took up church work served in voluntary roles at the parish level. They taught in evening and Sunday schools, sang in church choirs, participated in parish musical ensembles and theater troupes, cleaned and decorated the church, helped cook for parish events, and joined sisterhoods and altar guilds. This reflected the broader customs of the late imperial Russian church, despite long-standing efforts to transform its ingrained gender roles. The historian William Wagner asserts that from the 1860s in Russia, "the ideal of womanhood conveyed in Orthodox writings and the roles considered appropriate for women were contested and in flux, destabilizing structures of authority and providing women with alternative images that could be used to interpret, fashion, and give meaning to their lives."[57] Both in Russia and in American Orthodox Rus', there was much work to do in this regard by the turn of the century. Relegated to parachurch institutions and support roles by canonical restraints and entrenched custom alike, laywomen carved out as much autonomy and authority as was possible outside the male clerical ranks.

These activities were amplified for clergy wives, many of whom also came from multigenerational clerical families and received educations from church institutions. The wives of priests were not just a mother to their families; they were *matushka* to the parish, its "little mother."[58] By virtue of their husbands' ordinations, clergy wives assumed duties that were imbued with tacit expectations of leadership, selfless sacrifice, and outward grace—and that were hardly voluntary. Clergy wives understood well the expectations placed on them and the spaces they were deigned to occupy. This was especially true for those reared in clerical families, having been exposed from a young age to the public and private realities of the clerical vocation and parish life. The domain of the priest was ostensibly all of the church and its environs and radiated from the altar, a space kept separate by an iconostasis through which most women were canonically forbidden to pass. The labors of the priest's wife occurred in peripheral spaces to the altar and church: the choir loft, the kitchen, the parish hall, the classroom, the rectory. In public, clergy wives were expected to take leadership roles in parish spaces and institutions open to women, founding and helming sisterhoods, leading parish schools, conducting church choirs, organizing parish dinners, and overseeing charitable endeavors, all the while serving as eager and visible handmaiden for their husbands' ministries—whether or not they wished to do so. Their domestic obligations of child rearing and homemaking, ostensibly private, garnered scrutiny from the prying eyes of congregants who held both figurative and legal ownership of parish rectories and also the strings of the clerical family purse.[59]

The role of the clerical wife was also defined by her own Orthodox practice. A 1913 guidebook for clergymen prepared by a seminary instructor in Russia offered a long list of questions that might be asked of a priest's wife during the sacrament of confession. While these questions were offered as exemplary suggestions and might not have been asked in every instance, they offer insight into the public and private responsibilities expected of clergy wives in the late imperial Russian Church. Did she read edifying literature? Did she pray before and after meals? How did she dress and comport herself? Did her husband drink or possess a "propensity to a carnal worldly life," and did she dissuade him when he was inclined to sin? Did she "help him conduct a life worthy of his rank and position?" Did she keep a peaceful and quiet home, freeing her husband from any distraction from his duties? Did she attend services on Sundays and feast days? Did she conduct positive conversations with parishioners and "serve as a good example for them in chastity, abstinence, and piety?" And did she instill her positive qualities both in her children and in other women? Perceived through these questions, the Russian clergy wife emerges as a perfect helpmeet, a woman who held no ordained rank yet still was expected to project the same public image of moral purity and pious devotion as her husband. Her activities inside and outside the church were more important for the example they exuded than they were for her personal needs and self-esteem. The sacrament of confession was but one place where the clergy wife was made to understand this burden. Her salvation would come only if she ensured the same for her children, her husband, his parishioners, and especially other women. None of these suggested questions asked what she demanded of others, if she felt supported, or if her own spiritual, material, or emotional needs were being met. In contrast, the questions provided for the confession of a priest include but one passing mention of his family and no mention at all of his wife.[60]

Clerical Expectations and Parish-Building

When Archbishop Evdokim (Meschersky) arrived in Berlin, New Hampshire, at the newly completed Holy Resurrection church in October 1915, he was met at the church door by parish priest Arcady Piotrowsky. When the archbishop continued on to the parish rectory, he was greeted by Piotrowsky's wife, Mary. From their arrival in the US, Mary Piotrowsky helped her husband transition from relief work with the Russian Orthodox Immigration Society to the Orthodox priesthood. After a period in which their family crisscrossed the Northeast with each changing parish assignment, in 1915, Father Arcady was interim pastor of the St. Theodosius parish in Cleveland when he was asked to establish a church in the White Mountains of New Hampshire.

Berlin was a paper town in the vast softwood forests of northern New England. Russian laborers first came there around 1900, taking up the lowest-paying jobs pulping mills had to offer, what they considered "black work" (*chyornorabochii*), a casual euphemism from Russia describing taxing physical labor that would cake one's skin with dirt and grime. Over the next decade, the Russian-speaking population in Berlin grew to more than 250, mostly from Grodno, Volyn, Vilna, and Minsk. There were around thirty families, and the rest were single men. Over time, local industrialists became concerned over the habits and behavior of these Russian-speaking workers. Notorious for drinking away their wages as soon as pay envelopes were opened, many spent Sundays and holidays brawling in the streets. On Easter Sunday in 1914, town police could barely keep up tending to the drunken and bloodied Russians sprawled outside bars and saloons.

Town leaders attributed the situation to a lack of religious grounding. There were churches in Berlin for the mostly French and Irish laborers who dominated the mills, including Episcopalian, Congregational, and Catholic parishes. In comparison, Russian workers had only occasional visits from regional clergy, usually a priest from Boston, who first visited Berlin in 1907. Two paper-company executives, Orton Brown of the Berlin Mills Company and Robert Wolf of the Burgess Sulphite and Fibre Company, were concerned that the issues they perceived as endemic to their Russian workers were greater than what a visiting priest could address. They initiated dialogues first with the Boston priest and then with archdiocesan leaders in New York, who were keen to expand their missionary reach into the more remote corners of New England. The two mill owners pledged support and resources to ensure that an Orthodox church would be built in their town. Both thought the church might improve the productivity of the Russian workers employed in their pulp mills. And as devout Protestants with great local influence, it seems they hoped the new church might also encourage temperance.

The archdiocese assigned a monastic priest to Berlin during the spring of 1915. He turned back for New York City two weeks later, declaring the community too unruly and disorganized to build and support a church. Bishop Alexander (Nemolovsky) contacted Arcady Piotrowsky,

78 | "MY SADNESS IS BOUNDLESS"

whom he knew through their mutual work with the Russian Orthodox Immigrant Society. Alexander told Piotrowsky that "in Berlin, a broad field for missionary labor lies ahead." The situation required a priest who was "fully in command of the English language" and who could build close relationships with influential industrialists like Orton Brown and Robert Wolf. These were attributes Alexander knew that Piotrowsky demonstrated amply in the immigration courtrooms of Ellis Island. Piotrowsky set out from Cleveland in April with Mary and their children, taking residence in a Berlin hotel just in time for Holy Week and Easter.

Father Arcady made quick work of organizing a parish. He set meetings with Brown and Wolf and made informal contacts with their Russian workers. The Piotrowsky family moved into a small, three-room apartment appointed with furniture from Brown's storehouses. An inaugural liturgy was held at the local Episcopal church with the enthusiastic sanction of its pastor. A meeting afterward attracted 139 people, who responded with a single, unanimous voice that they desired a church. For Easter services the next Saturday evening, Piotrowsky rented the meetinghouse of the Berlin Unitarian Society, which often allowed other religious groups to use its building.[61] To his astonishment, "nearly a thousand Orthodox people had come down from the forests of New Hampshire and Maine, and from Canada," filling the corner church and spilling out into the street. A few Polish Catholics and even some "Americans" came as well. Piotrowsky's sermon "implored the people not to defile the Holy Feast with reckless drunkenness, and to spend the day as is befitting a faithful Christian." He learned later that unlike the previous Easter, not one Russian worker was arrested for drunkenness that day. Encouraged by these apparent signs of progress, Piotrowsky rented a garage from the city, once a fire station. "Washed and cleaned out, with an improvised iconostasis," he recalled, "the garage transformed into a very decent church."[62]

Within a month, local Russian workers, hired at a rate of $1.75 per day (later raised to $2, around $60 today), were using dynamite to clear rocks and boulders from a plot of land at the foot of Mount Forist. Piotrowsky selected the site of the new church himself, with Brown and Wolf's approval. Brown wrote a check to purchase the land and agreed to donate half of the construction materials. With the help of Brown's suggested contractor, the warehouse of Brown's mill provided the rest at half price. Parishioners paid the remaining construction costs themselves, with the final total amounting to nearly $10,000. A two-story church was planned. The ground-floor parish hall would be outfitted with a harmonium, appliances and dishware for tea service, fully stocked bookshelves, and a "magic lantern" slide projector. Above would be a church hailed as "a wonderful example of Russian church architecture, adapted to the conditions of American life." It was designed by John Bergesen, an Orthodox architect whose other works for the church included the archdiocesan cathedral in Manhattan. Bergesen also drew up plans for an iconostasis, to be custom-built by a local cabinetmaker. Piotrowsky designed the rectory himself.[63]

On October 9, 1915, Archbishop Evdokim (Meschersky) came to Berlin to consecrate the church, dedicated to the Holy Resurrection. When the bishop reached the site, perched atop the White Mountains, Piotrowsky and assembled clergy and laity sang the hymn "God Grant Many Years" for "the Sovereign Emperor, the Imperial House, the President of the United States, the Holy Synod, and His Most Eminence Archbishop Evdokim." The bishop paused to admire the panoramic view. "What a strikingly marvelous sight opens from here!" he remarked, gesturing to the town below. "Indeed . . . it is very good here. The soul is closer to God and one desires to pray!" After visiting the rectory and greeting Mary Piotrowsky, Evdokim and others set off in Orton Brown's eight-seat automobile for a long drive through the natural splendor of Mount Forist.[64]

The consecration service the next morning underscored that building Holy Resurrection was a missionary effort by Piotrowsky and the Russian Archdiocese and also a social project for Berlin industrialists and their Protestant brethren. "Americans" filled the church, including town officials, mill administrators, and parishioners from the local Episcopal and Methodist parishes. Edward Parker, the Episcopalian bishop of New Hampshire, and the Reverend Percival Wood of Berlin's Episcopalian parish stood inside the altar in their full vestments and followed along using English-language prayer books.[65] In a tearful sermon, Piotrowsky "thanked the American friends for their sympathy and help in the difficult struggle [podvig] of organizing a parish and building a church," just as he thanked "the Omnipotent Lord, . . . who did so much for the benefit of the Russian people, torn from the Motherland and not having their own corner in a foreign land, creating for them an ethnic refuge—a House of God!" When the cornerstone was blessed, Wolf and Brown each took turns at the trowel to seal the block with cement.[66]

With Robert Wolf's support, Piotrowsky expanded his missionary labors into neighboring towns. Situated a few miles to the northwest, Lincoln was a company town controlled by George Henry and his family's paper firm, J. Henry and Sons. Meeting with Henry in Lincoln, Piotrowsky described the new Berlin church and offered a letter from Wolf attesting to their successful collaboration. Henry was wary to offer similar assistance. "Being a Protestant," Piotrowsky recalled, "evidently, he mixed up Orthodoxy with Roman Catholicism." It took nearly three hours for Piotrowsky to ease Henry's concerns and secure an agreement by which Henry would help obtain construction materials, furnish the rectory, purchase vestments and liturgical items, and also obtain books for a school and a reading room. Henry also promised that mill owners underwrite the priest's salary. Piotrowsky was pleased, though he also knew that Henry owned or controlled much of the property in town, including the Protestant and Catholic churches. He told Henry that to continue with the project, "drawing up a notarized contract would be obligatory." The archdiocese could allow Henry to own the land but only if the parish (and its bishop) had claim and full use of what was built on it. Piotrowsky departed Lincoln confident that Henry would agree.[67]

As 1915 came to a close, Arcady Piotrowsky appeared to be overseeing a growing mission in the paper towns of northern New Hampshire. Behind the scenes, however, the priest had reached an emotional breaking point. Berlin town fathers thought that the church had ebbed the drunken rowdiness of local Russian workers. Piotrowsky saw a different picture. At several contentious parish meetings, "the question of ousting Fr. Piotrowsky from the city limits was openly discussed," necessitating that Orton Brown, Robert Wolf, and local Episcopalian clergy intervene on Piotrowsky's behalf.[68] In a letter to Evdokim in early February 1916 that was reprinted in the *Russian Orthodox American Messenger*, Wolf described issues that Piotrowsky omitted in his published accounts of founding the Berlin church. Wolf revealed that a group of local Russian men had opposed the building project. The constant antagonism of these workers, known more for patronizing local saloons than the church, stoked Piotrowsky's simmering breakdown. As Wolf explained, "the saloon element is making a last desperate effort to control things at the church and it seems [to] those of us who are interested in the welfare of your church here that the only way out of the matter is to absolutely prohibit these men being in any way connected with the Church Committee." Though not Orthodox, Wolf felt ownership over the Berlin church, having expended financial and material resources as well as his political capital for its construction. And as an Episcopal vestryman whose denomination had demonstrated long-standing concern and favor for the Russian Archdiocese, he also felt a sense of ecumenical duty for its upkeep. Wolf admired and respected Piotrowsky and was disappointed that a pastoral change seemed inevitable. "We, of course, need a man who understands the English language thoroughly," he suggested, "and also a man with enough force to handle the rougher element in the way they should be handled."[69]

Orton Brown, following his own conversation with Piotrowsky in those days, dispatched an equally impassioned letter to Evdokim, an expression of regret also published in the *Messenger*. "After talking with him for some time and trying to find out the situation," Brown wrote, "it seems to me the reason for his present state of mind is that he is nervously tired out and things that would not ordinarily distress him seem like mountains to him now." Brown suggested that Piotrowsky be allowed time to rest, offering his personal assistance and also his firm's resources to ensure that the priest would be financially secure and attended to during his recuperation.[70] Yet, as Brown and Wolf feared, Piotrowsky left Berlin for a new parish assignment in Watervliet, New York.[71]

The contrast between the triumphant exhilaration that Arcady Piotrowsky felt after the consecration of the Berlin church and his contentious departure only four months later speaks to the constant uncertainty and unpredictability of missionary work in American Orthodox Rus'. And that so many of his struggles there were described in the archdiocesan newspaper suggested the very public, perhaps invasive nature of clerical work. Clergy like Piotrowsky remade their religious worlds within the strange and demanding contexts of the US industrial workplace, reorienting their own beliefs and vocations within the insecurities and anxieties of a distant and multiconfessional missionary field. They felt the same pressures of assimilation and acculturation, the same linguistic barriers and social isolation, and similarly struggled to find their way in the bustle of the industrial city. Supporting wives and children, priests held the same anxieties over wages and employment conditions, toiling in a missionary field where their authority and job security were often in question. The building of American Orthodox Rus' centered around tensions between clergy and laity at the turn of the twentieth century and, as we will see, spurred some of the most contentious challenges to its survival in years to come.

3

"The Holy Church Is Their Mother"

The Aid and Education of Orthodox Youth

All your children shall be taught by the LORD,
and great shall be the prosperity of your children.
—Isaiah 54:13

When US public schools let out for the day during the early twentieth century, thousands of Orthodox children and adolescents headed to church for what they called "Russian School." These schools met in church basements, social halls, or classroom buildings for several hours into the early evening, usually under the watchful eye of clergy, clergy wives, or *psalomshchiki* (lay psalm singers). Cramming into rows of desks or around large tables, young people learned what it meant to be good Russian Orthodox Christians. They learned to decipher the complex Church Slavonic script used in worship and internalized the prayers and hymns of Orthodox liturgy. They drilled over Russian grammar and the history of Holy Orthodox Rus'. They memorized poetry and practiced folk songs, put on plays and formed balalaika ensembles. Some evenings there was choir practice, for on Saturdays and Sundays, they might be expected to sing in church. At the end of the year, students might anticipate a stern examination with their priest or perhaps a visiting bishop. By 1916, there were over 125 of these parish Russian Schools.[1]

For some, to remember these years was to recall disciplinarian instructors and hard-earned lessons. "Many of you may still remember the kneeling on the floor," one parish history noted of its Russian School, "or the sting of the rattan on the hand or the head."[2] Another recollected, "those of us who went to Russian School remember the sting of the rule and the weight of the books held over our head."[3] But for others, like Peter Mock of Homestead, Pennsylvania, there were warm and nostalgic reminiscences of hockey skates or playing endless games of tag. For Mock, the strongest memories were of lessons made fragrant with apples roasting on the corner stove. "There is nothing in the world," Mock remembered, "that smells so sweet or tastes so good as an apple baked in Russian class."[4]

Building American Orthodox Rus' depended on raising children like Peter Mock in two worlds, complementing their "English" or "American" schools with educational opportunities at church. When a lay missionary was ordained to the priesthood in 1900, Bishop Tikhon (Bellavin) advised the new clergyman, "the future of Orthodoxy in this land depends on church schools, and . . . these schools are especially crucial here, since in the public schools of this country, as you yourself know, the Law of God is not taught."[5] Even so, Tikhon knew that Orthodox parents did not hesitate to send their children off to public schools alongside their friends from the neighborhood, knowing that when the school bell rang in the afternoon, they would be off to Russian School to memorize verses of Pushkin and Lermontov, read the Bible, and learn about Orthodox liturgy, theology, and sacraments.

Church leaders insisted that embodied Orthodox instruction and religious life in the home were necessary complements to both "American" and "Russian" schools. "Teach the boy and girl geography and history," missionary priest Sebastian Dabovich argued in a sermon, "but if you do not train the child's will, in order not only to please you, its parents, but to bend before the holy will of Him, who is the only just rewarder of good and evil, then you are a failure as a christian [sic]." To Dabovich, who was born in California to a devout Serbian Orthodox family and later taught in several church institutions, the lessons children learned at Russian School only went so far if parents did not reinforce them at home. "It is the duty especially of parents to see that their children pray correctly, and also to pray with them together in an audible voice themselves," Dabovich insisted. He emphasized that this should be a mutually beneficial practice for parent and child and not rote routine. "This reasonable discipline, when you kneel by the side of tender childhood and see the little ones pray, will lighten your own heart—at the same time that it does in theirs—the fire of heavenly love."[6]

Just as American Orthodox Rus' offered social, material, and spiritual aid to vulnerable immigrant workers, it also built a safety net for their children, most of whom were born in the United States. This chapter looks at three examples of institutions established and funded by the Russian Archdiocese to impart that "fire of heavenly love" to young people. It begins with the Russian Missionary School and the Russian Theological Seminary, two educational institutions nurtured within the St. Mary's parish of Minneapolis, one of the largest and most significant communities of the Russian Archdiocese. It then moves to the Orphan Home in Springfield, Vermont, operated by women monastics to serve children and families from throughout the archdiocese. It closes with the St. Mary Women's College, a short-lived institution in Brooklyn, New York, that provided young women with an Orthodox education intended to steer them into lay vocations of serving the church as wives and mothers. Though the three institutions were geographically distant from one another, all were complementary aspects in how the Russian Archdiocese imagined its future in the United States.

In these three contexts, our perspective on American Orthodox Rus' shifts from a network of social and material aid serving a contemporary generation of immigrant workers to a church anticipating the needs of future generations of Orthodox Christians in North America. In these institutions, church leaders and young lay believers offered new conceptions of church vocations born not in the schools and academies of imperial Russia and the rigid constraints of the Russian clerical caste but rather in the factory and company towns of the industrial United States. The curricula of these institutions, as well as their wider social and religious framings, encompassed the general knowledge and practical experiences that were thought necessary for children and adolescents to continue contributing to American Orthodox Rus' as adults. This included familiarity with liturgics and church singing, knowledge of the Russian language, and a grasp of both Russian history and the history of the Orthodox Church. As the curricula premised that students were already receiving solid educational foundations in public schools, lessons served as complements to, and not replacements for, general US education standards.

Church leaders felt that children and adolescents stood at critical spiritual junctures in which the external pressures of US pluralism and popular culture clashed against the traditions and upbringings of the Orthodox home. As scholars of childhood note, these anxieties are common across the spectrum of US religions. "Faith sits at the intersection of internal and external experience, of self and other," the religious studies scholar Ann Braude observes. "At this intersection children, like adults, are capable of making the same religious motions either as concessions to conformity or as heroic personal commitments, or, most likely, at some indefinable point in between."[7] In this way, church schools and institutions acknowledged that the first US-born generation lived in two different worlds, living in a malleable time when industrialization and mass communication were making the world smaller and faster-paced. Through church-sponsored efforts in education and social relief, the ideals of American Orthodox Rus' maintained that industrial modernity was wholly compatible with Orthodox practice. Though the goals of American Orthodox Rus' with regard to education and social welfare were somewhat smaller in scope than those of more established denominations in the United States, they were great in ambition, seen as necessary steps for the building of a permanent and forward-looking Russian Orthodox missionary presence in North America.

One challenge in exploring social and educational endeavors for young people is the problem of received perspective. Period church newspapers published reports from teachers, administrators, and church workers, though not from the young people with whom they worked. These were written almost always by men, and usually by clergymen. The few retrospective accounts that describe what it was like for young people to live and study in these places come from former students glimpsing their younger selves in warm and nostalgic retrospection. To construct narratives of Orthodox childhoods in American Orthodox Rus', then, is to rely on either the adult gaze or the tenuous threads of memory. Even so, this chapter endeavors to present an image of an Orthodox childhood that provided great opportunities for young people while expecting much of them once they reached adulthood.

The Minneapolis Russian Colony and Its Missionary School

Of all the communities of American Orthodox Rus' at the turn of the twentieth century, few were considered as important as the St. Mary's parish in Minneapolis. In 1889, the widower Greek Catholic priest Alexis Toth arrived in the city and presented himself to John Ireland, the local Roman Catholic archbishop. When the outspoken proponent of Catholic Americanization learned that Toth had been married (his wife, Rosalie, died several years after his ordination), Ireland erupted into anger, announcing that he had no intention to accept Toth into his diocese. Nor did he consider the St. Mary's parish, which had invited Toth to their wooden church in the working-class immigrant Northeast neighborhood, to be Catholic. In late 1890, angered by Ireland's rejection, Toth and his community appealed to the Russian Orthodox consistory in San Francisco. Several months later, Bishop Vladimir (Sokolovsky-Avtomonov) traveled east to Minneapolis, where he accepted Toth and more than 360 of his parishioners into the Orthodox Church. For decades, parishioners of the St. Mary's parish prided themselves as the "first-called" of dozens more Greek Catholic parishes in the United States that would "return" to Orthodoxy.[8]

The "Russian colony" of the Northeast neighborhood emerged in the late 1870s, comprising mostly men from Austria-Hungary laboring in factories and the lumber industry. Throughout the early history of the St. Mary's parish, it would be defined by its distinctly Carpatho-Rusyn identity, though this somewhat eroded with the Russification encouraged both by Toth and the Russian hierarchy after the parish converted to Orthodoxy. These changes were most evident in the sanctuary. Built in 1887, the space appeared somewhat like a Roman Catholic church. It lacked an iconostasis. Its altar table was the tiered style common to Latinized Greek Catholics. There were fourteen statues depicting the Stations of the Cross. After the community embraced the Russian Church, the space gradually transformed into a more typically Orthodox worship space, cast in the gilded trappings and soft pastels common to the churches of late imperial Russia. By 1892, the statues were gone. An iconostasis was installed with icons ordered from Lviv, including four purchased by the Holy Synod in St. Petersburg. The tiered altar was replaced with a broad, flat altar table (*prestol*).[9] Worship practices changed as well. Their long-standing practice of congregational singing (*prostopinie*), which drew on common, internalized knowledge of Carpatho-Rusyn hymnody, gave way to an a cappella choir of eight voices directed by a *psalomshchik* assigned by the Russian consistory, Paul Zaichenko. "It was hard to teach them because none of them were vocally gifted," Zaichenko recalled. "Being hard, plain working men, concerned only with their daily occupation in cooper shops, giving all their physical power to it, it was not so easy for them to come to rehearsals four, five, six times a week, but nevertheless, in spite of all hardships, they came and attended rehearsals for twelve long years." In time, Zaichenko trained his workaday choir to sing complex works like the liturgical setting of Pyotr Ilyich Tchaikovsky—a substantial shift from *prostopinie* common chant. The altered worship space and the burgeoning parish choir demonstrated that the St. Mary's parish had embraced the artistic synthesis of polyphony and the florid aesthetics favored in the late imperial Russian Church. Diocesan leaders felt these exemplars of Russification were necessary for full and enduring incorporation into the Orthodox Church, establishing a model that would be repeated in their orchestration of other Carpatho-Rusyn Greek Catholic conversions in years to come.[10]

The role of St. Mary's in the Northeast Minneapolis Russian Colony centered just as much around the church as around the educational institutions associated with the parish. In 1893, the community built a two-story, wood-frame school adjacent to the church. Because of St. Mary's increasing size and prominence among the parishes of the Midwest, Minneapolis was chosen four years later as the location for a diocesan school. Housed in a new, larger brick school building across the street from the church, the Russian Missionary School was for both local children and promising students from across the diocese, who would live there as boarders.[11] The school was accredited by the state of Minnesota and overseen by administrators from the Minneapolis public school district. Each spring, the ruling bishop or his representative came from San Francisco for final examinations. This was also an opportunity to identify young men with potential church vocations. Bishop Nicholas (Ziorov) pointed to Minneapolis as a model for his diocese, imploring parishes to establish their own schools as "the foundation upon which [they would] build the present and the future church."[12] By its seventh academic year, there were 120 students: 77 boys and 43 girls.[13]

The missionary school immersed its students in the social and religious worlds of Northeast Minneapolis, particularly boarders living far from their homes and families. Students were allowed visits with family and friends on Sunday afternoons, and some traveled home during summer breaks. Even so, these were but fleeting moments amid a long school year. One of the first students at the school was ten-year-old

Basil Basalyga, who hailed from the anthracite coal town of Olyphant, Pennsylvania. Basalyga came to view St. Mary's parishioners as surrogate family, later recalling them as "loving and sympathetic, expressing pity that we had left our parents so young. Their tenderness took the place of parental love, and our happiness became their happiness, our sorrow, their sorrow." Educated at church expense and more or less raised by the parish, students embraced the activities of church life and became wound up in the exciting camaraderie of a school that expected great things of them. The school curriculum took some cues from imperial Russian primary and secondary schools, emphasizing language, literature, and Orthodox catechism. School days began and ended with prayer. Meals kept to the church fasting calendar. The St. Mary's choir director Paul Zaichenko drilled the students in church singing, building a credible junior choir of mixed voices. Saturdays were cleaning days, the older children supervising the younger with mops and brooms. Sundays and feast days were spent across the street at St. Mary's, where students read and sang and boys helped the priest at the altar. Liturgical worship and participation in the sacraments, including meticulous preparation for confession and communion several times each academic year, were matters of both religious devotion and school curriculum. Long hours spent in church were also a source of social support. "Through our participation in the church services," Basalyga later recalled, "we came in contact with the parishioners, and through them with the outside world."[14]

Priest Alexander Kukulevsky left diocesan administration in San Francisco in 1903 to accept a teaching post at the Missionary School. After some years in the US, Kukulevsky had considered returning home to Russia, but he found himself drawn to new opportunities in Minneapolis. "It was sad to leave California, where the roses bloom in January," he later wrote, for reality set in quickly. "Minneapolis gave me no friendly welcome," he recalled. "As soon as I stepped down from the coach a keen frost penetrated me." Kukulevsky found a school of children from across the United States, as far away as California. Nearly all were born in the United States to Carpatho-Rusyn families, a point of tension for church leaders invested in their Russification, an endeavor that Kukulevsky took for granted. "They came to the school with a very poor knowledge of the Russian tongue," he observed. "To counteract this situation, we demanded that only Russian should be spoken within the walls of the school."[15]

Kukulevsky also worked with other faculty to expand extracurricular offerings, taking his inspiration from period values of Christian masculinity rooted in health, fitness, and the creative arts. During this time, American Protestants and Catholics extolled the virtues of muscular Christianity, emphasizing health, exercise, sport, and physical toughness as exemplars of Christian "manliness." This approach was adopted by other religious groups, including American Jews.[16] These values were impressed in Minneapolis as well, where Missionary School students had access to a gymnasium with dumbbells and rudimentary exercise equipment. Kukulevsky purchased boxing gloves for a sparring program, "and very soon bruises and scratches could be seen on the happy and flushed faces of the students." In winter, teachers flooded the schoolyard to make a hockey rink. Even the school inspector and priest Anatole Kamensky laced up a pair of skates. Kamensky also shared with students his interest in photography, transforming a bathroom into a darkroom during school holidays and teaching the students to process and develop their own photographs.[17] When the lights went out at day's end, Kukulevsky remembered, "Only the glimmer of the lamp before the icon illuminated the children's bedrooms."[18]

Though the school oriented its activities toward educating well-rounded young people immersed in the life of the Orthodox Church, they remained adolescents nonetheless. One summer day, a Romani caravan passing through Minneapolis stopped for some time in the St. Mary's neighborhood. One of the Missionary School's older students, Peter Dobish, became enamored with one of the women, a fortune-teller whom singing instructor Paul Zaichenko recalled as "young and beautiful, dressed in bright colors as if ready for a masquerade." Zaichenko stood nearby as Dobish "fell head over heels in love," watching the girl tell fortunes "as one hypnotized, and devoured her with his eyes." That night, Dobish disappeared. In the morning, Zaichenko and another teacher set out to find the caravan and bring Dobish back to school. They met an old Romani man "in wide velvet pants with a red sash around his waist," who pointed them toward the young woman. They found Dobish sitting under a tree talking with some of the Romani. After some discussion, Dobish returned with his teachers. The next morning, however, Dobish and his belongings were gone. He had gone after the caravan. "Since then, nothing has been heard of him," Zaichenko wrote over thirty years later. "He disappeared without a trace, and left behind everything: his school, his friends, and the brilliant prospects of a future missionary."[19]

The regret expressed over Dobish's abandoned promise speaks to a fundamental goal of the institution. While there were female students, the Missionary School was oriented toward identifying young men who exhibited potential for church work and clerical ordination. As there was no Orthodox seminary in North America, Bishop Nicholas (Ziorov) secured several dozen scholarships to leading Russian theological academies specifically earmarked for young men from his diocese. In 1895, five recipients were chosen from the Missionary School. All five returned to the United States and became priests. Yet this arrangement was unsustainable. Sending young men to study in Russia proved inconvenient and cumbersome. Clerical needs in North America far outstripped the number of scholarships. And diocesan leaders recognized that the preparation that students received in Minneapolis and other parish schools in the US was far different from that of their potential classmates in Russia, and was certainly inferior, leaving them at a frustrating academic disadvantage when they enrolled in a Russian theological academy.[20]

In 1903, a commission met in Cleveland to discuss the establishment of a North American seminary. The commission felt that a dedicated and well-funded seminary could show that the diocese was a religious institution interested in, and congruent with, its North American context and that it was moving toward a model in which young people who were born, raised, and educated in North America would take up its missionary work. Yet it was also sensitive to perceptions both within and outside the diocese, perhaps most loudly from its Greek Catholic opponents, that the "Russian Treasury" (Russkaia Kazna) was paying priests from Russia, Austria-Hungary, Greece, the Ottoman Empire, and even some US citizens for "political aims." The commission emphasized that the seminary "should be a specialized school, a Theological school," and that it could not merely replicate or mirror the rigid and traditional approaches to clerical education in Russia. It envisioned a national educational system by which a young man could enter the Missionary School at eleven, matriculate to the seminary at seventeen, and graduate at twenty-one well prepared for the priesthood. Seminarians would receive instruction in theology, dogmatics, liturgics, church history, and music, all of which would contribute to their ability to articulate in "a land of thousands of sects and general heterodoxy . . . what distinguishes Orthodox from heterodoxy." Just as important, all classes would be taught by teachers holding advanced degrees from Russian theological schools. There would also be English-language instruction.[21]

A separate issue was location. The commission preferred a site near an Orthodox parish, preferably a cathedral, with a community large enough to support and enrich a theological seminary. One possibility was Minneapolis, though the potential seminary—"the building, the décor, living conditions and upbringing, and of learning, etc."—would need to be distinct from both the St. Mary's parish school and the Missionary School. "It is impossible to connect the future seminary with the Minneapolis school," the commission argued, "where children of both genders and various ages are being taught." Pennsylvania was another, perhaps more economical choice. Greater attention was afforded New York, though the commission feared that such a busy urban location would not offer enough green space and also that constructing a building large enough to house up to fifty resident students would be cost-prohibitive.[22]

Nearly two years later, the *Russian Orthodox American Messenger* announced that a new seminary would open in Minneapolis in the fall of 1905 on the premises of the Missionary School, whose existing building would house both classrooms and student residences. The Missionary School would close, though it would be partially reconstituted into a restructured St. Mary's parish school and, later, a smaller day school. As a result, many of its students would be dispersed. The majority were Minneapolis locals, who reenrolled in the city's public schools. Some of the male residential students were sent to a new missionary school attached to the St. Theodosius parish in Cleveland, an institution known as the "Bursa." The most significant result of the closure, however, was its impact on the education of women, as most, if not all, of the thirty-five young women enrolled in Minneapolis during the 1904–5 academic year lost their chance to pursue their formal religious educations at an archdiocesan school.[23]

The Russian Theological Seminary

The new Minneapolis seminary was divided into two, aged-based divisions. The initial upper-level class mostly comprised recent Missionary School graduates, who would be ready for ordination at the end of the academic year. Younger students would complete longer terms of study and were invited to apply for entrance examinations later in the summer. Preferential admission was offered to adults already serving as missionaries and *psalomshchiki*, who would not be required to live at the school. Nor would adolescents from Minneapolis, who could remain at home with their families. Tuition was set at ten dollars per month (less than $350 today).[24] Twenty students were enrolled by the 1907 school year, ten in each of the two grade levels. Eighteen were residential students.[25]

One early seminary instructor was Basil Bensin. Upon his graduation from the Moscow Theological Academy in 1903, Bensin expressed his wish to work as a lay missionary in the US. The following year, he made a critical and fortuitous connection with Bishop Nicholas (Ziorov), formerly of San Francisco, who was passing through Moscow on his way to St. Petersburg. Nicholas recommended Bensin to his successor in North America, Bishop Tikhon (Bellavin), who sent for the promising young academy graduate. Bensin arrived in New York in 1905 and headed west to Chicago. There he met with Tikhon for several days of deep discussion on the bishop's educational vision. "I have decided to found a seminary for young people born in America," Tikhon explained, "who intend, as most of the priests from Russia, to stay there for good." Tikhon echoed the findings of the seminary commission, stressing to Bensin that the school "would not be like the Russian Ecclesiastical Seminaries." In contrast, the bishop felt that his diocese "must establish a school that would suit the needs of people in America." Bensin boarded a train north to Minneapolis. "On my arrival at the school, the students were already gathered," Bensin remembered. "I was surprised at the diversity of their ages and scholastic training." He prepared for the academic year by immersing himself in the local public schools, working his way from kindergarten through high school classrooms to observe US teaching methods and improve his English. He also brushed up on his musical skills for a choir curriculum he modeled on that of the Kyiv School of Music. Through Bensin's influence, the seminary curriculum was tailored to the breadth required of a US-born clergyman. "The history of the United States and civics were included in the curriculum, and was taught in English," Bensin recalled. "Also I felt that the seminarians should be prepared to take the public school teacher's examinations, so that they would be well qualified to teach parish schools."[26]

The seminary's multilingual curriculum was tailored to provide the tools necessary to serve a Russian church situated in the context of a pluralistic and English-speaking United States. Courses of study included Russian and US history, church history, Hebrew Bible and New Testament, Russian literature (both "Little Russian," *malorusski* [Ukrainian], and "Great Russian," *obshcherusskii*), English, mathematics, physiology, psychology, dogmatic theology, patristics, liturgics, church singing, and Russian grammar. To learn homiletics, seminarians read Russian-language anthologies of sermons by Metropolitan Filaret (Drozdov) of Moscow and others. They learned liturgics from textbooks prepared by the Moscow Theological Seminary instructor Pyotr Lebedev for intermediate students in Russian seminaries. Their English-language textbooks included George Wentworth's *Elements of Algebra*, Andrew W. Phillips and Irving Fisher's *Elements of Geometry*, and Philip Van Ness Myers's *General History*, all in common use in US public schools.[27] They also had access to an English-language Orthodox catechism published by the archdiocese in 1901. In church, they used the English-language *Service Book of the Holy Orthodox-Catholic Apostolic (Greco-Russian) Church*, published in 1906 by its translator, the Episcopalian laywoman and Russophile Isabel Hapgood.[28] The school year ended with several full days of examinations overseen by a bishop and the seminary faculty.[29] Seminarians spent their summers working in parishes. They served and sang during services, helped with organizations like musical ensembles and parish brotherhoods, and taught in church schools. This attuned them to the diverse needs of congregations that they might one day oversee and also introduced them to missionary priests whom school administrators hoped would become their colleagues.[30] In the words of Leonid Turkevich, a young and energetic priest who arrived at the seminary in late 1906, graduates of the seminary would leave the school "by blood, kindred to their future flock by language and character, sons of the church and patriots of all Slavdom [*slavianstvo*]; in ministry, Orthodox in formation; in action, culturally engaged."[31]

Social and religious activities within the St. Mary's parish increased with the opening of the seminary, especially after the arrival of Turkevich. Just thirty years old, Turkevich came from Volyhnia, in western Ukraine, where his father was a priest and longtime assistant inspector of the Volyn Theological Seminary. Another son, Benedict, came to the US in 1898 and was ordained a priest four years later. As *popovichi* with deep roots in the Russian clerical estate, the Turkevich brothers numbered the seventh generation of priests from their family. In Minneapolis, Leonid Turkevich and his family lived at first in the seminary building. When he took on the additional role of parish priest in 1907, the family moved across the street into the St. Mary's rectory.[32]

The presence of Turkevich, Bensin, and other seminary personnel had practical benefits for St. Mary's, a large and growing congregation with increasing demands for sacraments and other pastoral duties. That the seminary faculty included several priests was a boon for a parish that otherwise might have been assigned only one. Between 1905 and 1912, St. Mary's averaged nearly 108 baptisms, twenty weddings, and nine funerals each year, labor made lighter by more clerical hands and readily available voices.[33] Seminarians could step in to assist with these and other pastoral duties, providing them hands-on learning opportunities. They taught Bible and Russian-language lessons for the two hundred students of the parish school. In the church, they read, sang, and served at the altar. They supervised a Saturday-morning liturgy for parish school students, as well as English-language vespers services on Sunday evenings. As Turkevich later recalled, from his earliest days in Minneapolis, he "noticed that the affairs of the Seminary were gradually involved in those of the parish." These ties strengthened with time.[34]

The inaugural group of seminarians included Basil Basalyga. After graduation from the Missionary School in 1902, Basalyga worked as a choir director and *psalomshchik* in western Pennsylvania. "Basil Basalyga was a favorite pupil of Bishop Tikhon," Paul Zaichenko later recalled. "The student's progress delighted the bishop and he often prophesied a brilliant future for him. What he foretold, came true."[35] Further study in Minneapolis confirmed Basalyga's career in the church, though these years brought exhilaration and isolation in equal measure. Basalyga was tonsured after his graduation, taking the monastic name

Benjamin. In 1911, he was ordained a priest, and in 1933, he became the first North American–born Orthodox bishop. For Bishop Benjamin, and for many of his classmates, church vocations began with enrollment at the Missionary School as a child and continued at the seminary as an adolescent and young adult. "After that first journey to Minneapolis, we seldom visited our home towns," Benjamin wrote of his and other early students' experiences nearly forty years after they came to Minnesota.

> Our whole life became a journey from one parish to another, from one city to another. Our unsettled life started early. Personally, it influenced me to be single and on my own, and later to take monastic orders. My circle of friends grew gradually smaller and smaller, largely due to the discords within the church. I sank deeper and deeper in my loneliness, and further away from this world and all its blessings. . . . Everything in us that is good, clean, and holy, everything that we have done for the Church and the Orthodox faith, and everything that we will do, we owe it all to our school years in Minneapolis, to the wonderful education that was given us.[36]

The central role of the St. Mary's parish in the curriculum of both the Missionary School and the seminary meant that students like Basil Basalyga matured with the congregation. They saw the dramatic changes to its worship space, where they spent long hours singing, reading, and learning the liturgical cycle amid the icons and clouds of incense. In 1904, a mysterious fire burned the wooden church to the ground; it was thought to have been ignited by an errant ash from the censer or a candle left smoldering after the funeral of an infant child. Though the parish had already decided to construct a new, larger church, it could no longer depend on anticipated funds from the sale of materials salvaged from the old building. In the evenings, students living at the Missionary School could look out their windows and see parishioners already tired from a full day's work digging the foundations for their new church with horse-drawn shovels. Day by day, students watched the building rise, constructed larger than planned at an estimated cost of $45,000 ($1.3 million today). And the students celebrated with their teachers when the gilded icons for the new iconostasis arrived from Moscow, painted on heavy wood panels by the monks of the Trinity-St. Sergius Lavra. The new church was consecrated in the summer of 1906, though it was by no means complete. The first, typically frigid Minnesota winter brought to light a critical, cost-saving measure: the new church was built without a heating system. "It was painful to say services, to sing, and to pray in the cold stone church, and to heat the basement classrooms with stoves was exhausting. Many people suffered that winter," Turkevich recalled. "But what joy there was in October or November, 1908, when for the first time steam travelled along the pipes and radiators. The pipes in the church began knocking, and old Stephen Reshetar started running to and fro, here to tighten a screw, there to repair a leak, and there to mop up the water. It was a real holiday for the children and the grown ups. But the church debt for the boilers increased by another two thousand dollars."[37]

After several academic years in Minneapolis, church leaders felt it would be easier to manage the seminary if it were located nearer to the archdiocesan cathedral and the numerous parishes of the New York metropolitan area. There were tensions in Minneapolis as well, where the seminary was becoming lost in the busying complexities of parish life at St. Mary's. Hundreds of parishioners belonged to brotherhoods and sisterhoods affiliated with various Orthodox benevolence and mutual-aid societies. There were sports teams, a youth club, and a temperance group. A library society kept a reading room several blocks north of the church and also sponsored a drama club. The church choir had grown in size and skill. Parish events often included performances by a brass band, led by a parishioner who would go on to spend more than a decade directing the University of Minnesota Marching Band.[38] "The Parish and the Seminary had developed to such an extent that it was necessary to separate them," Turkevich recalled, and so he "bade goodbye to Minneapolis."[39]

Turkevich and other faculty followed their seminary to a mansion in Tenafly, New Jersey, where it was renamed the St. Platon Russian Theological Seminary. The relocation brought significant changes in Minneapolis. The expansive educational program at St. Mary's, bolstered for years by the presence of clergy, lay faculty, and seminarians, was entrusted to a priest, a *psalomshchik*, and engaged lay parishioners. The legacies of its educational endeavors resonated for decades. Dozens of young men who studied at the Missionary School and the Russian

Figure 3.1. Russian Band, St. Mary's Russian Orthodox Greek Catholic Church, Minneapolis, Minnesota, ca. 1910. (Minnesota Historical Society)

Theological Seminary formed a new generation of clergy and church workers born in North America and trained to serve communities like those that reared them, ranks that included teachers, choir directors, deacons, and priests—and from the potential others in the church recognized in young Basil Basalyga, the first North American–born bishop.

Female Monasticism in the Russian Archdiocese

In late September 1911, four women arrived at St. Nicholas Cathedral in New York City. Mother Paulina, along with Sisters Andrea, Mikhaila, and Anastasia, were Greek Catholic nuns from Transcarpathia sent to the United States to help deter individuals and communities from joining the Russian Orthodox Church. Now they stood at "the door to all American Orthodox Rus'," as it was described, "fragrant through the prayers of tens of thousands of Russian immigrants," poised for reception into the Orthodox Church. They were the first female monastics in the Russian Archdiocese, and the description of their conversion in the *Russian Orthodox American Messenger* emphasized their unusual profile. The women were described to have shirked their mission as Greek Catholic church workers, which by their own description was intended "to damage Orthodoxy." And by doing so, they also were casting off the "Roman Church," which had "held them not by belief, but by force." The women stood in the Manhattan cathedral prepared to accept Orthodoxy "in view of all," wearing the habits of Roman Catholic women religious, "with massive iron crosses on their chests."[40]

Mother Paulina and her colleagues were entering an Orthodox setting in which female monasticism was rare and a church in which their vocational expectations were somewhat different. As Greek Catholics, part of the so-called Eastern or Oriental rites under Rome, they worked within a wider Catholic context that afforded women religious public ministries in church-operated settings like hospitals, schools, and orphanages. In traditional Orthodox practice, however, monasticism means a life of private repentance. While some monastic priests lived and worked in parishes, the most common monastic life was one of isolation, stillness, obedience, and prayer. Most Orthodox monasteries are sustained through measured communal life, but they also prioritize individual, even hermetic lives marked by prayer, physically demanding prostrations, and strict obedience to spiritual elders. In the United States, the sole Orthodox monastery was the male community of St. Tikhon of Zadonsk in South Canaan, Pennsylvania, established in 1905, and from its inception, it was a major center of spirituality and pilgrimage for the archdiocese. Yet Orthodox monasticism is not a male enterprise alone. In the Russian Empire, female monasticism was a fast-growing institution. As the historian William Wagner notes, there was a sevenfold increase in female monasteries in Russia between 1764 and 1914, as well as a nearly fourteenfold rise in female monastics and novices between 1825 and 1914—growth that far outpaced their male counterparts over the same time spans.[41]

While female monasteries were important and evolved institutions in late imperial Russia, there were no female communities or female monastics in North America until the conversion of Mother Paulina and her companions—women whose monastic formations occurred not in

Russia and its Orthodox Church but rather in Greek Catholicism as it was practiced in Transcarpathia. By 1915, their Holy Virgin Protection Convent was located adjacent to the Holy Trinity parish in Springfield, Vermont, a rural house church flanked by two larger auxiliary buildings. The four women established a prescribed division of labors. Mother Paulina was the abbess (*nastoiatel'nitsa* or *igumena*). Sister Andrea was the treasurer (*kaznacheia*), Sister Mikhaila was the sacristan (*riznichaia*), and Sister Anastasia was the housekeeper (*ekonomka*). Their attachment to a parish provided them a priest and confessor, the fullness of the liturgical cycle, and the opportunity to receive the eucharist. The pastor assigned to the Springfield parish was ordinarily a monastic himself. As newly converted Orthodox Christians in obedience to the Russian Archdiocese, the women carved out spaces for themselves in education and social work, most notably through the archdiocesan orphanage.

Established in 1905 by priest Alexis Toth, the Orphan Home (*Sirotskii Priiut*) was first located near the St. Tikhon's monastery in Pennsylvania. Operated by the male monastics there, the orphanage accepted three categories of Orthodox children from across the United States: those without parents; those with living parents facing poverty, debilitating injury, or disease; and those who came from families of means to raise them but who had been placed in foster care. Funds for its establishment and initial upkeep came from a variety of sources, including large sums from Bishop Tikhon and the Russian noble and statesman Count Sergei Witte and smaller donations from parish organizations and individual clergy and laity from across the diocese. Significant donations came from local brotherhoods of the Russian Orthodox Catholic Mutual Aid Society (ROCMAS). Both the orphanage and monastery also benefited, both financially and materially, from the yields of its farm.[42] In 1906, there were twelve children at the orphanage, more than double the number of monks.[43] By 1910, this ratio remained roughly the same. Ranging from ages three to thirteen, the children were born in the United States, nearly all to immigrant parents. Most had come from Pennsylvania, and others came from New York and Minnesota.[44] Speaking at the consecration of the new monastery church in 1906, Bishop Tikhon (Bellavin) addressed critics who questioned locating the orphanage at the monastery, asking if it was "appropriate for monks who have renounced the world to be preoccupied with cares other than the salvation of their souls?" Tikhon invoked the story of the ten virgins in the Gospel of Matthew, explaining that nothing more befitted a monastery than charity. Explaining that "monks cannot save themselves by virginity alone," the bishop maintained, "The orphanage is far from being superfluous to our monastery. In it the monks can serve these little ones with their own labor and with their monastery property, and in this way build their salvation." Tikhon implored the orphanage to remain in South Canaan.[45]

Over time, however, church officials became concerned that the rural monastery was too remote, especially from the area public schools where the children were enrolled. In 1914, the orphanage relocated to a building adjacent to the Holy Trinity parish in the Brownsville neighborhood of Brooklyn. In New York, the institution received a new and unusual sense of collective ownership and support greater than that afforded to most other archdiocesan institutions. Archdiocesan leaders and others in the Russian community made patronage of the orphanage a public act so as to encourage smaller donations from the parishes. Prominent donors included priests and bishops, as well as members of the Russian diplomatic corps. The Russian Orthodox Catholic Women's Mutual Aid Society, a suborganization of ROCMAS, made the orphanage its primary charitable concern. In Brooklyn, as the orphanage grew more intertwined with the congregation of the Brownsville parish, a culture of large- and small-scale philanthropy emerged. This included a local custom by which weddings and other social events included special collections for the children.[46] On December 25, 1914, "American Christmas," seventy-five donors sponsored a Nativity pageant, or *yolka*, for the children at the orphanage, a group that included Bishop Alexander (Nemolovsky), Russian ambassador to the United States George Bakhmeteff, priest and *Svit* editor Peter Kohanik, church architect John Bergesen, *Russkii emigrant* editor Gabriel Dobrov, and parish sisterhoods from Pennsylvania and New Jersey. The children staged a Christmas play and enjoyed a warm evening of holiday cheer. A description of the *yolka* in *Svit* closed with a request that readers "do not forget the orphans" during the season of New Year's and Christmas, because "for those orphans, the Russian family [*russkaia sem'ia*] is obligated to replace their father and mother."[47]

During the spring of 1915, the archdiocese purchased a large plot of land adjacent to the Holy Trinity parish of Springfield, Vermont, for use

Figure 3.2. Mother Paulina (*left*), Sister Mikhaila (*right*), and some of the children in their care standing on the lawn of the Russian Orphanage, Springfield, Vermont, 1916. (*Russian Orthodox American Messenger*, July 20, 1916)

by the relocated orphanage. Founded in 1905, the Springfield parish retrofitted a two-story residential structure into a church, installing a large steeple atop its roof. Its scenic, rural location and the ready availability of land made the parish a desirable complement to the orphanage. It was also convenient for Mother Paulina, who was granted space on the property for her Holy Virgin Protection Convent. "Soon the orphanage will be filled with orphans," Bishop Alexander (Nemolovsky) wrote. "My heart painfully aches: can it be that this holy endeavor will be lost? Will no one support it? In God and in you, holy American Orthodox Rus'," he wrote, "I place all hope."[48]

The archdiocese earmarked a portion of its annual stipend from the Holy Synod to underwrite the orphanage. Yet the construction and renovations required at the Springfield site necessitated a robust and extraordinary fundraising campaign. In the *Russian Orthodox American Messenger*, priest Leonid Turkevich suggested that archdiocesan parishes offer ongoing financial support for the orphanage, posing that supporting the institution was an urgent and shared imperative in a country whose social institutions were dominated by other faith traditions with greater resources. "Thousands of our Russian children are being lost from the absence of the loving arms of fathers and mothers," he wrote. "Hundreds are being taken away from us to strangers, into the arms of the non-Orthodox [*inoslavie*]. The orphanages of the non-Christians [*inovertsy*] are increasing, and what is more, on account of our children."[49] The archdiocese mounted a direct appeal to the parishes: $3.40 came from priest Arcady Piotrowsky and his parish in Berlin, New Hampshire; from remote Afognak, Alaska, came $15; the three daughters of a missionary priest in Seattle sent $2.50. In September 1915 alone, the Consistory collected nearly $250 of such small and heartfelt donations (around $7,200 today).[50] The progress and potential of the orphanage was such that less than two years later, another 160 acres of land were purchased for use as a vegetable and dairy farm. Students worked the farm, and its yield helped to fill their plates. A farmhouse on the property was renovated into an Orthodox chapel.[51]

The patronage of the people of American Orthodox Rus', clergy and lay, young and old, helped sustain the housing and education of fifty-three children at the orphanage, a figure that later exceeded one hundred. Boys could remain until they turned fifteen, and girls until age sixteen. Each day began at 7:15 with morning prayers in the recreation hall, at which boys and girls alike read the prayers. Just as in parish communities throughout American Orthodox Rus', the religious education of the children at the orphanage was not posed as a replacement for, but rather as complement to, US public education. After a quick breakfast, the children set off for Springfield public schools for six hours of instruction, for which the orphanage paid tuition. The children returned at three in the afternoon for an early supper. Then came ninety minutes at evening "Russian school," where the children studied Orthodox catechism, Russian language and literature, Church Slavonic reading, Russian history, and church singing. After two hours spent completing their "English school" homework, the children were off to bed.[52]

The Russian Orphanage was but one aspect in the rearing and education of young people in American Orthodox Rus'. The children who lived and studied there, whether or not their parents were living, were implored to feel that "the Holy Church is their mother."[53] Undertaken and overseen by Mother Paulina and her convent, the work of the orphanage was the most visible role in the Russian Archdiocese held by women, unmarried monastics garbed in the dark, Catholic-style habits and large iron crosses brought from Transcarpathia. For other women who chose to marry and raise families, however, opportunities were more limited and situated within everyday parish life: informal and auxiliary roles, the environs of the church and the kitchen, and in the parish school classroom. The model Orthodox family revolved around the church and demanded patriarchal structures that mirrored the social structures and divisions of labor found in the parish. In clerical families, these dynamics were even more pronounced. The Russian Orphanage and the monastic community that supported it were intertwined with another, short-lived educational institution intended for women.

The St. Mary Women's College

When the Orphan Home left Brooklyn in the summer of 1915, the archdiocese granted its former space to a new, church-sponsored endeavor. Reflecting the same impetus for social aid as the orphanage, the St. Mary Women's College boldly challenged ingrained gender dynamics, even as it served to reinforce their rigid and traditional notions of family and community.[54] The founding of the women's college echoed calls in early twentieth-century Russia for greater public roles for women, posing their labors as important individual efforts that served the greater moral good. As early as the mid-nineteenth century, church reformers advocated that educational opportunities mandated for the sons of clergy be offered to their daughters as well.[55] As the historian William Wagner argues, Orthodox thinkers across the Russian social and political spectrums were acknowledging that "although women remained primarily mothers and wives, they could also be social actors within boundaries defined by what they deemed their particular nature and divine calling as women." As a result, the proportion of women in Russian secondary schools and colleges steadily increased during the years preceding the First World War.[56]

Church leaders in the US were part of this ideological milieu, though adapted to their ministries to migrant workers in pluralistic industrial cities and factory towns. As one women's college supporter mused, "Is

Figure 3.3. Students of the St. Mary Women's College in "Little Russian costumes." With them are two of their instructors, priest's wives (*matushki*) Anna Mescherskaia (*left*) and Anna Turkevich (*right*). (*Russian Orthodox American Messenger*, August 3, 1916)

it really possible without profound melancholy to see the whole procession of young Russian girls in local cities, hurrying with the crowds early in the morning to time-enforced labor at factory machines? What is their fate? What is their future?" The anonymous writer, most likely priest Leonid Turkevich, felt it imperative to provide new opportunities for working women in American Orthodox Rus'. With most educational opportunities being either secular or reflective of other faith traditions, and given the pressures of assimilation and acculturation, the Women's College was an opportunity for transformation as both Orthodox and Russian women. Acknowledging the potential and autonomy of women, training them to be better teachers, nurses, church singers, homemakers, and community members was thought to ensure the lasting moral uplift of American Orthodox Rus', especially for its youth. "In the end, women should be conscientious, educated, Christian-educated participants in our general religio-church and public life," it was argued. "If she is better educated, then her labor for the common good is more valuable and skilled. If the woman is greater in mind and temperament, then so will be her entire family." From this perspective, educating women was posed as an essential undertaking. "Is it not clear that every step forward on the path of granting the Russian woman her inherent rights should be supported and welcomed with zeal and enthusiasm[?] The women's college is the beginning of the endeavor. It is but a door to a new and better future for us all."[57]

There were six students in the inaugural class, aged sixteen to twenty-five. Their applications consisted only of a letter to Archbishop Evdokim (Meschersky), who personally evaluated and accepted each applicant. Tuition was $15 (less than $450 today). Priest Basil Repella of Mayfield, Pennsylvania, wrote to recommend his wife, Martha, and sent along a dress pattern she had prepared for the college uniform. The priest of the parish in nearby Yonkers recommended four women from his congregation, including sixteen-year-old Olga Sirotyak. Another, nineteen-year-old Olga Adamiak, had completed only the fifth grade of "English school." Katherine Gress, sixteen, was the daughter of priest Nikita Gress. She came to New York City from her father's parish in Clayton, Wisconsin, a remote dairy and farming community where parishioners traversed logging roads cut through the surrounding birch forests to get to church.[58]

The college curriculum emphasized practical instruction in topics that would foster vocations for Orthodox women as wives and mothers, especially for those who were, or might become, clergy wives. Modeled on imperial Russian pedagogy, each school day began and ended with common prayer. There were courses in arithmetic, geography, and natural sciences, as well as language instruction in French, Russian, and English. There was also church singing, Old and New Testament study, church history, Russian history, home economics, hygiene, culinary arts, and needlework. To prepare them for work as educators, pedagogical and didactics practicums were held at the Brooklyn parish school.[59] In general, instructional priorities privileged the gendered divisions of labor found in model clerical families and parishes. There was nothing in the curriculum or stated goals of the college that might challenge the primacy of men in clerical roles or church leadership. Rather, the refined and educated graduate's domestic homemaking would complement her public life of obligatory, though unpaid, service to the church. The *Brooklyn Daily Eagle* noted in a feature on the college that "from among their number many will become the wives of future priests of the Orthodox Church, fully equipped, both educationally, socially and religiously, as helpmates to their husbands."[60]

Around half of the instructors were women. In the request of Evgenia Krilova, an older member of the community and a graduate of the Ekaterinoslav Institute, to become the college's dean, she offered her services for free. "Despite my advanced years," she wrote, "I dare think that my profound life experience helps me to serve the sacred cause with benefit and success."[61] Anna Turkevich, the school's principal, taught both general and Russian history. Dr. Eugenia Kohanik, a practicing dentist as well as a priest's wife, taught Russian. Anna Mescherskaia, a priest's wife, taught arithmetic and church singing. Z. I. Chernobaeva taught geography and French. Sister Andrea, one of the women monastics associated with Mother Paulina, taught hygiene, culinary arts, and embroidery. Another, Sister Mikhaila, taught home economics. Male instructors included priest Ingram Nathaniel Irvine, a convert from the Episcopal Church, who taught English. Gabriel Cherepnin, *psalomshchik* of the Yonkers parish, assisted with arithmetic, and monastic priest Feofan (Oblivantsev) assisted with church singing.[62]

The remainder of the faculty and staff suggests the degree to which the college was intertwined with the archdiocesan consistory, in both personnel and administration. Priest Leonid Turkevich, husband of Anna, dean of St. Nicholas Cathedral, and editor of the *Russian Orthodox American Messenger*, served as the college inspector. Priest Peter Kohanik, husband of Dr. Eugenia Kohanik, president of ROCMAS, and editor of its newspaper, *Svit*, taught liturgics and church history. Archbishop Evdokim, formerly the rector of the Moscow Theological Academy, took a hands-on role in both administration and curriculum development and also stepped in for pedagogy and didactics lectures. Student acceptance letters were dispatched on archdiocesan letterhead and signed in Evdokim's name. Faculty forwarded expense receipts to the archdiocesan consistory for reimbursement.

Home economics courses taught ecclesiastical tailoring, by which students produced vestments, cassocks, and other items to be sold in the diocesan store. And the women's college was afforded a stature and presence alongside other archdiocesan institutions, including the male seminary.

At the end of the first academic year, the archbishop, faculty, and local clergy proctored a week of final examinations. These culminated with college students and children from the Brooklyn parish school staging a Russian-language play, *At School* (*V shkolye*).[63] With final examinations completed, six women left the college with the primary knowledge and skill sets they would need as an Orthodox wife or, ideally, a clergy wife: to teach children, to sing in church, and to keep a home. What was more, a group of young women whose formal educations had lasted only into junior high school experienced a rigorous year of higher learning—mostly under the tutelage of other women. By these measures, the first school year was a success. In late August, applications were solicited for a second year of instruction, though one that portended changes.[64] Five of the seven instructors on the pared-down faculty roster were men.[65] When the autumn of 1916 came, however, pressing budgetary concerns made reopening the school a difficult proposition. The archdiocesan report for that year noted that "the Mission cannot boast of any success by this young institution," blaming organizational failures, funding problems, and "the low level of education of our faithful, the majority of whom are often simple blue-collar workers." The women's college closed, though the male St. Platon's Seminary did not. Despite the lofty goals of the St. Mary Women's College and a fruitful inaugural year, the brief experiment came to an unceremonious end.[66]

In Minneapolis, Springfield, and Brooklyn, church leaders tethered education to religious practice, posing that an Orthodox adolescence was one in which scripture, doctrine, and most importantly, liturgy were equally intertwined toward the making of a faithful adult. Young people in parish schools and church institutions learned to read, chant, and sing, to participate in the sacraments, and to perceive the Orthodox Church as an inseparable component of their identities. Church leaders never saw these endeavors as monopolistic or exclusive, however, and made a concerted effort to complement, if not replicate, the curricula and pedagogical techniques found in US public schools. Orthodox parents shared these ideals, showing little impulse to shelter their children in schools that taught only Orthodox points of view, nor did these working-class parents attempt to educate their children at home. Rather, they shared the concern of church leaders that the young people of American Orthodox Rus' needed to learn to reside in two worlds: their church and their pluralistic society, in which the Orthodox constituted a distinct minority. As a result, students trod off to "Russian School" only after their "American" school days concluded.

While warm memories of Russian Schools and archdiocesan educational institutions indicate the foundational role of such efforts for generations of parishioners, some clergy considered them inadequate for building a lasting Orthodox presence in North America. One priest, John Kedrovsky of Coaldale, Pennsylvania, thought so little of educational opportunities there that in 1913, he sent his son and daughter to Russia to live with an aunt and study in Petrograd instead.[67] That same year, in a report given to an Orthodox charitable group in Ukraine, priest and former North American missionary John Nedzelnitsky echoed this sense of the positive intentions yet clear shortcomings of Orthodox educational endeavors in the US. "The work of educating the Orthodox people in North America stands as poor for the time being," he observed. While many parishes had schools, he explained, few had a dedicated school building. He regretted that through lessons held only a few times each week, often in the church basement, "Russian children receive only the basics of Russian school instruction." Nedzelnitsky shared the hope of his former missionary colleagues that these students might enjoy the kinds of educational opportunities that other faith traditions offered in the United States, such as the Roman Catholics, who supported countless grade schools, seminaries, and colleges. "For higher education [Russian children] must go to a foreign school, where what is given to them is not in a Russian spirit," he lamented. "For now, the highest-level Russian school in America is only one seminary, though the mission expends on it considerable money, heartfelt attention, and zealous effort."[68] In 1914, clergy like Nedzelnitsky felt justified in their confidence that the North American archdiocese could address these inadequacies with ongoing efforts in social and educational aid for immigrant workers and also that the thrust of American Orthodox Rus' could be augmented to meet the needs of their children as well. Yet they could not anticipate the geopolitical changes that would make such dreams impossible to achieve.

4

"Let All America See"

The Russian-American Army in the Great War

Do not think that we desire that our names be entered into
history. No, we only desire your charity.
—Corporal Michael Basalyga, Corporal Peter Slimak, Private Phillip Nirka, and Private Alex Manko, United States
Army, Augusta, Georgia, October 27, 1917

In a January 1918 letter to *Svit*, Private Frank Hopko described the many
challenges facing Orthodox Christians in the United States Army. Born
to Carpatho-Rusyn immigrant parents in Poughkeepsie, New York,
Hopko was twenty-two when he enlisted in 1917. Soon after his arrival
at Camp Wadsworth in South Carolina, the young private discovered
that military life was not so easy for ethnic doughboys. Even though
he was a natural-born citizen, Hopko wrote that his bunkmates there
viewed Orthodox soldiers like him with suspicion. "As I am ready to
ask you that something must be done by our church leaders to save us,
young men," Hopko wrote in his English-language letter, "as I know a
lot of men, in fact right here, who are ashamed of speaking a word of
their mother tongue. Why? For the simple reason that our religion is
not represented by a chaplain in their army." Hopko heard of a Russian parish in nearby Spartanburg, though he later verified that it was
a Greek chapel where services seldom occurred, as there was no priest.
And while a clergyman visited Spartanburg in early January for the
Nativity feast, a measles epidemic in the barracks kept Hopko under
quarantine. It was the first time the young private had ever missed
Christmas services.[1]

Frank Hopko worried about his uncertain fate at the European front.
More important to him, however, was his eternal salvation should he
die in battle not having received the eucharist. What did it say about

his faith when his friends could access their Catholic or Protestant chaplains while Hopko was left only with his private devotions? How could his church not meet even the most basic spiritual needs of its own doughboys? In Hopko's words, "Here we are training to go across to fight for humanity and liberty and when the time comes for the final test, where are we to receive the Holy Sacrament. Are you going to let us go to death without it, or are you going to help us out? I myself do not want to go that way. I believe there are hundreds that feel the same way. So American Russia in civil life wake up and help your American Russians in khaki, as without your help we will be lost spiritually."[2] The newspaper's response to Hopko, probably penned by priest Peter Kohanik, described existing plans to appoint Orthodox "war priests" for the American Expeditionary Forces. An Orthodox priest was already in France as a chaplain with Canadian soldiers, and Bishop Alexander (Nemolovsky) wanted to embed his clergy with the Americans as well. The United States War Department agreed, having informed the church in November 1917 that "the appointment of priests of the Russian Orthodox Church as chaplains at large is contemplated." *Svit* accordingly included the department's instructions and application for becoming a chaplain.[3]

Several archdiocesan priests responded to express their willingness to serve. Among them was priest Arcady Piotrowsky, once the Russian Orthodox Immigration Society representative on Ellis Island, then serving a parish in Salem, Massachusetts. Piotrowsky received a terse response: "Those who want to become a priest in the American army are first of all obliged to be a citizen." Though Piotrowsky had been in the United States for more than a decade and filed his declared intent to become a citizen, he had not yet completed the process. In a mission still predominantly served by immigrant priests who—like their flocks—often did not consider US citizenship a pressing concern, a citizenship test was a significant obstacle, no matter their eagerness to volunteer. *Svit* asked concerned Orthodox doughboys to send appeals to Bishop Alexander, hoping an urgent groundswell within the army could prompt the War Department to "without fail deign to appoint for the army but one of those expressing a wish to serve in war work as priests."[4] On Armistice Day, however, "American Russians in khaki" remained without chaplains of their own.

The Great War was an unprecedented, cataclysmic conflict that pitted humanity's capacities to reason, relate, and rationalize against its many and increasingly destructive ways to maim, destroy, and kill. Death swam the seas, tunneled beneath the ground, and crawled and rumbled over the earth. It descended from the skies and lingered in the air. The war's destruction was total, its scope unparalleled, and its potential apocalyptic. That a doughboy like Frank Hopko felt spiritual dread at the prospect of facing battle without the sacraments indicates not just fear but a heightened inclination at the front to view oneself in relation to the divine. Across the globe, political leaders and observers alike posed the conflict as both a national and religious struggle, a conflict of differing views of the world that would determine the path of human development into a new and modern age. "We are at war to preserve a real world in the making," the American Protestant theologian Shailer Mathews wrote in 1918, "not a Utopia that men have dreamed."[5] Combatants felt their war to be an effort to reshape the world. The people of American Orthodox Rus' believed they had a rightful stake in determining how humanity might do that work.

This chapter addresses two experiences of the war effort within American Orthodox Rus': the transformative impact of war service for immigrant soldiers and families and the reorientation of US industry toward war production. While the Great War initially reinforced the transnational worldview of American Orthodox Rus', the entry of the United States into the conflict changed how the Russian Archdiocese ministered to its flock. Throughout the war, American Orthodox Rus' engaged in a performative patriotism that demonstrated loyalty and fidelity, expressing that Orthodox workers and their families were properly comporting themselves in a global age of insecurity. Marching in parades, attending meetings, dispatching letters and telegrams to public officials, purchasing Liberty Bonds, and other performing demonstrative acts, immigrant workers and their children (often US-born) displayed their loyalty to the United States while also foregrounding that they were Orthodox Christians. Such performative patriotism served to ease the perception that the Russian Orthodox Church was incompatible with life in the US. This was particularly important at a time in which an emerging federal surveillance state was beginning its foray into Russian communities to ascertain their loyalties and intentions.

Figure 4.1. Priest Leonid Turkevich blessing ambulances for war service in front of the Russian consulate, New York City, April 10, 1916. (LC-B2-3813-8, Bain News Service Photograph Collection, Library of Congress)

From the start of the conflict in 1914, the patriotic thrust of American Orthodox Rus' was oriented toward material aid and spiritual support for the Russian armed forces. Congregations donated money to the Russian Red Cross and helped obtain ambulances and war relief materials. They prayed for the tsar and his soldiers, drawing on imperial rhetoric of duty and sacrifice to support the "new patriotic war." Then came the events of early 1917. In Russia, the February Revolution brought the abdication of Tsar Nicholas II. In Washington, DC, several weeks later, President Woodrow Wilson abandoned the isolationism of his 1916 reelection campaign and brought the United States into a fight that many Americans had long hoped to avoid. The clergy and laity of American Orthodox Rus' deftly repurposed patriotic rhetoric once used to support the tsar to echo the ideals of a US president who posed patriotic language of duty, sacrifice, and loyalty in identifiably religious terms. Wilson did so to drive a massive military and war-industry mobilization not seen since the Civil War, a conflict that itself indelibly wove similar patriotic vocabularies into national discourse.[6] By standing behind Wilson, the clergy and laity of American Orthodox Rus' traded the global aspirations of one powerful empire for another. Hoping the war might repel both the German "Hun" and the Bolshevik "Red," they placed their trust in princes and sons of men so as to preserve the salvation of Russian Orthodox Christians across the world.

The Russian War Effort in American Orthodox Rus'

New Yorkers passing near Washington Square on April 10, 1916, would have been treated to an unusual sight. That afternoon, thirteen ambulances and three support automobiles were parked in front of the Russian consulate, fifteen of which were bound for Russia. Priest Leonid Turkevich and two attendants descended the consulate steps, finding hundreds of people crowded on the sidewalk. "Many stood with bared heads as the rector of the St. Nicholas Cathedral, resplendent in a cloth-of-gold robe, passed from one car to another, celebrating the ritualistic rites of the Greek Catholic Church," the *New York Tribune* described. "Marching in a circle about the car, they sprinkled it with holy water. Thus they passed down the entire line, nor did the solemn chant cease until the three had marched again into the consulate." Dignitaries and interested passersby gathered around the ambulances, whose canvas sides bore the imprimatur of the American Ambulance in Russia, the organization that raised the funds for the vehicles. Children were hoisted into the drivers' seats for playful photographs. The blessed ambulances were then driven across the Queensboro Bridge to a storage facility and shipment to Europe ten days later.[7]

The Russian declaration of war on Germany in August 1914 shifted the efforts of American Orthodox Rus' from immigrant aid to the imperial war effort. In Russia, this endeavor drew heavily from the material and personal resources of the Russian Church and its clergy. Just as critical, if not more so, was the power and reach of the church to mold the minds and ideals of a nation at war. The war inspired millions across the Russian Empire to think of themselves as part of a national community in new and more intimate ways. The historian Melissa K. Stockdale has termed Russia's wartime confluence of faith and fatherland the "sacred union," which she describes as "a grand patriotic narrative of unity, service, generosity, and sacrifice assembled at the start of the Great War."[8]

Stockdale notes that through its parishes, schools, and inroads within the armed forces, "the Russian Orthodox Church was uniquely placed to shape the narrative of the war's meaning and conduct."[9] The Orthodox Church held a central role in Russian public life, a religious institution imbued with the authority and credibility to influence how the Russian people would understand and undertake their mobilization into war industries and military service. Russia's victory over the dreaded "Teutons" would require the Orthodox Church to instill a sense of singular determination across a sprawling, multinational, and multiconfessional empire. "Nationalist discourse in Russia, as in many other countries," Stockdale argues, "did not simply draw on religion as a constitutive element: it was inflected by the familiar—and legitimizing—language *of* that faith."[10] After several decades in which increased print culture, emphases on pilgrimage and piety, and the close ties between church and the tsarist state changed the intensity and breadth of popular religious practice, Russian Orthodox Christians possessed a fervent vocabulary of devotion, obligation, and sacrifice. Acting on this vocabulary necessitated everyday action and performative patriotism throughout the Russian Church and in all places where Russian Orthodox Christians could be found, including North America.

From the war's onset, the Russian Archdiocese fostered an efficient network to disseminate information and drum up support for tsarist forces against the German "Hun." Church newspapers filled column inches with dispatches from France and Belgium. Coins dropped into collection plates to aid the wounded and displaced. Clergy weighed the theological implications of modern warfare. Laity and clergy alike were asked to exude personal support for the tsar's army, from public displays of loyal allegiance to material donations. Soon after Russia entered the conflict, priest Sergei Snegireff of the archdiocesan consistory mailed small tricolor flags to every clergyman and to the leaders of local Orthodox brotherhoods. "Every Russian person should have such a small national flag of their own in the home," Snegireff wrote, advertising that more were available for twenty-five cents each.[11] Russia's ambassador to the United States initiated a fundraising effort for the Russian Red Cross. "Donate, dear brothers and sisters, to the Russian soldiers, to the defenders of our dear Motherland," he entreated, asking support for those who were "carrying their own life to the altar of the homeland."[12] In response, the archdiocese authorized the formation of the Russian War Relief Society in early 1915, organizing Russian women in New York—many of them the wives of priests—in support of the Russian Red Cross. Parishes generated over $16,000 in small donations by the end of February (around $500,000 today).[13]

Church publications disseminated statements from both Tsar Nicholas II and the Holy Synod imploring all Russians to unite behind what they called the "new patriotic war." In a message reprinted on the first page of the *Russian Orthodox American Messenger*, the tsar invoked his own Orthodox devotion and the divine power he afforded his office to couch war as a holy struggle, declaring that he "would not make peace until the last enemy soldier withdraws from Our land." He pledged his support to his "army, united in heart and in soul, strong as a granite wall, and bless[ed] her to military service."[14] The spiritual efforts of American Orthodox Rus' were to align behind the tsar's army. In churches across North America, congregations would ask God to intercede for "our warriors" against the "calumnies of the enemy" and to ensure a speedy end to the conflict. "Thou who defendest those who hold the faith, send Thy arrows, O Lord, and create confusion among our enemies," one suggested petition beseeched. "Let Thy lightning flash and scatter them; send Thy power from above and bring them into submission, and deliver them into the hands of Thy faithful warriors and the hands of our Emperor; we pray Thee, hear us and have mercy on us."[15]

Supporting the imperial war effort was perfectly natural for much of the largely Russian-born clergy in American Orthodox Rus'. They generally shared the patriotic thrust of their counterparts in Russia in justifying the conflict as a matter of preserving humanity and civilization—even as they understood war as a violation against human life. From the pulpit and in the press, clergy drew on historical conflicts and animosities with "Teutonic" peoples to arouse anti-German sentiment and explain why war was necessary. "War, like murder, is a great evil and a great sin," Archbishop Platon (Rozhdestvensky) noted in a sermon offered shortly after departing North America for a position in Moldova. "No amount of riches can purchase a life lost, nor can anyone or anything bring the dead back to life. And yet for us this will be a most popular, most national war. It was foisted upon us, we are defending ourselves, and we never planned to attack."[16]

Clergymen on the domestic front of American Orthodox Rus' eagerly highlighted counterparts in Russia engaged in the important work of spiritual relief in Europe. Priest Adam Philippovsky wrote in April 1915 of "the enormity of the work carried out by the Russian Orthodox Church in relation to its people and Homeland" on the battlefields of Europe. Philippovsky pointed to widespread reports by war correspondents concerning "the gallant selflessness of those heroes armed not with a rifle, sharp saber, nor spear, but rather who walk with the holy cross raised high in their hand." He described how each of these Orthodox chaplains approached the wounded, "his appearance seeming to say, 'if we are to die, then we will die together, but together with valor and glory!'" Philippovsky argued that the very presence of these priests under fire not only bolstered the tsar's army in general but also reinforced to each dying soldier that their sacrifice had intertwined religious and national meanings. Chaplains offered words of consolation in equal measure to the sacraments, including confession and the presanctified eucharist. In this way, the Orthodox soldier was posed as a hero to his people and the fruit of a church that God ordained to bring the salvation of Russia. "Every Orthodox person looks to this work of their Mother Church with ecstatic joy," Philippovsky observed. "He is proud of the church, which has reared him to be a hero. He is proud of [the church], for at every turn she gives to him examples of the honest fulfillment of his duties before Tsar and Motherland [*Rodina*]." In the midst of a cataclysmic war, every Russian Orthodox Christian—especially those in uniform—needed to understand and value their own role within a church mandated to support the living, comfort the ailing, and pray for the dead. "We are Your flesh and blood. You are ours," Philippovsky wrote, addressing the Orthodox soldier. "United, holy, great and mighty Rus' has begotten and raised us all. May her glory endure forever and ever!"[17]

Away from the front, Philippovsky noted that notions of service and sacrifice prevailed in Russia and in "the land newly annexed by Russia," driven by a Russian Church eager and well equipped to house, clothe, and feed those who were affected by the conflict. Monastic communities sewed clothing and bandages, operated hospitals and infirmaries, and took in orphans and refugees. Pilgrimages and other activities were oriented to provide Orthodox vocabularies for wartime patriotism.

Seminaries were repurposed into hospitals. Priests, bishops, and members of the nobility gave up their homes to house refugees. "War is a great and terrible thing! It demands sacrifices and drags into the maw of destruction not just fathers and husbands," Philippovsky noted. "To their families it brings grief, misfortune, and need. How many forsaken, helpless wives and children are there already? And how many widows and orphans?" In areas that had seen battle, he told of villages devoid of adults, where "in the houses and in the forests are small children without clothing, food, and supervision. Fear has nearly stifled their very sense of life." Philippovsky asserted that church relief efforts could bring their salvation. "But you were not left orphans, without father nor mother!" he wrote of them. "You have lost them, loved ones, kinsfolk. Yet from now on, all Holy Russia shall be your father and mother!"[18]

Patriotism in American Orthodox Rus'

The United States entered the war on April 2, 1917, precisely as post-tsarist Russia hastened toward its exit. Similar to the imperial Russian "sacred union" of faith and duty, the US war effort wedded personal duty, national obligation, and enthusiastic patriotism so as to inspire closer personal identities with the state. The historian David Kennedy writes that as President Wilson mulled joining the conflict, Americans "entered on a deadly serious contest to determine the consequences of the crisis for the character of American economic, social, and political life."[19] Beyond its implications for Wilson's foreign-policy ambitions to "make the world safe for democracy," the war offered new justifications for eroding difference on the home front. The war accelerated an ongoing, nativist project of coercive immigrant assimilation long posed as essential for ensuring ideological unity and political orthodoxy—if not preserving democratic capitalism itself. It brought greater measures of immigration restriction. And in the name of national security, federal agencies gained broader surveillance, investigatory, and judicial powers—including the ability to deport noncitizen immigrants long after they arrived in the United States.[20]

When the United States joined the war, those elements of American Orthodox Rus' deployed for enthusiastic support of the Russian war effort shifted to back the United States' rapid mobilization for the

European front. Hours after Woodrow Wilson asked Congress to declare war, Archbishop Evdokim (Meschersky) deployed a telegram to the president expressing his thanks that Wilson had "so generously come forward to the defense of freedom for mankind—this high and precious gift of the Almighty to the sinful world." Though a relative newcomer to the United States, the forty-eight-year-old archbishop pledged, "I, the head of the Russian Orthodox [Church] of America, and millions of Russian people behind me, are not only loyal, but will fight for the great American people for the freedom of humanity to the last drop of blood." In doing so, Evdokim volunteered the former site of the St. Mary Women's College in Brooklyn to serve as a hospital "for the future suffering soldiers, who have fought for the Cause of Humanity." Evdokim wanted the president to know that all facets of American Orthodox Rus' would be redeployed to his cause, from the toil of factory workers to the exhortations of clergy and especially the lives of young men from its parishes taking up arms for the United States.[21]

For more than two decades, archdiocesan clergy puzzled over US patriotism. Few events perplexed them more than the Fourth of July, when Americans found just as much delight in civic pageants and patriotic parades as they did in blowing up fireworks and firing guns. On July 5, 1896, after offering prayers for the holiday marked the previous day, Bishop Nicholas (Ziorov) described his own curious interest. "Unfortunately, among all this fuss, the shooting and cracking of fireworks, we did not hear the ringing bell, we did not hear the Americans praying and thanking God for their freedom," he remarked. "And how I would have liked to hear that!" Nicholas searched for a Russian, specifically Orthodox, frame of reference. He suggested that day's feast, which commemorated the Vladimir Icon of the Mother of God and its miraculous deliverance of Moscow from a Tatar invasion in 1480. Instead of crowning "Goddesses of Liberty" and singing patriotic songs, Russians marched with icons and crosses and intoned sacred hymns, a solemn practice of religious commemoration that Nicholas clearly preferred. All the same, he wished to honor "the special relationship of America and Russia," marked by decades of mutual support and diplomatic relations, including the 1867 sale of Alaska. "We Russians should be grateful to the Americans," Nicholas said, "for we have the right to live among them and enjoy the protection of their laws."[22]

By the Great War, performative patriotism was posed as an appropriate and critical aspect of American Orthodox Rus' and the careful balance it encouraged between the United States and Russia. Archdiocesan leaders did not preach total isolation from life in the US. To the contrary, lay adherents were encouraged to become US citizens, vote in elections, and explore the world around them—though in ways informed by the Orthodox faith. The archdiocese recognized that concepts of citizenship and what it meant to become "American" were not about blood or ethnic identity but rather about entering a system of ideas and accepting a legal status. "In America there is no prohibition against faith or identifying with the Russian ethnicity," noted a 1909 editorial in the *Russian Orthodox American Messenger*. "Monroe's doctrine of 'America for the Americans' is understood here in a rather peculiar sense. In order to be an American (an American citizen), it is not required to be born in America, though it is necessary to live here a few years, and it is not hard to obtain documents to become a naturalized American and thus to enjoy all the rights of a son of the great transatlantic republic." Still, the author (almost certainly a priest) bemoaned that those who did become citizens often voted without knowledge of whom, or what, they were voting for—if they even went to the polls at all. He lamented that "Russian people themselves, not Americans, put themselves in such a position that, for Russian people, the most important events in American political life pass completely unnoticed."[23] Some outside observers felt that Orthodox migrants were isolating themselves in their own habits and customs and prioritizing religious activities over the secular world around them—all the while ignoring a US political system whose immigration and citizenship policies very much affected their lives. As another 1909 editorial lamented, "Americans did not learn of the existence of Russians by their participation in the political life of America, but rather through religious processions, grand archpastoral services, and a special type of church with eight-pointed [triple-barred] crosses."[24]

Performative patriotism was more important than ever in American Orthodox Rus' in 1917, when national fears arose that Russian-speaking immigrants would unleash their own political revolution on US soil. To counter such fears, some within the archdiocese focused on public displays of devotion through displaying and honoring the US flag. In May, a church-affiliated firm on the Lower East Side of Manhattan advertised for sale lapel pins and tie clips bearing both the Russian and US flags, imploring potential buyers that they should "express particular sympathy to our new ally America."[25] That same month, Archbishop Evdokim participated in a "ceremony of consecration of the American Flag" (*torzhestvo osviashcheniia Amerikanskago flaga*) in Watervliet, New York. Five thousand people gathered to watch the fully vested bishop march in a parade alongside four other vested Orthodox clergymen, the town's mayor, a state supreme court justice, representatives from an "American school," and members of the local Russian community. The parade ended at a rostrum festooned with the Stars and Stripes. In a ceremony blending Orthodox ritual with US patriotic pageantry, Evdokim sprinkled holy water on a US flag, blessing the symbol most associated with US patriotism. His cathedral archdeacon, Vsevolod (Andronoff), intoned in English the traditional Orthodox chant "God Grant You Many Years." At the close of the ceremony, all sang "My Country, 'Tis of Thee."[26]

During the Great War, national symbols became more potent and ubiquitous. As the Watervliet flag consecration ceremony shows, few symbols grew in prominence more than the US flag. Old Glory long enjoyed a privileged space in national discourse, especially since the Civil War. Though Americans began to informally celebrate June 14 as Flag Day in the 1880s, it was only in 1916 that it became a national holiday.[27] "The language of the flag became mystical," Arnaldo Testi notes of shifts in patriotic symbology during the war. "In the orations of the time, the Stars and Stripes was spoken of as a sacred thing, which comes from the hands of God, which the Americans should adore like the Israelites adored the Ark of the Covenant."[28] When the United States entered the war a year later, the flag was already a venerated object whose stars and stripes bore the nation's aspirations and exemplified a carefully cultivated history of (largely "Anglo-Saxon") national triumph. During the war, the flag transformed into a shibboleth for identity and loyalty, even a frightening manifestation of nativist coercion. Through groups like the Grand Army of the Republic and the Daughters of the American Revolution, the flag became a positive symbol of the nation's military sacrifices and the possibilities of a (largely white) United States democracy. On the other hand, nefarious groups such as the Ku Klux Klan and the American Protective Association used the flag to further their racist, nativist, and anti-Catholic agendas. In repeated incidents during the war, individuals who were perceived to be disloyal—and who were usually foreign-born—were subjected to ritualized shows of devotion involving the flag, even compulsory veneration of the flag itself. These "flag-kissing ceremonies" reflected domestic insecurities about syndicalism just as much as nativist fear, calling on those who were thought most likely to be politically subversive and inimical to the war effort—immigrants and especially Germans and Slavs—to prostrate themselves before the most potent symbol of US patriotism to the point of humiliation.[29]

Viewed in this context, Archbishop Evdokim's public blessing of a flag was a patriotic performance intended to show that local Russians—as well as Greeks, Syrians, Armenians, and other Orthodox ethnic groups in attendance that day—were visible members of the community and loyal to their adopted country. A similar display took place that spring in the textile town of Fall River, Massachusetts, on Patriots' Day, a New England holiday marking the Battles of Lexington and Concord, fought in 1775. In the celebration, which occurred only days after Congress declared war, priest John Semanitsky and members of the Falls River parish brotherhood marched in the town parade to demonstrate their patriotism and dedication. It was a rare and emboldened moment of public visibility for members of Semanitsky's parish. "All who turned up considered, and think of themselves as Russians," the priest recalled. "They passed through the street to much applause from the public, who for the first time saw and recognized that there are Russians in Fall River."[30]

The Russian-American Army

While Russian Orthodox Christians took eager parts in the spectacle and performativity of Wilsonian wartime patriotism, the war could not be won with parades and flag blessings alone. Young men from American Orthodox Rus'—foreign- and native-born alike—numbered among the hundreds of thousands of doughboys in the American Expeditionary Force. On June 5, 1917, the United States conducted a draft registration, inaugurating the first conscripted military service since the Civil War. From seven in the morning until nine that evening, millions of men ages twenty-one to thirty lined up to register. Selective service was intended, as David Kennedy observes, "to serve primarily as a way to keep the right men in the right jobs at home."[31] It was also a way to determine service opportunities for the foreign-born. Those classified as "alien enemies" were ineligible for conscription. Other foreign-born men were funneled into menial, noncombat roles, where their limited commands of English were less impactful. Many early Orthodox enlistees trained at Camp Gordon in Augusta, Georgia, a frequent destination for Slavic immigrants within the polyglot US Army. While military service was seen as a vehicle for Americanization, some people felt that foreign-born soldiers were detrimental to efficiency, morale, and decorum. As the historian Nancy Gentile Ford argues, the army worked alongside leaders of religious and ethnic groups alike to develop "an approach similar to that used by many Progressive social welfare workers who preserved Old World traditions while they slowly assimilated immigrants into the American culture."[32]

Orthodox soldiers often needed far more assistance than the military was willing or able to provide. Some turned instead to *Svit* (*The Light*), the newspaper of the Russian Orthodox Catholic Mutual Aid Society (ROCMAS). From the earliest days of the conflict, the paper reflected the ardent wartime patriotism of editor and priest Peter Kohanik. Born in 1880 to a Greek Catholic family in Carpathian Rus', Kohanik came to the United States in 1892; there his family numbered among the thousands of Carpatho-Rusyns who converted to Orthodoxy through the efforts of priest Alexis Toth. Kohanik studied in Minneapolis at the diocesan Missionary School, then received a coveted scholarship for seminary training in Russia. After his studies in St. Petersburg, he returned to the United States in 1902 to work as a missionary priest in Pennsylvania. When the war began, Kohanik was one of the most decorated clergymen in the archdiocese and an outspoken leader within its significant Carpatho-Rusyn flock. He helped establish parishes across the Northeast, worked to build the Russian Immigrant Home, and served in administrative positions for both the archdiocese and ROCMAS.[33] For many people, Kohanik was synonymous with the Ruthenian-language *Svit*, whose coverage of the war outweighed that of most other periodicals with wide circulation within American Orthodox Rus'. Most issues printed a war-related cartoon from the US press on the front page. *Svit* also advertised Liberty Loan drives and War Savings Stamps, provided information about war registration, and ran patriotic articles encouraging its readers to back the war effort.

Beginning in January 1918, *Svit* published its own muster rolls for what it called "our Russian-American Army" (*nasha Russko-Amerikanskaia Armiia*), listing the names of "our Russian heroes" from industrial cities and company towns across the United States, from Chicago and Detroit to Carnegie and Coaldale. One pair of soldiers hailed from Sitka, Alaska. Week after week, the updated list appeared as a patriotic infographic, usually a uniformed doughboy holding a numbered banner or service flag inset with that week's total spelled out with stars. The first list included the names and home towns of 60 men. By the final installment, there were 747, so many that they were listed only by the number from each city or town. While it is not clear how many of them lost their lives in military service, it is almost certain that the last was infantryman John Loss, who enlisted in February 1918. One of the 81 soldiers who hailed from the St. Mary's parish of Minneapolis, Loss was wounded in action on November 8. He died from his injuries two days later, mere hours before Armistice Day dawned.[34]

Once soldiers like John Loss found their way into US khaki, *Svit* mobilized its readers to come to their spiritual and material aid. Early in the conflict, Kohanik began sending issues of *Svit* to servicemen. He published the responses he received from them, offering readers insight into how the Russian-American Army perceived war service. An October 1917 letter from four such soldiers stationed for training at Camp Gordon thanked Kohanik for appealing to archdiocesan clergy to pray for Orthodox soldiers like them. "Our hearts gushed with joy," the men wrote. "You made us equal with our brothers, who at the moment are injured or are dying in the fields of battle. We are not worthy of that; we are only preparing to take their place, in order to stand up for our country and faith. We do not fear death." The soldiers felt they were at war for the salvation of Russia just as much as that of the United States. To the paper's readers, the soldiers entreated,

> Dear Orthodox brothers and sisters, do not give up in spirit, but fervently pray to the Lord for us, and at the same time buy "Liberty Loan Bonds," with which you help not only us, but our brother Russian soldiers, who are now, in essence, like orphans without father and mother. Do not

forget that you have sons who will also go in our footsteps when we give up the body for our loved ones, for luminous "freedom." Do not think that we desire that our names be entered into history. No, we only desire your charity. Know that your sacrifice will be accepted as Jesus Christ accepted the widow's two mites.[35]

These same sentiments were echoed in a March 1918 letter from Private Peter Telep. A twenty-six-year-old immigrant from Austria-Hungary, Telep settled in Cleveland in 1907 and enlisted for war service ten years later.[36] Telep wrote *Svit* from France to request Russian-language reading materials at the front. His brother was sending him copies of *Svit*, but Telep hoped for regular distribution through the YMCA. "Since I had gone to the army, I had no Russian paper or book to read, which made me very lonsome [*sic*] about our people and our language," Telep wrote. "What we desire from all Russian people in U.S. of America—is please make such an organization which will help our soldiers in the U.S. Army in supplying them with Russian books [and] papers." Kohanik promised Telep in response, "from now on, until the end of the war, our 'Svit' will be found in the reading rooms of the U.S. Army Y.M.C.A."[37]

The Home Front

The overwhelming majority of Russian Orthodox Christians who contributed to the US war effort did so not in Europe but rather in war industries on the domestic front. War contracts subsumed nearly every facet of US industrial production, while the conflict itself redefined the very nature of industrial work. Laborers who once made consumer products like automobiles and everyday clothing found their workplaces retooled to produce airplanes, medical supplies, and uniforms. Immigrant workers in these industries were encouraged to understand their insoluble connections with soldiers at the front, measured in each monotonous assembly line task or scoop of a mine shovel. Theirs was an extraordinary domestic struggle of patriotism, sacrifice, and duty, one that represented just as much the drudgery of US industrial labor as an enforced sense of belonging in a noble pursuit for global freedom.

Orthodox workers did not always blend seamlessly into this US war machine. In August 1918, the assistant district representative of the

United States Fuel Administration wrote a terse letter to the archdiocese concerning the work habits of Orthodox coal miners in Pennsylvania, later reprinted in *Svit*. The administrator wrote, "reports are continually coming to us that members of your church are laying off from work on week days to attend church services and Holy-day celebrations." Placing aside his outrage that miners might be lying about church attendance to slough off work, the administrator maintained that even legitimate absences could have significant national security implications. "This cuts down on the production of coal and coke, which is so necessary for the prosecution of the war," the official noted with alarm. "Anything which interferes with production now is against the best interests of the United States Government." He warned that absences would be recorded and reported and that government administrators would follow up with priests to confirm that absent workers had indeed been in church.[38]

This stern letter suggests that Russian workers attended services in the fullness of the Orthodox liturgical calendar and that they valued such liturgical participation so much as to prioritize worship over work. To the faithful, this was an unquestioned devotional obligation. To the state, however, it suggested a community of wartime slackers. Bishop Alexander (Nemolovsky) responded on behalf of the archdiocese in a strongly worded exhortation that he demanded be read in all its churches. "All living beneath the starred flag of America," he implored, "citizens and noncitizens," had a responsibility to "join hands in one desire, in one task." He began with miners, as "without coal, the ammunition factories will stop working, and the war fleet and transports will not set out upon the waters." To ensure that wartime industry continued, he implored his flock to "toil diligently, with sufficient strength to sweat blood." Alexander explained that individual religious devotions could not cause anything "that takes us away from the desired day of victory," even if it meant missing liturgical services. "On Sundays, pray and rest," he instructed.

> But on holidays that occur during the week, let the priests pray in the churches, and you hurry off to work. It's war now. Every moment of labor is precious. And each person who lets this minute slip by is an unwitting traitor of his motherland, of the United States, and of those glorious warriors fighting the Huns. Remember that many thousands of Russian

warriors are in distant France under the glorious flag of America, laying down their soul for us. We shall be worthy of them. To work! To work! Glory and honor to all who labor. Shame and disgrace to slackers and the negligent![39]

Alongside responsibilities to war industries, workers were expected to assume a financial stake in the general war effort. Jolting the nation from isolation to preparedness required billions of dollars, funds the government did not have. The American people would need to underwrite the costs through a variety of war bonds, including Liberty Loan (and later Victory Loan) certificates and less expensive Thrift Stamps and War Savings Certificates. These bonds were presented as substitutes for other spending. Putting one's purchasing power behind the federal government instead of consumer goods freed manufacturers and industrialists from expending production capacity for nonmilitary products. The Yale economist Irving Fisher reasoned that if consumers bought Liberty Bonds in amounts equal to what they would otherwise spend on an automobile, for example, "we have done our duty in the full sense of the word, because we have not only given Uncle Sam the funds but we have gotten out of his way in industry, and the same labor and capital which would have made my pleasure car will make a motor truck."[40]

The government advertised Liberty Loan bonds to ethnic communities, producing templates and advertising copy that could be translated and augmented for foreign-language periodicals. These advertisements emphasized that to assume a personal financial stake in the war effort helped one become an American. Bonds were portrayed as wise investments that demonstrated patriotic duty, even though it meant that workers with little savings were placing their limited funds in investments that would not mature for a matter of years. (Some bonds remained unpaid well into the 1930s.) One such advertisement, published in *Svit* in October 1918, portrayed Liberty Bonds as "'Service Stars' on your Pocket Book." The advertisement proclaimed, "If you are Foreign-born[,] They prove your patriotism and loyalty to this country, which you have chosen for your own. They prove that you have a stake in this free America, and that you are determined to be 100% AMERICAN IN THOUGHT AMERICAN IN SPEECH AMERICAN IN HEART AND American in the Will to Win this War."[41] Purchasing a bond also instilled a sense of national pride. Another advertisement showed a family of five—a workman father, a mother holding an infant, and two sons—watching doughboys on parade. The father holds his hat over his heart. The mother flashes a proud smile. One of the children wears a replica uniform, waving with one hand as a toy gun rests in the other. Below, in parallel English and Ruthenian translation, Liberty Loan bonds are presented as important ways for an immigrant to "PROVE YOU ARE A 100% AMERICAN." To buy a Liberty Bond was to show respectability, assimilation, and patriotism. If one bought a bond and embraced other markers of being "100% American"—learning English (or helping someone else to do so), preparing for or completing the citizenship process, obeying the law—the immigrant would "have the right to say with pride, 'I AM AN AMERICAN.'"[42]

War Saving Stamps were a smaller yet no less rhetorically powerful measure to do the same. These often were advertised in terms of what their lesser denominations would purchase in material goods for the front. One 25¢ Thrift Stamp bought a pair of wool socks, two stamps a first-aid kit. One $4.17 War Savings Stamp (around $85 today) supplied an iron hospital bed or a doughboy's helmet. These purchases, the National War Savings Committee said, "[buy] the necessary equipment for our boys—YOUR BOYS, PERHAPS—in order that they may be armed better, supported better, fed better, housed better, and receive more protection than any of their adversaries!"[43] Mail carriers sold thrift stamps door-to-door. They could also be purchased in stores, businesses, banks, and post offices. Whereas Liberty Loan certificates offered a somewhat significant return on maturation, these were low-yield bonds. A War Savings Certificate purchased for around four dollars in 1918 could be redeemed five years later for only around a dollar more.[44] Even so, the broader meaning was made clear. "Every time you buy a stamp . . . you are buying a bullet that may save an American soldier's life, or helping to buy a pair of shoes or a warm blanket that may keep him from having pneumonia," one advertisement noted. With every stamp, purchasers were "bringing the defeat of the kaiser just that much nearer." And to do so also demonstrated fiscal responsibility. "You will find it a mighty comfortable nest egg for that rainy day which may come sometime, and you will never miss the money with which you bought it."[45]

Sales of war bonds, stamps, and certificates relied on sympathetic, accommodating industrialists and employers who were willing to encourage their employees to open their pay envelopes for the war effort. Some even made employee donations mandatory. In the automotive factories and machine shops of Detroit, Liberty Loan posters went up like wallpaper. Four-Minute Men from the federal government Committee on Public Information (CPI) halted assembly lines for bond drives. Liberty Bonds sold in these contexts ranged in value from $50 to $250 (between around $1,000 to $5,000 today), a significant portion of a working-class pay stub. Detroit workers also had small amounts of their wages diverted to the Red Cross and the Detroit Patriotic Fund. One Orthodox Detroiter later said that this was a standard practice in the shops where he worked during the war. "They collected from me thru the factory," he recalled. "They took it from the wages. Some places took more than others, some took a dollar every month, and some $1.50, but they took it every place thru the factory."[46] Another working in a rubber and tire plant reported having $100 taken in four $25 increments to help another man buy his own Liberty Bond. "The company said we should buy them," the man recalled, "so I bought them."[47]

The strongly encouraged, if not coercive, nature of these bond purchases demonstrated that performative patriotism was a way for Orthodox workers to ensure stability in an uncertain and punitive labor market. When one man was asked if he would have made any of these donations without his employer asking, if not requiring him to do so, he responded, "No, if nobody had asked me I would not have contributed."[48] Another recalled, "The Boss in the Shop where I am working came over to every employee, and he asked if he wants to buy, and my answer was I was going to buy." This man claimed that he "bought freely"—"I had money and I bought them"—though the power dynamics of the wartime industrial workplace suggest that he might have felt little choice. This same man recalled that his $200 in bond purchases—made through his employer, the Ford Motor Company—were compulsory, though not without critique. He reported that some of his "Bolsheviki friends" advised others "not to buy bonds because they served to help kill our brothers."[49]

Performative patriotism grew in importance as the war progressed. During the spring of 1918, President Wilson declared the Fourth of July holiday as "Loyalty Day," a moment for all to channel their boisterous celebrations toward the nobler goal of unity behind American doughboys. The birth of what Wilson called "the New Democracy" depended on a spirit of national harmony among native-born and immigrant Americans alike. Wilson specifically called on immigrant communities to participate. "Nothing in this war has been more gratifying than the manner in which our foreign-born fellow citizens and the sons and daughters of the foreign-born, have risen to this greatest of all national emergencies," Wilson wrote in a special message to "Ethnic Societies." Wilson hoped this Fourth of July would be "the most significant in our national history," calling on those who were born in the United States to join with their immigrant neighbors to "celebrate the birth of a new and greater spirit of democracy, by whose influence," he said, "we hope and believe, what the signers of the Declaration of Independence dreamed of for themselves and for their fellow countrymen shall be fulfilled for all mankind." Celebrating immigrant Americans' "eager response to calls for patriotic service," Wilson emphasized that devotion to their adopted country made "all distinctions of race vanish" and, as a result, would make the collective, amalgamated nation "feel ourselves citizens in a republic of free spirits."[50]

As Loyalty Day neared, Bishop Alexander decreed that parishes across American Orthodox Rus' should "arrange everywhere festive manifestations—processions in the streets with American and Russian flags, with inscriptions conveying sympathy for the allies and our loyalty to our second country—the free land of Washington and to the noble head of the United States of America President W. Wilson." Congregations were to participate in a celebration that Alexander hoped would also be "for our unlucky Rus'" a good harbinger of liberation from the wicked Teutons and their shameless and faithful servants—the Bolsheviks." Alexander noted the sacrifices of the Russian people to fight back German aggression—three million killed and seven million injured—as a crucial supplement to the doughboys marching into Europe "for the defense of the freedom of all, even the smallest of peoples." To carry a flag in a parade or listen to a Four-Minute Man might preserve the "great transatlantic republic" of the United States, a nation fighting for Russia's salvation. If their congregations did march that day, Alexander wanted a photograph taken and sent to English-language newspapers as well as to his consistory office, so he could then forward them to Washington as proof of their fidelity. "Let all America see that we Russians feel profound gratitude to the United States of America," Alexander wrote, "and as if for our Holy Rus', are prepared to stand behind them to the end."[51]

On the Fourth of July, foreign-born communities across the US answered Wilson's appeals for participation and national unity. In Washington, DC, a parade along Pennsylvania Avenue ended at the steps of the Capitol with a "final tableaux" titled "Democracy Triumphant," including participants "from various parts of the country and even from foreign lands to make the demonstration truly an allied pageant."[52] The *Chicago Tribune* proudly declared that "Americanism, aggressive, undefiled, flaming in its patriotic fervor and inclusive of every element that enters into the makeup of the nation, will find its exemplification in Chicago today in the celebration of the greatest Fourth in the city's history."[53] An "Americanization Parade" down Detroit's Woodward Avenue culminated with the unfurling of a giant flag atop the newly installed "Liberty pole" in Cadillac Square. Revelers progressed east to the city park on Belle Isle, where a thousand-person cast staged a pageant called "A Mingling of the Forces of American Life."[54] And in Virginia, a delegation representing thirty nationalities led a pilgrimage to Mount Vernon to hear President Wilson deliver his "Loyalty Day" message, which would be cabled across the globe to be read at events later in the day.[55] In the speech, Wilson declared that the Founding Fathers "were consciously planning that men of every class should be free and America a place to which men out of every nation might resort who wished to share with them the rights and privileges of free men. And we take our cue from them, do we not?"[56]

One of the places Americans might have seen Orthodox Christian commemorations that day was in Detroit, where the forty-two-year-old locksmith Matthew Mazur led a Loyalty Day parade through the east-side neighborhood surrounding the All Saints church. Mazur and fellow members of a neighborhood brotherhood organization, the Russian National Home, proudly marched the streets of their immigrant neighborhood with small US flags pinned to their lapels. That evening, fellow Russian immigrant Hendry Sirgenkof came to Mazur's home and took him to task. "You should be ashamed to march under a United States flag," Sirgenkof assailed, telling Mazur that it would be better if Germany were to win the war. This was not the first time Mazur encountered Sirgenkof, an alleged member of the Industrial Workers of the World (IWW) who had been fired from his position at Ford for distributing Wobbly propaganda at work. Mazur responded "that the United States flag and country was alright and good enough for [him]," grabbed Sirgenkof off his feet, and threw him out of the house.[57]

That an account survives of Matthew Mazur's Loyalty Day confrontation with Hendry Sirgenkof is because Mazur described it to a federal investigator. Several weeks had passed when agent T. C. Wilcox came to Mazur's downtown locksmith shop and asked about Sirgenkof. As Mazur "appeared very frightened and did not want to talk," Wilcox walked him to a Bureau of Investigation field office in the nearby Owen Building. In addition to Sirgenkof, Mazur named eight men said to be "active workers in the Russian Anarchist Society, Bolsheviki and IWW. in this city," including a socialist lawyer allegedly helping "young Russians who are slackers" to evade military service. Finally, Mazur claimed that "the I.W.W. and Bolsheviki had a plan nearly perfect to start a Revolution in Detroit last November and seize the city government by force of arms" and that the "arms and ammunition needed, were to be furnished by German interests."[58]

Matthew Mazur's extraordinary claims reflected shifts in national discourse as the war neared its end. His account began with the performative patriotism of a Loyalty Day parade and the contrasting disloyalty of a fellow immigrant alleged to be a radical Wobbly and ended with audacious allegations of German-backed revolutionary violence. His story was grounded in the performative patriotism and appeals to loyalty demanded of foreign-born communities during the war years, tailor-made to match wartime military intelligence interests like unpatriotic disloyalty, sedition, and draft evasion. It also portended a Red Scare dominated by domestic intelligence concerns over Russian Bolshevism on US soil. For Mazur and others who composed American Orthodox Rus', the war years were as transformative as they were bewildering. Yet as his account demonstrated, there were new and more tenuous challenges yet to come. We now broach difficult years of crisis and uncertainty in American Orthodox Rus', a period marked by immense political change abroad, the ravages of a viral epidemic, and the crushing onslaught of financial crisis and administrative instability within the North American Archdiocese. At the dawn of a Bolshevik age that was more permanent than anticipated, in American Orthodox Rus', it seemed there was no going back.

PART II

The Toil

5

"Waves of Anarchy"

Making Meaning of 1917

No good tree bears bad fruit, nor again does a bad tree bear
good fruit; for each tree is known by its own fruit. Figs are
not gathered from thorns, nor are grapes picked from a
bramble bush.
—Luke 7:43–44

In 1981, the Orthodox priest and theologian Alexander Schmemann visited Springfield, Vermont. "An old house church," he described in his journal, "at one time there was a women's monastery and orphanage here. And everything ended somewhat grimly and ugly."[1] During the autumn of 1917, the secretary of the Vermont State Board of Charities and Probation went there as well. William H. Jeffrey found sixty-one children in the care of Mother Paulina and her small community of female monastics. Jeffrey was alarmed to find children "so seriously underfed" that he deemed it his duty "to call upon the proper officials of the town of Springfield to provide, at public expense, additional food supplies." He deemed several children "mentally deficient," others "so delinquent as to make it necessary to either deport them or place them in the state institutions." Suspecting that Mother Paulina intended to bring several hundred more children into her care, Jeffrey dispatched an urgent report to the state attorney general.[2]

William Jeffrey had discovered what church officials already knew: the Orphan Home, like so many archdiocesan institutions, was in crisis. Though fundraising for the orphanage was a constant archdiocesan concern, these efforts accelerated beginning in early 1916, when its charitable patrons learned the extent of need at the institution. This included capital projects like a new steam heater, but it also concerned everyday needs, such as reliable access to nutritious food. Donations from archdiocesan parishes raised nearly a thousand dollars during the first half of 1916. A benefit pageant was planned in New York that summer, alongside other festivals, concerts, bazaars, and balls aimed at socialites and well-heeled archdiocesan benefactors. The archdiocese also sold a promotional booklet featuring photographs of the orphanage, the convent, and the adjacent church. "But this is a drop of water in the sea," Bishop Alexander wrote in November 1917 in a front-page notice published next to a photograph of Mother Paulina and the children. "All should know that the other day a warning was received from the city government of Springfield that if we do not act now so that the children do not starve, . . . the orphanage will be closed and all the children sent home or handed over to other orphanages (Roman Catholic and Protestant)." Fundraising efforts continued for several years but never alleviated the orphanage's shaky finances. As of 1920, the orphanage still owed the town of Springfield hundreds of dollars in unpaid public school fees for the children's educations. Even so, the Springfield town council recognized that "Rev. Mother Paulina has done a heroic work in getting the money to support so many children," feeling "that few American women could have done it." Mother Paulina's efforts were just not enough to overcome a troubling calamity beyond her control, which remained in the historical memory of the Springfield parish many decades later.[3]

This chapter explores how clergy and laity in American Orthodox Rus' confronted the two Russian Revolutions of 1917. After the February Revolution came the abdication of Tsar Nicholas II, and with Red October came the consolidation of Bolshevik rule. Within the Russian Church, these events proved altering, if not calamitous. There was no general consensus within American Orthodox Rus' as to how these new and changing realities should be navigated, nor was there reliable, even coherent information about developments in Russia. Many favored retrenchment, preserving the former conditions of the transnational Russian Church even when faced with the cessation of funding and then with a hostile regime whose antireligious efforts hampered normal ecclesiastical functions. Others, as we will see in subsequent chapters, advocated for radical changes to hierarchical church administration, perhaps even abandoning it altogether. And against the backdrop of this administrative and financial chaos came the postwar Red Scare, by which the suspicious gaze of a growing wartime federal surveillance infrastructure shifted from the German "Hun" to the Russian "Red." The shifting geopolitics of the Red Scare forced the clergy and laity of American Orthodox Rus' to balance the ongoing, external imperative to prove congruency with US democracy with their spiritual and material reasons for maintaining ties with an institutional hierarchy in Bolshevik Russia. These intertwined dynamics defined the experience of the Red Scare and its aftermath in American Orthodox Rus'.

The political changes of 1917 underscored the many ways that the North American Archdiocese remained dependent on Russia and the institution of the Russian Church. From operating funds and ecclesiastical guidance down to church wares, service books, and clerical pay, American Orthodox Rus' still struggled to remain standing on its own after more than a century of missionary labors. As the situation worsened, attempts within the church to forge a new path became increasingly politicized and divisive. At stake was what it meant to identify as a Russian Orthodox Christian within a church transformed by rapidly changing geopolitical circumstances, especially at a moment of increased external scrutiny. What emerged were acrimonious disputes that tore apart the archdiocese from within. "It seems as if all the powers of hell have gathered together for the purpose of sinking our Church in the waves of anarchy," Bishop Alexander (Nemolovsky) wrote in 1918. "Not just strangers, but also our own people."[4]

The February Revolution from Afar

March 18, 1917, was a relatively normal Lenten Sunday but for one notable difference: the Russian Orthodox Church would not be offering prayers for Tsar Nicholas II, whose abdication three days earlier cast Russia, and its church, into startling uncertainty. The first stirrings of the February Revolution were an escalating series of protests in the streets of Petrograd expressing outrage over anticipated food shortages in the capital city. On February 27, four days after the protests began, Nicholas ordered the use of violence to clear the streets, only for the soldiers to mutiny and abandon their posts. Away from the capital as the emerging crisis unfolded, Nicholas dissolved the State Duma and attempted to return to Petrograd. On March 2, coming to accept that he would no longer have support to operate his government, the tsar abdicated. The next day, Grand Duke Michael, his brother and heir apparent, declined the throne. After more than three hundred years, a hastily assembled provisional government had supplanted the Romanov imperial house, promising democratization and liberal reforms.[5]

In the United States, outsiders looked to local Russian churches with curiosity. In Manhattan, an archdiocesan official assured the *New York Times* that a change in political leadership was not so drastic as it might appear for the church. He declared the Russian Church "the most democratic in the world. It tolerates no pews in which a man may separate himself from his neighbor's [sic]. It makes Czar and peasant stand next to each other and receive the blessing from the lips of the same humble priest." He harbored optimism that the revolution would not separate the Russian state from the Orthodox Church, "because the State and the people, no matter what changes may take place, cannot do without the Church. In the absence of a permanent form of Government the Church will be more necessary than ever to keep the masses under control and prevent them from leaping into all kinds of brutal excesses to which revolutions give rise."[6] When Archbishop Evdokim omitted the usual prayer for the tsar at the Manhattan cathedral for the first time, one worshiper shouted in broken English, "Hello—the Russian freedom!"[7]

The enthusiasm of this anonymous Manhattan congregant suggested a future with limitless possibilities. The reality was that elsewhere in the cathedral complex, ledger books showed that the archdiocese was in a precarious financial situation that surely would worsen once American Orthodox Rus' could no longer count on the resources and support of the former regime. Within weeks, stipend funds from Russia ceased. The archdiocese fell behind on mortgage payments for church properties. At the New York cathedral, bills for coal, oil, and church candles went unpaid. Missionaries reported bounced salary checks, if they even arrived at all—funds for clerical pay had run out in March 1917, mere days after the revolution. In Kenai, Alaska, one missionary priest wrote in a desperate letter to his vicar bishop that after more than a year of delayed or missing paychecks—a situation that began as early as 1916—his family was hopelessly indigent. "Given the present situation," the priest wrote, "I cannot rely on the Ecclesiastical Consistory anymore."[8]

During the peak years of prewar transatlantic migration, the North American Archdiocese grew faster than did its financial resources.

Though the First World War had slowed transatlantic migration, the church still maintained its wide-reaching efforts in educational, social, cultural, and material assistance. These efforts were underwritten in part by individual philanthropy at the parochial level, as well as through the support of parachurch organizations and external philanthropists. Most of the budget came from a stipend granted by the Most Holy Synod in Petrograd, the governing body of the Russian Church. This sum remained unchanged for some years, even as consistory officials long argued it was inadequate. In 1916, the synod invited Archbishop Evdokim to propose a new archdiocesan budget. He requested approximately $1 million (around $29 million today), prioritizing budget increases for clergy and lay missionary salaries, support for parish-level "Russian schools" (*tserkovno-prikhodskiia shkoly*), and the operating budgets of archdiocesan institutions like the St. Mary Women's College and the Springfield orphanage. The Holy Synod consented to only $550,000 — much of which was never allocated.[9] By 1917, archdiocesan debts exceeded $100,000 ($2.4 million today). Within two years, the debt more than doubled.[10]

Some hope arose during the summer of 1917 when word reached New York that the Russian Church would at long last convene a local church council (*sobor*). The first to be held since the seventeenth century, the council was first proposed in 1905, though it was postponed repeatedly. With the reform-wary Tsar Nicholas II no longer in power, plans resumed, and preconciliar meetings commenced, with the support of the fledgling Provisional Government. "Virtually every aspect of church life was on the agenda," note the religious studies scholars Scott Kenworthy and Alexander Agadjanian in regard to the council's anticipated possibilities. Many observers hoped the council would reflect the fullness of the Russian religious revitalization that began in the late nineteenth century and embrace a more democratic model of church governance, or *sobornost* (conciliarity). Other proposals included the liturgical use of vernacular Russian, increased lay influence over church administration and finances, stronger emphases on parish life and congregational autonomy, and greater gender equity in church life. More radical were calls for innovations like the married episcopate, eroding the power differential between the "black" (monastic) and "white" (married) clergy. Most notable, however, were calls for the restoration of the ecclesiastical office of Patriarch of Moscow, abolished in 1721 by Peter the Great and replaced by the Most Holy Synod. The potential for welcomed change seemed immense, including for church life in North America. In July, Evdokim received instructions to select three delegates from his archdiocese—one bishop, one priest, and one layman. Ultimately, Evdokim and priests Leonid Turkevich and Alexander Kukulevsky were sent to Moscow, ignoring the council's stated goal to enfranchise a significant lay delegation.[11]

Before the delegation departed for Moscow, Evdokim prepared a report on the many financial and administrative inadequacies that had so hamstrung missionary efforts in North America, details he hoped would inspire his superiors and other bishops to improve their support and treatment of the distant archdiocese. Evdokim described arriving there in 1915 and finding nearly every archdiocesan institution or endeavor in debt. The financial situation only worsened, he claimed, from a combination of the Great War and delays, indifference, and broken promises on the part of the Most Holy Synod. Evdokim had difficulties maintaining enough clergy for the parishes—a recent journey along the Pacific Coast included visitations to five churches, none of which had a resident priest. In Los Angeles, some congregants had never even seen a bishop. Evdokim claimed that the leadership void invited incursions from proselytizing "Holy Roller" sectarians and others. For these reasons, he declared that the current organizational structure "ought to be immediately filed in the archives. It is in no way possible for the archbishop, who lives on the East coast in such a vast country as the United States of North America, to have time to be everywhere, even were he to possess considerable abilities and physical powers." Evdokim suggested that ignorance of US law and financial regulation on the part of the Most Holy Synod, compounded by the understandable pitfalls of overseeing a faltering mission from afar, necessitated perhaps "to give the Mission the appearance of autocephaly [self-rule]," a measure he considered only "out of the unavoidability of finding some favorable way out of a difficult situation." At the very least, Evdokim suggested restructuring the archdiocese as an exarchate, a status that was lower than autocephaly but that would offer American Orthodox Rus' greater self-determination. Building on the model Archbishop Tikhon described as part of the initial, ultimately halted preconciliar process of 1905, Evdokim envisioned an exarchate adapted to the unique needs of a mission whose Orthodox communities were diverse, polyglot, and locally contingent. Within the core "Russian" portion of the archdiocese, thirty-one geographical deaneries would become six ecclesiastical districts, each fitting within a more democratized local governing structure that was less reliant on the Most Holy Synod. Other ethnic groups would enjoy a level of autonomy within an ecclesiastical hierarchy that remained under the Russian Church. Administrative tasks would be more defined and delineated and assigned to the New York cathedral clergy and other priests. "The Mission considers it its duty to warn the Most Holy Synod that we can no longer live as we have been," Evdokim declared. "If the Most Holy Synod remains deaf to the petitions and needs of the Mission, all the Mission's activity will totally cease, all the affairs of the Mission will come to a halt, and the Mission, unable to govern itself on the basis of funds at hand, will destroy itself."[12]

Evdokim left for Moscow in July prepared to argue that American Orthodox Rus' could be revitalized only if the Holy Synod and the council granted it greater autonomy and more reliable financial support. In his stead, he left written instructions that "the administrative journals [*pravlenskie zhurnaly*] be dispatched to His Grace Alexander for approval," specifying too that if need should arise, Alexander should be invited "for immediate participation in the affairs of the Consistory [*Pravlenie*] in New York."[13] A month later, Evdokim amended his instructions, cabling the New York consistory on August 31 to ask that "Bishop Alexander take government of [the] Mission," as council sessions were expected to last through Christmas. Evdokim requested of the priests who edited church publications, "inspire [and] acquaint our people in [the] press and talk about [the] splendid sobor." And he relayed a small victory for his priests, reporting that "all missionaries receive pensions."[14]

Despite optimism of what Evdokim stated was a "splendid" council, the archbishop knew well that its delegates were continuing their work under fast-changing, adverse political conditions. Events of that summer, including the July Days demonstrations in Petrograd and the Kornilov Affair, a failed military coup staged in August, suggested that the tenuous Provisional Government would not hold. In both the council sessions in Moscow and the consistory offices in Manhattan, opportunities for lasting and meaningful reforms now appeared fleeting at best. Dwindling funds and fears of imminent violence in Moscow spurred the council to quicken its ambitious agenda. In late October, discussions began on perhaps the most notable measure left to be considered: the restoration of the patriarchate. On November 1, delegate Leonid Turkevich rose to speak in favor of the proposal. The American missionary priest described how administrative vagaries and financial shortfalls often made labors more difficult for himself and other North American missionaries, suggesting the need for more decisive leadership and structural change. Without drastic transformations in both administrative policies and material support from Russia, he argued, American Orthodox Rus' would wither on the vine. "If you care to hear it, I will say that we have not received salaries for three months, and do not know when we will get them," Turkevich explained. "Our missionary institutions are perishing from a lack of resources, and we do not know whom to turn to. When the Russian government itself fails, who will pay attention to us?"[15]

Six days later, Bolshevik revolutionaries stormed the Winter Palace and seized power from the Provisional Government. In the confusing days that followed, delegates cut short debate and voted to reestablish the patriarchate. Gunfire and cannons were audible in the streets outside. Facing increasing levels of intimidation and violence, a delegation of bishops, priests, and laypeople bearing candles and icons set out across Moscow on the morning of November 14, walking in procession behind white flags sewn with red crosses. Upon arriving at the at the Bolshevik headquarters on Tverskaya Street, the group was turned away save Metropolitan Platon (Rozhdestvensky), the former archbishop of North America, who received a private audience with a Bolshevik commissar. The imposing metropolitan, one of the most powerful churchmen of his day, begged on his knees before the uniformed commissar for an end to the violence—and in turn, to ensure that a patriarchal election could occur.[16] Four days later at the Cathedral of Christ the Saviour, a blind, elderly monk reached into an urn and chose one of three slips of paper, that bearing the name of Metropolitan Tikhon (Bellavin) of Moscow. As the Russian Church entered the unsteady waters of Bolshevik rule, its new leader would be a fifty-two-year-old hierarch with vision and idealism significantly forged in American Orthodox Rus'. Tikhon was enthroned sixteen days later as the first Patriarch of Moscow in nearly two hundred years. A few hundred yards away near the Kremlin wall, dirt settled atop the first mass burials of the Bolshevik dead.[17]

The patriarchal election was received with warm jubilation in Tikhon's former archdiocese. Yet, as weeks and months passed, the patriarch proved to be one of several former North American missionaries whose experiences under Bolshevism became touchstones for how the October Revolution was immediately received and understood in American Orthodox Rus'. Another was priest John Kochurov. The son of a village priest, Kochurov came to the United States in 1895 when he was twenty-four, shortly after his graduation from the St. Petersburg Theological Academy and ordination to the priesthood. Sent to the Holy Trinity parish of Chicago, Kochurov was instrumental in the planning and construction of its Louis Sullivan–designed church and also responsible for the establishment of missionary parishes in nearby industrial towns. Kochurov and his family left North America in 1907, though Chicago never left his mind. He treasured and often wore a pectoral cross gifted him by the Holy Trinity parish brotherhood on his tenth ordination anniversary. "Let this be my support in difficult moments," he said that day. "It has no place in the grave. Let it remain here on earth for my children and their descendants as a family relic, and as clear evidence that brotherhood and friendship are the most holy phenomena on earth, without which life has no beauty."[18]

On the evening of November 12, 1917, Kochurov led a procession in Tsarskoye Selo, the former imperial residence south of Petrograd, and gave a short speech in support of the Provisional Government. The Bolshevik bombardment of the city began hours later. Accounts differ on what happened next. By one, Red Army soldiers seized Kochurov from a local cathedral and shot him in the street outside, then beat his body with rifle butts. Another, somewhat confusing version describes Kochurov trying to intervene on behalf of other priests arrested in the siege, only to be taken himself and transported to a nearby airfield. Before a crowd (which possibly included his teenage son), Red Army soldiers shot Kochurov. A lone voice then emerged above the din: "Finish him off like a dog." All accounts agree that on November 13, 1917, John Kochurov became the first Orthodox clerical martyr of the Bolshevik era.[19] When a friend saw his body laid out at a hospital, the prized pectoral cross from Chicago was gone.[20]

Through the martyrdom of John Kochurov and also the well-publicized persecution of Patriarch Tikhon, clergy and laity in American Orthodox Rus' drew on intimate connections and strong memories to put human faces on the changes that befell Russia after Red October. By February 1918, church newspapers were commemorating Kochurov as a New Martyr (*novyi muchenik*), a person of faith who had lost his life to a heretical regime. In March, the *Russian Orthodox American Messenger* published a photograph of his funeral bier. Writing of Kochurov's murder, as well as that of Vladimir (Bogoyavlensky), the martyred metropolitan of Kiev and Galicia, Bishop Alexander wrote, "All Rus' prayed and is praying for them *together*," ranks that included the faithful of North America. Of a strange new world in which two esteemed clergy would be so openly and brutally killed, Alexander pondered, "Are these not the times of the Antichrist?" He recalled Kochurov as "a favorite of the entire mission. . . . The creator of the Chicago parish, the builder of the wonderful Chicago church, organizer of the parishes in Streator and Joliet, Fr. John Kochurov was one of the chief missionaries in the mission's golden age. . . . And his departure from the mission brought among the missionaries and the flock no little regret." Alexander expected that Kochurov and Vladimir were the first of untold more martyrs. "But why these vain deaths? What is their meaning?" Alexander wrote. "Prostrating before the unreasonable ways of the God of Providence, we can only boldly cry out: Hieromartyrs crowned by Christ with blood, pray to Him for the salvation of our unhappy mother Holy Rus.'"[21]

Material Realities

When Evdokim departed for Moscow to attend the church council, he left behind idealistic plans to revitalize archdiocesan institutions and establish new endeavors to meet emerging or long-overlooked needs—premised on his faith that the council would provide him greater resources to do so. And there were so many problems to address. The advent of Bolshevism and the subsequent Russian Civil War amplified the more immediate, everyday struggles to maintain church life in American Orthodox Rus', worsening existing challenges of maintaining a transnational church amid a cataclysmic global war to the point of stark and opaque impossibility. The conflict in Europe had greatly disrupted transatlantic migration, shipping, and communication and had even delayed Evdokim's travel to the United States to replace Archbishop Platon. When he arrived in 1915, Evdokim discovered upward of twenty priests serving without a blessed altar cloth (*antimension*), a canonically required item to celebrate a eucharistic liturgy that could be acquired only from the Most Holy Synod itself. Some priests were using printed icons as substitutes. Evdokim received guidance on how to obtain more, though wartime mail disruptions caused his requests to go unfulfilled. "However sinful or unsinful, however permissible or impermissible this may be," he wrote, "the Mission decided to print *antimensia* on its own press, using an old *antimension* as a pattern."[22]

The availability of other church goods slowed as well. The diocesan store in New York City was one of the only Orthodox religious goods suppliers in the United States, buying much of its stock wholesale from well-established church goods manufacturers and book presses in Russia. It also did steady business with Greek Catholics, whose needs were better met there than from Roman Catholic suppliers. Evdokim considered the store essential, for without it, he said, "our believers would resort to Catholic stores, and we would with our own hands be spreading Catholicism throughout the parishes." During the war, the store strained to fill orders for important items like icons and liturgical implements, for which there were no domestically produced replacements. Following lengthy delays, most items ordered from Russia failed to arrive, seemingly lost alongside the funds forwarded to pay for them. By early 1917, the diocesan store stopped taking orders altogether. Evdokim proposed to establish in the US icon studios, metalworking and woodworking shops, and ecclesiastical tailoring operations that could meet local demand until cheaper and better-quality goods could be imported from Russia once again—an ambitious idea that, like so many others, failed to come to fruition.[23]

From an institutional perspective, the archdiocese was struggling to keep up. The Russian Immigrant Home was in financial freefall, serving virtually no new arrivals and inhabiting a building that Evdokim described as "old and tumble down. No remodeling will set it aright or shore it up." A new building was needed if immigrant relief work was to resume, and it needed to be built soon, as Evdokim feared that imminent changes to US immigration policy would make reviving aid work impossible if the archdiocese waited much longer. There were also widespread irregularities in legal incorporations, property deeds, and state charters for parishes, church institutions, and even the incorporation of the archdiocese itself. Evdokim worried that this had caused the archdiocese and other constituencies to miss out on significant revenue and legal protections—all issues that required individual attention and great cost to rectify. Evdokim also reported discovering that a number of priests were using hand-copied liturgical texts instead of printed books. The diocese placed a $2,000 order with the synodal press in St. Petersburg. When the books never arrived, the consistory learned that the press had applied the money to previous, unpaid invoices instead, necessitating that the archdiocesan press in New York attempt to replicate its work. Problems were aggregating in every corner of the archdiocese, from outstanding debts and tattered service books to crumbling buildings and beleaguered institutions. It seemed that any hope for transformation and renewal was disappearing beneath piles of unpaid bills, urgent requests, and bank notices.[24]

Few, if any, bishops could have reversed the circumstances facing American Orthodox Rus' at the end of 1917. Yet Bishop Alexander, despite his long history in North America, seemed uniquely incapable of doing so. He arrived in 1901 as a newly ordained celibate priest, spending his early missionary years mitigating conflicts between Orthodox and Greek Catholic factions in the Northeast. He also edited the church-adjacent newspapers *Russkaia zemlia* (*Russian Land*) and *Russkii emigrant* and later the *Russian American Orthodox Messenger*. Consecrated to the episcopate in 1909, Alexander first served as the vicar bishop for Alaska and then as administrator for the Canadian parishes. Rail thin with bushy hair and a tightly cropped beard, Alexander was described by Metropolitan Evlogy (Georgievsky), who knew him later in life, as "a curious type of archpastor. Enthusiastic in performing services (he serves daily) he is an ascetic, a faster, and an agitational American-style preacher with political shadings in his sermon content."[25] Other intimates thought Alexander ineffective, even naïve. Boris Bakhmeteff, the ambassador of the Russian Provisional Government to the United States and one of the most important allies for the archdiocese at the time, considered Alexander "a hierarch totally deprived of economic and administrative ability."[26] Metropolitan Platon thought him "a totally unselfish man. Acquiring funds sometimes by dangerous means, he least of all was thinking about his personal needs, and often he lived in real poverty."[27] For another, far less sympathetic contemporary, Alexander represented nothing less than an "American Rasputin."[28]

In January 1918, Alexander announced that an archdiocesan council would meet in Cleveland that April to consider the question of his election and to address the many pressing issues facing American Orthodox Rus', asking parishes to provide financial support and pledge their participation. The council would utilize new procedures of conciliar governance established with the Moscow council, particularly in the democratic election of an archdiocesan bishop by clergy and lay delegates. These procedures would be refined over time as the council approached, later drawing from the observations of priest Alexander Kukulevsky, a clergy delegate to the Moscow council, when he returned from Russia in August. Alexander's appeal in January, however, received affirmative responses from only a quarter of the parishes. Several dozen more expressed their intentions not to send delegations at all. Alexander postponed the council until November, hoping to rally both interest and funds over the summer, intending to use the time to bolster support and enthusiasm for the conciliar process.[29]

What happened instead was month after month of acrimonious debate. Much of this came through church-related newspapers, which became sounding boards for clergy and laity—and even Alexander himself—to proffer contrasting opinions on the embattled hierarch. These differences were made particularly evident in the pages of two Orthodox newspapers with wide circulation within the archdiocese: *Golos tserkvi* (titled in English *Voice of the Church*), published in Pittsburgh by the Russian Orthodox Clergymen League, and *Svit* (*The Light*), published in Wilkes-Barre, Pennsylvania, by the Russian Orthodox Catholic Mutual Aid Society. Established in 1917 as a resource for priests, *Golos tserkvi* was openly favorable toward Alexander and became a favored mouthpiece for his consistory, especially since the publishing schedule of the archdiocesan organ, the *Russian Orthodox American Messenger*, had become infrequent since the departure of its editor, Leonid Turkevich, for the Moscow council during the summer of 1917.[30] In contrast, priest and editor Peter Kohanik used the Ruthenian-language *Svit* to publish contrarian opinions, especially those from Carpatho-Rusyns who resented that Evdokim had not designated Bishop Stephen (Dzubay) of Pittsburgh, a former Greek Catholic from Transcarpathia, as his temporary administrator. Their largest grievance, however, was their perception that Alexander was stifling opposition to the council in order to ensure his own election.

Throughout early 1918, published letters and petitions suggested that a significant portion of clergy, laity, and their congregations remained with Alexander. At the local level, parishes and regional deaneries ratified statements of support. After one such meeting in Detroit, priest Arcady Piotrowsky disseminated the unanimous sentiments of area priests and *psalomshchiki* (psalm singers) "that only HIS EMIN[INENCE] *vladyka* ALEXANDER can save the Orthodox Church in a foreign land [*na chuzhbinye*] from total collapse," begging "every priest and *psalomshchik* to come with love to the aid of our ARCHPASTOR, who has dedicated his entire life to the good of the church and the people [*narod*]."[31] Alexander recognized the risks of such pronouncements. "For a long time, the enemies of Orthodoxy have spread the sorrowful news that the Mission is collapsing," he wrote in a message to archdiocesan clergy. "But thank God, the Mission is standing strong, despite the lack of material support from Russia. This is to Your credit." He appreciated their telegrams, letters, and statements of support, empathizing with the weighty consequences clergy might experience for their loyalty. "I bow down [*zemnoi poklon*] to those who were prepared to sacrifice everything for my sake," he wrote, "excellent parishes, careers, their entire futures, even including the possibility of removing their cassock." Alexander acknowledged that their aid even ensured his own material existence: "for everything that I have, from my cassock down to my shoes and underwear, was sent by You—my dear brothers." Without their help, he admitted, "I would not have been able to buy even a bit of bread."[32]

Alexander also knew that a growing, vocal minority of priests and parishes was not so supportive. In a heated back and forth played out in the two papers, the archdiocesan treasurer and priest Sergei Snegireff took aim at Kohanik, a priest he knew well from their shared tenures at the New York cathedral and the consistory. Snegireff, born into a prominent Russian clerical family, launched a biting attack at the Carpatho-Rusyn Kohanik, masking ethnic insults with barbs about class, education, and professional ambition. "At the time you came to America in 1902 and were earning money, I was hauling the heavy strap of academic life at the Spiritual Academy in Kyiv," Snegireff wrote, boasting that after completing a hard-won *magesteria* (the equivalent of a master's degree), he spent six low-paying years as a seminary instructor. "I *did not flee* to America," he emphasized, but rather came because Archbishop Platon expressed an "urgent conviction" that Snegireff "work with and for him in America." Snegireff alleged a clear contrast: Kohanik graduated from a lesser clerical school in Crimea and leapt for the easy money of missionary work in the United States (and where, as Snegireff failed to mention, the remainder of Kohanik's immediate family still lived), while Snegireff furthered his knowledge with a higher degree from an elite institution, then paid his dues in seminary work.[33] Kohanik responded in kind, assailing Snegireff as a smug elite unable to shake his roots in the Russian clerical estate. "I am a peasant, it is true," Kohanik wrote, "but I have never been called a noble and an archpriest's son, like Father Snegireff. . . . Recall this about the members of our Mission: are there among them more sons of archpriests, or of peasants?" And while Kohanik acknowledged clear differences in training, he resented the insinuation that education alone defined a priest and recoiled from Snegireff's patronizing suggestion that ethnic origin said anything about the worth of a Carpatho-Rusyn missionary. After all, Kohanik claimed, no one less than Archbishop Platon considered him "more 'Russian' than 'Russians' from Sovereign Rus.'"[34]

That priests—and even their bishop—were unafraid to turn on other clergy in widely read church newspapers indicated that that Bolshevism had strained the bonds of clerical friendship and collegiality past the breaking point. In the summer of 1918, following months of public spats like those between Snegireff and Kohanik, hundreds of priests met in New York and Pittsburgh. These were ostensibly billed as preconciliar clergy meetings (*predsobornoe sobranie dukhovenstva*), yet they focused far more on the mounting discord among the clerical ranks. Throughout the year, both *Golos tserkvi* and *Svit* were replete with announcements of clerical suspensions levied by Alexander and the archdiocesan consistory, each describing specific canonical violations concerning proper discipline and ecclesiastical fealty. Those who attended the preconciliar meetings welcomed Alexander's suspensions of priests like John Kedrovsky, though they wished he would go further. The New

York meeting named eight priests who publicly condemned Alexander, two of whom were already suspended. Meeting attendees demanded Alexander "exclude from the Church [*iskliuchit' iz Tserkvi*]" these and six others, including Peter Kohanik, Sebastian Dabovich, and Theofan Buketoff, three of the most prominent and well-connected priests working in North America. The eight clergy had published material in *Svit* alleged to be written "in a blatantly 'demagogic' tone" and "composed in a spirit of 'Bolshevism,' detrimental as such to the foundations of any democratic country, and threatening to bring the same 'bolshevist' spirit into the common life of Russian Americans [*russkie Amerikantsy*]."[35]

Archdiocesan and church-adjacent newspapers were important venues for molding how clergy and laity in North America understood rapidly unfolding religious and political developments in Russia. Their editors rejected Bolshevism as an ideology, seeing it as an existential threat to the spiritual unity and physical survival of the Russian Church. They framed objections in personal terms, both for Orthodox Christians facing Bolshevik oppression and for Bolshevik revolutionaries themselves. Invoking the martyrdom of the former American missionary priest John Kochurov or the tribulations of the embattled Patriarch Tikhon placed Bolshevik revolutionary violence and antireligious policies within the lives of people whom many in American Orthodox Rus' knew well. In contrast, the ideological stakes and motivations of Bolshevism were more abstract, imposed by obscure, pseudonymous revolutionaries with scant public profiles in North America. Church publications filled the information gap by drawing on prejudices commonly held in late imperial Russia and shared by prominent clergy. One popular strain furthered in the church press was the conspiratorial myth of Judeo-Bolshevism. An emergent ideology within Russian émigré circles, Judeo-Bolshevism framed the February and October revolutions as plans masterminded by German-backed Jews, leading to both selective persecution of Christians and the affirmation of a mysterious world order centered around Jewish control of global politics and finance. In 1919, *Svit* republished a lengthy article from the *Brooklyn AntiBolshevist* that blamed Bolshevik revolutionaries, Jewish financiers, and the Jewish press for political unrest in New York City, declaring in a subheadline that "Jews seek to dominate the world."[36]

The dissemination of antisemitic conspiracy theories in church publications speaks to both the centrality of antisemitism throughout the Russian Church and the aspirations of archdiocesan leaders to stir up emotional responses against Bolshevism within American Orthodox Rus'. Lieutenant Boris Brasol was a fiercely anti-Bolshevik émigré active at the New York Cathedral. In prerevolutionary Russia, Brasol was a lawyer, military officer, and participant in the Black Hundreds, a violent and antisemitic monarchist group. He arrived in the United States in 1916 as a tsarist military appointee, carrying with him a rare copy of the fraudulent, antisemitic tract *The Protocols of the Elders of Zion*. From their initial publication in 1903, the *Protocols* were a touchstone for antisemitism in Russia, stoking everyday prejudices, amplifying conspiracy theories about Judaism, and reinforcing the prejudices of more conservative and reactionary Orthodox clergy. With Brasol's participation and support, the *Protocols* were translated into English for the first time and published in Boston in 1920. The translated text was bookended with anonymized analyses in which Brasol argued that developments in Russia confirmed that the *Protocols* were authentic, as they described the exact process he alleged Jewish Bolsheviks had used to seize power: instrumentalizing the press; manipulating financial, political, judicial, and educational institutions; infiltrating organized labor; and—most of all—enacting the violent persecution of Christians, principally the Orthodox. "The fact that the Jewish race has taken such an active part in the Russian Bolshevist movement, with its international ramifications, has been attributed in some quarters to the motive of revenge on the part of Jews for what they regard as a long era of persecution," Brasol asserted. "If this be so, is it impossible that Jews in various parts of the world imagine that now is their chance not only for revenge but for world domination?"[37] In his conclusion to the volume, Brasol claimed that "the motives which actuated the publication of this book are not anti-Semitic," even though he had framed and invoked the *Protocols* themselves in those terms. "The object . . . is to call the attention of the American people to a document which may throw important light upon the international Bolshevist movement which menaces directly the vital interests of the United States."[38]

Brasol found a sympathetic patron in the Detroit industrialist Henry Ford, who published one of Brasol's anti-Bolshevik pieces in his

Dearborn Independent newspaper in 1919. A year later, Ford launched a serialization of the *Protocols* in the *Independent*, giving the hoax text national distribution through Ford Motor Company dealers. Though Ford later acknowledged that the *Protocols* were a cruel and malevolent hoax, the damage was already done. Granting the text his lofty platform bolstered not only the enduring place of the *Protocols* in international hate movements but also Boris Brasol's long career as an anti-Soviet and antisemitic operative. During the early 1920s, Brasol became a leader in *Pravoe Delo* (Right Cause), a reactionary monarchist group that conducted meetings at the archdiocesan cathedral and whose eponymous newspaper received public support from church leaders. A decade later, Brasol's anti-Soviet and antisemitic ideals drove him to be one of the most notorious Nazi partisans in the United States.[39]

Another of Brasol's patrons was Bishop Alexander, whose conservative political sentiments—and antisemitism—were not uncommon for a clerical son who came of age in the late Russian Empire. As the editor of church-related newspapers like *Svit* and *Russkii emigrant*, Alexander filled column inches with antisemitic diatribes and jokes. Years later, his response to Bolshevism showed that these views remained central to his worldview. In a January 1918 missive republished in *Golos tserkvi*, Alexander echoed Judeo-Bolshevist tropes that Russia had been overtaken by "an occupying force (the Bolsheviks (the majority of whom are Jews [*evrei*]))."[40] Six months later, Alexander asked parishes to endorse a set of public resolutions condemning Bolshevism. "The Russian Bolsheviks are leading a vile campaign of agitation in America . . . to create a feeling among Americans that almost all Russians are Bolsheviks and, consequently, that America is virtually compelled to recognize the Bolshevik government," he wrote. "This is a lie." For Alexander, Bolshevism confirmed prejudices deeply held. "Down with the Bolsheviks," Alexander wrote, "with German agents, with Jewish [*iudei*] traitors."[41]

Wartime Surveillance

Bishop Alexander's reference to "German agents" was an appeal to another prejudice with politicized currency in the United States. During the First World War, the federal government launched a multifront effort to root out syndicalism, subversion, and dissent, much of it focusing on German Americans. This manifested a permanent and pervasive federal surveillance infrastructure that emboldened hyperpatriotic federal agents to watch, to hide in plain sight, and to document and catalog what they had seen. Amid the most fearsome military conflict ever seen, an enduring federal surveillance state was born. Between 1917 and 1919, haphazard military domestic intelligence efforts gave way to an increasingly potent and effective collaboration between several intelligence-gathering agencies, from the quasi-official American Protective League to the Justice Department's Bureau of Investigation (BI). "Americans recognized that their soil had become a playing field for the manipulations and subversions of friend and foe alike," the historian Theodore Kornweibel notes. "Thus several bureaucracies began to conduct their own independent investigations and were soon competing jealously for dominance."[42] Alongside restrictive immigration laws, these measures granted the federal government unprecedented leeway to deport or exclude immigrants from the nation's shores. As the scholars Sylvester Johnson and Steven Weitzman assert, federal surveillance hinged on the meticulous collection and internal dissemination of knowledge about religion and religious institutions, first with the Bureau of Investigation and then with its successor institution, the Federal Bureau of Investigation (FBI). This led to the enduring reality that "the government in the form of the FBI has infiltrated religious life in the United States (both literally and metaphorically), and that American religion has likewise infiltrated the culture of government."[43]

By 1918, federal domestic intelligence efforts placed American Orthodox Rus' in a precarious position. Whereas BI agents and other government officials had once perceived German syndicalists and radical anarchists to be the most dominant threats to wartime national security, their prevailing fears shifted toward an imminent Bolshevik revolution on US soil. Fervent Americanists portrayed Bolshevism as an ideology diametrically opposed to US democracy. The historian Robert Murray argues that Bolshevism's global aspirations and anticapitalist impulses "ran counter to all accepted American traditions of political philosophy and economy and struck terror into the heart of the average American conservative."[44] A national bulwark against Bolshevism would save the United States from political peril, economic ruin, immorality, and irreligiosity. As an outsider immigrant religious community whose hierarchy was based in Bolshevik Russia, American Orthodox Rus' aroused suspicion as a community where Bolshevism and anti-Americanism could run rampant. The Russian Archdiocese, awash in the tumult of Bolshevism abroad, became but one target of federal suspicions of a potential revolution on US soil—interest sometimes based on information provided from within the church itself.

In early September, priest John Kedrovsky and his Brooklyn parishioners asked a federal agent from the War Department Military Intelligence Division to intercede in the affairs of the Russian Archdiocese, claiming that their church "for strange and inexplicable reasons is being oppressed by Bishop Alexander Nemolovsky and his Consistory." Claiming that Bishop Alexander and the consistory "have during the whole time of war . . . been trying to spread discord among the Russian people in America," the parish considered the federal government to be its last refuge. "Nemolovsky is hurriedly selling the Church and the property of the Church to unknown people," they alleged, "and places us in the road." Thanking the intelligence agent, who had visited the parish rectory a few days earlier, Kedrovsky's congregation also extended gratitude to President Woodrow Wilson and the US government for sympathizing with their interests. Kedrovsky and his flock concluded with a simple request: "Do not abandon us."[45]

John Kedrovsky was born in 1879, the son of a deacon in the Kherson Governorate, in present-day Ukraine. He followed the typical path of a *popovich* and enrolled in the local Ecclesiastical School. Graduating as an otherwise undistinguished student from the lowest level of Orthodox clerical education, Kedrovsky took a position in Kherson as a *psalomshchik*. In 1901, local church administrators cited Kedrovsky for "drunkenness and assault committed against the priest and the deacon [of the parish], as well as for violence and fighting," and imprisoned him in a monastery.[46] Upon release in 1902, Kedrovsky was sent for missionary work in Alaska. Though the assignment was intended to be part of his penance, Kedrovsky never made it to Kodiak, citing his wife's ill health and securing a more desirable posting in Pennsylvania. Even with his sordid past and middling credentials, in 1905 Kedrovsky was ordained as a deacon and then a priest. Serving in Brooklyn in 1918, Kedrovsky rose to prominence among those who shared his frustrations with Alexander and other archdiocesan leaders, a group calling itself the Federation of Clergy and Laity of the Russian National Orthodox Church.[47] The bulk of the group's somewhat-scattered grievances were with Alexander, tailoring its charged accusations to the wartime concerns of outside observers, especially the federal government. It painted Alexander as an un-American, anticapitalist radical, and an ecclesiastical usurper. And the group charged that the bishop and other clerics at the Manhattan cathedral were living lives of luxury on money set aside for missionary clergy and Russian orphans and that they maintained nefarious and geopolitically charged connections with the German government. "We call to all Russians to stand for America as our best friend," the group wrote in a pamphlet assailing the bishop, "to join hands with the American people for common cause and to follow in everything Washington-Lincoln-Wilson as great and unselfish friends of humanity and real democracy here and all over the world."[48]

Kedrovsky also knew that in July 1918, the Justice Department, the Internal Revenue Service, and United States Customs agents executed raids in New York City in order to learn more about how Alexander and other archdiocesan leaders were addressing the financial crisis. Federal agents served warrants at St. Nicholas Cathedral and the church-operated St. Vladimir Russian National Home on East Seventeenth Street, filling trucks with piles of material alleged to show a conspiracy between archdiocesan clergy, German officials, and perhaps even Bolshevik leaders in Russia. Further raids on the apartments of priests Leonid Turkevich, dean of St. Nicholas Cathedral, and Sergius Snegireff, the archdiocesan treasurer, yielded trunks crammed with yet more documents.[49] "We found nothing among the effects of the priests which would indicate that they were engaged in any *Bolshevik Activities*," an agent wrote in his report on the raids. "Nevertheless, we seized a large quantity of literature printed in Russian which was sent to the Customs House with other papers and books taken by the Internal Revenue men."[50] When a Russian-speaking agent reviewed the material the next day, he reported to a disappointed United States Attorney that he found nothing seditious.[51] Even so, publicity around the raids, including coverage in the English-language press, further damaged an already-floundering church administration. Within a week, Alexander had suspended Kedrovsky and several other like-minded priests from their positions.[52]

Some weeks later, on the evening of Sunday, September 1, 1918, Captain A. V. Dalrymple of the Military Intelligence Branch traversed New York City on an investigation of his own, acting on information provided to him by Kedrovsky. Dalrymple stopped first at Kedrovsky's Brooklyn rectory. Kedrovsky was out, though his wife, Priscilla, was willing to discuss the situation. She expressed frustration that her husband's suspension meant that there had been no services at the church for two weeks. She lodged charges of financial impropriety involving priest and archdiocesan treasurer Sergei Snegireff and a Russian Jewish businessman, Adolf Hunau, alleging that "the jew [sic] had been in a conspiracy with the Rev. Snegireff, to do something since the days of the Revolution." And she described her own wariness of Alexander, stemming from the bishop's visit to the Kedrovskys' home the previous summer. Priscilla Kedrovsky claimed that when she kneeled to ask Alexander's blessing, he instead placed his hands on her and suggested that they "commit an immoral act." In her own words, from that moment, she "distrusted the Bishop" and realized that "all the rumors about his immorality" she knew "could not have been invented."[53]

Following Dalrymple's salacious conversation with Priscilla Kedrovsky, he proceeded to the Russian Immigrant Home on the Lower East Side. There, Russian Orthodox Immigration Society priest John Kozitzky admitted that the archdiocese was in financial ruin. Despite an influx of $24,000 ($490,000 today) from former Russian ambassador Boris Bakhmeteff, who was using funds from his defunct embassy to prop up Russian interests and institutions in the United States, the situation remained dire. Kozitzky disclosed that he had not received a salary in four months. Dalrymple heard more of the same when he visited the Ninety-Ninth Street apartment of priest Leonid Turkevich, where federal agents had seized two trunks of documents that summer. The raid came mere days after the priest returned from Moscow and the ill-fated church council, having made a harrowing escape through Siberia to Japan and a ship steaming across the Pacific.[54]

Few clergymen were as well informed about both archdiocesan administration and the situation in Russia as Turkevich. The priest confirmed much of what Dalrymple already learned, providing background on archdiocesan finances that corroborated Father Kozitzky's account. Turkevich too had not received his $35 monthly salary since the early summer (around $725 today) and strained to meet the $60 rent on his family's eight-room apartment (around $1,225 today). They were getting by on what little money Turkevich could earn writing articles about Russia for US publications. Dalrymple also inquired about rampant rumors concerning Evdokim's departure from the United States, a salacious tale of an affair with a young female instructor at the St. Mary Women's College. "That is so, unfortunately," Turkevich said, describing how the woman, her mother, and a young child—purportedly fathered by Evdokim—lived in the cathedral apartments.[55]

In Dalrymple's report on the investigation, he expressed wariness about the priests he encountered in New York—save John Kedrovsky, whose assertions he seemed to accept. "The books of the Consistory have been seized by the Department of Justice, . . . and some queer things are expected to leak out," Dalrymple wrote. "I do not trust Rev. Turkevich, either," he added, suspicious of how the priest described the worsening situation. In addition, he claimed that Turkevich admitted to being "a monarchist." Though this made Turkevich anti-Bolshevik, to be an avowed monarchist indicated to Dalrymple loyalties contrary to US democracy. The agent suggested that "a copy of this report be sent to [the Department of] Justice to be used for what it is worth in connection with their investigation."[56] Others agreed with Dalrymple's general impressions. The BI file concerning Alexander and archdiocesan finances includes a tattered jotting from Alfred Bettman, special assistant to the attorney general for Espionage Act cases, to BI director A. Bruce Bielaski: "Watch this fellow and get something better on him."[57]

The spring of 1917 portended momentous change for the Russian Orthodox Church and also for its North American Archdiocese, an opportunity to begin the world anew through the long-awaited church council. The abrupt shift of Red October, marked by revolutionary violence and the rapid marginalization and persecution of the church, changed the conditions of possibility once again, and just as quickly. In Russia, an embattled Patriarch Tikhon fought to preserve the rights of his faithful to continue their religious practices. Across the ocean in North America, Bishop Alexander struggled to maintain unity, much less the archdiocesan coffers. The ambitious slate of reforms that many observers in North America hoped would be enacted, and in turn would revitalize and stabilize missionary work abroad, never materialized.

The Moscow council jolted to an inauspicious end in September 1918, its funds exhausted and meeting spaces confiscated by the state. Its final session concluded with the reading of the names of 121 known victims of revolutionary violence—bishops, priests, monastics, laity, all considered martyrs and confessors for their faith. It was a strange and confusing new world that was just as bewildering when perceived from American Orthodox Rus', especially during the summer of 1918, when reports of the executions of the Romanov family and their personal attendants reached the US. Bishop Leonty (Turkevich), the former Father Leonid, wrote decades later of his reaction to receiving the news, a moment he placed (probably mistakenly) during the slow and harrowing transoceanic journey that returned him to the US after nearly a year in revolutionary Russia. "But I could not bear in my soul the terrible news," he remembered, "that . . . over the radio . . . The Anointed Tsar [*Tsar'-Pomazannik*]. The God-Bearing People [*Narod-Bogonosets*]. And an execution in a corner of Russia on order of the executive committee! What horror! What quiet horror! I wanted to sob and to pray."[58]

6

"Under the Cloak of Religion"

Heretics, False Priests, and the Making of Independent
Orthodox Parishes

Brother will betray brother to death, and a father to his child,
and children will rise against parents and have them put to
death; and you will be hated by all because of my name. But
the one who endures to the end will be saved. When they
persecute you in one town, flee to the next; for truly I tell
you, you will not have gone through all the towns of Israel
before the Son of Man comes.
—Matthew 10:21–23

In August 1918, priest Vladimir Alexandrof of San Francisco published
an open letter in the Russian-language newspaper *Russkoe slovo* (*Russian Word*) advocating for "the freedom and progress of the Russian
Orthodox Church in America," which he had served as a missionary
for over twenty years. After the February Revolution in 1917, Alexandrof
traveled to Russia on sabbatical (*otpusk*), arriving in time to witness the
immediate changes brought by the long-awaited national church council. He also served as an attaché for the Root Commission, an unofficial
delegation bearing messages of support from the United States to the
Russian Provisional Government, the Russian Orthodox Church, and
the Russian people.[1] Having returned to American Orthodox Rus' by
year's end, Alexandrof praised the development in Russia of what he
called "truly People's Churches," whose "long-suffering pastoral martyrs
and their flocks were messengers of long-desired rational freedom for
Orthodox Christians in the work of church administration." He claimed
that these churches embraced conciliarity (*sobornost*), allowing clergy
and laity to manage the church together. Alexandrof was proud to have
been "a personal witness and participant of the reorganization of the

162 | "UNDER THE CLOAK OF RELIGION"

All-Russian Orthodox Church along democratic principles and Electoral Rule," and as he wrote, "I believe that this is the correct path for our church toward a good future."[2]

Alexandrof noted that some parishes in North America were already pursuing this path, drawing from both Russian church reforms and Western democracy. "In America there are already a significant number of People's [*Narodnye*] Russian Orthodox Parishes in the very largest cities . . . with many thousands of followers," he wrote, and "indeed it may be said with certainty that every parishioner (with a few exceptions) not only wants, but with great impatience all are expecting a National *Sobor*, which should . . . spare the church from the old unjust regime and from individuals, who are totally and arbitrarily managing the great work of the church." Yet Alexandrof claimed that archdiocesan leaders perceived democratic control and *sobornost* as grave threats. Alexandrof wrote, "I have lost faith in the Episcopal grace of Bishop Alexander," the temporary administrator of the archdiocese since the summer of 1917, whom Alexandrof felt was dragging his feet to convene an archdiocesan council to elect a permanent bishop. Priests who advocated a truly democratic council, Alexandrof claimed, "were quickly exposed by the consistory priests and were horribly repressed and persecuted by the Bishop." Until a council convened and American Orthodox Rus' embraced reform, Alexandrof could not consider himself a priest of the North American Archdiocese. He telegrammed the archdiocesan consistory to announce his resignation, saying, "I am continuing to serve for the good of the Free National Russian Orthodox Church in America, in the manner I already began to serve in Russia in 1917, where the church was reorganized before my eyes, and with my participation, and became National and Conciliar."[3]

This chapter concerns the emergence of ecclesiastically independent parishes in American Orthodox Rus', first in Chicago in 1912 and then in Baltimore in 1919, probing how such communities challenged clergy and laity to reconsider their places in their eucharistic communities as well as their roles in church governance. Ensconced in the monolithic ecclesiastical power structures of American Orthodox Rus', clergy like Vladimir Alexandrof expected great control over their parishes, with lay influence kept at careful remove. In contrast, many lay congregants wanted a louder, even determinant voice, feeling that their role in founding and maintaining their churches entitled them to the congregationalist power dynamics they saw in other religious denominations. In forming independent parishes, clergy and lay believers drew on antiauthoritarian and congregationalist impulses to propose reforms to Orthodox church life in the US. They wanted to control their religious worlds and embrace the promise of a postimperial democratic society. Some independent church reformers even sought to blend their Orthodoxy with socialist and communist ideologies, associating with various leftist social and political organizations prevalent within Slavic immigrant communities. And they maintained that their parishes were Orthodox in liturgy, scripture, and dogma, even if they disregarded its ecclesiastical hierarchy.

In response, archdiocesan leaders and local clergy set out to stop "independents" in their tracks. Within American Orthodox Rus', many considered it audacious, even outrageous, that anyone would claim to be Orthodox without obedience to any hierarch, and it necessarily followed that there were very real liturgical and sacramental ramifications as well. "How people debunk fakes reveals what is important to their conception of the real," argues the religious studies scholar Charles McCrary.[4] From the perspectives of Russian Archdiocesan leaders, local clergy, and many believers, independent parishes represented nothing less than a counterfeit form of Orthodoxy, even if independent clergy and laity unambiguously identified themselves as Orthodox Christians. Church authorities launched robust attacks on independent clergy and parishioners, both in person and in the Russian press, calling them schismatics (*raskol'niki*) and heretics (*eretiki*) and their clergy false priests (*lzhesviashchenniki*) and impostors (*samozvanetsy*). They warned lay independents about marriages and baptisms that would be considered illicit and of departed souls whose bodies would be lowered into the ground without valid prayers. Church newspapers became sounding boards for clergy and laity to impugn the character and personal lives of independent clergy and laity and for public notices of clerical suspensions and other official actions of ecclesiastical discipline. Was the Orthodox faith sustained in unity of practice or in the institution of the church? At stake was where the boundaries of authenticity were drawn, of what was "real" Orthodoxy and what was not.

These efforts included the willing collaboration of archdiocesan clergy and laity with a federal surveillance state then emerging from the

164 | "UNDER THE CLOAK OF RELIGION"

First World War. As described in chapter 5, with the dawn of the postwar Red Scare, surveillance measures and bureaucracies grew in both complexity and scope, consolidating myriad wartime intelligence-gathering agencies into the Bureau of Investigation (BI). Once a small division of the Justice Department, the BI strengthened to address a new perceived threat to national order: Bolshevism. As we have seen, one place federal agents looked for Bolshevism in the early days of the Red Scare was at the highest echelons of the Russian Archdiocese. And as this chapter describes, another was independent Russian Orthodox parishes, where agents and archdiocesan officials alike suspected that ecclesiastical grievances could actually be fronts for leftist political subversion.

Before continuing, a critical clarification in terminology is necessary. As described previously, the statute that governed the Russian Archdiocese since 1909 classified parishes as either "independent" or "dependent," an administrative categorization based on whether or not a community had the resources to build or obtain a church and support a full-time clergyman. These independent parishes were referred to using the Russian adjective *samostoiatel'nyi*, the state of being self-sufficient, literally to stand on one's own. The independent parishes discussed in this chapter used the adjective *nezavisimyi*, meaning administrative or political independence, of being nondependent or nonsubordinate. This subtle semantic difference spoke volumes. In places like Chicago and Baltimore, *nezavisimyi* independence emphasized missionary growth within a single congregation, defying both Orthodox ecclesiology and the administrative reach of the Russian Archdiocese. While independent parishes in the United States drew on period debates in Russia over conciliarity (*sobornost*) and ecclesiastical governance, they were just as indebted to American Protestant impulses toward congregationalism and republicanism and American Catholic debates over trusteeism. They resisted efforts to redeed properties to the national church, favored local committees with greater power over finances and parish life, and desired greater checks against the clergy—both their local priests and faraway hierarchs.[5]

Independent congregations afforded just as much, if not more, importance to financial control as they did to ecclesiastical administration. Forgoing archdiocesan authority also meant forgoing access to archdiocesan resources like supplementary funds for clerical salaries. This increased pressure on independent congregations, which would need to rely even more on what their working-class parishioners could give. Localized donation practices and systems of giving spread financial accountability across the entire parish, cumulatively obtaining meaningful sums from people who made and possessed little money themselves and as a result cared greatly about transparency over the parish purse. Regular donations were recorded in small ledger books issued as a marker of church membership. These often included the portions of local and national church statutes outlining the rights and duties of lay church members in church governance, as well as their financial obligations. Parishioners supplemented their membership donations with donations at the church candle stand, particularly on feast days, and also offered periodic donations for intercessory prayers for the sick and memorial services for the dead. Specialized fundraising campaigns addressed pressing needs or building improvement projects. Involving both communal prayer and personal devotion, localized giving suggested lay ownership over parish life, in turn inspiring disagreements about who collected, controlled, and spent parish funds. Such debates resounded time and again in virtually every parish in American Orthodox Rus', achieving their most extreme form—and proposed solution—within independent parishes.

In an independent parish, one could remain devotionally and dogmatically Orthodox while eschewing the structures that had governed church life for centuries. Clergy and laity alike identified themselves as Orthodox Christians and were interested in sustaining religious communities, even if their critics disagreed with their motives, tactics, and strategies. This factor has echoed throughout decades of church historiography, which has painted independent parishes as schismatic aberrations undertaken to destroy the church from within. Yet, in their disagreements with hierarchs and their overlap with radical political ideologies, as the historian Edward Roslof has argued of ideologically similar reform movements in Russia, the independent congregations of American Orthodox Rus' "generally acted out of genuine religious conviction."[6] In a spirit of interrogation and experimentation, independent parishes like those of Chicago and Baltimore declared that Orthodox eucharistic communities could exist outside a hierarchical, clergy-controlled church. As we will see, independent parishes *were* Orthodox, even if they disagreed with the structures that ordered church life.

Independent Orthodoxy in Chicago

In the 1906 muckraking novel *The Jungle*, Upton Sinclair described how when searching for entry points into the US industrial economy, many working-class migrants like Jurgis Rudkus, Sinclair's Lithuanian protagonist, "knew that one word, Chicago—and that was all they needed to know, at least, until they reached the city."[7] Chicago's infamous stockyards relied on a steady stream of immigrant labor, which in turn made the city a major center for progressive reformers, the birthplace of Hull-House and the Industrial Workers of the World, and a crossroads for socialist and anarchist figures like Eugene V. Debs, Emma Goldman, "Big Bill" Haywood, and Peter Kropotkin. Chicago's "Russian Colony" began in the 1880s with the arrival of migrants from Russia and the Austrian and Hungarian Empire. Its working-class people labored in stockyards, factories, foundries, and service industries, with their toil making the city a central player in industry, transportation, commerce, and food production. In 1892, the St. Vladimir's parish was established on the near west side to serve a combined congregation of Russians and Greeks. The parish emerged, then, in parallel to the rise of Daniel Burnham's White City and the World's Columbian Exposition and was bolstered by Bishop Nicholas (Ziorov) using the church as one of his home bases during his summer at the fair. The bishop's presence jump-started parish growth. Within a decade, the Greek portion of the congregation began a parish of its own in what would become Chicago's Greektown. At the same time, the Russian congregation, buoyed by a donation from Tsar Nicholas II to purchase land for new churches in Chicago and New York, eyed a sturdy replacement for their wooden building.

In 1902, a cornerstone was laid and blessed several miles to the northwest at the corner of North Leavitt and West Haddon. Designed by the famed modernist architect Louis Sullivan, a rare masterwork from the waning years of his long career, the church and adjoining rectory that rose over the next year blended Prairie School modernism with traditional Russian aesthetics. Sullivan came to the project through the Chicago industrialist Charles Crane, a Russophile and longtime archdiocesan patron whose family firm, Crane Co., frequently employed Sullivan. Along with Tsar Nicholas II, Crane was one of the most significant

Figure 6.1. Designed by the noted modernist architect Louis Sullivan, the Holy Trinity Church in Chicago was one of several showpiece temples built in American Orthodox Rus' at the turn of the twentieth century, seen here soon after its completion in 1905. Note Sullivan's colorful stucco exterior on the church and its adjoining rectory, which repeated maintenance issues soon necessitated be refinished in white. (DN-0002191, Chicago Daily News Collection, Chicago History Museum)

underwriters for the new church. The lengthy design process and costly construction, overseen by Sullivan in consultation with both the archdiocese and the local Russian consulate, culminated with the architect donating half his fee back to the congregation. Under the leadership of its energetic pastor, John Kochurov, and a new spiritual patron, the Holy Trinity parish became a hub for Orthodox missionary activity in the Upper Midwest.[8] After Kochurov returned to Russia in 1906, however, the congregation descended into acrimony. The new and ornate church required constant, costly repairs, a fate common to the ambitious designs and construction innovations of modernist architects like Sullivan and his protégé Frank Lloyd Wright. Parishioners struggled to maintain Sullivan's bespoke steam heating system. The multicolored stucco exterior required constant repair and repainting, necessitating that Sullivan's intricate, stenciled design be resurfaced in a more convenient white. While a masterpiece, Sullivan's church was driving the parish further and further into debt.[9]

Priest Vladimir Alexandrof arrived in Chicago in 1910 and set out at once to implore the congregation to repay its debts, which brought a brief respite to their acrimonious conflicts. This, however, did not last. The archdiocesan statute ratified in 1909 mandated that all church properties be deeded in the name of the ruling bishop. The statute was written to ensure that should a former Greek Catholic parish return to the Catholic fold, its properties would stay with the Russian Archdiocese— and with those parishioners who wished to remain Orthodox.[10] For the archdiocese, this was a means to prevent costly litigation and property loss at a time when Greek Catholic conversions to Orthodoxy were still fluid and fervent efforts from both churches swayed parishes back and forth. Many parishioners from Holy Trinity resisted, feeling it an unnecessary and unwelcomed intrusion. Father Alexandrof, acceding to pressure from his ecclesiastical superiors, pushed them to comply.

On May 1, 1912, several hundred dissenters—mostly members from two of the three parish brotherhoods—combined into a new organization under the patronage of St. George the Victorious. It was an apt choice. St. George's hagiography holds that the warrior saint was fearless and audacious. In iconography, the saint is often depicted on horseback, thrusting his spear into the mouth of a dragon. Calling themselves *georgievtsy* (Georgians, not to be confused with those from the nation in the Caucasus or the US state), the group charged Alexandrof with habitual financial mismanagement. They claimed nearly that $6,500 in parish funds were missing (around $212,000 today), including large donations from Charles Crane and the Chicago industrial heir Harold McCormick and a smaller yet sizable sum from the Russian Orthodox Catholic Mutual Aid Society. Fearing what might happen if their priest also wrested away the property deeds, the *georgievtsy* demanded a full accounting of the parish ledger.[11] As one of the early *georgievtsy* later recalled, their group resented that "they were paying good money to the priest for performing the church rites and donated money for the adornment of the church, but they did not have the right to demand from the priests any reports concerning the spending of the money."[12] Alexandrof was dismissive. "This is not your business," he responded to their requests for financial transparency. "If you want to stand here, stand here. If not, you can beat it."[13] He enlisted Chicago police to watch over the *georgievtsy* at services. Then his frustrations became violent. He allegedly struck parishioner Martha Chubik in the mouth as she leaned in to venerate the priest's gilded cross after liturgy, breaking her teeth. When a group of *georgievtsy* cornered Alexandrof on a subsequent Sunday, he used the same cross to point out twelve people whom he felt the police should apprehend, all of whom were jailed and fined.[14]

Though Alexandrof left Holy Trinity soon after these events, the grievances of the *georgievtsy* remained. By then, their ranks had grown to upward of three hundred people, including thirty-five children.[15] On March 24, 1914, they legally incorporated themselves as the Russian Orthodox Congregation of St. George. From the start, their congregation was governed by a democratically elected president, secretary, and cashier.[16] Consistory officials and the local deanery administration initially supported the move. They stipulated, however, that a new church could be established only if the *georgievtsy* chose a location at least six blocks away from Holy Trinity and deeded the property to the diocesan bishop—all restrictions that echoed the *georgievtsy*'s core objections. In the absence of any other Orthodox ecclesiastical body in North America, the *georgievtsy* decided to abandon the Russian Archdiocese and go it alone. One early congregant later recalled that it was a choice driven by defiance and indignation. "We no longer need tsarist consuls, nor government-appointed eminences in whose name our church property would be

170 | "UNDER THE CLOAK OF RELIGION"

written," he wrote. "We ourselves shall manage our church; we ourselves shall manage the priest; also we shall order him about, not he us."[17]

In building their independent parish, *georgievtsy* allied themselves with the Russian Independent Mutual Aid Society (*Russkoe Nezavisimoe Obshchestvo Vzaimopomoshchi*, hereafter RIMAS). Established in 1912, RIMAS was one of several national mutual-aid organizations that provided Slavic workers injury, death, and funerary benefits. Beyond their importance for individual security and protection, local brotherhoods or sisterhoods, known colloquially as a *bratstvo*, served as social auxiliaries and sources of financial support at the parish level. Among the largest of such organizations was the Russian Orthodox Catholic Mutual Aid Society, which retained close ties to the Russian Archdiocese and allowed clergy to become members. In contrast, RIMAS was established without ecclesiastical affiliation. While it respected the Orthodox Church as a critical part of the Russian cultural world, RIMAS was far more ethnonationalistic than it was religious. "An ethnic, purely Russian atmosphere prevails in every section of RIMAS," one early member wrote, describing the organization as "truly a large Russian family in a foreign land," which had "preserved not only their language, habits, and customs, but a deep, purely filial love for Mother Russia."[18] RIMAS offered the St. George congregation critical financial and institutional support, forging an enduring symbiosis with the St. George parish, maintaining ethnic Russian schools, clubs, musical groups, and other organizations across Chicagoland for decades to come.[19]

In 1914, RIMAS spent $9,500 (around $300,000 today) to purchase two adjoining structures at 917 North Wood Street. Formerly a German Lutheran school, the site was less than a mile from Holy Trinity and near where most of the *georgievtsy* already lived. Yet it also pushed against the geographical radius that the archdiocese stipulated when the *georgievtsy* set out on their own. "As religious people, the *georgievtsy* decided to organize their own parish and renovated one of the buildings into a church for believers," one early RIMAS member recalled, "and the other structure into a hall and school for free-thinking people."[20] In the church building, two floors were combined into one to create an airy worship space. Installed atop the roof was an onion-dome cupola with a three-barred Orthodox cross. The St.

George congregation held the property deed. By so flaunting the stipulations of the archdiocese, the *georgievtsy* determined to go it alone.[21]

The *georgievtsy* and their independent parish required more than a building; they also needed a priest. Whereas the diocesan bishop ordinarily would assign them one, the *georgievtsy* democratized the process: they held auditions. The winner was Timothy Peshkoff, a thirty-year-old purported monastic. Born in southern Russia, Peshkoff was raised in an observant Orthodox home. His older brother once journeyed a thousand miles on foot from Astrakhan to Kyiv to venerate holy relics kept there. Peshkoff embarked on wanderings of his own, participating in the 1905 Russian Revolution before coming to the United States. In the US, he lived the life of an itinerant laborer, working as a janitor and candymaker in Colorado, existing as "a hobo . . . tramping about, as many other migratory workers."[22]

Peshkoff later tramped to Indiana and Valparaiso University to study engineering and then to Chicago to continue his studies. There he encountered the *georgievtsy*.[23] "For almost a year these people were wandering without a leader and without a church," he later wrote. "These people asked me several times to be their priest, but I refused and tried to persuade my friend, who was a good young man, the son of a Russian priest." His friend declined to pursue ordination, however, and in time Peshkoff himself would relent to become an independent priest. "This act was a great risk, sacrifice, and responsibility on my part," Peshkoff recalled, "but I knew that the Lord was with us. I knew that we were not separated from God but we were seeking to love him more."[24] Though he was a man who would otherwise never be ordained an Orthodox priest, lacking even the most basic ecclesiastical credentials, Peshkoff presented himself as a suitable and qualified candidate, with enough acquired knowledge to suggest he was capable. "The people themselves examined him at the church," one observer remembered of the audition. Parish leaders watched and listened as Peshkoff and another candidate celebrated the liturgy and delivered a sermon.[25] Peshkoff's competence, however, proved shaky. The same observer recalled in another account some years later that Peshkoff appeared as but a "semiliterate man," and his success in the audition was the result of "the even greater semiliteracy of his rival."[26]

The *georgievtsy* had chosen their priest, Timothy Peshkoff. And while they relished their independence from the archdiocese and its "tsarist" bishops, certain ecclesiastical standards remained essential. Peshkoff was a lay monk, and their new altar on Wood Street remained unconsecrated. As with their selection of a pastor, the *georgievtsy* would need to stray from Orthodox conventions. They turned to Archbishop René Vilatte and his Chicago-based Old Roman Catholic Church. Referred to by the historian of the independent churches Peter Anson as a "buccanneer [*sic*] ecclesiastical adventurer," Vilatte was the most notorious of the so-called *episcopus vagantes*, bishops who emphasized the apostolic succession and validity of their ordinations over allegiance to established churches.[27] Usually outcasts and discards from mainstream denominations, these were religious travelers who transformed and reinvented themselves with each newer and greener pasture. They were keen to take on new names (Vilatte was also known as Mar Timotheus I), dress in sumptuous (sometimes incongruous) vestments, and affiliate with increasingly diverse and obscure churches (however briefly) to further gird their claims to legitimacy. Yet with episcopal independence often came instability and scorn, requiring constant motion and abrupt change. In Anson's appraisal, Vilatte "never had the slightest scruples about changing his allegiance from one denomination according to the circumstances in which he found himself at the moment. . . . He was always an opportunist but never to any purpose. Unfortunately, none of the horses he backed proved winners."[28]

Vilatte, hoping the *georgievtsy* might join his church, chose to back St. George. On August 15, he came to North Wood Street to consecrate the church and ordain Peshkoff to the priesthood. Dressed in the Byzantine episcopal vestments of an Orthodox bishop, his long hair flowing beneath a domed miter, Vilatte celebrated the liturgy in English. Peshkoff and choir director Timothy Karablinoff led the responses in Church Slavonic.[29] Later evidence suggests that parish leaders may not have told other congregants the truth about Vilatte's affiliation. It seems that most assumed Vilatte to be an Orthodox bishop who was merely unknown to them, leading them to believe in turn that he had made Peshkoff an authentic Orthodox priest and consecrated a valid altar table.[30]

For some time, the independent status of the St. George parish was an outlier. This seems the result of a sustained and heavy-handed campaign from archdiocesan leaders who feared independent success in Chicago could sway parishes elsewhere into independence. "Synodal [Consistory] clergy called them schismatics [raskol'niki] and heretics [eretiki], and put on them an anathema," one later history recalled, "persecuting them in every possible way, and with all their might endeavored to nip [the georgievtsy's] affairs in the bud."[31] One St. George member recollected, "They called us renegades [otshchepentsy] and schismatics [raskol'niki]. . . . But our pioneers were not frightened by these protests, waving a hand at all of this nonsense."[32] Others long remembered being "bombarded" on the street with leaflets against Peshkoff and the St. George church. According to Peshkoff, one such pamphlet warned in the name of ruling bishop Archbishop Evdokim,

> T. Peshkoff and his followers have been formally excommunicated from the Russian Orthodox Church, and for this reason I ask the Orthodox people of Chicago to give the names (of those who are the members of the newly formed Independent Church) to Father Kukulevsky, the official priest of Chicago, so that I may send them to the Holy Synod and to the Russian government for publicity, excommunication from the church, and to be anathematized. Those who are christened and married in Peshkoff's church are not to be recognized by the civil Russian government and the church. I give my warning to all the faithful Orthodox Russian people of Chicago that those who shall associate or communicate with Peshkoff or his followers commit deadly sins.[33]

When the New York consistory learned of Peshkoff's ordination, it dispatched Bishop Alexander (Nemolovsky) to investigate the Orthodox communities of Chicago and quell the situation. Alexander visited all three of the city's archdiocesan churches across a whirlwind Sunday in October—the Russian and Serbian parishes on the west side and a Carpatho-Rusyn congregation on the near south side.[34] A report on the visit, published in the name of all three parishes, admitted little surprise that an independent parish had emerged in Chicago. "Famous in all the Mission for the rebelliousness of many of its members and an abundance of unsavory characters," it noted, "the Chicago parishes had an urgent need for archpastoral guidance," particularly in that they were "at a remote distance from the bishop's cathedral (more than two thousand

174 | "UNDER THE CLOAK OF RELIGION"

miles)" and thus "deprived" of the attention afforded parishes in the Northeast. Following liturgy at Holy Trinity, Alexander stood before the altar and denounced "the *georgievtsy*, those renegades who have betrayed the covenants of their ancestors, caved to the influence of enemies of Orthodoxy and the Russian people, 'sold themselves . . . for pride and money.'" Knowing a few *georgievtsy* were in attendance, Alexander did not mince words. "Harsh words fell like the blows of hard earth on the lid of a coffin; not one stray hung his head," recalled one account. In response, "with despair in his heart," Alexander "cursed both their weakness of will and those who pushed him down the wrong path."[35] This explicit denunciation was a boon for Chicago clergy, who were struggling to counter an alleged misinformation campaign by the *georgievtsy*. Priestmonk Timon (Muliar) of the near south side parish later recalled his own outrage that the *georgievtsy* had "assured a simple-minded Russian audience" of Peshkoff's legitimacy, circulating a document bearing Alexander's signature and the claim that Peshkoff's ordination "was committed by a Romanian Orthodox archbishop." It was warm solace for Timon that Alexander "publicly called Peshkoff 'a false priest [*lzhesviashchennik*] and an impostor [*samozvanets*].'"[36]

It seems these critiques affected Peshkoff's position at St. George. His working-class roots had manifested some solidarity with his congregation—in 1916, for instance, Peshkoff pointedly marched with corn-processing workers during a deadly strike in Argo, a suburban Chicago factory town where RIMAS was active.[37] Yet he also struggled with everyday pastoral work, perhaps a reflection of the fact that the Russian Archdiocese would have balked at the notion of ordaining someone with his lack of education or credentials. One observer cited inexperience as the reason for Peshkoff's ultimate failure in Chicago. He recalled Peshkoff as "a clever, hearty and unsophisticated person," though "not intellectually developed, and knows very little; that he must first learn himself if he hopes to teach others." In the end, Peshkoff "could not agree with some people; he could not satisfy others."[38] Peshkoff left Chicago in April 1917. He later enrolled in a seminary program at Boston University and became a Methodist minister.[39]

With passing decades, aging *georgievtsy* remembered their early years of independence as essential catalysts for long-lasting congregational bonds, beginning with the inciting slights and abuses of priest Vladimir

Alexandrof. One founding member wrote in 1937, "I should here thank Fr. Alexandrof for his conduct, inflicted on [future society members] in 1912. None other than Fr. Alexandrof with his ultra-police measures gave us the impulse to move forward. Through his repressions he taught us how to organize to the advantage not only of our membership, but to the benefit of the entire Russian colony."[40] In the markers of Alexandrof's excesses—their broken mouths, jail cells, and court hearings—the *georgievtsy* found the courage to take a bold and unprecedented step: founding their own church. Under the patronage of Saint George the Victorious, their independent parish was free from archdiocesan control and the brunt of Alexandrof's golden cross. And though they did not know it in 1912, their endeavors paved the way for other congregations to do the same.

An Independent Parish in Baltimore

The Holy Trinity Russian Independent Orthodox Church of Baltimore began in much the same way as St. George in Chicago. The Baltimore Russian community emerged at the turn of the twentieth century, large enough by 1907 to establish the Holy Resurrection parish. In early 1919, priest Vasily Kurdiumoff traveled from Philadelphia to meet with a group of Holy Resurrection parishioners who were angered by their priest, Constantine Seletzky. The parishioners accused Seletzky of a fantastical embezzlement scheme, claiming he had absconded with a large sum of money earmarked for the church mortgage, demanded exorbitant sacramental donations (*trebi*), and even charged a fifteen-cent admission fee for each service—raised to a dollar on Easter. They hoped Kurdiumoff could help them form their own, independent parish, free from Seletzky's control. This idea came from Nestor Nikolenko, a former priest who had been defrocked by the archdiocese and who was now offering the group his counsel. Speaking on their behalf, Nikolenko alleged that Seletzky was serving against their wishes and that "with the fall of Czarism in Russia, Seletzky's throne shook." Yet the Holy Resurrection church was deeded to the archdiocesan bishop, meaning that their independent parish would need to begin anew. "On February 9 of this year was laid a corner stone of 'love and justice.' And the National Church was established," Nikolenko wrote. "And Seletzky's throne based

176 | "UNDER THE CLOAK OF RELIGION"

on the decayed foundation of autocracy fell in abyss with his assistants. Let him be cursed forever and for Independents long life."[41]

On March 18, 1919, Holy Trinity Independent Russian National Orthodox Church incorporated with the state of Maryland. "The purpose and object of this corporation," its parishioners reported, "is to be for divine services according to the ritual and consistently with the practice of the Russian Independent Orthodox Church." Within weeks, Nikolenko and several hundred former Holy Resurrection parishioners were conducting services in the rented basement of a Lutheran church located less than a mile from Seletzky's parish. They bought the building in May, staking the entire $15,000 purchase price ($266,000 today) in cash. This substantial sum seems exorbitant for a working-class immigrant parish to obtain so quickly. Some of it came in small donations from 250 parishioners. It seems, however, that much more came from Leon Rasst, a former imperial Russian consul to Mexico, described by members of Seletzky's church as "the director and organizer of this congregation."[42] He bore a dodgy past, having left Mexico with a substantial fortune earned through a bungled arms deal for Victoriano Huerta's military dictatorship, a misadventure that landed Rasst in a Mexican prison. Upon release, he took what was left of his fortune to Baltimore and appeared to enter the guncotton industry, though it seems he was actually engaged in an elaborate counterfeiting scheme. A wealthy man with few compunctions, Rasst drew on his wealth and his shrewdness to establish himself in Baltimore.[43]

Sustained by the mysterious Leon Rasst, the Holy Trinity parish became synonymous with the political leanings of its congregation and precisely as the nation entered the early throes of its postwar Red Scare. In a newspaper report describing Baltimore's otherwise uneventful May Day celebrations, the city police commissioner commented that there was "a man [in East Baltimore], reported to be a renegade priest of the Russian church over there who is preaching [Bolshevik] doctrines," referring to its chosen pastor, Nestor Nikolenko, intimating that he was "the cause" of what the commissioner alleged were the only stirrings of Bolshevism in Baltimore. A former monastic, Nikolenko came to the US as a missionary in 1911. While serving a parish in Connecticut six years later as a purportedly celibate priest, Nikolenko married and subsequently fathered a child with a Russian woman sixteen years his junior.

Though the archdiocese defrocked Nikolenko, he comported himself as a married priest. Expelled from the archdiocese and having broken his monastic vows, his only option to continue serving as an Orthodox priest was to find an independent parish that would take him.[44]

That local police were aware of Nikolenko was the result of communications from Father Seletzky, whose vested interest in stalling an independent parish run by a defrocked clergyman prompted him to contact federal law enforcement agents as well.[45] On May 20, Justice Department agent William Doyas surveilled Nikolenko and the Holy Trinity parish for the first time. He reported that "This group of Russians comprises 90 percent of the 1500 Russians living in Baltimore and surroundings, who refused to be members of the regular Russian Church . . . of which Rev. Constantine Seletzky is pastor." He charged that its "entire membership" belonged to the Union of Russian Workers and had left Seletzky's parish for political reasons. "The only reason for breaking away from the regular church is because Rev. Sletsky [*sic*] is opposed to Bolshevism and is now and has been loyal to the United States from the very beginning of the War," Doyas wrote on May 31, "and is looked upon as a traitor to Russia and the Russian Workingmen . . . solely on the grounds of being loyal to this country and opposed to the Bolsheviks."[46] Shortly after Doyas's initial reports reached Washington, acting BI chief William E. Allen advised the Baltimore bureau that "the activities of Nikolenko and his congregation be carefully watched and that copies be obtained of all the literature he distributes among his followers."[47]

On June 5, Seletzky dispatched an envelope to J. Edgar Hoover, head of the BI Radical Investigation Division, which probably contained a report about the community. BI agents in Washington used this report to assemble a comprehensive dossier on the Holy Trinity parish. It included the names of "Bolshevist Anarchists" alleged to associate with Nikolenko, details about Rasst's private life, and information on the origins of independent parishes. The Justice Department seemed convinced that Holy Trinity was a well-funded effort by Bolshevik leaders "to make Baltimore the headquarters for Bolshevist propaganda, because of its proximity to Washington and the comparative freedom from interference." They concluded, "The Bolshevists here want to destroy the Russian Greek Church . . . which is a barrier to the successful spreading of their propaganda."[48]

The Baltimore BI office sent an agent from the local immigration control office to observe services at Holy Trinity. They chose the Polish-born, Russian-speaking agent Charles Laskowski, "for reason he was never seen by these Russians before and Mr. Laskowski has the appearance of a Russian, therefore would not arouse suspicion." Laskowski attended liturgy on June 8, finding some three hundred parishioners crammed into the Lutheran church basement. During the morning liturgy, Nikolenko "delivered a very good sermon, strictly adhered to explaining the meaning of the Gospel." According to Laskowski, Nikolenko mentioned that the congregation would take possession of the building the following Sunday, a sign of their self-sufficiency. In contrast, Nikolenko argued, Seletzky had "received assistance from the Old Russian Government and from other sources in support of his church and [had] accomplished nothing." As to the interests of the BI's investigation, Laskowski reported that Nikolenko "absolutely made no radical remarks during the entire sermon, and nothing was said against the United States, or in any manner suggested Bolsheviks should be established in this country."[49]

Charles Laskowski emphasized in his report that what he had seen and heard at Holy Trinity was scriptural, spiritual, and ecclesiastical but not political. Even so, Justice Department officials determined to hire a confidential informant to infiltrate the parish. "It is deemed advisable to place a person in subject's church this day to cover subject's preaching, without the least suspicion," Doyas wrote in his request to instigate surveillance of Nikolenko, "who would be looked upon by subject as one of his own." Doyas once again turned to Seletzky for help. The priest responded favorably, accompanying the Holy Resurrection parishioner Joseph Kamensky to the Baltimore bureau office several days later. Kamensky told Doyas that he earned around $4 per day assembling railroad cars (around $70 today), but as the agent reported, "he was satisfied to stay away from work to do what he could for the Government, that he knew all the anarchists and Bolsheviks of [Nikolenko's] congregation, in fact he knows entire congregation together with Nikolenko are radical Bolshevik, and that he is able to get directly among them, that they look upon him as their friend." Doyas asked Kamensky to attend a Holy Trinity picnic at Liberty Park on June 21, agreeing to pay Kamensky the equivalent of his daily earnings, cover the twenty-five-cent admission fee, and "remit all expenses for all literature which he might be able to buy at the park, sold by any member of the congregation." Kamensky attended the picnic and kept close to Nikolenko all afternoon. Doyas went as well. Though he kept a comfortable distance, he was immediately noticed by a man he had once interrogated and left the picnic early. According to Doyas, the man "cautioned every Russian on the grounds to be careful, pointing me out as a detective." Kamensky later told him that Nikolenko gave a short speech calling for action: as "Bolshevikes [*sic*] and Socialists, they are the leaders who know the principles themselves and we must support them." Nikolenko also led the crowd in an IWW song, the lyrics of which were printed on five-cent postcards that a picnic attendee was selling from his coat pocket. Kamensky bought a postcard and a copy of the anarchist newspaper *Khleb i volia* (*Bread and Freedom*). He returned to the BI offices the next day to describe the picnic and file his expense report. "For services rendered June 21, 1919," Doyas recorded, Kamensky received his daily wage of $4.[50]

The Baltimore BI monitored Nikolenko and events at Holy Trinity throughout the summer. In late July, Doyas had a chance encounter with the man who had identified him at the church picnic. The man boasted that he was openly "spreading Bolshevik propaganda in the Independent Russian Church of which Nikolenko is pastor" and "that nobody can stop them, because they know the government agents and they cannot catch them." Doyas now felt it necessary to rely only on confidential informants. He turned once again to Kamensky, whom he considered to be "quite an intelligent Russian, makes a fine appearance," and whom he found "sincere, truthful and reliable." Doyas also valued that Kamensky was "bitterly opposed to Bolshevism and is willing to assist the Government in apprehending the agitators." Doyas instructed Kamensky to infiltrate Holy Trinity under the guise of a prospective new member. Kamensky was also instructed to attend an IWW meeting in hopes of finding independent parishioners there. "I instructed Kaminsky never to come to the office," Doyas reported, explaining, "I would call at his home for such information which may have obtained and same would be held strictly confidential."[51] In collaboration with the Baltimore Postmaster General, the BI also monitored Nikolenko's mail. Its weekly summaries show that Nikolenko kept frequent contact with *georgievtsy* in Chicago, as well as with other independent congregations in Philadelphia, Detroit, San Francisco, and Ohio.[52]

180 | "UNDER THE CLOAK OF RELIGION"

By September, the Justice Department had collated its surveillance of Holy Trinity into a dossier intended to secure Nikolenko's deportation. "It appears that Nikolenko, under the cloak of religion, is spreading and advocating the cause of Bolshevism," its report summarized, and "Seletzky is very much inflamed over the fact that Nikolenko has converted from his (Seletzky's) congregation of loyal Americans, so many disciples advocating and agitating the cause of Bolshevism." Agents outlined charges of financial irregularity, emphasized Nikolenko's status as a lapsed monk, and described his alleged indignation toward Seletzky and the Holy Resurrection congregation. The report drew from contacts with Holy Resurrection parishioners to suggest that the BI found Seletzky's archdiocesan parish preferable and honorable and Nikolenko's independent congregation to be irregular, if not un-American. "While Fr. Seletsky [sic] is very anxious to see the Government deport Nikolenko," the report described, "he has frequently expressed his willingness to assist the Government in running down radicals and he and the entire membership of his church claim to be loyal Americans."[53] The BI closed its investigation into Nikolenko shortly after the report was filed. Nikolenko had left Baltimore for Chicago and St. George. Yet the BI would continue to investigate Holy Trinity and its new pastor, John Zeltonoga, a suspended archdiocesan priest already the subject of federal investigation in the Windy City—an investigation that amplified in scope once he reached Baltimore.

Holy Trinity and the Growing Independence Movement

During the spring of 1918, priest John Zeltonoga of Donora, Pennsylvania, wrote a letter announcing his resignation from the Russian Archdiocese and his intention to become an independent Orthodox clergyman. Zeltonoga had come to the US in 1911 at age twenty-nine and became a lay *psalomshchik* (psalm singer) in New Jersey. Ordained a priest two years later, Zeltonoga served as a missionary in Alaska, Massachusetts, and New Jersey. In 1914, he accompanied priest Alexander Hotovitzky and the boys choir from the New York cathedral on a trip to the White House, where they performed for President Wilson.[54] Four years later, Zeltonoga emerged as a dissenting voice against Bishop Alexander (Nemolovsky) and his struggles to manage the difficult situation in the North American Archdiocese following the October Revolution. Declaring himself an independent priest, Zeltonoga set off for Chicago to succeed Timothy Peshkoff at St. George. Bishop Alexander, renewing his zealous efforts to quash the independent *georgievtsy*, announced in archdiocesan newspapers that Zeltonoga had "departed to the pastorship of the independent church in Chicago, turning up under the jurisdiction of René Vilatte, incorporated as a bishop of the Old Roman Catholic Church," and was "banned from priestly service."[55]

Like Nikolenko, Zeltonoga's outspoken politics and identification as an independent priest made him a focus of intense and sustained federal surveillance. In March 1919, a United States Attorney in Kansas City asked the BI office in Chicago for information on Zeltonoga, then on a speaking tour of Russian communities across the Midwest. "This office [is] suspicious he is Bolshevik Lecturer," the attorney wired in a terse telegram. "[The] Russian Population inclined to Bolshevism here are advertising this man to deliver speeches in Kansas City Kansas." A BI agent dispatched into Chicago's Russian Colony determined Zeltonoga to be a "very radical laborer advocating recognition of Russian soviets," who was "adored by Russians for his Bolshevist tendencies." The Chicago BI opened a file on Zeltonoga.[56]

Like other communities in American Orthodox Rus', the independent St. George parish struggled to maintain community momentum in the chaotic years after 1917. By the summer of 1919, Zeltonoga's first in the city, the parish was struggling to support a full-time pastor. When Zeltonoga was an archdiocesan missionary, he could receive additional funds to supplement his salary. As an independent priest, however, he was wholly dependent on the *georgievtsy*, who could no longer pay him a living wage. Zeltonoga mulled other vocational opportunities. He already served as an assistant editor of the RIMAS newspaper *Daily Free Russia* (*Svobodnaia Rossiya*), whose offices were not far from the Wood Street church. The paper provided Zeltonoga supplementary pay—and a ready platform. In August, Zeltonoga published a letter to Ludwig Martens, the nonrecognized Russian ambassador to the United States, announcing his intention to work for the unofficial embassy that Martens operated, the Russian Soviet Government Bureau. "I wish to be close to the nation. I wish to enter into the very heart of national life," Zeltonoga wrote. "I wish to go to the nation even in the ranks of the Red,

182 | "UNDER THE CLOAK OF RELIGION"

victorious army, into the struggle for the national ideals and national freedom; freedom of the working class and the Russian peasant farmer." And Zeltonoga wanted to do so as an Orthodox priest. "I wish to be one of the first national preachers in the number of fighters for the soviets and for Soviet Russia," he wrote, "and if it is possible I am asking you to accept me as one of your helpers here in America." He touted his skills as a writer and orator, as well as his nationalistic ideals. "Being a son of great and free Soviet Russia, being a son of the nation, I am ready for anything which I would be assigned to do here or in the Homeland."[57]

Some days after the letter appeared in *Daily Free Russia*, BI agent A. H. Loula covertly approached Zeltonoga. The priest defended himself, saying that he needed to support his family. What was more, parishioners were questioning whether his radical rhetoric was genuine. Zeltonoga had recently gone to the Chicago suburb of Argo to speak with Russian workers once again on strike from a corn-processing plant. There remained a RIMAS chapter in Argo, though despite Timothy Peshkoff's outreach to strikers there in 1916, there was still no Orthodox parish. "After the strike broke out I went to this town and begged the Russians there, who were very militant, to strike peaceably and not use force and bloodshed to win the strike," Zeltonoga explained. He claimed that a Bolshevik agitator had radicalized the workers toward violence. "Had it not been for me the town officials from the mayor down to the officials of the Corn Products Co. would have been murdered by the strikers and the plant seized by the workers," he claimed. "I prevailed upon them to conduct themselves peaceably and not to riot and cause bloodshed." Parishioners felt that Zeltonoga had backed factory management and the town government, by extension repudiating Russian workers for striking. Zeltonoga thought publicizing his letter to Ludwig Martens would prove his political credentials. "I had a 2-fold reason for doing this," Zeltonoga told Loula. "By the letter becoming public, I would again be placed in the correct light in the eyes of my congregation; and, on the other hand, I had a chance of obtaining a good position."[58]

The letter did not work, neither for Zeltonoga's pastorship in Chicago nor for his job prospects with Martens. Zeltonoga moved to Baltimore in the late fall, swapping positions with Nestor Nikolenko. The Justice Department increased its surveillance of Zeltonoga there, hiring no fewer than six additional confidential informants to attend services, parish meetings, and social events at Holy Trinity. One informant reported that a service there in late November was "packed to suffocation" and that he deduced that "the attitude of the Russians are that if they are permitted to return to Russia they intend to do so and forsake the church, which they now occupy for religious purposes." The informant said Zeltonoga's sermon expressed that the parish was a space for both Orthodox worship and political organization. "There is no doubt that the present Pastor of said Church is extreme Bolshevist," BI agent William Doyas concluded. "Said church will be covered closely at every meeting, and the services will be covered."[59]

Confidential informant Thomas Mirnoff, code-named M-20, attended services at Holy Trinity for the next two Sundays. After attending services on December 9, Mirnoff reported alarm over what he observed. "I am informed by Informant, who is a Russian himself, that the religious services are not conducted in any manner as they should be," Doyas reported, "but it appears that the service is a meeting place for the Russian colony in Baltimore, for spreading propaganda, agitating and advocating hatred of the capitalists and laws of organized government." Mirnoff said that Zeltonoga invited the 350 congregants to an evening social event at which his children would sing and a three-act play on revolutionary Russia would be performed. And in his sermon, the priest allegedly offered a message heavy in both religious and political rhetoric. "Here you see the Capitalists do not give you what you earn, but give you a portion of it to live on until they need you again," Zeltonoga allegedly assailed.

> You know yourselves that they treat us as a herd of sheep. Whenever they want to shear wool off of us, they do so; if they need meat, they will kill us and cut us up because we are afraid of the Capitalists. This is the time now people to realize that you have to work as slaves for them and give up yourselves to them, and they will kill you as they do now. Be brave and go forward and be not afraid of death for that which you need and for that which your brother has already obtained.

From Mirnoff's observations, the Baltimore field office deduced that "there is no question about [Zeltonoga] being a radical Bolshevist." To the BI's chagrin, however, Mirnoff reported that the congregation was so inspired as to deposit $736 in the collection plate (more than $13,000 today).[60]

184 | "UNDER THE CLOAK OF RELIGION"

BI officials in Washington suggested that Mirnoff covertly interview Zeltonoga. The Baltimore bureau office feared, however, that this might arouse suspicion too early in its investigation. Doyas favored sustained, more focused surveillance, hoping to "learn their leading members of the congregation and their attitude and activities, ascertain conclusively who is in possession of the membership book and learn their connections with the leading bolsheviki [*sic*] propagandists in the United States." Instead, Doyas instructed Mirnoff to begin paying membership dues at Holy Trinity. Mirnoff volunteered to do so, "in order to get in on the inner circle where it can be learned the secret activities of the pastor and the congregation." Mirnoff filled out an application, and Doyas forwarded $16 (around $280 today) for his membership fee. Mirnoff was accepted as a parish member two weeks later. The report describing Doyas's handling of Mirnoff, including Mirnoff's handwritten summary of a service at the church, was alarming enough to reach the desk of J. Edgar Hoover.[61]

Mirnoff's surveillance yielded extensive and detailed summaries of Zeltonoga's sermons, especially those purported to be anticapitalist. A sermon delivered on December 29 used a parable assailing the American commercialization of Christmas to raise money in defense of imprisoned Russian radicals. Zeltonoga's parable juxtaposed the fruits of working-class immigrants' labor against their unseen, wealthy consumers, describing an informative stroll through Baltimore on Christmas Day "to learn how Capitalists live and also how lives the working class of Baltimore City." Gazing through the house windows of a wealthy neighborhood, he said, "I saw there everything which the working class produced." There were Christmas trees, "all decorated with most expensive ornaments and illuminated by electricity, and around these trees Capitalists were sitting with their children and their friends." Nearby he saw two newspaper boys, the "ragged and hungry" children of political prisoners and their overworked wives, who "must drag around the streets and earn money to support themselves and their mothers." Zeltonoga used his parable to encourage his congregation to think of themselves as an oppressed people with a responsibility to help those who were exploited by capitalists like the holiday revelers. And he called for solidarity with those who were caught in the late-autumn Justice Department raids on organizations like the IWW. "They are doing this with us because we are not dummie [*sic*] Russians," he said, "because we are regular fighters for freedom of people, from the yoke of capitalism, and went in [and] cut the heads off the capitalist Government in Russia."[62] By early January, these confidential reports attracted the attention of assistant BI director Frank Burke, who instructed agents in Baltimore to pursue evidence to ensure Zeltonoga's deportation.[63]

Zeltonoga knew well that federal agents and confidential informants were surveilling his parish and knew how to recognize them, given that he had already spoken with at least one agent in Chicago. And from Doyas's experiences at the Holy Trinity picnic the previous summer, it seems that parishioners were acutely aware as well. The Palmer Raids of early January 1920, a coordinated series of mass arrests by the Justice Department in major cities across the United States, exposed the severity of these kinds of antiradical measures. The raids also revealed the intricate efficiency and coordination of the Justice Department's domestic intelligence networks. In thirty-three cities spanning twenty-three states, federal agents arrested thousands of alleged "radicals," most of whom were eastern European immigrants. The national press hailed the raids for their scope and heavy-handedness. In cities like New York and Detroit, agents racked up hundreds of indiscriminate arrests through raids of large meetings and events. Arrests in Baltimore were more targeted and top-down in contrast, numbering around thirty-five people holding leadership roles in local groups.[64] Baltimore radicals fretted that the arrests meant that the BI's work there was only beginning. The confidential informant Thomas Mirnoff reported that Zeltonoga spoke about the dangers of surveillance for Holy Trinity. "You know we have no badges or no names with Russian letters for them (meaning spies) to read them off to the United States Government Officers," Zeltonoga allegedly said in a sermon in early January. "Secondly, we have Brothers with us same as Christ had Judas, with whom [Christ] worked with and [who] sold [Christ] to the Government as an enemy. For that reason we must know with whom we speak and not use the same words as we do to our workers for our benefit."[65]

The Baltimore BI bureau office heightened pressure on Holy Trinity after the Palmer Raids, hiring two additional confidential informants by mid-January. Luka Lamokin was assigned to shadow Mirnoff and corroborate his accounts of Zeltonoga's sermons. Another, Thomas Gajewski, was "an honorably discharged soldier, and a citizen of the United States, nationality Polish," whose familiarity with the Russian language would allow him to blend into the congregation. Three more were added by April, allowing the BI to deploy multiple informants at a time. As 1920 unfolded, these confidential informants documented what they alleged to be the heightening radicalization of the parish, both in rhetoric and in external associations. In late January, informant Joseph Kamensky summarized a sermon in which Zeltonoga allegedly declared that "the United States Government was at least 1000 years behind that of Russia and compared all of the people of this Country with an overgrown mushroom, which is worthless, and likewise compared the brains of the American people with this mushroom." Kamensky reported that the priest claimed that "the American people are educated to worship gold and not God" and that while communists and anarchists were hostile to religion by definition, Zeltonoga said that "what he is doing for his followers he is doing good for all of us who love the Church." To meld these ideologies with their Orthodox faith, in other words, could hasten socioeconomic progress. Yet Zeltonoga was careful not to say too much, telling his congregation, "I cannot step out to the front but I must suggest ideas to you."[66]

Recognizing the appeal of strident revolutionary rhetoric within the Holy Trinity congregation, Zeltonoga tried to build bridges between his parish and leftist political groups in Baltimore. The BI confidential informants surveilling Holy Trinity also documented alleged ties between the parish and the local branch of the Communist Party. Joseph Kamensky observed in January that the Palmer Raids suspect and local communist Alex Volkov "was present and was quite intimate with the Pastor at the close of the Church services." Several months later, Zeltonoga encouraged the parishioner Natali Vovechek to attend a Communist Party meeting in order to publicize a church-sponsored ball. Party leaders were also considering using the church as a meeting hall, though local branch head Louis Hendin quashed the idea. Even if party members worshiped there, he believed allying with the church undermined the party's antireligious character. Zeltonoga still sought appeasement. In July, an informant alleged that Zeltonoga held a requiem service (*panikhida*) for deceased revolutionaries, reporting that he "offered a special prayer for the success of Bolshevik rule, praying the red flag which conquered Poland will conquer the entire world for nothing can stop the red flag." The informant quoted Zeltonoga as stating, "The red flag will not only prevail in Russia but over the entire world." By October, William Doyas was convinced of Zeltonoga's Bolshevism, reporting that the priest "together with his entire organization are pronounced rabid Bolsheviks, co-operating with [the] Workers Relief Society, an amalgamation of the Union [of] Russian Workers and 1st Russian Branch [of the] Communist Party," which had staged a ball whose admission tickets bore the Holy Trinity parish seal.[67]

Another perspective on Zeltonoga's views was published in the Russian-language *Volna* (*The Wave*) in September 1920. *Volna* was an anarcho-communist journal critical of both Bolshevism and religious adherence. The cover of most editions bore an elaborate illustration depicting, in part, an Orthodox priest standing on a rocky island, holding aloft in each hand a cross and a censer as protection against an oncoming, menacing wave. "The adaptation of religion to bolshevism may be noticed not only in Russia, but in the United States," wrote the pseudonymous Ivan Bezzubyi ("Ivan the Toothless"). "One of the independent churches, the leader of which is the priest Zeltonoga, might serve as an example. This farsighted priest has already managed to adapt to Bolshevism. He is now a 'genuine' Bolshevik." Bezzubyi thought that the political syncretism of independent Orthodox Christians like Zeltonoga and their recent, hastened emergence embodied what typical anarcho-communists liked least about the Orthodox Church and its historical place within Russian social and political life. "He did this, of course, not because the liberation of workers is dear to him," the author argued, "but for the simple reason that circumstances compelled him to do so." Bezzubyi suggested that the increasing numbers of Orthodox adherents who flocked from archdiocesan parishes to independent congregations after the Palmer Raids had been deluded into believing that radicalized priests like Zeltonoga were in solidarity with their struggles as industrial workers. Instead, Bezzubyi assailed, they had cast their lots with frauds. "Now they pray, they make prostrations against the grimy floor," he wrote, and "they are doing this only because Zeltonoga became a 'radical,' or rather 'a wolf dressed in sheep's clothing, in order to draw closer to the sheep.'"[68]

188 | "UNDER THE CLOAK OF RELIGION"

John Zeltonoga left Baltimore and its independent parish in 1923, returning to Chicago and his former position at St. George. Through his labors, and that of other independent priests, the bonds of independent community would endure, both on the Chesapeake and in the Windy City. In Baltimore, the Holy Trinity congregation maintained ties with leftist political groups well into the 1920s, including cooperation with the local branch of the Communist Party. The local party head taught children the Russian language there as late as 1926. The parish shed its independent status by the early 1930s, affiliating first with the Russian Orthodox Church Outside of Russia (ROCOR) and then the Moscow Patriarchate, under which it remains today.[69] St. George similarly abandoned independence and entered ROCOR in 1929. Zeltonoga was at its altar table when an Orthodox bishop placed a blessed altar cloth (*antimension*) on it for the first time. Still, the parish retained some elements of its early years. When a new priest arrived there in 1951, he discovered portraits of Soviet leaders in the parish hall and a red Soviet flag in the church. "It was necessary to explain to the people that Marxism and religion were not exactly compatible," a later parish history recounted, "and that a Marxist flag did not have a place in a church." Today St. George is a cathedral parish of the Orthodox Church in America (OCA).[70]

The clergy and laity of independent Russian Orthodox parishes, from their first stirrings in Chicago, transformed a marginal idea into a fledgling movement that by 1920 numbered a dozen independent parishes throughout the United States and Canada.[71] Though they rejected normative Orthodox ecclesiology, independent parishes did not wish to change other aspects of how they lived their faith in their local eucharistic communities. These congregations valued the integrity of the church's message of salvation and its liturgical cycle, scriptures, and traditions. What they wished to change was how—and by whom—the church was administrated, who owned and controlled parish properties, and who had a say in the assignment and employment conditions of clergy. "It may appear bewildering how plain Christian believers could undertake such a revolutionary feat as to secede from the Synod Mission and to found their own Independent Orthodox Church," Timothy Peshkoff later recalled, "to elect a priest who would suit them, to issue their own certificates of birth, which prompted the Mission and the tsar's consulates in America to persecute severely those who did it."[72]

Despite fierce criticism and intense scorn, thousands of working-class people in American Orthodox Rus' did exactly this, forming churches that were Orthodox in practice and self-identity while congregational in structure. "We were not rebels against the Church and the motherland [*rodina*]," an early independent parishioner maintained, "but at the time of the revolution, when many fell away from the faith, we continued to preserve our Orthodox faith and church."[73]

7

"We Go Fearlessly into the Maw of Death"

Mutual Aid and the Influenza Epidemic of 1918

A Helper and Protector, He has become my salvation
This is my God, and I shall glorify Him
The God of my father, and I shall praise Him
For gloriously has He been glorified.
—The Great Canon of Saint Andrew of Crete (circa seventh
century CE)

On Sunday, September 29, 1918, priest Alexander Lupinovich celebrated the Divine Liturgy at the Holy Annunciation parish in Maynard, Massachusetts. That afternoon, he dined with friends in the parish rectory, telling jokes and bouncing his young daughter on his knee. After a short rest, he went to church for a meeting of the Annunciation Brotherhood, the local chapter of the Russian Orthodox Catholic Mutual Aid Society. When he returned home, Lupinovich complained to his wife of a sore throat and runny nose. Natalia Lupinovich rubbed her husband's body with camphor oil and sent him to bed with a mug of tea and a warm blanket. During the night, the priest developed a severe fever. A doctor was summoned. It was influenza. For days, Lupinovich floated in and out of consciousness, enduring delirium, vomiting, and a temperature that hovered over 104 degrees. On Thursday, he was alert enough to receive Holy Communion and Holy Unction. By Saturday, the sixth day of his illness, there were few signs of life. Late that dark evening, as a thunderstorm rolled in from the west and flashes of lightning lit the sky, Alexander Lupinovich died. He was twenty-eight years old.[1]

Between 1918 and 1920, a global influenza epidemic struck an estimated five hundred million people, a third of the world's population. At least fifty million people died. A quarter of the United States population, an estimated twenty-five million people, were afflicted, of which 675,000 perished. One of them was Alexander Lupinovich. The epidemic altered nearly every aspect of life in the US. State, county, and municipal health departments set restrictions on social gatherings, commerce, and religious activities to slow the rate of infection. Cloth masks became common. Hospitals filled with patients. Cemeteries buried the dead around the clock. It was a virus widely felt, with swift onset and debilitating symptoms, and for many, it brought a gruesome death. As the historian Nancy Bristow observes, "for millions of Americans, both those who suffered from influenza and those who lost loved ones to the disease, the 1918 pandemic lived on in vivid memories and in lives indelibly marked by those experiences."[2]

Among those in the United States who were so "indelibly marked" were Orthodox Christians. While it is difficult to determine how many believers across American Orthodox Rus' contracted influenza, it almost certainly numbered in the thousands—men and women, young and old. Hundreds died, though perhaps far more. Few, if any, communities were spared. Despite such wide reach within Orthodox communities, however, the epidemic was an experience that was generally forgotten. This was not uncommon. Like so many others, Orthodox Christians constructed what Bristow calls a "preferred narrative," minimizing their historical memory of profound loss—individual and communal alike.[3] What is more, as Patricia Fanning notes, the epidemic "was felt most by those with least access to the authoritative written word: poor military conscripts, Native Americans, laborers, and immigrants."[4]

From this perspective, as a religious community composed of working-class immigrants, it is little surprise that the influenza epidemic is obscure in both church historiography and historical memory of American Orthodox Rus'.[5] In contrast to these omissions of memory and history, a significant archival record exists to show that the influenza epidemic was a deeply interwoven medical, spiritual, and social crisis that altered the social and religious worlds across the spectrum of American Orthodox Rus'—clergy and lay, women and men, young and old (though mostly young)—at catastrophic degrees. Much of this record was documented by the Russian Orthodox Catholic Mutual Aid Society (ROCMAS) in the pages of its weekly, Ruthenian-language newspaper, *Svit* (*The Light*), published from the society's headquarters in Wilkes-Barre, Pennsylvania. One of several fraternal and benevolence societies operating within American Orthodox Rus', ROCMAS comprised working-aged men and women and was unique in that it had administrative ties to the Russian Archdiocese and permitted clergy to become members.[6]

Influenza adversely affected the ability of parachurch institutions, especially those like ROCMAS, which maintained networks of financial and social support for working-class Orthodox people. The primary function of a mutual-aid society was to ensure injury, illness, and mortality benefits for its dues-paying members, which required the regular publication of membership statistics and financial statements as a matter of transparency. Those published by ROCMAS during and immediately after the epidemic provide general insight into how the epidemic affected ROCMAS as an institution but, more importantly, also offer intimate perspectives on how the society's predominantly Carpatho-Rusyn membership experienced the influenza epidemic. In late 1918 and early 1919, *Svit* listed the names, ages, and chapter affiliations of over two hundred influenza victims across more than a hundred communities in American Orthodox Rus'. Each name offers a poignant point of entry for understanding how influenza affected Orthodox believers, their families, and their churches. The disproportionate impact of influenza on working-aged adults amplified the importance of the society's fraternal bonds but strained its financial resources and even threatened the organization's very survival.

The Epidemic in American Orthodox Rus'

The morning after priest Alexander Lupinovich died, two clergymen traveled twenty miles from Boston to Maynard. Singing the Trisagion and chanting psalms, the priests cleaned and anointed Lupinovich's body, then dressed him in his *riassa*, a simple black cassock.[7] His casket was arranged for viewing in the rectory dining room. For hours, Natalia Lupinovich stood next to her husband's body as grieving parishioners filled their home. One of them was a friend who had lunched with Lupinovich mere hours before he fell ill, attended to the family's needs throughout the week, and was present at the priest's deathbed. Their account of the funeral visitation described a scene almost too difficult to bear. "On the very same table at which we had so recently had fun," they wrote, "in a poor, cheap coffin (for on account of the epidemic and frequent deaths, it was impossible to obtain a decent casket), lay our dear father." The time came for the casket to be taken to church for memorial prayers, after which Lupinovich would be transported more than 250 miles west to St. Tikhon's Monastery in Pennsylvania for his funeral and interment. Outside the rectory, members of the parish brotherhood and the church choir assembled behind a processional cross and icon banners. Singing a hymn from the seventh-century Great Canon of St. Andrew of Crete, "A Helper and a Protector," they carried candles as they bore the casket to the church. "This unusual spectacle in an American city attracted quite a crowd of people, which the large church could not sufficiently contain," the friend wrote. During the service, "the singing mingled with *matushka's* desperate cries. . . . The entire temple was filled with sheer, indescribable sobbing."[8] This significant display of public grief was all the more notable, if not alarming, for as another observer reported, "At that time in Maynard, Massachusetts, it seemed there was not a single house where there were not influenza patients."[9]

Throughout the epidemic, most especially in the autumn of 1918, American Orthodox Rus' trod a thin line between the church's aspirations to be a spiritual hospital—a "helper and protector" for the sick and suffering—and the need to adapt to public health measures addressing the temporal realities of a fearsome viral strain that has perplexed scientists, medical experts, and historians of medicine for more than a century. A strain of the H1N1 virus, the 1918 influenza virus, commonly (and pejoratively) called the Spanish flu, was unique for its unusual morbidity and mortality distributions. Typically, age-specific curves plotting the mortality of viral epidemics are U shaped, indicating greater vulnerability for children and the elderly and lower risk for working-aged people. In 1918, however, the curve formed a peculiar W shape, indicating heightened mortality for people between twenty and forty—the dominant demographic of American Orthodox Rus'. While there have been many hypotheses, none has proven conclusive. The epidemiologist David Morens and the immunologist Anthony Fauci deem this anomaly as "perhaps the most important unsolved mystery of the pandemic."[10]

Scientists and historians alike link influenza's rapid spread in communities like those of American Orthodox Rus' with environmental factors such as working conditions, social habits, living environments, and health-care access.[11] As described in earlier chapters, living conditions were generally poor in the most heavily concentrated regions of American Orthodox Rus', the soot-buried coal and steel towns of Pennsylvania. Immigrant laborers often suffered from poor nutrition, pointing to weight loss as a sign of struggle in the US, and were more vulnerable to getting sick. Work-related health conditions were common, especially tuberculosis and other respiratory ailments, as was physical debilitation from overwork. And though less quantifiable in objective terms, Orthodox religious practices might also have played a factor in the spread of influenza. In church, worshipers stood in close proximity, venerated the same icons and crosses, embraced one another, and successively kissed clergymen's hands in blessing. Those who approached the chalice received the body and blood of Christ from a common spoon, then drank warm red wine from the same *zapivka* (washing down) cups. At work, at church, and at home, the living conditions and environmental factors that parishioners endured troubled clergy and other church workers. "There is not one who has lived to be sixty in my parish," one priest lamented.[12]

Though faced with widespread health, safety, and environmental risk factors, Orthodox workers often had only sporadic access to quality medical care. Some harbored wariness of medical practitioners. What medical guidance workers received was of mixed quality, usually from Russian-language newspapers. Such newspapers—especially religious publications—were important sources of church news as much as they were for information on practical matters like health care. These included the ROCMAS-published *Svit*, a newspaper that was tailored to its working-class, Carpatho-Rusyn readership and that regularly advertised medical quacks and unproven treatments. Its pages touted patent medicines like Richter's Pain Expeller, a liniment composed of 45 percent alcohol and sold by a purported doctor trained at a nonexistent medical school.[13] Another longtime advertiser was the Wilkes-Barre physician Dr. Mendelson, a "Russian doctor" who treated patients with "the very finest and most pure medicines, serums, and injections" for ailments ranging from blood infections and rheumatism to "loss of masculinity."[14] A period study on medical access found that Russian workers were susceptible to such enticements. As a Chicago doctor observed, they would "look upon everything printed in the newspaper as absolute truth. They do not understand even that an advertisement is written and paid for by the advertiser, and innocently think it is the newspaper that praises these physicians because they are so good."[15]

Svit printed its usual fare of sensational medical advertisements during the epidemic. Yet it also published practical and scientifically sound guidance on caring for the sick and slowing viral transmission. At the outset of the epidemic, the paper warned readers to avoid crowds, limit excursions, cover coughs and sneezes, wash their hands, and sterilize their eating utensils. It instructed them to isolate the sick in separate rooms and to call a doctor on the third or fourth day of illness. The paper also dissuaded against folk remedies like wearing a pouch of camphor around the neck, advising instead more effective and scientifically proven medications.[16] Elsewhere in *Svit*, however, were accounts of those who moved beyond science to interpret the mysterious illness as divine punishment, wondering, as one Minneapolis parishioner wrote, "if all who live in America had dealt more piously, God would not have punished the entire country with such widespread illness." Through *Svit*, the writer was aware of the great prevalence of influenza in places like Pennsylvania and New York and bemoaned that the epidemic had at last reached their "distant place" in the Upper Midwest at a similar scale. "We only hope that if we start praying to God more," they wrote, "he will have mercy on us and spare us His punishing right hand."[17]

Missionary Work in an Epidemic

Clergy and church workers shared such religious interpretations of the epidemic, though adapted them to their own, often horrifying insight on its impact. Four archdiocesan priests died during the early months of widespread illness, including Alexander Lupinovich, each contracting influenza while attending to the sick and dying.[18] Priests considered their duties to the sick to be a clerical imperative; during an epidemic, it was a mortal risk. As we have seen, the clergy of American Orthodox Rus' navigated complex relationships that were simultaneously pastoral, social, and material. They were expected to be mediators between their congregants and the unfamiliar world around them, to intervene in moments of trouble or danger, and to do so selflessly. And when influenza struck, they served within an archdiocese straining to maintain operations and support missionary clergy.[19] While church leaders recognized the danger of ministering to influenza patients, they demanded that clergymen do so, even though little or no guidance on personal safety or suggestions on altered practices to mitigate the virus were provided. Priests obligingly rushed from bed to bed and house to house as their congregants fell ill. This was especially taxing for priests whose duties also included serving isolated adherents and communities without priests, necessitating endless travel at a moment's notice and stark confrontations with the severity of loss. The granddaughter of priest Constantin Buketoff later wrote that in 1918 her grandfather "worked literally day and night at the grim task of giving Communion to all the dying and of keeping up with the overwhelming number of funerals. The pressure was such that burials in the cemetery went on into the night, around the clock!"[20]

Priest Maxim Bakunoff contracted influenza from a parishioner in Whitman, West Virginia, an Appalachian coal town where he was organizing a mission parish. On the evening of October 23, 1918, one of his parishioners woke from a dream in which he saw "that our dear *batiushka* [father] had given [his] soul unto God." Rushing to Whitman, eight miles from his home, the man discovered Anna Bakunoff grieving beside her husband's body. Whitman was a remote and underserved community; the closest neighboring parish was in Moundsville, more than two hundred miles away. With no nearby clergy to prepare Bakunoff for burial, parishioners pooled money to buy a casket, cleaned Bakunoff's body, and dressed him in his white vestments—a dreadful task, given the disfigurement that influenza often inflicted on its victims. Members of the congregation then transported their priest almost three hundred miles to his former parish church in Allegheny, Pennsylvania, where his funeral was held.[21] "Despite a ban by the authorities," by one account of the service, "a sizable number of people gathered in the church, and even more were on the church porch."[22] In a graveside eulogy, Bishop Alexander (Nemolovsky) extolled "our dear Fr. Maxim," who had endured "an early, yet glorious death, having contracted a terrible illness from his own flock" while hearing the confessions of the afflicted and administering the eucharist. The bishop framed this as evidence of Bakunoff's missionary zeal and as the natural end to a challenging pastoral assignment. Alexander saw Bakunoff as a model missionary whose labors in Whitman yielded a strong parish "in a very short time." Yet the bishop also knew that it had been difficult toil. Bakunoff, his wife, and their three young children shared a single room and slept together on the floor. Addressing Bakunoff himself, Alexander imagined the priest arriving home at the end of a long day, entering "secretly in the night, afraid, as if you would be asked for bread you didn't have." Turning to Bakunoff's loved ones, Alexander's gaze fixed on the priest's children, the youngest only an infant. "Who will warm them?"[23]

The struggles of the young Bakunoff family illustrate the demands routinely laid on clerical families and even more indicate how influenza exacerbated the difficult conditions and relationships that defined their lives. As we have seen, clerical families were integral parts of the religious and social networks of parish life, especially in smaller missions. Clerical wives and children were expected to be visible and exemplary parishioners, to silently endure financial and residential arrangements that left them wanting, and to accept the demands and responsibilities that could keep their husbands and fathers occupied, day or night. Demands on clergy and clerical families only increased during the epidemic, when the needs of the afflicted and their families surpassed the hours of the day. And just as priests contracted influenza, so did their kin. Thirty-six-year-old Anna Solanka contracted influenza while aiding her husband, Father Andrew, as he ministered to ill parishioners in Slovan, Pennsylvania. Theirs was a crowded home; their ten children ranged from ten months to eighteen years. When Anna succumbed to influenza-related pneumonia on December 5, 1918, Father Andrew and their eldest two children were sick themselves, though all three recovered. From their family, only Anna's brother was healthy enough to travel to Scranton for her funeral.[24]

In early November, Bishop Alexander publicly addressed the concerns of clergy and clerical families. Twenty priests had contracted influenza. Four had died. Echoing his words at Bakunoff's graveside, Alexander wrote in praise of archdiocesan priests for their "heroic *podvigs*," great spiritual endeavors, amid an epidemic "raging with all the strength of hell" as a "terrible retribution God has sent to all America." Alexander expressed his admiration that priests continued to go into hospital wards and private homes, even ministering to Roman Catholic and Greek Catholic patients, "without any kinds of safety masks and disinfectants." He described a frightened clergy wife in Pennsylvania who challenged her husband as he left their home to hear the confessions of eight afflicted parishioners, even though he had no personal protective equipment. The priest responded by making the sign of the cross, explaining, "No other remedies will help!" Another missionary showed similarly little concern, even after he contracted influenza from a parishioner. "What if I die?" he exclaimed when Alexander visited his bedside. "On a missionary post, why, this is good fortune!" The experiences of his clergy led Alexander to see the epidemic as an opportunity for them to model selfless devotion, even martyrdom. "We are not afraid of any disease," one priest told him. "We go fearlessly into the maw of death."[25]

Public Health and Orthodox Practice

Though Alexander directed priests to bravely sustain their *podvigs* among the sick and dying, public health policies intended to curb the spread of the virus sometimes limited their ability to do so. Measures such as closing saloons, restricting commerce, and canceling public events had a profound impact on slowing infections, though they were unevenly applied. Some municipalities delayed or even cut short their directives. Others were reluctant to close churches and synagogues, even as they shuttered physically similar spaces like theaters.[26] Influenza rippled across northeastern Pennsylvania, a region where archdiocesan parishes and ROCMAS chapters were numerous. In Philadelphia, an ill-timed Liberty Loan parade in late September caused a citywide spike in cases, prompting mitigation measures that included church closures. By mid-October, the state's health commissioner recommended, but did not require, that municipalities do the same.[27]

The enforced church closures in Pennsylvania affected a number of archdiocesan parishes. Alexander responded by declaring the epidemic "purely of the Antichrist" and providing guidelines for how devotional practices should be adapted. "But can we really cease to pray and remove Divine protection from American Orthodox Rus'?!" he asked. "No!" If general worship was prohibited, he reasoned, "no one will forbid a priest and *psalomshchik* [psalm singer]—just the two of them—to enter a church and serve the Divine Liturgy on behalf of all those absent out of sad necessity." Even in reduced form, Alexander wished church life to continue. "So then serve the Divine Liturgy EARLY, fathers and brothers," he wrote; "let not our churches be silent on Sundays and feast days!" Alexander assumed that parishioners remaining at home already maintained prayer rules and possessed sophisticated liturgical knowledge and thus could manage their own substitutes for common worship. "I know that some Godly families have the custom of gathering together in the best room," he wrote, "and here under the direction of the head of the house sing the vespers, matins, [and] liturgy." Priests were instructed that this was a suitable, though only temporary, stand-in for church prayer. "Explain to the people, persuade them that each Sunday morning, all Orthodox families ought to gather in their own homes in common prayer," he wrote. "If they do not have books, or if they are not able to sing the vespers or matins, let them sing a few church songs or pray aloud."[28]

Alexander's instructions suggested that believers were improvising ways to adapt familiar patterns of devotion to the uncertainties of a viral epidemic. In Wilkes-Barre, Pennsylvania, numerous members of priest Peter Kohanik's parish contracted influenza. In a letter to the parish, Kohanik offered bitter consolation that the tragic death of ten parishioners was less than other parishes he knew of that had experienced upward of twenty or thirty. "It was God's will to unleash this unprecedentedly contagious illness upon our country, and likewise upon the environs of Wilkes-Barre," Kohanik wrote in *Svit*. "Aside from medical and physical precautions already described in previous editions of *Svit*, as Christians, we should offer prayers to the Lord for our speedy deliverance, and that of our loved ones, from this disease." While Kohanik valued personal devotions, he felt that "church prayer is higher than home prayer." Given the open-ended nature of the church closure order, Kohanik would hold a weekly prayer service (*molieben*) for the health of all parishioners, at which each family would be represented by a single candle. Kohanik designated parishioners from each of the city's neighborhoods to collect much-needed donations from interested families. A shuttered church, after all, meant the lost revenues of a closed candle stand.[29]

While Kohanik and other clergy worshiped alone in their churches, other aspects of liturgical life were moved outdoors. This was most evident when communities attended to their dead. Shuttered churches meant funeral services held in cemeteries, often within a day or two of death, and with only a few family members or friends present. In Colver, Pennsylvania, Dimitrii Varga was mourned only by other men from his ROCMAS brotherhood, of which he had been a particularly zealous member. Varga was just as devoted to the Colver parish, where he was a lay chanter and church board trustee. A friend wrote in *Svit* that with Varga's loss, "a heavy blow struck our parish," as to bury such an active member without a funeral in their church felt sad and incomplete.[30]

Regular eucharistic worship occurred outdoors as well. In mid-October, a ROCMAS member named Aleksandr Pyza traveled to attend an open-air liturgy at a church in Erie, Pennsylvania, in fact a renovated home in the shadow of the city's iron and steel foundries. The Erie ROC-MAS chapter was instrumental in forming the parish, Erie's first. Pyza arrived to find a large crowd outside a "well-decorated and beautifully adorned" house church, including Russians and Romanians and even some Episcopalians (Angliki) and Italian Catholics. ROCMAS members lined up to hold candles on either side of the improvised altar. Vespers and the liturgy were celebrated in the yard in Church Slavonic and Romanian. Pyza felt that what he experienced felt little different from a "cathedral service," impressed that "here Russian Orthodox people are gathered round, here children stand with mothers, women and men sing at the *kliros* [choir stand]." The community's eagerness to worship with such comfort and confidence in the yard of their house church made Pyza feel "as if a church had stood in Erie for twenty years."[31]

Public gathering bans altered church activities at the archdiocesan level. As previously mentioned, the rise of Bolshevism and the administrative ambiguities of Bishop Alexander's position as temporary archdiocesan administrator prompted the calling of a local church council. Initially planned to convene in Cleveland in January 1918, financial issues and general discord within the archdiocese caused the council to be postponed until November. As the scheduled council approached, Cleveland's acting health commissioner, H. L. Rockwood, enforced stringent mitigation measures to curb an outbreak across northeastern Ohio. The city cleaned its streets, distributed thousands of cloth masks from the Red Cross, and waged a "war on spitting." It also closed schools, restaurants, and saloons. In mid-October, Rockwood shuttered places of worship as well. Over protests from Christian and Jewish communities (a hundred clergymen went door-to-door to drum up support), Rockwood extended his order into November.[32] Archdiocesan leadership still hoped to hold the council as scheduled. When two Cleveland-area priests approached Rockwood for the necessary city permits, however, he politely turned them down. Bishop Alexander acknowledged the prevalence of influenza in his archdiocese and expressed agreement with Rockwood. He instructed parishes to delay their elections of council delegates. In the meantime, he instructed that "priests should not go away from their parishes, but remain in place for comforting the sick and burials of the dead." A council convened in Cleveland, though not until February 1919.[33]

Orthodox Mutual Aid and the Epidemic

Priest Alexander Lupinovich's casket was taken by train from Maynard to New York, where clergy from the St. Nicholas Cathedral in Manhattan offered a *panikhida* (memorial prayer) for the deceased priest on the railway station platform.[34] The journey continued to Scranton en route to St. Tikhon's Monastery. Before Father Alexander was buried, Natalia Lupinovich insisted that his body be transferred into a copper coffin. She hoped that in time, his remains might be disinterred so that they could be buried together in Russia. Like many others, it seems their family saw missionary service in the US as a temporary adventure that would advance Father Alexander's long clerical career. Their well-laid plans were now tragically dashed.[35] Soon after the funeral, Natalia filed for her husband's $750 ROCMAS mortality policy.[36]

Founded in 1895 in Wilkes-Barre, Pennsylvania, ROCMAS served important ethnic, spiritual, and fraternal roles for its members. "Our society is RUSSIAN," it was explained, "for it aims to spread in America the ideal of a united, indivisible Rus' . . . and generally endeavors for the enlightenment of the Russian people in a Russian spirit, in feelings of love and devotion to Russian nationality [*narodnost'*]." It was Orthodox, "for it endeavors for the spread and adoption of the Orthodox Christian Faith in America and the creation of Orthodox churches here" and because "only a person Orthodox in faith may be a member."[37] Within the Russian Archdiocese, this multifaceted emphasis served an important purpose. Ministering to a flock significantly composed of former Greek Catholics who defined themselves in nuanced ethnic terms, the

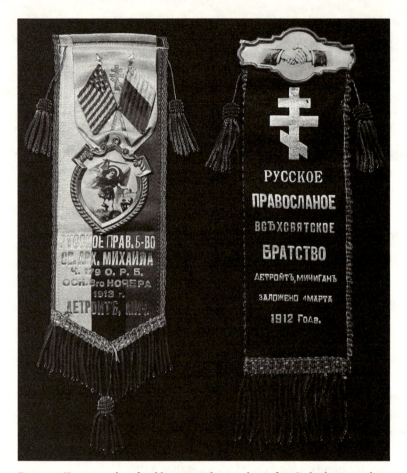

Figure 7.1. Two examples of emblems worn by members of an Orthodox mutual-aid society brotherhood (*bratstvo*). These double-sided ribbons, both from Detroit, were produced for the Russian Orthodox Brotherhood of the Holy Archangel Michael, chapter 179 of the Russian Brotherhood Organization (*Obshchestvo Russkikh Bratstv*), and the Russian Orthodox All Saints Brotherhood, ROCMAS chapter 212. The black reverse was displayed on somber occasions, such as funerals. (From the author's collection; photograph by the author)

archdiocese encouraged the Russification of newly converted Carpatho-Rusyn believers, most of whom still maintained familial and social ties in their former religious communion.[38]

While much has been written about the critical role of mutual-aid and fraternal societies within vulnerable religious, ethnic, and racial minority groups in the early twentieth-century US, the histories of such Orthodox organizations are less known. ROCMAS was an Orthodox solution to common problems of social aid and crisis intervention for working-class immigrants. Such organizations had existed in Europe, then were brought to North America with myriad ethnic and religious groups.[39] Slavic migrants had known precarity in Europe, as the sociologist Ewa Morawska has noted, but experienced it anew in the industrial United States and on more befuddling terms. They harbored what Morawska identifies as a "fundamental concern with security."[40] The migrant believers of American Orthodox Rus' valued organizations that could offer both fraternal support and material aid, especially in moments of acute need. The difficulties, hardships, danger, and low pay of industrial work were consistent struggles for Orthodox workers, whether one ladled molten steel or shoveled coal, manned an assembly line or fed cotton into a loom. Though some benefited from early forms of corporate welfare, few looked forward to company pensions. Federal Social Security benefits were still decades away. Though states like Pennsylvania required companies to pay medical costs for workers who were injured on the job, period evidence suggests that these benefits were inconsistently disbursed. Instead, workers and their families turned to ethnic and religious organizations like ROCMAS.[41]

The society was overseen from a national office in Wilkes-Barre, though the bulk of social support and even some financial benefits were handled at the local level. Named after a spiritual patron, a ROCMAS *bratstvo* (brotherhood) typically operated in parallel to a parish, usually with the cooperation of its pastor. In absence of a parish, a *bratstvo* substituted for many of its social purposes until one could be established.[42] Parishes founded from preexisting ROCMAS brotherhoods often built their churches using society grants.[43] By 1918, most of the society's 225 chapters were found in coal and steel towns of Pennsylvania and other industrial centers of the Northeast. There were also chapters in far-flung places like Cle Elum, Washington, Hartshorne, Oklahoma, and Slovaktown, Arkansas, where remoteness and somewhat smaller Orthodox populations only heightened the need for familiar institutions.

The viability of a benefits-based fraternal society like ROCMAS depended on its ability to maintain membership levels, collect dues, and carefully balance available funds against anticipated policy

Figure 7.2. The $1,000 policy certificate of ROCMAS president and priest Peter Kohanik, 1913. (*Russkoe pravoslavnoe kafol. obshchestvo vzaimopomoshchi v syevero-amerikanskikh soedinennykh shtatakh XX-lyetnemu iubileiu, 1895–1915* [New York: Svit, 1915])

disbursements. In 1918, ROCMAS offered four levels of mortality policies: $250, $500, $750, and $1,000 (between $5,100 and $20,500 today). Monthly dues followed calculation tables prepared by the National Fraternal Congress of America and were set proportional to age (ROCMAS membership was limited to people aged sixteen to forty-five). Members who suffered debilitating illness or injury were guaranteed between thirty-one and forty-six weeks of benefits, depending on their policy. In case of death, their beneficiaries received the full policy amount.[44] Each member held a small stake in the society's finances, and its accrued resources ebbed and flowed with enrollments, expulsions, and deaths. Membership changes were meticulously listed by name in *Svit*, which also published general membership statistics and financial statements. In the summer of 1918, these reports showed ROCMAS on solid financial footing, buoyed by the monthly dues of ninety-seven hundred members. The society's available funds and reserve accounts were sufficiently full and its benefits disbursements timely. Over the first nine months of the year, ROCMAS received an average of six mortality claims per month and never more than nine. In any given month, the society might have disbursed as little as $250 or as much as $9,000 in policy disbursements (between $5,100 and $194,000 today), all very manageable amounts.[45]

Then came influenza. In October 1918, ROCMAS received ninety-two mortality claims. Fifty-six came in November, then sixty-five in December. Over the last three months of the year, 213 ROCMAS members died from influenza, amounting to just over 2 percent of the society's total membership. They were men and women ranging in age from their midteens to early fifties, though most were in their twenties and thirties. At least 107 ROCMAS chapters—around half of the total number—reported at least one influenza death. Losses were greatest in Pennsylvania, where many coal and steel communities had multiple chapters. The St. Nicholas Brotherhood of Edwardsville, Pennsylvania, a coal town near Wilkes-Barre, lost ten members, seven in November alone. The greatest losses were in Wilkes-Barre: nineteen members across its four chapters. Collectively, ROCMAS owed the beneficiaries of influenza victims $146,000 in mortality disbursements (nearly $3 million today).[46]

Each of these 213 claims reflected its own tragic story. There were six ROCMAS chapters in Mayfield, Pennsylvania, a heavily Slavic coal town between Scranton and Carbondale. During October and November, twenty-eight influenza victims were buried in its Russian Orthodox cemetery. Nine were children or infants. Nearly half were male coal workers, from a fourteen-year-old slate packer to a fifty-four-year-old miner. There were housewives, domestic workers, and a "silk girl." Many of the adults were ROCMAS members. Among them was Anna Serafin, thirty-four, of the Assumption Sisterhood. Six others belonged to the Ss. Boris and Gleb Brotherhood, including thirty-eight-year-old Michael Serafin, Anna's husband.[47] The stories of Anna and Michael Serafin's difficult lives underscore the importance of ROCMAS for working-class Orthodox families in coal towns like Mayfield, where life revolved around anthracite. The mines under the town were dusty and dangerous, prone to cave-ins and accidents, and harsh on workers' bodies and lungs. Families knew to listen for the ominous whistle and dread the sight of metal tags still hanging on the check board. Anna first married in 1903, when she was eighteen. In 1910, her husband died in a mine collapse, leaving her alone with their two sons. A widower and father of two, Michael himself suffered hip and leg fractures in a mining accident and found safer work running a hotel. Michael and Anna married in Mayfield in 1911, then had two children of their own. On October 20, 1918, the day after their youngest daughter celebrated her second birthday, Michael served as the informant on Anna's death certificate and on that of another family member, "Still Born Serafin." Michael died the next day. All three were buried in the Russian Orthodox Cemetery on October 22. The $1,000 ROCMAS mortality policies that Michael and Anna each held helped provide for their surviving children.[48]

The Lasting Impact of Influenza on American Orthodox Rus'

As those who were laid to rest in Mayfield suggest, ROCMAS was a subset of American Orthodox Rus'. And because of its membership criteria, influenza-related mortality statistics reflect only the deaths of working-aged members. They do not account for nonfatal cases of ROCMAS members or the illnesses and deaths of thousands more Orthodox adults, elders, and children who did not belong to the society. Even so, ROCMAS statistics and subsequent research on the epidemic offer preliminary clues for how influenza affected American

Orthodox Rus'. Health experts speculate that 25 percent of the United States population contracted influenza during the epidemic. At its onset, ROCMAS had around ninety-seven hundred members, meaning that it is possible that nearly twenty-five hundred members fell ill. Yet given the unusually high morbidity of the 1918 influenza strain within the society's exclusive demographic, working-aged adults, the actual figure was probably higher. And when projected across all of American Orthodox Rus', total morbidity and mortality almost certainly was much greater as well.[49]

The prevalence of influenza infections shows that the frightening experiences and heavy responsibilities of the epidemic certainly were shared across communities, and by necessity. To a significant extent, adult adherents arrived in American Orthodox Rus' alone. Workplaces, neighborhoods, and parishes replicated the multigenerational and wide-reaching kinship networks they left behind. Often it was not family but friends, coworkers, and fellow parishioners who stood as wedding parties, served as godparents, and mourned the dead. In ROCMAS chapters, mutual aid meant more than policy benefits. When someone from a brotherhood or sisterhood died, other members assumed responsibilities that were otherwise taken up by kin. One such example occurred in Boswell, a coal town in southwestern Pennsylvania. Across three days in October, Yurii and Maria Kovach and two of their four children succumbed to influenza. The secretary of the Holy Spirit Brotherhood turned to ROCMAS for help in aiding the surviving children, aged three and five. "The trouble is that a place cannot be found for them in these times," the secretary explained. He inquired if the church-operated Russian Orphanage in Springfield, Vermont, might take them in and asked what should be done with Yurii and Maria's mortality benefits. Priest Peter Kohanik responded with advice and comfort. "Your sadness is truly without precedent," he wrote, "yet we are all obliged to kneel before the will of the Lord God Almighty." He advised that the orphaned Kovach children be sent to Springfield and promised that ROCMAS would transfer their parents' policy funds there.[50]

Kohanik's public pledge to the Boswell *bratstvo* came as he was fretting privately over the society's worsening financial situation. In truth, ROCMAS lacked sufficient reserves to meet its obligations to beneficiaries like the orphaned Kovach children. Society leaders feared that public meeting bans like those in place across Pennsylvania would cause members to delay making deposits into their chapter accounts precisely when the national organization needed them to do so. State insurance regulations limited the extent to which ROCMAS could draw on reserve funds once its mortality account emptied. The society's statutes obligated its general membership to cover the outstanding amount. In early November, chapters were instructed not to wait until their brotherhoods could meet to remit monthly dues to the Wilkes-Barre national office.[51] There were already 120 death claims and more coming each week. When Kohanik called an extraordinary meeting of the society's leadership in mid-December, there was $120,000 in outstanding disbursements. By month's end, the sum had grown to $146,000 and would ultimately top $160,000 ($3 million and $3.3 million today). For ROCMAS to remain solvent and honor its policy responsibilities in a timely manner, it needed to raise additional funds—and quickly.

The National Fraternal Congress of America advised that a special monthly assessment be imposed in the amount of one-tenth of 1 percent of each member's policy amount. Each member would pay between 25¢ and $1 each month, amounting to between $4.50 and $18 over the eighteen months needed to pay the balance in full (between $80 and $320 today). Members were to remit their assessment payments to the local brotherhood with their regular monthly dues. The national office planned to take out short-term loans each month, to be repaid as special assessment funds arrived. Barring another wave of illness, the influenza deficit would be met by late 1920, with minimal impact on normal operations.[52]

By the time the special assessment went into effect in early 1919, perhaps more than half of influenza-related death claims, upward of $100,000 ($1.78 million today), remained outstanding.[53] Unexpectedly, however, around one-third of the organization—seventy-four chapters—refused to pay their share and participate in the special assessment. Among them was the Assumption Brotherhood of Maynard, Massachusetts, whose members had carried their pastor through the streets of their town only months earlier, then helped Natalia Lupinovich claim her husband's mortality benefits.[54] ROCMAS expelled these chapters, and their members, from the society, at the risk of a drastic, costly shift in membership levels. Since ROCMAS's founding in 1895, it had endured only two, rather slight annual membership losses. In 1919, the society expelled an unprecedented 3,268 members. In less than a year, expulsions and influenza deaths combined for a net membership decrease of more than 20 percent.[55]

The disagreement was rooted in suspicions within the society that the extra assessment was necessary because of mismanagement, not misfortune. On the one hand, ROCMAS consistently put forth a public image of frugality and financial transparency. Issue after issue of *Svit* published detailed membership reports and long lists of financial contributions—no matter how small. And in 1915, the society's twentieth-anniversary commemorative booklet gave a detailed appraisal of its properties and assets, down to a ten-cent water tankard in the Wilkes-Barre front office.[56] Dissenting chapters like the Maynard *bratstvo* maintained, however, that when ROCMAS was handling thousands of dollars of income and disbursements each month, it was also failing to file proper financial statements with state regulators. In a letter to the Pennsylvania Insurance Commissioner, a lawyer representing a dissenting chapter in Pittsburgh argued that given the lack of financial reports, "the department should institute proceeding [*sic*] to prohibit the society from doing business."[57] Kohanik responded by opening the society's files to the commissioner, who discovered that ROCMAS had indeed failed to file proper reports until mid-1918. In his determination, however, this was "due to pure ignorance and to being misinformed by their attorney." The commissioner felt that ROCMAS had acted within its bylaws both when it imposed an extra assessment and too when it expelled chapters that refused to pay. What was more, the commissioner was made to understand (probably by Kohanik, who used *Svit* to broadcast his own US patriotism throughout the Great War) that "the majority of the brotherhoods have paid the extra assessment and that most of these members are American citizens; while those opposed . . . are not American citizens and no doubt, have little or no intention of remaining in this country."[58]

While ROCMAS leaders encouraged the insurance commissioner to interpret the noncompliance of so many chapters and their dues-paying members as unpatriotic disloyalty, it perhaps more accurately indicated preexisting tensions between chapters and the national organization or within chapters themselves. These disagreements were exacerbated by influenza. One such example was the St. Gregory Brotherhood of Homestead, Pennsylvania. "Many brotherhood members went where there is no return" during the epidemic, a chapter history later noted. Those who remained recoiled at an extra assessment intended to ensure that the mortality benefits of their fellow, recently departed members were paid. The chapter was expelled. Shortly thereafter, less than half of its membership came to accept the need for the assessment and restarted their *bratstvo*, though they imposed a strange stipulation that former members "were invited to return only after a new examination by a doctor." It was retribution disguised to ensure that only healthy members joined the chapter. These stipulations continued for more than five years, a period recalled as "a time of troubles [*smutnoe vremia*]" for the Homestead community, in which "it became difficult to attract new members into the Brotherhood's ranks." It was only in 1926, with new leaders and a vigorous membership campaign, that the St. Gregory Brotherhood recovered.[59]

At the national level, with shrinking membership numbers and extra assessments slow to roll in, ROCMAS struggled to remain solvent. In the summer of 1920, as its twenty-fifth-anniversary convention approached, an article in *Svit* asked a simple question: "Why are we not financially strong?" The answer was the lingering influenza deficit.[60] Some of the expelled brotherhoods wished to rejoin and be represented at the convention, even as they continued to criticize the society in the press. Kohanik bemoaned that these former members had "woken up" only after other chapters had done their part, having "set off a great fiasco" by demanding that the state insurance commission shut down the society.[61] Meeting in Wilkes-Barre with the dissenting chapters conspicuously absent, the society's general convention ratified nearly two hundred changes to its bylaws. These included state-mandated increases to monthly membership rates. These were set slightly higher for new members—including, pointedly, any former member who had been expelled.[62] This was not a warm entreaty for former members to rejoin. In 1920, ROCMAS membership sagged further. When the epidemic began, the organization had around ninety-seven hundred members. ROCMAS membership would never again exceed seventy-five hundred.[63]

The Epidemic Ends

Month after anxious month in late 1918 and early 1919, American Orthodox Rus' struggled through the shared traumas of a terrifying viral epidemic. When churches closed, clergy and their congregations generally complied, modifying religious obligations, liturgical activities, and even rites of memorial and burial to meet the circumstances of an invisible and terrifying viral epidemic. Priests continued to minister to the afflicted and comfort those who mourned, in spite of perilous risks to themselves and their families. Influenza placed increasing pressures on other forms of church-driven assistance and comfort, especially in the bonds of material aid found in local chapters of benevolence societies like ROCMAS. When the influenza epidemic ebbed in the United States in early 1919, cotton masks came off, and patterns of normalcy resumed. While the material ramifications of influenza on institutions like ROCMAS are clear, the lasting emotional and spiritual impacts of the epidemic on American Orthodox Rus' prove harder to measure.

With passing decades, those Orthodox Christians who endured influenza in the United States tended not to dwell on their experiences. The legacy of the "forgotten" epidemic as it was experienced in American Orthodox Rus' might be quantified in opportunities lost and potentials unfulfilled. In a matter of months in 1918, missionary priest Maxim Bakunoff built a growing mission in Whitman, West Virginia, at great cost to himself and his young family. Their dreams of a church faded with his death, leaving only a ROCMAS chapter. There would never be a permanent parish in Whitman.[64] And there were the subtle ways that influenza dead remained in local memory. For aging believers whose habits and religious devotions included visits to parish burial grounds like the Russian Orthodox Cemetery in Mayfield, Pennsylvania, the graves of influenza victims were as much tangible testaments of absence as reminders of collective trauma and loss. "In the year of 1918, when the world was plagued with the flu," the steel worker and lifelong Homestead, Pennsylvania, parishioner Peter Mock wrote in 1964, "many hearts were broken with the horrible toll of deaths of our parishioners and especially of the children. Evidence of the heartbreak can be seen today at the old section of our cemetery which had just then been acquired. The long row of small graves along the fence with tiny, some broken, headstones, attests to the magnitude of the sadness within our church."[65]

Such experiences and legacies of the influenza epidemic of 1918 challenged believers' senses of individual and communal security in a new land, underscoring that working-class believers placed their well-being and survival within the wavering grasp of American Orthodox Rus'. What did it mean to fall ill so quickly or to watch others around you approach death when they were well only hours before? What was it like to provide information for a spouse's death certificate, knowing that your own time was dreadfully near? How did it feel to prepare the remains of the disfigured dead, then mourn them without a church funeral? Who would offer comfort if your priest had died? Who would provide if a breadwinner was gone? These questions resonated across American Orthodox Rus' in 1918, even if their traces were elusive, and sometimes imperceptible, with the passage of time.

8

"These Radicals"

Litigating Orthodox Ecclesiology in Red Scare Detroit

I have other sheep that do not belong to this fold. I must
bring them also, and they will listen to my voice. So there
will be one flock, one shepherd.
—John 10:16

As the winter of 1919 turned into spring, priest Dimitri Darin felt uneasy.
He had come to the east side of Detroit the previous summer to become
the pastor of All Saints Russian Orthodox Church, taking residence with
his wife and children in the adjacent rectory at the corner of Hendrie
Street and Jos. Campau Avenue. The fourth priest of All Saints in its five-
year history, Darin knew that each of his predecessors had locked horns
with parish trustees over salary and administrative control. And he suspected that the majority of his parishioners were "Bolsheviki." As the
postwar Red Scare inched toward its underwhelming apex, the Palmer
Raids of late 1919 and early 1920, Dimitri Darin was girding himself
to protect his job and, more dramatically, his parish. He saw red banners and portraits of Vladimir Lenin and the American socialist leader
Eugene V. Debs hanging in the parish-affiliated Russian National Home,
located a block down Hendrie Street. When going about his duties in the
church, Darin heard men singing political songs in the parish hall below.
As acrimony grew within the congregation, Darin asked police to watch
over services. He denied the communion chalice to those whom he suspected to be "Reds" and even enlisted loyal parishioners to eject from the
church those whom he claimed "worked and agitated against the church
and went against the rules of the church." And Darin knew that Joseph
S. Apelman, a Justice Department agent in charge of "radical" investigations in Detroit, was keeping close watch for alleged political subversion
in the parish neighborhood, and perhaps the priest even sanctioned it.

214 | "THESE RADICALS"

As Darin later testified in court, "naturally, being an American citizen, I would like to see this country cleaned up of these radicals."[1]

Dimitri Darin appeared on the witness stand because a politicized conflict within the All Saints parish had fractured the congregation into two antagonistic factions. In March 1919, parishioners with ties to Darin met with Apelman and swore to affidavits against more than a dozen others alleged to be fomenting a Bolshevik plot to take over the parish. Weeks later, thirteen men from the parish community were arrested in federal raids in the surrounding neighborhood, including one on a meeting at the Russian National Home. The day after the first arrests, five hundred parishioners gathered at the National Home. An overwhelming majority voted to remove Darin, replace members of the parish committee, and make the All Saints parish independent from the national archdiocese. Their congregation and its new trustees would hold their church properties and determine parish decisions by democratic vote, tilting the balance of power away from their pastor.

By May, two legal entities were incorporated with the state, each claiming to be the lawful All Saints parish. They spoke of themselves and their opponents in factional terms, a "majority" (bol'shinstvo) that favored independence and a "minority" (men'shinstvo) that backed Father Darin and the Russian Archdiocese. To the majority, Darin and the archdiocese had subjected their congregation to authoritarian and arbitrary measures intended to minimize lay influence and remove their say in financial matters. Maintaining loyalty to Darin, the minority faction considered the controversies nothing less than a Bolshevik plot to seize the parish property deeds, close the church, and transform it into a social club. To blend Orthodox Christianity with Bolshevism was a prospect too abhorrent to bear, even disqualifying from the faith. "They were church members," one Darin ally told federal investigators, "but they ain't now—they became Bolshevikies."[2]

This chapter traces this dispute over the All Saints parish, which lasted from 1919 until 1923, four years in which members of the working-class parish turned church properties into proxies for a political split within their congregation. In the words of one parish trustee, "I just wanted the people to own the property but the method of worship I wanted left the same."[3] Tethering Orthodox ecclesiology to property ownership and driven to fracture amid rampant fears of a Bolshevik revolution on

US soil, a small subset of the community employed the highest levels of federal policing and state jurisprudence to mitigate what was more or less a conflict about assets, property, and institutional control. Then they turned to the courts.

Though brought in July 1919, *All Saints Russian Orthodox Church v. Dimitri Darin, et al.* did not reach trial until September 1921. The case was heard on appeal by the Michigan Supreme Court in 1922 and again in 1923. In each iteration, the case demonstrated how the rise of Bolshevism and disruptions to church life caused by antireligious persecution in Russia prompted Russian Orthodox Christians abroad to closely consider, if not greatly obsess over, the hierarchical structure of their transnational church. In the courtroom, All Saints parishioners and their lawyers adapted, finessed, and even manipulated traditional understandings of Orthodox ecclesiology to make their faith legible at the bar and garner their desired legal outcomes. Such litigation laid bare that beneath the spiritual and religious meanings that Orthodox adherents afforded their church lay the stark realities of property, of salaries and employment benefits, of mortgages and loans and repair bills—the temporal elements that provided an Orthodox community a reliable home and its pastor his livelihood. It exemplified many tensions inherent to the world-building project of American Orthodox Rus' during the early twentieth century. It also was a harbinger of new conflicts to come.

All Saints was a typical parish composed of working men and women who drew on the Russian Archdiocese for spiritual support, social uplift, material aid, and vocational advancement. The church, rectory, and Russian National Home stood in the shadows of several major automotive plants—Ford and Briggs, Fisher and Packard. As laborers embedded in the world's most transformative industrial economy, toiling in a city whose dominant industry relied on the malleability and replaceability of its immigrant workforce, All Saints parishioners were not immune from the rise of left-leaning political and labor activism in the Motor City. They were exposed to and engaged with socialist, communist, and anarchist ideas, literatures, and groups. It was all of these dynamics—worlds of work and faith, the lifeways of their immigrant neighborhood, the fast pace of the industrial city, the shifting political tides of the Progressive era—that defined the All Saints parish and the solidarities within its congregation. Yet, beginning in 1919, it was all of these things that

216 | "THESE RADICALS"

also threatened to tear them apart. At the heart was a simple question with no clear answer: What values defined and bound together Russian Orthodox Christians outside Russia's borders at the dawn of the Bolshevik age?

Detroit's East Side Russian Colony

During the early twentieth century, Detroit transformed from a city that made carriages, stoves, and cigars into a sprawling regional economy driven by the automobile. Putting the world on wheels relied on a diverse labor force of immigrant workers. Accustomed as they were to the most menial labor, as demonstrated in previous chapters, hundreds of working people from across American Orthodox Rus' made their way to what was already being called the Motor City. As a result, Orthodoxy emerged somewhat later in Detroit than in other midwestern industrial metropolises. In 1907, Carpatho-Rusyn migrants on the southwest side founded Detroit's first Orthodox parish, Ss. Peter and Paul.[4] Five years later, their priest, Isidore Salko, noticed a new "Russian colony" emerging across town on the east side, composed of Orthodox workers from the western regions of imperial Russia. They were mostly men employed by Fisher, Hudson, Ford, Packard, and other automotive firms, as well as in light industrial labor in smaller shops and car-related industries along the Detroit River. Their common place of origin reflected certain peculiarities of Detroit within the bigger picture of American Orthodox Rus' and, from a wider perspective, Eastern Christianity in North America. In a report that Salko sent to his superiors early in the parish's development, he noted that All Saints was composed almost exclusively of Russians and Serbs, while "Galicians and Hungarians" attended Ss. Peter and Paul. Salko also reported that unlike most other major metropolitan areas with archdiocesan parishes, Detroit had no Greek Catholic presence, "and therefore there is no struggle with them."[5]

In 1914, the east side "Russian colony" purchased a church at the corner of Hendrie Street and Jos. Campau Avenue, whose former Methodist congregation had relocated several blocks north. After minor renovations, it was consecrated as All Saints Russian Orthodox Church that summer.[6] Once a rural corner of town tilled by German Lutheran farmers, the blocks surrounding All Saints had become a dense grid of light industry and multiunit homes rented out to mostly eastern European automotive workers, inspiring its lasting moniker of Poletown East. In this fast-changing corner of Detroit, All Saints became one node in a network of neighborhood institutions serving the needs and interests of its largely Slavic population. In 1916, the parish purchased a building at the corner of Grandy and Hendrie, a block southwest of the church, and opened it as the Russian National Home (RNH). A social hall for the eponymous society that met there and an overflow space for larger parish events, it was also a job-training center, fitted with $2,500 of instructional factory equipment and a well-stocked technical library.[7]

Vocational education and self-improvement were critical for advancement within Detroit's dominant industry, whose many demands All Saints parishioners understood from personal experience. On Wednesday, January 7, 1914, an estimated five to eight hundred Greek and Russian workers at Ford's Highland Park assembly plant took the day off to attend Christmas services in their Orthodox parishes. The next morning, the employees returned to work to learn that they had been fired. With Ford's unprecedented five-dollar daily wage soon to take effect, the terminated Orthodox workers had no choice but to join the thousands of job seekers who crowded in front of the factory each morning hoping for a coveted position on its assembly line. It was a hard lesson that to gain and retain employment in a fast-growing industrial city required both skill and the appearance of assimilation, tailoring one's religious obligations to the expectations of one's employer. As factory management turned fire hoses on those who were huddled outside the hiring office in the brutal winter cold, including not a few of the fired Orthodox men, a company spokesman told the *New York Times*, "if these men are to make their home in America they should observe American holidays."[8]

Social and educational endeavors at the RNH developed alongside others in the neighborhood. Nicholas Baikowsky, a printer and newspaper editor by trade, was an All Saints parishioner and RNH regular who also taught mathematics and literature classes from the living room of his rented home on Jos. Campau, located between the church and the RNH. Walter Grinewsky, the principal of the RNH vocational school, cotaught arithmetic, technical drawing, and mechanical theory classes at the neighborhood public library. The Americanization Committee of Detroit, a consortium of industrialists, businessmen, and civic leaders concerned with immigrant assimilation, offered courses a few blocks south at Ferry Elementary School, lighting a red, white, and blue lantern over the door when classes were in session.[9] Next door to the RNH was the Russian Consultation Bureau, which kept late hours and space for socialization and provided everyday services like banking, private mailboxes, and steamship-ticket sales. Anchored by All Saints, the RNH, and these other types of immigrant-driven spaces, the neighborhood bustled day and night with the changing of the shifts and the comings and goings of men and women who leaned on these many resources to make livings—and lives—in the Motor City.

Parish Administration

A new pastor came to All Saints during the summer of 1918. On the eve of his arrival, the congregation ratified a new parish statute that they hoped would eliminate the disputes that had driven out three predecessors over just four years. Previously, an elected committee oversaw parish affairs, including the supervision of clergy. Troubles emerged when parishioners discovered how much money their first priest, Isidor Salko, was receiving from *trebi* donations for sacraments and incidental services. Because All Saints was one of only two archdiocesan parishes in Michigan at the time, Salko's ministry extended throughout the state, as well as across the Detroit River to Ford City, Ontario, and a nascent congregation of automotive workers. Though often amounting to just a few coins, *trebi* donations added up quickly to substantially supplement Salko's meager salary. Wasili Rybko, the president of the parish committee at the time, later recalled that the committee launched an investigation. There was but a dollar in the parish safe at the time, yet in contrast, "Father Salko has so much money coming, seven hundred a month." A general parish vote capped Salko's monthly salary at $100 and require him to surrender any *trebi* fees earned in Michigan, though he could keep what he received in Canada. "Well, [Salko] don't like that rule, he said," Rybko recalled, "and he stay after that, month or two months" before returning across town to Ss. Peter and Paul. When Salko's successors too questioned these policies, Rybko reported that priests Wasil Oranovsky and Arcady Piotrowsky were told, "if you won't work on that rule, and that money, it is all right, if you don't you got to move out." Both did.[10]

The new parish statute that was passed in August 1918, shortly after Piotrowsky's departure, further solidified the committee's supervisory role, defining "under what conditions the new priest and his assistant are to remain." The priest was charged to serve as an intermediary "in the case of an accident with a Russian in the street, shop or in the suburbs of the city," in which case he "ought to offer his services and ought to investigate the accident." He and his family (if he had one) would live in an eight-room rectory, located next door to the church, where the parish owned the furniture and fixtures, down to the kitchen utensils. His monthly salary was kept at $100 (around $2,000 today). While this was somewhat higher than the average clerical salary in the Russian Archdiocese, it was still paltry, especially for a married priest.[11] The priest was to document *trebi* donations and meet with the committee chairman each Saturday evening to report what he had earned. By accepting these conditions, the statute explained, the pastor agreed that as a salaried employee, he had "no right whatsoever to manage the affairs of the church" and would "have nothing to do with the business affairs in the parish." Should he stray too far, a general parish vote could remove him.[12]

Above all, the statute underscored the great importance of control to working-class congregations like All Saints, juxtaposing the autonomy that lay adherents desired over a dominant institution in their lives against the hierarchical power dynamics and financial structures that otherwise governed an archdiocesan parish. At work, All Saints parishioners toiled on assembly lines and docks and labored in machine shops, beholden to overbearing bosses and paternalistic factory cultures of surveillance and supervision. As "floaters" and "five-day men" in Detroit's flexible, though sometimes fluctuating, labor market, they experienced the ebbs and flows of automotive production and the intentional replaceability of their scientifically managed labor, which made employment a constant question. At church, however, they were the managers and administrators. They fixed and paid their priest's salary, wrote the statute setting the conditions of his employment, and owned the rectory where he and his family lived. Parishioners privileged above all the feeling that their priest worked for them and that parish life depended on their choices.

Congregations like All Saints placed great emphasis on control, particularly in regards to finances. Parishioners took out the loans to purchase and renovate their church and made the mortgage payments, as was true for the RNH as well. Maintaining these and other budgetary commitments required a culture of small-scale giving embedded within parishioners' regular Orthodox practice. The statute that the congregation wrote and adopted in 1918 defined parish membership through monthly dues, which the committee treasurer recorded in a small ledger booklet issued to each member. Parishioners gave through *trebi* donations for sacraments and prayer services and dropped coins into candle stands and collection boxes. The parish also depended on supplementary support from parachurch organizations. These included the All Saints chapter of the Russian Orthodox Catholic Mutual Aid Society, as well as the unaffiliated brotherhood at the RNH. Both groups held great influence over parish administration. To belong to All Saints meant accepting such constant small-scale giving and parachurch participation, driving widespread lay assumptions that their persistent investments of time and treasure bought them greater say in parish management.

By the end of 1918, disagreements over parish administration and finances were pushing All Saints to the brink of collapse. Parishioners expressed increasing frustration with the archdiocese, beginning with the controversial and ineffectual Bishop Alexander (Nemolovsky). These misgivings also extended to the young clergyman whom Alexander sent to Detroit that summer. Twenty-seven-year-old priest Dimitri Darin was born and raised in Alaska, where he was a beneficiary of the church's social safety net for nearly all of his early life. Of mixed Russian and Alaska Native ancestry, Darin came from Ninilchik, a tiny settlement on the Kenai Peninsula. His father, Stephen, was a fisherman of Russian descent. His mother, Evdokia, came from the interconnected *kreol* kinship network that constituted the village from its founding as a missionary outpost in the 1840s, most of whose members could trace their ancestry to a single Alutiiq woman named Agrafena.[13] The Darin family was devout, with several family relatives holding leadership roles in the village's Orthodox parish. At the age of seven or eight, Dimitri was sent to live with an uncle at Fort Kenai and enrolled in its church-operated missionary school. With the death of his father two years later (probably by suicide), Dimitri was orphaned. Before Stephen Darin's passing, he expressed his wish that the church would care for his only son. Dimitri was taken in by the seminary at Sitka. In 1911, he was one of three seminarians selected by Archbishop Platon (Rozhdestvensky) to study in Minneapolis at the Russian Theological Seminary, where Darin met his future wife. Born in New Jersey to a Carpatho-Rusyn family, Anna Capitola was raised in Minneapolis near the St. Mary's church. The couple married there in 1912. Darin was ordained to the priesthood two years later and accepted a newly opened parish in Homestead, Pennsylvania. In August 1918, Bishop Alexander sent Darin to Detroit.[14]

The young priest's troubles began as soon as he arrived. The parish committee, emboldened by its new local statute, insisted that Darin and his family share the rectory with the parish *psalomshchik*, a stout man in his early thirties whose bachelor habits and unruly demeanor clashed against a clerical household with three young children.[15] Darin also argued with the committee over his meager salary. Parishioners who toiled in machine shops and automotive factories resented the idea that Darin would earn more than they did for what appeared to be far less time-consuming and physically demanding work. Though a priest for six years, Darin was around the same age, if not younger, than most of his parishioners, a difference that seemed to factor into how the congregation determined his labor conditions. When the committee offered $100 per month and use of the rectory, it was far less than the going rate if Darin were to go to Henry Ford's personnel office for a job on the assembly line. They further suppressed Darin's wages at weekly meetings, where they expected the priest to remit much of his *trebi* earnings, even though his growing family needed the money. Salary disputes were routine, even accepted in American Orthodox Rus'. Darin's parishioners knew that he weighed the demands imposed on him—expectations of time, attention, and intervention and also his limited earnings—against his fealty to the clerical vocation. The congregation expected that Darin would accept their conditions out of duty to his higher calling. If not, he easily could be reassigned to another, more amenable parish. After all, three far more experienced priests had left All Saints over similar issues of authority.

It was another issue, that of property, that elevated commonplace parish tensions to extraordinary heights. Like other priests in the archdiocese, including Vladimir Alexandrof in Chicago several years earlier, Darin pushed his parishioners to redeed their property in the name of the ruling bishop, not local committees or individual trustees. Around the time he came to Detroit, Darin attended one of the preconciliar clergy meetings convened to condemn priests mobilizing against Bishop Alexander (Nemolovsky) and knew the extent to which the archdiocese desired to make it more difficult for these and other clergy to take their parishes into independence, as his new parish seemed intent to accomplish for themselves—a move Darin found unacceptable.[16] As one All Saints parishioner later said, Darin "wants the church to belong to the bishop and we want the church shall belong to the people that are members of the church." The differences seemed insurmountable, yet Darin pressed the issue—risking a parish schism.[17]

Controversy

In reality, the property question at All Saints was a proxy battle for political disagreements within the congregation. By the spring of 1919, at the height of the postwar Red Scare, anarchist, socialist, and Bolshevik ideologies were commonplace in the All Saints neighborhood. Some parishioners took great interest in the political changes occurring in Russia after 1917, even eyeing a return to take part in the revolutionary transformation of the former empire. Red banners and portraits of Lenin and Debs hung in the RNH. The men who met there also gathered less than two miles south at the House of the Masses, a former German beer hall owned by the Michigan Socialist Party.[18] From early 1918, the building housed events for immigrant Detroiters, including Russian theater, German literary circles, and Ukrainian balls. A weeklong "Proletarian Bazaar" in February 1919 was restaged each evening for a different ethnic group, including Russians.[19] Often, the posters and handbills that advertised these events were produced at First Russian Typography, operated by the All Saints parishioner and RNH regular Nicholas Baikowsky. Located near the church on Chene Street, Baikowsky's print shop also stocked Russian-language socialist and anarchist books.[20]

Another fixture at the House of the Masses was the Detroit branch of the Soviet of Workers' Deputies. A pro-Bolshevik labor council, the group emphasized moral uplift, material support, self-determination, and community organization. It also had international policy ambitions, intending, "by means of agitation, to familiarize the American population of the city with the principles of the Soviets of Russia," doing so "in the struggle to support the principles of the Russian revolution."[21] In early 1919, representatives from the RNH began attending the Soviet's meetings and participating in its advocacy work. A unanimous resolution from the RNH to the group's New York headquarters demanded it "to petition the President of the United States to recognize the Soviet Government . . . and to open up the borders of the United States for the Russian Citizens, for those who want to return to Russia at once."[22] The RNH also depended on the Soviet for material aid. When the RNH mulled the construction of a larger building, Nicholas Baikowsky went to the House of the Masses to ask the Soviet for support.[23]

Darin blamed these political connections for the mounting discord in the congregation, claiming that those who were attempting to remove him from All Saints were acting out of loyalty to Bolsheviks and socialists and not to the Orthodox Church. The priest reported that revolutionary songs reverberated from the church basement during services and that once-pious and respectful parishioners disrupted worship with laughter and taunts.[24] Some allegedly demanded that Darin offer prayers for the Bolsheviks, just as he had once done for the imperial house. "At first they formulated plans to compel the priest to commemorate the Soviet authorities instead of the bishop," a church newspaper reported, "then to replace the icon of St. Nicholas the Wonderworker with a portrait of their patron Father—Nikolai Lenin."[25] With Bolshevism already becoming a fearsome byword in the United States, an icon of Lenin suggested potent and frightful implications. Federal investigators considered this an urgent threat in Detroit, where the conditions of automotive and industrial labor caused workers to seek out ideas and vocabularies that made meaning out of their lives in the Motor City. Some found them in socialist, communist, and anarchist groups. Under Darin's predecessors, perceptions of disloyalty and Bolshevik ties prompted a short-lived means for parishioners to mitigate encounters with the police. "A number of Russians were arrested; they could not speak English, and they were entirely at a loss as to what to do," one parishioner recalled, so "they were supposed to carry these cards in their pockets, and in case of any trouble, that in case of arrest, they would notify their Father, the priest of the church," who would then explain that the person "is a member of the church and not the radical, not the bolshevik."[26]

By late 1918, with parishioners frequenting spaces like the House of the Masses, Darin felt his tenuous grasp over the congregation slipping away. He no longer waited for authorities to contact him, instead proactively asking police to watch over services in the church and manage the unruly crowds gathered outside.[27] Tensions came to a head after an annual parish meeting, held on January 5, 1919. A new committee had been elected, whose composition mapped onto disagreements within the congregation over both the property issue and Darin's continued employment at the church. Two additional parish meetings held in January and February further demonstrated that there were now two factions, a majority of parishioners in opposition to Darin and a minority who maintained allegiance to the priest and the archdiocese. The divide was also tangibly political, in that the majority also constituted men who belonged to the RNH and broadly favored more revolutionary ideologies like those found at the House of the Masses. The majority was also advised by defrocked priest Constantin Leontovich, formerly of Lawrence, Massachusetts, who was now operating as an independent clergyman. Leontovich instructed the majority to take the church by force, change the locks, oust Darin, and declare All Saints an independent parish.[28]

On the evening of Saturday, March 8, the minority group loyal to Darin met in the basement church hall to discuss "a very critical and disorderly situation, that is owing to the agitation of the anti-church and bolshevik, their efforts to organize an independent church, and the others to completely destroy the church, and also to their interference in the church work, existing up to the present time, the order [of which] was entirely destroyed." These parishioners felt that the solution was to ensure that only "real members who attend services, and who uphold the church with their contributions" would manage parish affairs, what they called "the remaining true members" of their congregation. They proposed the formation of a new organization with "the sole object to protect the Russian All Saints Orthodox Church."[29] Three weeks later, around seventy people gathered again at the church hall, having received a postcard inviting them there. They heard the Darin loyalist Andrew Miniewsky and the parish committee chairman Anthony Mazur describe the formation of a "Church-Protecting Society" in support of

Darin and the archdiocese. Mazur alleged that the majority faction consisted of "anti-church members and bolshevists . . . [and] outsiders such as Polish and Jews" under the sway of the defrocked Leontovich, while their minority group constituted the "remaining true members" of All Saints. Mazur invited the parish committee secretary Makary Skurko to speak. Skurko was a leader of the anti-Darin faction and was to explain his group's position. He expressed his objections to Bishop Alexander and his archdiocese, expressing the need to reorganize All Saints "on the new fundamentals,—according to the wishes of comrades-bolsheviki!" The pro-Darin group listened, then voted to oust four parish committee members who had joined the majority faction, including Skurko, and to take back the parish records and books that Skurko retained—vowing to utilize civil courts if needed.

The minority group also drafted a new parish statute that they hoped would prevent the majority group from seizing parish properties, settling on a list of policies and regulations that their lawyer could later refine into proper, legal terminology. They defined All Saints as a parish under the authority of the archdiocese (the "Russian Mission") and served by a priest assigned by its ruling bishop ("Preferring the one the parishioners would like"). And they would deed parish properties in the names of "firm, faithful Orthodox people." Minutes of their meeting record that at this point the gathering was interrupted by "some of the anti-Church men," who "managed to get in and tried to break it up." Anticipating this, the parish committee had asked local police to be present. The officers stepped in and threw the offending individuals out of the church. The minutes bear fifty signatures, though others did not sign due to illiteracy or the need to return home. Affixed to the end of these minutes is a peculiar, unsigned addendum. It reiterated that the "Church-Protecting Society" was not a separate group but rather *was* the parish, "good members, religious, respecting the church and who do not belong to the Anti-Church organization." A structure of membership dues would make it possible for them to discern a church member from a nonmember and allow a voice to churchgoing parishioners whom the committee felt were marginalized by more boisterous, radical members who were said to seldom attend services. Though much smaller than the majority group, the society saw itself as "the only hope of restoring order to the parish and thereby saving the church." They did not wish to

226 | "THESE RADICALS"

close the church's doors to anyone. Still, they pledged to expel "all those that are known to be agitating against the church." To further distinguish themselves from the majority, or "Bolsheviki," faction, members of the Church-Protecting Society agreed to no longer refer to one another as "Comrade."[30]

Several Church-Protecting Society members were also engaged in a simultaneous and separate endeavor to destabilize the majority faction. On March 21 and 22, three men—the tailor Andrew Miniewsky, a tailor, and Peter Dobritzky and Wassil Pastuchak, both automotive machinists—met with Joseph Apelman. In collaboration with other BI agents, Apelman had been surveilling the All Saints neighborhood since 1918, including the RNH, which the agents considered to be a "Bolshevik hall." Apelman met his informants next door at the Russian Consultation Bureau. Over two evenings, the three men signed a series of affidavits against thirteen others, all concerning a meeting at the RNH on March 9. The informants alleged hearing statements that criticized the US government, decried US capitalism, and offered vague threats against public officials—all of which aligned closely with specific examples of prohibited speech outlined in a critical subsection of the Immigration Act of 1918. The thirteen men were leaders at the RNH, and most were dedicated All Saints parishioners. None were US citizens. Apelman paired each affidavit with a request for an arrest warrant and the initiation of deportation proceedings.[31]

Arrests in the neighborhood began on April 12. Some suspects were roused from their beds and had their homes ransacked for "radical" literature. Others were rounded up at the RNH. Friends and loved ones traveled downtown to stand vigil at the Wayne County jail, passing food and cigarettes through the bars. A meeting convened at the RNH to pool resources for bail bonds, assembling for collateral stacks of Liberty Loan certificates purchased during the war. The arrests cast a heavy pall over the All Saints neighborhood. Most parishioners cast blame on Darin and his small group of followers. Initially, most of the men were represented by lawyers affiliated with the Michigan Socialist Party.[32] One of them, Lazarus Davidow, told the *Detroit News* that the situation allegedly "came from advocates of the plan of the priest, who came to the church six months ago," and that an immigration inspector privately told him as much. Davidow claimed that the inspector said that "he really knew nothing about the men and that as far as he knew the trouble might have grown out of the church controversy."[33]

No longer were parishioners' primary grievances those long-standing clashes over administrative control or disagreements about *trebi* donations and salaries. Now it seemed as if their priest was a double agent with political motivations. BI investigation files show that Darin was familiar with Apelman and knew of BI surveillance in the neighborhood. Later, Apelman hired Darin to serve as a paid government translator for immigration hearings, including several involving his own parishioners. Many in the neighborhood took this to mean that the priest was an informer (if not a federal agent) and that he supported the potential result of the hearings—the permanent deportation of parishioners under his spiritual care. Yet there is no evidence that Darin directly informed on any of the men, and he took great pains in later court testimony to separate himself from the deportation proceedings. "There was not one affidavit made out in my church," he said. Yet it was a careful choice of words, for Darin could have been just as aware that affidavits were being signed at the Russian Consultation Bureau instead.[34]

On Sunday, April 13, the morning after the first arrests, Darin was handed a slip of paper with an announcement for a general parish meeting that afternoon at the RNH. At the end of services, he pulled the note from under his vestments, read the announcement, and made it clear that he would not attend. Hours later, 400 parishioners met down the block and cast ballots on the fate of their priest; 385 voted that Darin be removed, stating their intentions "to invite another Reverend who will act in accordance with the wish of all the parishioners of the above church and serve them as a Reverend Father and honest leader of the parish community."[35] Their statute allowed for this. Under most circumstances, an expelled priest would pack up and accept another parish assignment. Yet the clear political divide within the parish, and the ardent support of a vocal minority, made Darin think twice. He also had the support of Bishop Alexander, who told the priest to "stay at his guns." Darin refused to leave, reasoning that because he had not chaired the meeting and also because it had occurred at the RNH instead of the church, the voting attendees had violated their statute. His message to the congregation was clear: "I defy you to put me out."[36]

Given Darin's tacit support of the arrests, as well as his open threats against the congregation, parishioners saw his periodic government employment as a breach of trust, if not a clear betrayal. According to Nicholas Baikowsky, one of the first to be arrested, Darin claimed that "he 'would get' those who opposed him." Baikowsky later wrote that he believed that "this promiscuous arrest of innocent persons has utterly terrorized the congregation of the Russian Orthodox All Saints Church, and that a great many of the congregation are living in daily dread of being arrested and deported."[37] Darin's presence in immigration courtrooms as an interpreter provided him insight into the government's cases against his own parishioners, as well as the ability to perhaps mold their testimony toward his interests. "The result of this action on the part of the government has been to create grave doubt in the minds of the Russians who belong to the Church as to any protection they can expect under the laws of the United States Government," the lawyer Lazarus Davidow wrote in an appeal to Attorney General A. Mitchell Palmer. "Men have been arrested at all hours of the night, taken from their beds, brutally beaten up and kept incommunicado in jail for periods of two to three to four days before being allowed to see their attorneys or friends. The purpose of Rev. Darin, namely to intimidate the members of the Congregation and thereby crush all opposition to him is being very nicely accomplished as to what has taken place and Rev. Darin has threatened would take place in the future regarding any others who would dare oppose him."[38]

On May 4, four hundred people met at the Russian National Home to ratify a message to the Department of Justice from the "Russians of Detroit." The statement alleged that in retaliation against the arrests, "the minister personally and through some of the members of the [former] Board commenced to make a series of unfounded and unsupported complaints and charges against the new Board of Trustees to the Resident Agent of the [BI]" and, in doing so, was "charging the men with various crimes along the lines of alleged revolutionary affiliations of these members, to-wit, Anarchistic, Socialistic, Bolshevist, and what not." They felt that Justice Department agents had inserted themselves into an internal community dispute and, "on account of their ignorance as to what was actually transpiring in this church row, lent their assistance of officers of the law, thereby taking sides in a purely private matter, with which said officers ought not have had anything to do." With their community "in a state of great agitation and despair," they felt that the federal government threatened their well-being. "It has reached now the point where the parishioners and particularly members of the newly elected Board are unable to fulfill their duties as officers of the church," they claimed, "and even any of the parishioners is prevented from mentioning a word against the minister or some of the members of the old Board, being in constant fear of being immediately apprehended, thrown into jail and having proceedings commenced against them by the immigration authorities under the request of the officials of the Department of Justice."[39]

Darin and his backers engaged the state in order to preserve the east side Russian Colony. Instead they shattered it from within. Many of those who were involved in the cases saw the arrests as a misstep that occurred only because of the church dispute. In the words of Immigration Inspector John Clark, "it is to be regretted that our Service has been made the instrument through which certain disgruntled persons of the church mentioned have sought to injure others of the congregation."[40] For Walter Nelson, the attorney who represented both the majority faction and many of the arrested men, the local situation was a national disgrace. "Verily is our proud flag not the emblem of law and justice, but the cloak of scoundrels," Nelson wrote in defense of one All Saints client, "and the eagle has become the croaking parrot of their lies and calumny."[41] The deportation cases of All Saints parishioners were inching through a US immigration infrastructure bogged down with thousands of other investigation files generated during the Red Scare. In the meantime, the parish controversy moved from immigration hearings into civil courtrooms, placing the future of the congregation in the hands of lawyers and judges and the whims of church property litigation.

Property Litigation

Filed in July 1919, *All Saints v. Darin et al.* joined a long discussion of US jurisprudence on property ownership in hierarchical churches that began with American Catholic disputes over "trusteeism" during the nineteenth century As Roman Catholicism expanded in the antebellum United States, congregations clashed with their church over clerical employment, financial control, and most of all, property ownership. Navigating a patchwork of state laws and local practices governing religious incorporation in a country dominated by congregationalist Protestants, Catholic communities empowered boards of trustees to manage parish life. Predictably, clashes erupted between clergy and laity and also among the laity themselves. Patrick Carey observes in his history of trusteeism that while certainly rooted in the European experience, the controversy "arose from American republicanism, legal structures, changing social conditions, and the hegemony of American Protestant ecclesiastical practices."[42] Diverging from the Vatican and diocesan bishops, many lay American Catholics favored a sense of voluntarism at the local level, feeling ownership over land, buildings, church fixtures, and liturgical items that they had bought and paid for—knowing that their clergy believed that these things actually belonged to the church. American Catholic bishops largely stamped out trusteeism before the Civil War. Yet the top-down, hierarchical system of property ownership enforced in their dioceses still contrasted with how state courts perceived other religious property claims.[43]

The United States Supreme Court clarified questions of religious property in *Watson v. Jones* (1872), a dispute over a Presbyterian church in Kentucky. Under the precedent set in *Watson*, state and federal civil courts were to adjudicate other religious property cases using neutral principles of law, sidestepping questions of dogma or belief to focus instead on property deeds, articles of incorporation, and institutional bylaws. In general, courts employed such evidence to determine only the highest identifiable ecclesiastical authority, which the court would permit to follow its own respective decision-making and administrative processes. This test of authority became the determinative factor in assigning property rights.[44] In light of *Watson*, the All Saints case is an early and rich example of how Orthodox churches struggled to present their religious traditions in court. "The American courts have almost no idea of what Orthodoxy is, and often even confuse it with Judaism, since the Jewish communities in America also use the title 'Orthodox,'" Archbishop Evdokim (Meschersky) noted in 1917. "Our church laws are for American judges an empty sound."[45] For subsequent generations of Orthodox believers in the United States, contorting their beliefs, practices, and senses of authority to achieve intended legal outcomes affected how

Orthodox Christianity would be practiced in North America. "While church language migrates unevenly across legal and political domains and back," the religious law scholar Winnifred Fallers Sullivan argues, "there is a kind of phenomenological exchange between how law imagines law and religion and their relationship and how religion imagines them."[46] Russian Orthodox clergy and laity of the Progressive era struggled in similar ways to adapt their church and its structures to US understandings of church governance and jurisprudence. The All Saints factions engaged this delicate dance of making their faith legible to the court, just as the court endeavored to fit Orthodoxy within precedents established with very different religious traditions in mind.

The All Saints case revolved around a critical fact: there were two All Saints congregations registered as religious corporations with the state of Michigan. From the founding of All Saints in 1914, the parish had operated as a voluntary, unincorporated religious body with its properties deeded in the name of the parish committee. The congregation had little awareness of incorporation and its legal importance. When the parish fractured in early 1919, property deeds and incorporation defined how each faction articulated its position. Having installed a new committee to supplant the one elected at the regular parish elections that January, the majority faction incorporated with the state in early May as the Russian Orthodox All Saints Church of Detroit. Three weeks later, the minority faction did the same, incorporating themselves and a separate slate of trustees as the All Saints Russian Orthodox Greek Catholic Church. Both claimed to be the legal All Saints parish. In July, the majority faction brought suit, asking the court to determine which group truly was the parish and, in turn, which parish committee owned its properties.[47]

For more than two years, the case lingered on the court docket. On the east side, community life in the All Saints neighborhood slowed. Shuttered by a court order from separate civil litigation, the RNH fell into ruin. Neighborhood boys made a game of breaking its windows with rocks, and the front door dangled from its hinges. During the harsh winter of 1920–21, the building's pipes burst, ruining the RNH society's technical library and encasing its instructional factory equipment in ice and snow.[48] Down the block, parish activities at All Saints halted. Darin, with the minority faction and the archdiocese behind him, remained the pastor and also the dean of the Detroit district and still lived with his family in the rectory. Yet the majority faction still held the keys to the church and did not permit him to offer services. As one parish history later recalled of this period, there had "in fact been no All Saints parish."[49] Darin remained defiant, though he was known to be considering a new career in business.[50]

The congregation still reeled from the arrests of parishioners during the Red Scare. Dozens had been detained, the first as a result of the parish controversy and yet more in the Palmer Raids of January 1920, perhaps as many as one hundred. Some cases remained active for more than a year. Suspects awaited deportation decisions under indefinite and constraining bail agreements, while their family and friends struggled to secure the return of precious savings and liquid assets that bond companies still held as collateral. Some of those who were most adversely affected by the controversies of 1919 had left Detroit, if not the United States. A few were formally deported. Others set sail on their own accord, enamored by the utopian possibilities of Bolshevism. For yet more, poor job prospects in Detroit's sagging industrial economy drove them from the city. The closing of lucrative military contracts caused shops and factories to slash employment rolls. To make matters worse, consumer demand for automobiles had gone stagnant. The Motor City had produced so many, and made them so well, that most Americans who wanted a car already had one and had no need to buy a newer model that was little different from what they already owned. As a result, the congregation litigating the case in 1921 was markedly different from that which brought the case two years earlier, smaller and with fewer resources.

When the case reached trial at last in September 1921, the majority faction offered three rationales for their legal rights to become an independent parish and control the property. First, they claimed that Darin was a financially corrupt and heavy-handed administrator, absconding with *trebi* donations, excluding those with whom he disagreed (and even contributing to their potential deportations), and ignoring the will of the congregation. He denied majority faction leaders the eucharist, called police to monitor services, and most egregiously, participated in, and even contributed to, the arrests and threatened deportation of more than a dozen men. Plaintiff witnesses expressed outrage that Darin had served as a translator at immigration court, taking it as evidence that their priest had been a federal informer or even an agent. And they claimed Darin took more money than was allowed under their parish statute. To prove this, the plaintiffs called to the stand a former All Saints parishioner, Julia Rymchanko, to prove that Darin had absconded with church funds. Julia and her husband, Mike, kept a grocery store and butcher shop at their home on Newton Avenue, north of All Saints at the border of Detroit and Hamtramck. On March 8, 1919, Mike was socializing with his next-door neighbor when a third man, Carl Sowka, shot him to death in a dispute over three hundred bottles of whiskey, presumably to be sold under the counter at the grocery store.[51] Darin ministered to Julia after Mike's murder, visiting her home, presiding over the funeral and burial, and offering several requiem (*panikhida*) services, for which Julia gave Darin a *trebi* donation. The day before the trial began, Makary Skurko and another plaintiff, Wasili Rybko, visited the grocery store to buy cigarettes. They pressed Julia to reveal how much money she had given Darin. Julia was hesitant, as she had remarried and fallen away from All Saints and was loath to revisit the trauma of Mike's murder. On the witness stand, Julia was no less reluctant, alluding that her husband "was killed" and offering vague, evasive responses about what happened after his death. She suggested that her *trebi* donation was between 25 and 50 dollars, covering three home visits, the funeral, several cross-town trips to Woodmere Cemetery, and requiem prayers. Skurko claimed, however, that Darin pocketed much of the money. "He was not entitled to it, the committee had to receive the money," Skurko said. "I received from him a voucher, only $12."[52]

Second, the majority claimed that after Evdokim's departure in 1917, Alexander had assumed control of the archdiocese as an illegitimate and morally dubious usurper, meaning that there was no valid ecclesiastical hierarchy to appoint Darin to the parish a year later. The majority faction offered a convoluted and counterfactual argument to explain their position, leaning heavily on a misconception common to the prerevolutionary era that the ecclesiastical head of the Russian Church had been the tsar himself.[53] The abdication of Tsar Nicholas II in 1917, they argued, shifted the church into subservience to the Bolsheviks, the prevailing government in Russia. The Russian Church had prayed for the tsar. Now it should pray for Lenin. But as the Bolsheviks had not stepped in to replicate such an arrangement, the Russian Church was now a defunct institution with no ecclesiastical authority. The chain had been broken, with its constituent parishes subsequently free to do as they wished. In America, they asserted, Alexander had convened a rigged church council to ensure his own election as the permanent head of the archdiocese. By their account, Alexander had little standing or reputation, more or less a man off the street and not a long-standing missionary clergyman in North America, with no right to assign Darin to All Saints.

What was more, they alleged that Alexander was dangerous, even morally corrupt. They introduced into evidence an incendiary pamphlet, "How Thinks, How Feels and How Teaches about America Alexander Nemolovsky, Canadian Bishop." It reprinted passages from articles published in the parachurch newspaper *Russkaia zemlia* (*Russian Land*) in 1916, which were translated into English by the suspended priest Paul Beskishkin of Bayonne, New Jersey. Beskishkin asserted that their pseudonymous author, "Black Diamond," was in truth Alexander. Each passage painted the bishop as anti-American, critical of the US government and US social norms, culture, and moral values. Beskishkin appealed for Russians to mobilize against Alexander, to "join hands with the American people . . . to follow in everything Washington-Lincoln-Wilson as great and unselfish friends of humanity and democracy here and all over the world." It was a strange inversion, deflecting against charges of radical and anti-American ideologies by asserting that the true radical was the archbishop himself.[54]

And third, the majority faction claimed that even if Darin had been appointed to the parish, its congregation was within their legal rights to incorporate with the state, adopt a statute, and follow its tenets when terminating his employment. That statute, passed prior to Darin's arrival in the city, comprised fourteen relatively brief points that tilted most power toward the congregation. It considered the pastor little more than a hired liturgical hand with a variety of social, educational, and even janitorial duties. The pastor (and his assistant, if a *psalomshchik* or deacon was also employed, at a salary of $60 per month) was to operate schools for children and adults, intervene on behalf of parishioners who suffered accidents "in the street, shop or in the suburbs of the city," and even to "look after the cleanliness of the church and the outside, for they live right there." Yet they were to do so only under the close supervision and judgment of the parish. Upon arrival, they were to "apply to the church committee first," which would then "state under what conditions the new priest and his assistant are to remain." They were "not to receive anything into church without the consent of the committee and the parishioners" and would "perform sermons and all church duties promptly and on time." For those parishioners who might "hire them" to perform sacraments, they were to keep close records and report their income each Saturday night. And above all, "they have no right whatever to manage the affairs of the church, for they receive a salary and have nothing to do with the business affairs of the parish." A parish meeting would be called if they did not "live up to their duties."[55] In the estimation of the plaintiffs, Darin had not done so. "The duties of the priest of the church is only to attend to the services, read masses," a parish trustee for the majority faction explained. "It has nothing to do with general economic standing of the church; it has to do with the religious part of the church only." The congregation had adhered to their statute when they called a meeting to discuss Darin's "failure" as pastor and also when they voted to remove him. They asserted that as the legal and valid All Saints parish, their congregation had every right to manage their own affairs through democratic consensus and were doing so.[56]

Darin's defense countered with a seemingly straightforward, though tenuous, argument. The priest maintained that he had been sent to the parish by Alexander, a valid bishop under the ecclesiastical supervision of the Moscow Patriarchate. As the legitimate pastor of All Saints, Darin asserted the right to determine who constituted its congregation. In his estimation, the majority faction had abdicated their standing in the Orthodox Church because they were "Bolsheviki." They held parish elections and convened meetings at the RNH in his absence, facts he offered as proof that the majority had left the congregation. His several weeks of interpreting work aside, Darin denied serving as a federal agent or informant or having sworn affidavits against any parishioner. He admitted calling on the police to preserve order at All Saints but countered that doing so did not make him a government agent. Darin repeatedly stressed that his motivations were twofold: that the Russian Orthodox Church, his lifelong faith, be protected from Bolshevik antireligious antagonism and that the United States, his native country, be preserved from Bolshevik revolutionaries. Backed by both the archdiocese and his supporters from the Church-Protecting Society, Darin felt he was doing nothing less than saving the All Saints parish from radical "Reds" who aimed to close the church and defile it as a social club. These congregants, he testified, were those "that have broken away from the church, after the revolution in Russia naturally were spreading their propaganda right here in the United States, and here in Detroit that had big influence on the church," and people, he claimed, "wanted and tried to destroy the church as I know real well, wanted to destroy the church I am in."[57]

The defense struggled to make this case. Judge Charles Collingwood denied their attempts to call an Episcopalian clergyman who could testify to Orthodox ecclesiology and the post-1917 Russian Church.[58] Darin strained to articulate his connections to the archdiocese, fumbled in his attempts to explain the circumstances of Alexander's ascendance as temporary administrator and the proceedings of the church council in Cleveland that had elected Alexander as bishop, and struggled to help the court understand the nuances in how the 1909 archdiocesan statute defined "independent" and "dependent" parishes. When pressed to provide documentation that Alexander had assigned him to Detroit, Darin offered instead contrarian impatience, then pointed to his name in a list of pastoral changes printed in the Russian Clergy League newspaper *Golos tserkvi* (*Voice of the Church*). His claims that majority faction meetings and votes were invalid held little weight, as it could be demonstrated that many parish meetings were held in the Russian National Home, as opposed to the cramped quarters of the church, and that his chairmanship was unnecessary under the parish statute. And despite the stakes of the case and archdiocesan support for Darin's position, the national church offered little material or evidentiary support. It provided no affidavits attesting to Darin's pastoral authority, nor did it dispatch expert witnesses or informed advisers to bolster his case. It seems that the minority faction was on its own. Darin and his defense team, building their case using Red Scare political rhetoric and their notions of religious fidelity instead of on established legal precedent, could not help Collingwood recognize the forest for the trees.

In the September 1921 decision, Collingwood acknowledged the time of troubles at All Saints after the Bolshevik Revolution. He found that Darin "was not in sympathy with the political ideas of the majority of the original congregation" and inferred that Darin's opposition to the majority faction "was aided by the facts that not only did he represent the spiritual authority of the church, but by inference at least, he represented our Government to [which] he had been most useful." Collingwood considered Darin to be generally honest "but strongly prejudiced by the outcome of the Revolution in Russia." The judge was not convinced that Darin and his followers had legal claim to the properties. Because the majority faction committee had incorporated first, consistently kept to their established statute, and retained and continued to use the original parish ledgers and record books, Collingwood determined that they constituted the true All Saints parish. Collingwood concluded, "this Court is not aware of any method in law or equity by which the priest or pastor can organize a minority organization which shall deprive the majority of their property rights even though this majority sympathized with the Bolsheviki." In other words, even Bolsheviks had a right to property. In a decree issued two weeks later, Collingwood ordered the church, rectory, and all pertinent documents transferred to the majority committee. In his view, "this church, parish and congregation . . . is an independent parish."[59]

Almost concurrently with Collingwood's decision, the archdiocese reassigned Darin to a parish in Chisholm, Minnesota, two hundred miles north of Minneapolis. Instead, Darin went sixty miles north of Detroit to Flint and joined the Greek Catholic Church, which received him as a married priest.[60] The move angered his supporters at All Saints, who had defended their embattled priest through two difficult years only for him to leave the Orthodox Church to become—of all things—a Greek Catholic. "Though Fr. D. Darin has abandoned us and has caused us great resentment," minority faction representatives wrote Alexander in 1922, "through the mercy of God and Your Most Eminence we are fighting and will win the Church into our hands."[61] As the minority's appeal awaited a hearing, they obtained a court order to prevent the majority faction from installing another priest at All Saints, and then another.[62] They also resisted efforts by the archdiocese to name a priest as well, taking the counsel of their attorney that to do so might damage their legal position. Community life continued at a stalemate. The All Saints church remained locked.[63]

In March 1923, the Michigan Supreme Court issued its final ruling in the case. The previous summer, the minority faction's appeal had argued that a civil court "had no jurisdiction to try the titles of church dignitaries and declare the election of archbishops to be illegal and unlawful, unless said archbishop is made a party to the suit." Arguing that they had never "closed the doors to any person . . . for worshipping purposes in a peaceful and quiet manner," they argued that Darin was within his rights as pastor to turn away those who he felt were disruptive to parish life. And since the majority faction were "Bolsheviki," they had not even been church members in good standing.[64] The Supreme Court disagreed. In its decision, the justices found the argument that the majority faction had abandoned the Orthodox Church by denying its hierarchy and forming an independent congregation to be an "extreme view" that was "not well sustained by convincing evidence." Merely saying one's opponents were no longer Orthodox did not make it so, nor did an institutional schism necessarily represent doctrinal differences. "There is little proof beyond assertion by defendants of any religious schism or division by reason of diversity of opinion on matters of faith and doctrine," the justices wrote. "While abundance of ill-feeling and intolerance is manifested, both parties strenuously claim adherence to the tenets and doctrines of the church."[65]

The justices also molded their decision to their reading of how the 1909 archdiocesan statute defined an independent parish. As described previously, the statute set out an administrative system intended to foster missionary growth. An "independent" parish was a congregation that was able to financially support a church and a pastor and that was a missionary hub for smaller, "dependent" parishes. In Russian, such a parish was described using the adjective *samostoiatel'nyi*, the state of being self-sufficient, literally to stand on one's own. This was a different concept of independence from parishes like St. George in Chicago, which used a different adjective, *nezavisimyi*, or the state of administrative independence. This was the terminology used at All Saints as well. This subtle difference was of great importance, yet the court's opinion lacked any such nuanced reading. Presented only with the English translation of the statute, an "independent parish" was taken at face value and, apparently, without a careful reading of the paragraph in which the term was explained. More importantly, the court followed precedent from similar church property cases and determined that adjudicating theology, dogma, and the legitimacy of religious authority was outside its purview. The justices agreed with Collingwood that the majority faction had maintained the parish books, had followed the spirit of their parish statute, and had established a system by which a voting majority could remove a pastor at any time. As such, it spoke for the parish. "So far as the temporal affairs of this congregation are concerned they are subject to that sound principle which underlies all our civic institutions," the justices wrote, "that in every organized society the controlling power rests with the majority."[66] In other words, as a parish governed by congregational rule, a majority vote of the parish was necessary to resolve disputes over property.

Rather than handing over the property to the majority, the justices remanded the case back to the lower court and instructed the Wayne County Circuit to oversee a parish election to determine who constituted the parish committee. Collingwood's 1921 decision would remain in place until the congregation could have its say. Only those whose names were on the January 1919 membership list, the final recorded ledger before the split, would be allowed a ballot.[67] The court-ordered election was held on April 21, 1923, at the Wayne County Building in downtown Detroit. It was overseen by a local lawyer who was not affiliated with the case. On the ballot were slates proposed by each faction. At the final tally, the majority slate won a predictable and decisive victory. The court ratified the election two days later. The minority faction sent a representative to a majority faction meeting to announce their intention to mount yet another appeal. For the moment, however, the archdiocese had lost All Saints.[68]

Between 1918 and 1923, the All Saints congregation ruptured over the question of what it meant to belong to the Russian Orthodox Church after the rise of Bolshevism in Russia. That the conflict even occurred at all was because elements of disagreement common to the parishes of American Orthodox Rus'—finances, property, clerical administration—took on greater, politicized meanings in the tinder box of Red Scare Detroit. From BI investigations to court-room dramas, All Saints parishioners marshaled the power of the state to adjudicate what all recognized as a political clash rooted in a church disagreement. First, political disagreements brought federal surveillance, congregational schism, and arrests of parishioners on allegations of radicalism. Then came litigation, which made church properties surrogates for ideological disagreements within the parish. Finally came negotiation, restructuring, and rebirth into a new All Saints congregation that would remain at the corner of Hendrie and Jos. Campau for another seventy-five years. Yet this was a lengthy and acrimonious ordeal that many parishioners were inclined to forget. As one of the first Orthodox parishes in the United States to litigate the ecclesiology of their church, All Saints parishioners portended more than a century of similar Orthodox property jurisprudence, several examples of which reached the United States Supreme Court.[69]

The All Saints dispute was also a tale of xenophobia and hysteria, trampled civil liberties and tightening immigration policies, and over time, the lasting scars of the Red Scare on Detroit's east side. Several men were deported, and others lost significant financial resources in securing bail for parishioners arrested in the raids of April 1919. By lodging allegations of radicalism, community members—and their priest—instrumentalized the nativism and paranoia of government officials, placing fellow Orthodox Christians at the mercy of the Red Scare surveillance and deportation state. It is clear that the majority of All Saints parishioners had embraced radical political ideologies to some degree. These concepts helped them to understand how Detroit industry thrived on their labor, and they sought a path toward social stability and economic prosperity that depended on investment and involvement in their immigrant neighborhood. As Darin and his followers saw it, however, the question was whether those ideologies were inimical to the Orthodox Christian faith. The majority faction did not see it that way. Contrary to Darin's allegations, they wished to keep their church open and continue parish life on their own terms. After all, for Darin to deny alleged "Bolsheviki" the chalice, they had to desire the eucharist—and they did. Through their "daily dread," as the arrested parishioner (and eventual self-deportee) Nicholas Baikowsky called their plight, the All Saints congregation saw their social and religious worlds wither before a nation that could not see them as anything other than "reds."

There is one more story of All Saints that bears telling. It begins with an unusual letter preserved in the archives of the Orthodox Church in America, the institutional successor to the Russian Archdiocese. Writing to Bishop Alexander (Nemolovsky) in late 1918, All Saints pastor Arcady Piotrowsky reported that one of his most fervent parishioners, Evdokim

Swirid, wished to obtain an ecclesiastical divorce by mail. Swirid came to the United States in 1912 intending to return to his wife and sons in a rural village of the Volyn region, today in northwestern Ukraine. Six years later, after the changes of 1917 and the outbreak of the Russian Civil War, he had decided to remain in the Motor City. Russian Church guidelines for granting a divorce had recently changed, and with apparent difficulties contacting Swirid's wife, Mokryna, it seems that neither Alexander nor Piotrowsky could sort out the situation.[70]

When Piotrowsky departed All Saints later that year, the divorce question remained unresolved. Evdokim Swirid took an active role in the parish dispute under Piotrowsky's successor, Dimitri Darin. Though once a member of the fraternal society at the Russian National Home, Swirid joined the Church-Protecting Society in support of Darin. He served on the minority faction committee and was its unsuccessful candidate for parish president in the court-ordered election of 1923. Later that year, Swirid chaired a community meeting that helped steer the still-divided factions toward a resolution in the property controversy. Under an agreement settled on in September 1923, the minority faction paid the majority group $6,000 and assumed $10,000 more in unpaid mortgage principal and interest, receiving the church and rectory in return. The majority faction kept the Russian National Home and agreed to dissolve their state incorporation. The minority group took possession of the church—despite majority stalwart Makary Skurko attempting to empty the building of its contents before doing so—and reopened under the leadership of a new monastic priest, Paul Gavriloff. Within months, the reunified congregation reestablished the All Saints brotherhood, ratified a more ironclad parish statute, and raised more than $5,000 to pay down their debts. In 1924, the archdiocese rewarded them by raising All Saints to the status of a cathedral and making it once again the seat of the Detroit deanery. After years of acrimony, All Saints was back in the archdiocesan fold.[71]

During these years, Evdokim Swirid served as a parish trustee and also as its *starosta* (parish elder). In 1926, he became a US citizen, using the onetime BI informant and fellow Darin supporter Andrew Miniewsky as one of his character references. Soon thereafter, Swirid obtained his long-sought divorce. Evdokim was given a choice: he could send money to Mokryna and her sons, or he could bring two of the boys to Detroit. They would arrive as US citizens and work on their father's bee farm in suburban Royal Oak. Because of Evdokim's decision, two emaciated teenagers arrived at his door in the spring of 1928. One of them was my grandfather, Ioann Evdokimovich Sviridov.

Epilogue

Stories of Knowing

For now we see in a mirror, dimly, but then we will see face
to face. Now I know only in part; then I will know fully, even
as I have been fully known.
—1 Corinthians 13:12

In early 1914, Wasil left New York City for Detroit and Henry Ford's five-dollar daily wage. Once he was hired at Ford's famed Highland Park assembly plant, Anna boarded a train with their three young children. She was visibly pregnant with their fourth, my grandmother, who was born in the Motor City that summer. Two years later, Anna wrote from Detroit to St. Nicholas Cathedral to obtain their family's sacramental records from their time in New York City. In the Manhattan consistory offices, the cathedral deacon pulled out the heavy books of sacramental records and carefully transcribed into a preprinted form the entries for Wasil and Anna's marriage and the baptisms of their three eldest children. He handed the document to priest Leonid Turkevich, who signed it and affixed the cathedral seal.

Nearly a century later, early in the research for this book, I sat with my grandmother at her kitchen table. I had been thinking a lot about the Manhattan cathedral and wondered if she had documentation for her parents' marriage there. I followed her to her bedroom. She sat on the edge of the bed and opened the bottom drawer of the metal file cabinet where she kept her important papers. A few moments later, she passed a manila folder over her shoulder. On the weathered pages inside, I recognized at once Turkevich's meticulous, spidery signature. And there was the name of priest Alexander Hotovitzky, who baptized Olga, my grandmother's eldest sister, and also that of priest John Slunin, who baptized Mary, the last of the children to be born in New York. But it was

244 | EPILOGUE

the entries for Wasil and Anna's marriage and the baptism of Vladimir, their first child, that brought me pause. Each bore the name of a priest whose name I did not recognize: Father Ilia Zotikov.

My great-grandparents married at St. Nicholas shortly after it became the center of the North American Archdiocese. Wasil was a social club porter in the city, and Anna was a cigar roller across the Hudson in Passaic. Both worshiped at the cathedral, and their first three children were baptized there in the bustling epicenter of American Orthodox Rus'. Two more entered the world in Detroit, the boomtown center of US industrial production and already one of the largest and most diverse Orthodox regional communities in the United States. For people and families like them, immigrant and first-generation Americans whose personal ties bound them mostly to the western reaches of the Russian Empire and the Carpathian Mountains of Austria-Hungary, American Orthodox Rus' was a transnational space that connected them with an idealized vision of Holy Orthodox Rus' as much as it was a source for social, material, and spiritual aid. In their transnational community, priests like Alexander Hotovitzky and Ilia Zotikov were sources of spiritual support as much as everyday counsel and assistance. With the passing years, however, their paths diverged. Ford's assembly lines drew Wasil and his family to Detroit. For Hotovitzky and Zotikov, the priests who helped them in New York, the transnational institution of the Russian Church beckoned them back across the ocean, where each began new positions for the church at the cusp of the First World War. Just as shared histories in American Orthodox Rus' tied them together, so were they linked by the tragedies that befell the Russian Orthodox Church under communism, hardships felt both in the United States and in the Soviet Union.

My grandmother was a toddler in Detroit when Tsar Nicholas II abdicated his throne in a rail car idled outside Pskov. Her adult life blossomed at the outset of the Cold War, when to be a Russian Orthodox Christian in North America meant situating oneself within an ecclesiastical identity that aligned believers just as much with an Orthodox bishop and "jurisdiction" as it did a general geopolitical thrust. These dynamics began across town on Detroit's east side when on April 2, 1924, priest Leonid Turkevich and Bishop Theophilus (Pashkovsky) celebrated a Liturgy of the Presanctified Gifts and service of thanksgiving (*molieben*) at All Saints Cathedral. These services marked the opening of a church council convened to address the many crises affecting the North American Archdiocese. For the people of American Orthodox Rus', the changing political landscape in Russia after 1917 was a tangible and personal phenomenon, one that affected the Russian Church in general and their ecclesiastical ties to its administration. The small All Saints sanctuary, however, could not facilitate a meeting of nearly 150 clergy and lay delegates. When services concluded, the council relocated downtown to the parish house of the Episcopal Cathedral of St. John for its first plenary session.

The Detroit council aimed to restore administrative regularity to American Orthodox Rus' in the face of continuing financial crises and ongoing property litigation. They turned to instructions from Patriarch Tikhon, by then subjected to imprisonment and house arrest, who in November 1920 offered a critical directive for bishops and dioceses who found themselves outside Russian borders and out of contact with their ecclesiastical leaders. In such cases, he instructed that "the bishop immediately enters into relations with the bishops of neighboring dioceses for the purpose of organizing a higher instance of ecclesiastical authority for several dioceses in similar conditions (in the form either of a temporary Supreme Church government or a Metropolitan district, or anything else)."[1] Given the ambiguous situation in Russia and the domestic challenges in North America, some in the archdiocese envisioned an unanticipated yet necessary separation from the Russian Orthodox Church. The legal counsel of the archdiocese advised, "[We] must exist self-dependently (on our own) in the future. No one must either appoint or recall or dismiss Bishops without the approval of the North American Orthodox Church. We must establish the Church Authority ourselves."[2]

On the council's first day, delegates voted to temporarily sever their ecclesiastical relationship with the Russian Orthodox Church. While they retained spiritual bonds and maintained eucharistic communion with their mother church, the North American Archdiocese now considered itself temporarily self-autonomous. A telegram was sent to Patriarch Tikhon in Moscow explaining that "these actions were taken as a way of self-preservation."[3] Another message informed President Calvin Coolidge that the "Orthodox Church in America" had declared itself to be "self-ruling" (*samoupravliaiushchiisia*), "and henceforth will act as a national American religious self-sufficient structure." Offering blessings to Coolidge and all Americans, the telegram expressed the "church's feeling of devotion and boundless loyalty to the United States," which it called, "our second great nation." The transformative model born from the 1924 Detroit council, that of an autonomous jurisdiction reluctantly separated from its mother church, was controversial. Yet it suggested that while American Orthodox Rus' once planted its feet on two continents and an imagined and useful past of Holy Orthodox Rus', the North American Archdiocese now took a tenuous step into an unanticipated future. Echoing the Psalmist, the descendants of automotive workers in Detroit and coal miners in Mayfield, and those of foundrymen in Gary and weavers in Maynard, would "sing the Lord's song in a foreign land," the United States, their "second great nation."[4]

The 1924 Detroit council affected ordinary believers like my grandmother's family, untethering them and their Ss. Peter and Paul parish from the transnational spiritual administration of the Moscow Patriarchate. At far remove from the Soviet Union in the remnants of American Orthodox Rus', this event manifested decades of intracommunity conflicts that constantly defined these believers' social and religious worlds. In 1926, Wasil and Anna were among sixty-nine Carpatho-Rusyn parishioners who split from Ss. Peter and Paul to form their own parish, dedicated to St. Michael the Archangel. At first, their fledgling congregation met down the street on the upper floor of a social hall and then around the corner in a repurposed Lutheran church. Outside the bounds of the Russian Metropolia, the jurisdiction established at the 1924 council (mostly comprising the core "Russian" parishes of the old North American Archdiocese), St. Michael's entered into a loose confederation of other Carpatho-Rusyn parishes that in 1933 coalesced into a new exarchate under the Moscow Patriarchate. The St. Michael's church was within eyesight of Ss. Peter and Paul. Their respective congregations remained neighbors, coworkers, and kin, yet the communities did not mix. In 1950, my grandparents married at St. Michael's amid a minor neighborhood scandal. How could a founding daughter of the parish marry the choir director from Ss. Peter and Paul?

In these and many other ways, the jurisdictional fracturing mapped the geopolitical implications of Bolshevism onto the fragments of American Orthodox Rus'. These shifting lines of demarcation brought communities on these shores in and out of three dominant jurisdictions: the

Russian Metropolia, the Moscow Patriarchal Exarchate (MPUSA), and the Russian Orthodox Church Outside of Russia (ROCOR), all holding slightly different yet defining perspectives about the Soviet Union. Established in Serbia in 1920 and first emerging in North America later in the decade, ROCOR maintained the implicitly anti-Soviet thrust of a membership significantly composed of exiled nobility, former tsarist officers, and conservative clergy. From the establishment of the MPUSA in 1933, it aligned with a weakened Moscow Patriarchate subservient to, if not infiltrated by, the Soviet state as a means of self-preservation. Despite its administrative ties to Russia, most MPUSA congregations comprised immigrant and first-generation Carpatho-Rusyns like my grandmother's family, people whose religious and cultural associations with Moscow were rooted in decades of Russification imposed by archdiocesan missionaries intent on converting Greek Catholics from Austria-Hungary into strong adherents of American Orthodox Rus'. The Metropolia situated itself somewhere in between, aligning with ROCOR at various times, then briefly appealing to Moscow for reunification immediately after the Second World War. By the 1950s, however, as the Cold War set in, clear lines of demarcation existed between the three groups and its flocks. The situation eased after 1970, when Moscow resumed eucharistic ties and granted the Metropolia autocephalous (self-ruling) status as the Orthodox Church in America (OCA), though several dozen MPUSA parishes—and the former archdiocesan cathedral in Manhattan, hard won by Moscow after years of property litigation— were allowed to remain with the patriarchate. In 2007, in a ceremony held under the watchful eye of Russian Federation president Vladimir Putin, ROCOR accepted autonomy under the Moscow Patriarchate, ending nearly a century of acrimonious, politicized division.

Despite the easing of eucharistic relationships over time, institutional divisions and other signs of difference remained. These boundaries defined my mental map of the Orthodox communities of metropolitan Detroit, conceptions that grew more complex on those Sunday evenings every winter when our family drove with my grandparents to another corner of the city for "pan-Orthodox" Lenten services. Our area was replete with Orthodox parishes, many of them with origins in American Orthodox Rus', and it seemed like my grandfather, an OCA priest, had friends in all of them. But certain differences remained palpable.

I knew that the MPUSA St. Michael's in suburban Redford, where my grandmother remained a member, was different from the OCA Ss. Peter and Paul in Southwest Detroit, where my grandfather was assigned in his retirement, though he frequently served at each of their altars. And I understood that these parishes were both different from the suburban ROCOR parish, once part of the OCA, where my grandfather could not don vestments for the funeral of his own brother. I internalized how these divides were made real for my grandparents and those whom they held dear, rooted in the same moments of geopolitical rupture and sustained as a fact of life even after the long-anticipated moment came in 1991 when the Soviet Union was no more.

The institutional cultures of these Russian Orthodox jurisdictions ebbed and flowed with what adherents abroad could make out through the dim glass that separated them from the Soviet Union, particularly in regards to state antireligious persecution and violence. As we have seen, American Orthodox Rus' became a primary conduit for such information from the earliest moments of Bolshevik revolutionary violence and a place of refuge for Orthodox Christians fleeing its reach. As communication with church leaders in Moscow became more difficult and accounts harder to verify, archdiocesan leaders in New York recognized that non-Orthodox figures could gain entry to places in Bolshevik Russia that Orthodox clergy and laity could not, turning diplomats and journalists into informants, couriers, and intermediaries between Moscow and Manhattan. One of the most poignant aspects of this work, undertaken by ecumenical allies that included YMCA missionaries to Russia and eastern Europe and Anglican clergy operating from the Lambeth Palace offices of the Archbishop of Canterbury, was obtaining information about the safety and security of high-ranking clergy, especially those still warmly remembered in North America.

In 1918, religious publications in the US reported that priests Alexander Hotovitzky and Ilia Zotikov had reunited in Moscow at the Cathedral of Christ the Savior in support of their former archdiocesan bishop, Tikhon (Bellavin), now the Patriarch of Moscow. Faced with the daunting challenge of steering the Russian Church through a brutal civil war and escalating pressures from a regime hostile toward religious practice, Patriarch Tikhon surrounded himself with trusted clergymen, some of whom were old colleagues from North America. Hotovitzky was named sexton (*kliuchar*) of the patriarchal cathedral, and Zotikov was appointed its sacristan (*riznichii*), echoing their administrative arrangement in Manhattan two decades before. Writing in an American Episcopalian quarterly, priest Leonid Turkevich considered Hotovitzky's appointment a sign that "the Church in Russia is on the way to be built up firmly from the foundation upward." Yet Turkevich surely realized as well that as a prominent priest with close associations to the patriarch, Hotovitzky was in a precarious position.[5]

Donald Lowrie, an American Protestant relief worker with the YMCA, went to Moscow in October 1920. Weeks later, already knowing he would be deported, Lowrie hastened to see an old friend, arriving unannounced at the apartments adjoining the patriarchal cathedral after Sunday-morning liturgy. Lowrie recalled that when priest Alexander Hotovitzky answered the door, he looked "a little thinner" than when Lowrie had last seen him, "and noticeably more worn." Hotovitzky did not recognize his old colleague at first, though he soon enveloped Lowrie in a warm embrace, repeating over and over, "And you are actually here, in Moscow again!" Lowrie knew that Hotovitzky had been imprisoned and that state agents frequently searched the apartment. "No one I have met here has felt more keenly the terrible isolation in which Russia exists," Lowrie wrote, "no news from the outside world, no new books to read, no touch with the thought of the world." Lowrie brought Hotovitzky up-to-date on Orthodox affairs abroad, noting with some sadness that "it was almost pathetic to see his joy at learning that things were going well with friends in America." Hotovitzky cut the visit short so as to attend evening vespers. Lowrie, taking his leave, was shaken by the realization that Hotovitzky was in his late forties yet appeared far older, noticeably nervous and ominously world-weary. "Before I left he asked me if it would be all right to tell the [Cheka] that I had been to see him," Lowrie recalled. "I said of course it would be all right. He warned me that it might get me into trouble, but I had nothing to conceal." Lowrie returned around midnight the following Thursday, the only time Hotovitzky had free. He found the priest and his wife, Maria, in their study, "heated by a tiny stove with sticks of wood so small as to be scarcely more than splinters." It was Thanksgiving Day in the United States, and the couple had set out tea for an impromptu celebration. Lowrie produced a small chocolate cake smuggled in from New York, to

Maria's clear delight. The scene reminded Lowrie that behind the indignities and dangers that clergy like Father Alexander faced in Bolshevik Moscow were also the private, tortured sufferings of their wives. "The past two years have been very hard upon her nerves, and she weeps at any mention of the distress they two have endured," Lowrie wrote of Maria. She welcomed the cake, for as Lowrie observed, "she has few pleasures, poor woman." Lowrie wrote to Leonid Turkevich shortly after the visit, insisting on strict confidence to ensure Hotovitzky's safety. "[Father Alexander] really lives without knowing what may come to him tomorrow," Lowrie recounted, "and his face and manner show the result of this long strain." Yet Lowrie fretted more over Maria, "so worn out with the long uncertainty that she would do almost anything to be free for a while." Lowrie recalled that when she briefly left them, Father Alexander confided that he had just learned that he was to report to the Cheka again the following day. "He said he would not tell his wife until morning."[6]

In March 1922, Hotovitzky and Zotikov were among sixty-nine Muscovites arrested for counterrevolutionary activities. Alongside two other priests from the Moscow cathedral, they were charged with "opposition to the confiscation of church valuables, distributing the appeal of Patriarch Tikhon, the call to mass and open resistance to the decision of the VTsIK [the All-Russian Central Executive Committee] concerning the confiscation of church valuables." It was Hotovitzky's third arrest and Zotikov's first. Tried before the Moscow Revolutionary Tribunal in December, Hotovitzky received ten years' imprisonment, while Zotikov received three years.[7] In 1923, Donald Lowrie made note of Hotovitzky's arrest and subsequent exile in a searing report about the recent plight of "one of the most talented preachers in Russia," now under severe state pressure. "Perhaps the reason he was not executed was that he was too popular in Moscow," Lowrie surmised. "He has been condemned to ten years hard labor."[8] The archdiocesan patron and Chicago businessman Charles Crane, whose friendship with Hotovitzky began in New York and was later rekindled in prerevolutionary Russia, received another account from a colleague in Moscow: "The priests Alexander Hotovitzky and Zotikov now have been dispatched to the countryside to work. Mr. Hotovitzky is happy to breathe the air of the fields after many months of solitude. Even in prison he earned the esteem of his warden." It was a euphemistic turn, perhaps for the sake of political expediency. To be "dispatched," after all, was but another way to describe forced exile.[9]

By early 1924, the Hotovitzkys were back in Moscow. When the YMCA relief worker Ethan T. Colton visited with Maria that spring, he wrote to Crane that she appeared fine but that "the strain on her has taken effect in a nervous condition that affects her ability to walk." She reported that Father Alexander also suffered from various physical ailments "but is better than when [he was] released from prison." Too outspoken and charismatic to be allowed a parish assignment and holding unabashed loyalty to Patriarch Tikhon, Maria said that her husband served and preached only occasionally. The couple knew that Crane was trying to extract them from the Soviet Union, and Colton said, "my expectation is that they will avail themselves of it if they will be allowed to leave." Colton gave Maria one hundred dollars and made plans to visit with Father Alexander on a planned return trip to Moscow in a month's time.[10] Yet Colton's account recognized that efforts to secure the Hotovitzkys' emigration would depend on whether Father Alexander could prioritize their safety over his long-standing loyalty to the patriarch and the faithful of Moscow—and whether he recognized the urgency to reach such a determination before it was too late. Patriarch Tikhon died under house arrest a year later, fundamentally changing the conditions of possibility for the Russian Church and its clergy. And as Soviet statecraft evolved, so did the ability of foreign groups to function within its borders, leading to the liquidation of the YMCA's Moscow offices and the expulsion of its key leaders. What chances existed for people like Ethan Colton or Donald Lowrie to visit Alexander and Maria Hotovitzky disappeared, as did any hope for the couple to reach the West.[11]

If Father Alexander did arrive in the United States, he would have found American Orthodox Rus' in a moment of transition. Though it was ecclesiastically separate from Moscow, communication channels were still maintained, even if they were increasingly unreliable. In 1930, the *Russian Orthodox American Messenger*, which Hotovitzky established nearly thirty-five years before, printed a brief announcement of his death at the age of fifty-eight. A promised longer obituary was never published.[12] For years, this was assumed to be his fate, even though Father Alexander was still very much alive in the Soviet Union, continuing to serve and preach when permitted. He was arrested once again on June 17, 1937, and charged with belonging to "an anti-Soviet terrorist fascist organization of clerics." Father Alexander Hotovitzky was executed on August 19, 1937, at the age of sixty-five. His body was taken to the only crematorium in Moscow, a stark, utilitarian facility retrofitted atop a former church of the once-influential Donskoy Monastery. Incinerated alongside the remains of two bishops and three priests, Alexander Hotovitzky was one of more than thirty-three hundred cremations there in 1937, the height of Stalin's Great Terror. Their remains were placed in one of three mass graves dug at Donskoy, the final resting place for an estimated sixty-five hundred victims of the Soviet state.[13]

In contrast to Alexander Hotovitzky, priest Ilia Zotikov received far less attention from former friends and admirers in the West. Of the three articles published in the *Russian Orthodox American Messenger* in 1923 and 1924 attesting to Hotovitzky's liberty, none mentioned Zotikov, despite his shared experiences of tribunals, exiles, and incarceration.[14] Zotikov's second arrest came in 1927 when a search of his apartment uncovered several handwritten poems. There was a copy of the anti-Soviet "Solovetsky Memorandum," written by bishops imprisoned in what was once one of Russia's most historic and influential monasteries.[15] Zotikov had also sent money to an exiled priest, though surviving records apparently do not record his name. (At the time, tantalizingly, Hotovitzky was exiled to the small Siberian town of Turukhansk.) Released after a month in Moscow's Butyrka prison, Zotikov was exiled over one hundred miles east to Vladimir, having been barred from taking residence in major cities like Moscow or Leningrad. In Vladimir during the autumn of 1930, he was arrested again.[16] One night in October at the former Nativity of the Virgin Monastery, Zotikov and two other prisoners—deacon Michael Lebedev and priest Mikhail Sokolov—were taken from their cells to stand before a firing squad. It is believed, however, that Zotikov did not make it that far. "When they were leading him to the execution, on the way to the wall of death Father Ilia died from a rupture of the heart," an acquaintance later reported, "not having received from the murderers a bullet to the back of the head." Father Ilia's remains were interred in the cemetery of his small church in Vladimir.[17]

By the mid-twentieth century, the fractured Russian Orthodox presence outside the borders of the Soviet Union described victims of Soviet antireligious violence as martyrs, assembling lists of names and piecing together accounts of their lives, deeds, and fates. Among the first and most influential were those compiled for ROCOR by priest Mikhail Polsky, the first volume of which was published in 1949. His second, published in 1957, listed both Zotikov and Hotovitzky.[18] In a ceremony conducted in New York City in 1981, ROCOR included Zotikov but not Hotovitzky among the hundreds of clergy and laypeople glorified (the term used by Eastern Christians for the recognition of a new martyr or saint) as New Martyrs and Confessors of Russia, though this act was not universally recognized within the wider spectrum of global Orthodox Christianity.[19]

Interest in such glorifications mounted in the Soviet Union with the state-driven resurgence of the Moscow Patriarchate in the lead-up to 1988, the one thousandth anniversary of the baptism of Kyivan Rus', bringing the glorification of Patriarch Tikhon in 1989. The process hastened with the fall of the Soviet Union two years later. In 1994, the Moscow Patriarchate and the OCA jointly glorified Alexander Hotovitzky and fellow American missionary John Kochurov, bridging their missionary legacies in North America with their respective fates in Russia. In these years, Russian archives opened, information flowed freely, and calls began for a national reckoning with the crimes of the Soviet past— including the mass glorifications of yet more New Martyrs and Confessors. Yet under the increasingly repressive leadership of Vladimir Putin, popular interest in glorification has clashed against mounting state insecurities over the legacies of Soviet repression and public memory of the Gulag. As a result, the glorification process has slowed. As of the early 2020s, Zotikov's status as a saint remained uncertain, long awaiting a decision by the canonization committee in the Eparchy of Vladimir.[20]

The increasing availability of information from Russia during the 1990s provided new and evolving insight about the lived experiences of Russian Orthodox Christians under Soviet antireligious policies. How did Ilia Zotkov endure those difficult years of exile in Vladimir? What lay behind the brave face Alexander Hotovitzky put on for sympathetic foreign visitors? As often is the case with those who disappeared into remote exile or brutal prison camps, we have only fragmentary vignettes. For Hotovitzky and Zotikov, these witnesses were aging Soviets who as young people knew both priests well and who lived and prayed with

254 | EPILOGUE

them during times of tribulation. They were those who survived the years of terror and fear and lived long enough to have the luxury—and freedom—to remember. All recalled both priests as luminous beacons in dark times, when churches were closed and priests were few. One was a man who knew Zotikov during his exile to Vladimir, remembering the priest as "having served with Saint Tikhon in America, formerly a pastor of the church of Christ the Saviour," and too recalling his association with deacon Mikhail Lebedev, another close associate of Tikhon from the Moscow patriarchal cathedral, who walked with Zotikov to their fate before the firing squad that October night. "All of them have departed long ago," the man regretted, but "they left behind bright, warm memories."[21] Another was a famed Soviet theater actor who knew Alexander Hotovitzky late in his life, when the heavy physical toll of his repeated imprisonments and exiles was clear. Even so, the actor remained transfixed by the power of Hotovitzky's gaze. "Even today I remember Father Alexander's eyes," he remembered. "It was a feeling I had when I saw the blessed Patriarch Tikhon. . . . The light shining in [his eyes] speaks of his holiness."[22]

Andrei Kozarzhevsky was a professor of literature and ancient languages at Moscow State University. In 1992, he described for the *Journal of the Moscow Patriarchate* church life in Moscow and its environs during his childhood. Born in 1918 to parents of German and Russian ancestry, Kozarzhevsky was baptized a Roman Catholic. In 1921, after his father's death, Kozarzhevsky was received into the Orthodox Church through Chrismation (anointing) at Hotovitzky's apartment. Zotikov stood as his godfather.[23] Kozarzhevsky considered this his first real memory, recalling in clear detail that he stood naked on a chair next to Zotikov as Hotovitzky dabbed holy oil onto his body. "Through the window, through the telegraph wires," he recalled in his mind's eye, "I see the Cathedral of Christ the Saviour and its surrounding square."[24] Both priests became memorable figures in Kozarzhevsky's upbringing. When he was a boy, the Kozarzhevsky family chose to follow Zotikov into exile in Vladimir, where young Andrei assisted the priest at the altar of a tiny church by then serving as the cathedral of the local diocese. As a teenager, Kozarzhevsky heard Hotovitzky preach in Moscow, recalling that he was still of strong voice, though hunched and grayed beyond his years. By then, neither Hotovitzky nor Zotikov were the young men they had been in the US. Both were widowers nearing their sixties. For years, they lived each day in constant terror. They had seen the prisons. They had witnessed violence and death, perhaps anticipating their own grim fate. And yet they continued to live each day as Orthodox priests.

Like others, Andrei Kozarzhevsky knew well the importance of American Orthodox Rus' in the ministry and legacy of Alexander Hotovitzky and also that these missionary years were critical for understanding how the priest endured his fate in postrevolutionary Russia. As an old man, Kozarzhevsky still preserved what few personal effects remained from Hotovitzky, items obtained by a devoted follower who had seen the priest in exile. The bundle included photographs, letters, and a battered prayer book that Hotovitzky used in prison. There was also a manuscript of an unpublished poem. Written in New York City during the summer of 1910, it was an ode to a "triple event" in the life of Ilia Zotikov: his name day, the fifteen-year jubilee of his ordination to the priesthood, and his imminent departure from American Orthodox Rus'. For over a quarter century, through the crucibles of tribunals and exile, the indignities of prison, the rapid decline of his body, and the criminalization of his clerical vocation, Alexander Hotovitzky carried the scrap of paper in memory of a brother priest, of a four-decades-long bond forged in a Manhattan townhouse and sustained across time, distance, and mutual struggle. It was a fleeting remnant of American Orthodox Rus' still held dear even through the most harrowing of crucibles. Kozarzhevsky noted that the top of the page was a short inscription in Hotovitzky's hand: "Dedicated to my best friend, Father Ilia Zotikov."[25]

ACKNOWLEDGMENTS

"Everything that happens has a small beginning," writes Saint Mark the Ascetic, "and it grows the more it is nourished." This project began as a paper for Leslie Stainton's first-year writing seminar in the Residential College at the University of Michigan. Twenty years later, it is a book. Throughout these long years, many people and institutions have self-lessly and generously supported my work. Just as all mistakes in this study are my own, so too are errors of omission in my expressions of gratitude. Research and writing has been underwritten by fellowships from the University of Chicago Master of Arts Program in the Social Sciences and the Northwestern University Graduate School, an NEH Dissertation Completion Fellowship from the Fordham University Orthodox Christian Studies Center, graduate and postdoctoral fellow-ships from the Nicholas D. Chabraja Center for Historical Studies, and a postdoctoral fellowship from the John C. Danforth Center on Religion and Politics at Washington University in St. Louis. I have benefited from research and conference travel grants from the Northwestern University Graduate School, the Northwestern History Department, the Daugh-ters of Vartan, and the Religion at Home and Abroad Project, sponsored by the Buffett Center for Global Studies and the Henry Luce Foun-dation. Funds from the Northwestern Graduate School and History Department Alseth language study grants underwrote two summers of Russian-language learning at the Kathryn W. Davis School of Russian of Middlebury College.

Portions of this study have benefited from being presented at nu-merous workshops and conferences, including regional and national meetings of the American Academy of Religion; the Association for Slavic, Eastern European, and Eurasian Studies; the Association for the Study of Eastern Christian History and Culture; the European Asso-ciation for the Study of Religion; and graduate student conferences at Northwestern, Harvard University, the University of Michigan, Miami

University, and Queen Mary University of London. Several chapters were workshopped at the Northwestern University North American Religions Workshop, the Newberry Library Urban History Dissertation Group, the Fordham Orthodox Christian Studies Center Fellows Workshop, and the History Department American History Dissertators' Workshop. Portions of chapters 1 and 8 include material from an article published in the *Journal of American Ethnic History*. Chapter 7 is a revision of an article that appeared in the *Journal of Orthodox Christian Studies*.

This project has benefited from the collections and staff of a number of libraries and archives. Thank you to Bill Creech of the National Archives and Records Administration in Washington, DC, Elena Silk of the Father Georges Florovsky Library at St. Vladimir's Orthodox Theological Seminary, St. Nicholas Russian Orthodox Cathedral in New York City, and Deacon Michael Suvak at the Holy Virgin Protection Orthodox Cathedral in New York City. The late Ray Gadke's acquisitions of rare Orthodox and Eastern Catholic materials for the University of Chicago's Joseph Regenstein Library were of critical help. I appreciate the diligent librarians and interlibrary loan staffs in the library systems of the University of Michigan, the University of Chicago, Northwestern University, Garrett-Evangelical Theological Seminary, and Washington University in St. Louis. And I appreciate most the warm hospitality of Alexis Liberovsky during a brief visit to the Archives of the Orthodox Church in America in Syosset, New York, early in my research for this project, though I regret that ongoing renovation and relocation plans prohibited further utilization of this rich resource.

I am a proud product of Michigan's public schools. I became a historian because I walked into Joseph Cislo's classroom at Northville High School, where I learned to keep my eye on the details. At the University of Michigan, mentors Leslie Stainton and John U. Bacon helped me to hone my narrative voice. Robert Hunter Greene, Olga Maiorova, and Matthew Herbst inspired me to incorporate the Russian Orthodox Church into my undergraduate interest in Soviet history. William Rosenberg supervised this project as a senior thesis. Most of all, Gerard Libaridian made a special effort to challenge me to dream bigger. To all, Go Blue!

At the University of Chicago, Richard Weyhing and Avi Sharma helped me consider historical work as a professional endeavor. And I am most thankful to Kathleen Neils Conzen for taking pity on an excitable master's student with very complicated project and helping to transform it into a prize-winning thesis. At Northwestern University, I was lucky to enjoy two academic homes, first in the Department of Religious Studies and then in the Department of History. Cristina Traina and Kate Masur moved heaven, earth, and untold bureaucratic barriers to help me pursue the best path for my doctoral training. I cannot thank them enough for their advocacy. I appreciate the mentorship of Lauren Stokes, Henry Binford, Michael Sherry, Daniel Immerwahr, Michelle Molina, Daniel Greene, Geraldo Cadava, Beth Hurd, and Scott Sowerby. For my long association with the Nicholas D. Chabraja Center for Historical Studies, I thank Sarah Maza, Jonathon Glassman, and Elzbieta Foeller-Pituch. A special thank-you to all the administrators, staff, and undergraduate workers in both departments for their tireless labors in helping all of us succeed. From my arrival in Evanston, Robert Orsi believed in this project and empowered me to tell this story in my own way and continued to offer his eager support long after I left Northwestern. I am also thankful for the mentorship of Sylvester Johnson and for Kevin Boyle's enduring patience, kindness, and good cheer and especially for long conversations about our shared and beloved hometown of Detroit.

I completed this book as a postdoctoral research fellow with the John C. Danforth Center on Religion and Politics at Washington University in St. Louis. I am thankful for the mentorship of R. Marie Griffith, Leigh Eric Schmidt, Mark Valeri, Laurie Maffly-Kipp, and Anna Bialek, and also for fellow postdoctoral fellows Susanna De Stradis, Esra Tunc, Eric Stephen, Michael Baysa, Judah Isseroff, and Cody Musselman. A center-sponsored manuscript workshop generated a rich day of generous conversation with Melani McAlister. Marie Griffith facilitated a fortuitous meeting with Laura Levitt, which brought this book to NYU Press and the North American Religions series. I am thankful for the guidance and patience of editor Jennifer Hammer and the editorial staff and for the generative comments of two anonymous readers.

Much of this book was written and revised as a contingent academic, including periods of under- and unemployment during the COVID-19 pandemic. I am grateful to those who provided me work, wages, and lifelines to continue working: Gerard Libaridian, Kevin Boyle, Bethany Harding, the Northwestern University Kellogg School of Management,

University of Texas at Austin OnRamps, and the Augusta Webster, MD, Office of Medical Education at the Northwestern University Feinberg School of Medicine. It has not been easy, and I regret that so many fantastic colleagues have not enjoyed the same opportunities. I pledge to pay it forward.

In our little world of Orthodox Christian studies, thank you to Scott Kenworthy, Nadieszda Kizenko, George Demacopoulos, Aristotle Papanikolaou, Patrick Lally Michelson, Nicholas Chapman, Matthew Namee, Fr. John Erickson, Vera Shevzov, the late Roy Robson, Heather Bailey, Elena Kravchenko, Jacob Lassin, Candace Lukasik, and Sarah Riccardi-Swartz. I thank Richard Custer of the excellent blog *Carpatho-Rusyns of Pennsylvania* for identifying the cover photograph as the Holy Trinity parish of McAdoo, Pennsylvania. A hearty *spasibo* to all who made for two unforgettable summers at Middlebury College, including Alice Volkov, Marek Eby, Peter Worger, Sharon Miller, Michael Rendelman, and especially Svetlana Harlan and Leigh Winstead.

Many friends and colleagues at Northwestern University and in Chicago have been important to my work. I am grateful for the friendship of two Northwestern graduate cohorts, first in religious studies and then in history. I appreciate the warm community of the North American Religions Workshop and all NARWals past and present, as well as the Newberry Library Urban History Dissertation Group and the Northwestern American History Dissertators' Workshop. Winnifred Fallers Sullivan was generous with her time to help me think about church property litigation. I express solidarity with my colleagues in the Northwestern University Graduate Workers. And I am particularly grateful for collegial friendships with Hannah Scheidt, Stephanie Brenzel, Joel Harrison, Benjamin Ricciardi, Jennifer Callaghan, Candace Kohli, Ariel Schwartz, Stephanie Brehm, Jeff Wheatley, Sarah Dees, Courtney Rabada, Ashley King, Eda Uca, Kate Dugan, Monica Mercado, Matthew Cressler, Matt June, Laura McCoy, Keith Clark, Bonnie Ernst, Sian Olson-Dowis, Alvita Akiboh, Andi Christmas, Vanda Rajcan, Leigh Soares, Amanda Kleintop, Myisha Eatmon, Lucy Reeder, and most especially Michael Falcone, Melanie Hall, Kyle Burke, Andy Baer, and Hayley Glaholt.

To complete a project like this required nonacademic friends eager to share the grandest adventures Chicago could muster. John Rodriguez and Dave Wendland are my brothers, always there with a spare concert ticket, taco, and a drink or three when I need it the most. Thanks to all those who sail with us, including Jaime Endick, Jillian Lamb, and Dr. Jen Paruch. I thank Humphrey Shoon for his good counsel. I am proud to have become a third-generation member of the Chicago and Evanston Armenian communities, which nurtured two of my paternal great-grandparents as refugees from the Armenian Genocide. I am profoundly grateful for my adopted family at St. James Armenian Apostolic Church, especially Ani Tokat (my beloved "church mom"), Dr. Larry Farsakian, Gary Rejebian, and the *asbedner* of Avarayr Lodge #4 of the Knights of Vartan. I remember fondly Tenny Arlen. Those of us who had the good fortune to know Tenny mourn her keen and creative mind, though we grieve most her radiant empathy, kindness, and deep concern for the dignity of all creatures. Most of all I thank my brother deacon Dr. Kavork Hagopian for incorporating me into his wonderful family and for becoming a beloved part of mine.

I am fortunate to have a large and loving extended family, including my grandmother Nina Sarkisian and aunts, uncles, and cousins in the Derderian, Houhanisin, Rupas, Kazarian, and Sarkisian families. I am thankful also for those who extend the meaning of family, including Dr. Jeff and Ilze Hammersley, Dr. Jerry Morris and Lynn Parkllan, and the Bell, Kazanjian, Apkarian, and Ohanian families. My sister, Sara Sarkisian Bell, and Morgan Bell have loved and sustained me in every way. Sona and Anya Bell, it is my joy to be your Uncle Tattoo. My parents, Dr. Edward Sarkisian and Anna Svirid Sarkisian, did more than anyone to help me reach my potential. Their advocacy for public education, libraries, and the arts helped me to know the importance of vibrant, progressive communities working toward the common good. Truly, we are stronger together. And I am thankful beyond words for the love and support of Diana Ohanian, for bonds strengthened through a pandemic and the difficulties of distance and for her patience with the mountains of books and records that follow me wherever I go. Ours is a joyful little world, and this book is all the better for Diana's insight and curiosity—especially chapter 7.

This book is dedicated with deepest love, admiration, and thanksgiving for my maternal grandparents. Archpriest Ioann and Matushka Melanya Sviridov were lifelong Russian Orthodox Christians who loved their church and lived its faith. My grandfather's death came just as I

262 | ACKNOWLEDGMENTS

began work on this project. His immense personal library and inclination to save every scrap of his past nourished my work in unexpected, often fortuitous ways, and his memory sustains me each day. It is most fitting that my work on this book concluded in his beloved St. Louis. My grandmother was my foundation, best reader, and greatest friend. Many of my best ideas began over her kitchen table and then were refined by her insistence on reading and then commenting on everything I wrote, no matter how minor, even past her hundredth year. While I mourn that they did not live to see this book, to know that you are reading it would cause them to rejoice and be exceedingly glad.

NOTES

ABBREVIATIONS

AOCA   Archives of the Orthodox Church in America, Father Georges Florovsky Library, St. Vladimir's Orthodox Theological Seminary, Crestwood, New York.

APV   *Amerikanskyi pravoslavnyi vyestnik* (*Russian Orthodox American Messenger*)

CFLPS   Chicago Foreign Language Press Survey, the Newberry Library, Chicago, IL

FBI BSF   Records of the Federal Bureau of Investigation; Investigative Records; Bureau Section Files, 1920–1921; Records of the Federal Bureau of Investigation, Record Group 65; National Archives and Records Administration; National Archives Microfilm Publication M1085 (Digitized by Fold3.com).

FBI OGF   Records of the Federal Bureau of Investigation; Investigative Records; Old German Files, 1915–1920; Records of the Federal Bureau of Investigation, Record Group 65; National Archives and Records Administration; National Archives Microfilm Publication M1085 (Digitized by Fold3.com).

GTs   *Golos tserkvi* (*Voice of the Church*)

IHRCA   Immigration History Research Center Archives, Elmer L. Anderson Library, University of Minnesota, Minneapolis, Minnesota.

INS   Subject and Policy Files, 1893–1957. Records of the Immigration and Naturalization Service, 1787–2004, Record Group 85, Entry 9. National Archives Building, Washington, DC.

IUS I   *Iubileinyi sbornik v pamiat' 150-lyetiia russkoi pravoslavnoi v syevernoi amerikye, chast' pervaia* [Jubilee anthology in commemoration of the 150th anniversary of Russian Orthodoxy in North America, part one] (New York, 1944)

IUS II *Iubileinyi sbornik v pamiat' 150-lyetiia russkoi pravoslavnoi v syevernoi amerikye, chast' vtoraia* [Jubilee anthology in commemoration of the 150th anniversary of Russian Orthodoxy in North America, part two] (New York, 1945)

RIMAS UIC Russian Independent Mutual Aid Society records, Special Collections and University Archives, University of Illinois at Chicago, Chicago, IL.

ROGCCA LOC Russian Orthodox Greek Catholic Church of America, Diocese of Alaska, Records, Manuscript Division, Library of Congress, Washington, DC.

INTRODUCTION

1 Will Herberg, *Protestant, Catholic, Jew: An Essay in American Religious Sociology* (Garden City, NY: Doubleday, 1955), 45n28. See also Kevin M. Schulz, *Tri-Faith America: How Catholics and Jews Held Postwar America to Its Protestant Promise* (New York: Oxford University Press, 2011).

2 For histories of the Russian Orthodox Church in Alaska, see Sergei Kan, *Memory Eternal: Tlingit Culture and Russian Orthodox Christianity through Two Centuries* (Seattle: University of Washington Press, 1999); Gwenn A. Miller, *Kodiak Kreol: Communities of Empire in Early Russian America* (Ithaca, NY: Cornell University Press, 2010); Ilya Vinkovetsky, *Russian America: An Overseas Colony of a Continental Empire, 1804–1867* (New York: Oxford University Press, 2011); Susan Wiley Hardwick, *Russian Refuge: Religion, Migration, and Settlement on the North American Pacific Rim* (Chicago: University of Chicago Press, 1993).

3 Synthesis church histories and general studies include Constance Tarasar, ed., *Orthodox America, 1794–1976* (Syosset, NY: Orthodox Church in America Department of History and Archives, 1975); Gregory Afonsky, *A History of the Orthodox Church in America, 1917–1934* (Kodiak, AK: St. Herman Seminary Press, 1994); Mark Stokoe and Leonid Kishkovsky, *Orthodox Christians in North America, 1794–1994* (New York: Orthodox Christian Publications Center, 1995); and Thomas FitzGerald, *The Orthodox Church* (Westport, CT: Greenwood, 1995).

4 For accounts of transformations within the Russian Church during the late imperial period, see Nadieszda Kizenko, *A Prodigal Saint: Father John of Kronstadt and the Russian People* (University Park: Pennsylvania State University Press, 2008); Vera Shevzov, *Russian Orthodoxy on the Eve of Revolution* (Oxford: Oxford University Press, 2004); Robert Hunter Greene, *Bodies like Bright Stars: Saints and Relics in Orthodox Russia* (DeKalb: Northern Illinois Press, 2009); Jennifer Hedda, *His Kingdom Come: Orthodox Pastorship and Social Activism in Revolutionary Russia* (DeKalb: Northern Illinois Press, 2007).

5 Many church histories repeat the claim that this meant that the Russian Archdiocese held jurisdiction and maintained oversight over every parish found there until the founding of the Greek Archdiocese in 1921. The church historian Matthew Namee challenges this "myth of past unity," asserting the many ethnic parishes (especially Greeks) situated outside the Russian Archdiocese and its ethnic vicariates never looked to the archdiocese for ecclesiastical leadership, instead maintaining ad hoc relationships with mother churches abroad. See Matthew Namee, "The Myth of Unity," *Orthodox History*, January 29, 2018, https://orthodoxhistory.org; and Matthew Namee, "The Origins of the 'Myth of Unity,'" *Orthodox History*, November 4, 2009, https://orthodoxhistory.org. Namee suggests that the phrase "myth of past unity" may date to 1927 and the historical claims of the American Orthodox Catholic Church, a controversial offshoot of the Russian Archdiocese. See Hiero-Monk Boris, "The Holy Eastern Orthodox Catholic and Apostolic Church in North America," *Orthodox Catholic Review*, January 1927, 7–16.

6 James Jorgenson, "Father Alexis Toth and the Transition of the Greek Catholic Community in Minneapolis to the Russian Orthodox Church," *St. Vladimir's Theological Quarterly* 32, no. 2 (1988): 119–37. See also Alex Simirenko, *Pilgrims, Colonists, and Frontiersmen: An Ethnic Community in Transition* (Glencoe, NY: Free Press, 1974). Greek Catholic conversions to Orthodoxy became transnational when emigrants to North America remigrated to Transcarpathia. See Joel Brady, "Transnational Conversions: Greek Catholic Migrants and Russky Orthodox Conversion Movements in Austria-Hungary, Russia, and the Americas (1890–1914)" (PhD diss., University of Pittsburgh, 2012).

7 *Zapivka* (washing down) cups contain red communion wine diluted with warm water, which along with a piece of unconsecrated communion bread (*antidoron*) serves to wash down any remnants of the eucharist and ensure they are not spit out. A communicant will ordinarily progress immediately from the chalice to consume both together.

8 Robert A. Orsi, *The Madonna of 115th Street: Faith and Community in Italian Harlem, 1880–1950*, 2nd ed. (New Haven, CT: Yale University Press, 2002), xiii–xix. See also David D. Hall, introduction to *Lived Religion in America*, ed. David D. Hall (Princeton, NJ: Princeton University Press, 1997), vii–xiii; and Robert A. Orsi, *Thank You, St. Jude: Women's Devotions to the Patron Saint of Hopeless Causes* (New Haven, CT: Yale University Press, 1996).

9 Shevzov, *Russian Orthodoxy on the Eve of Revolution*, 13. See also Vera Shevzov, "Letting the People into Church: Reflections on Orthodoxy and Community in Late Imperial Russia," in *Orthodox Russia: Belief and Practice under the Tsars*, ed. Valerie Kivelson and Robert H. Greene (University Park: Pennsylvania State University Press, 2003), 69. Here Shevzov contrasts the study of lived religion with the Russian historiography of "everyday Orthodoxy" (*bytovoe pravoslavie*). See also Heather J. Coleman, "Studying Russian Religion since the Collapse of Communism," *Journal of the Canadian Historical Association* 25, no. 2 (2014): 311; Heather

J. Coleman, "Faith and Story in Imperial Russia," in *Orthodox Christianity in Late Imperial Russia*, ed. Heather J. Coleman (Bloomington: Indiana University Press, 2014), 1–21; and Christine D. Worobec, "Lived Orthodoxy in Imperial Russia," *Kritika: Explorations in Russian and Eurasian History* 7, no. 2 (Spring 2006): 329–50. There has been also a limited turn toward "popular religion" in the study of Russian religiosity, though this has not engaged with lived religion as an analytical category. See John-Paul Himka and Andriy Zayarnyuk, eds., *Letters from Heaven: Popular Religion in Russia and Ukraine* (Toronto: University of Toronto Press, 2006).

10 Richard Callahan, *Work and Faith in the Kentucky Coal Fields: Subject to Dust* (Bloomington: Indiana University Press, 2008), 4.

11 E. P. Thompson, *The Making of the English Working Class* (New York: Vintage, 1966), 12–13.

12 Thompson, 13.

13 Dimitry Grigorieff, "The Historical Background of Orthodoxy in America," *St. Vladimir's Seminary Quarterly* 5, nos. 1–2 (1961): 15.

CHAPTER 1. "THIS BABYLON"

1 Edward Hagaman Hall, *The Catskill Aqueduct and Earlier Water Supplies of the City of New York* (New York: Mayor's Catskill Aqueduct Celebration Committee, 1917), 92–95; J. M. Matthews, "Electric Power in Building the World's Greatest Aqueduct," *Engineering Magazine*, November 1912, 161–62.

2 David Grann, "City of Water," in *The Devil and Sherlock Holmes: Tales of Murder, Madness, and Obsession* (New York: Doubleday, 2010), 193.

3 Fr. Alexander Hotovitzky, "Russkie v Amerikye," *APV*, January 28, 1912, 33.

4 Hotovitzky, 34.

5 Hotovitzky, 32.

6 "Russkaia Emigratsiia," *APV*, September 28, 1907, 351–54.

7 US Immigration Commission, *Reports of the Immigration Commission*, vol. 3, *Statistical Review of Immigration, 1850–1910* (Washington, DC: Government Printing Office, 1911), 53.

8 "Politicheskaia rol' pravoslavno-russkago dukhovenstvo v S. Amerikie," *APV*, June 14, 1909, 198–99.

9 Daniel E. Bender, *American Abyss: Savagery and Civilization in the Age of Industry* (Ithaca, NY: Cornell University Press, 2009), 133.

10 Emily Greene Balch, *Our Slavic Fellow Citizens* (New York: Charities Publication Committee, 1910), 5. See also Matthew Frye Jacobson, *Barbarian Virtues: The United States Encounters Foreign Peoples at Home and Abroad, 1876–1917* (New York: Hill and Wang, 2000); David R. Roediger, *Wages of Whiteness: Race and the Making of the American Working Class*, rev. ed. (New York: Verso, 1999); Robert H. Wiebe, *The Search for Order, 1877–1920* (New York: Hill and Wang, 1967).

11 Oscar Handlin, *The Uprooted: The Epic Story of the Great Migrations That Made the American People* (Boston: Little, Brown, 1951), 5.

12 Father Peter Kohanik, "Russkoe Emigrantskoe Delo v S. Amerike," IuS I, 225.

13 Father Alexander Hotovitzky, "Iz dnevnika," *APV*, December 1, 1908, 422–26.

14 Robert A. Karlowich, *We Fall and Rise: Russian-Language Newspapers in New York City, 1889–1914* (Metuchen, NJ: Scarecrow, 1991), 57, 189–97.

15 John D. Klier, "*Zhid*: The Biography of a Russian Pejorative," *Slavic and East European Review* 60, no. 1 (1982): 1–15. See also Benjamin Nathans, *Beyond the Pale: The Jewish Encounter with Late Imperial Russia* (Berkeley: University of California Press, 2000), esp. 186–94, 292–95. For a more general discussion of violence toward the Jewish communities of the Ukrainian shtetl and the borderlands of Poland in late imperial Russia, see Yohanan Petrovsky-Shtern, *Golden Age Shtetl* (Princeton, NJ: Princeton University Press, 2014), 164–80.

16 Frank Bondarenko, hearing transcript, April 16, 1919, File 54709/568, Box 3496, INS.

17 US Immigration Commission, *Reports of the Immigration Commission*, vol. 4, *Emigration Conditions in Europe* (Washington, DC: Government Printing Office, 1911), 245; Daniel Beer, *The House of the Dead: Siberian Exile under the Tsars* (New York: Knopf, 2017).

18 Charles Steinwedel, "Making Social Groups, One Person at a Time: The Identification of Individuals by Estate, Religious Confession, and Ethnicity in Late Imperial Russia," in *Documenting Individual Identity: The Development of State Practices since the French Revolution*, ed. Jane Caplan and John Torpey (Princeton, NJ: Princeton University Press, 2001), 67–82; Nicholas V. Riasanovsky, *Russian Identities: A History* (Oxford: Oxford University Press, 2005), 167–210; Eric Lohr, *Russian Citizenship: From Empire to Soviet Union* (Cambridge, MA: Harvard University Press, 2012); Richard Pipes, *Russia under the Old Regime* (New York: Charles Scribner and Sons, 1974), 314; Mervyn Matthews, *The Passport Society: Controlling Movement in Russia and the USSR* (Boulder, CO: Westview, 1983). See also S. Janovsky, "Russian Law and Emigration," in US Immigration Commission, *Reports of the Immigration Commission*, vol. 4, 251–64.

19 "Spravachnyi Otdel," *Russkii emigrant*, June 13, 1912.

20 US Immigration Commission, *Reports of the Immigration Commission*, vol. 4, 253.

21 Mike Kot, hearing transcript, November 27, 1919, File 54709/552, Box 3495, INS.

22 Mike Kot, rehearing transcript, November 18, 1919, File 54709/552, Box 3495, INS.

23 Dirk Hoerder, "Immigration and the Working Class: The Remigration Factor," *International Labor and Working-Class History* 21 (Spring 1982): 28. See also Mark Wyman, *Round Trip to America: The Immigrants Return to Europe, 1880–1930* (Ithaca, NY: Cornell University Press, 1993).

24 "Po Emigrantskomu Voprosu," *APV*, November 4, 1915, 464–65.

25 Priest Alexander Hotovitzky, "Russkie v Amerikie," *APV*, January 28, 1912, 32–34.

26 Priest John Slunin, "Poyezdka moia na rodinu," *APV*, December 28, 1911, 433–36. White Army officers evacuated the Kursk Root Icon to Siberia in 1920. The icon is now kept by the Russian Orthodox Church Outside Russia at the Cathedral of the Sign on East Ninety-Third Street in New York City.

268 | NOTES

27 Erika Lee, *At America's Gates: Chinese Immigration during the Exclusion Era, 1882–1943* (Chapel Hill: University of North Carolina Press, 2003); see also Anna Pegler-Gordon, "Chinese Exclusion, Photography, and the Development of U.S. Immigration Policy," *American Quarterly* 58, no. 1 (March 2006): 51–77.

28 Mae Ngai, *Impossible Subjects: Illegal Aliens and the Making of Modern America* (Princeton, NJ: Princeton University Press, 2005); Alexandra Minna Stern, *Eugenic Nation: Faults and Frontiers of Better Breeding in Modern America* (Berkeley: University of California Press, 2005); Matthew Frye Jacobson, *Whiteness of a Different Color: European Immigrants and the Alchemy of Race* (Cambridge, MA: Harvard University Press, 1998); Thomas Guglielmo, *White on Arrival: Italians, Race, Color, and Power in Chicago, 1890–1945* (New York: Oxford University Press, 2003).

29 "Dieiatel'nost' o. prot. Arkadiia Piotrovskago v Russkom Emigrantskom o-vie i Domie v N'iu-Iorkie (1912–1914 g.g.)," IuS I, 227–28.

30 Fr. Peter Kohanik, "Russkoe Emigrantskoe Dielo v S. Amerike," IuS I, 225.

31 A. P[iotrovs]kii, "Ellis-Ailandskie Siluety," *Russkii emigrant*, August 21, 1913.

32 For 1913 statistics, "Otchet russkago emigrantskago doma za 1913 god," *APV*, February 14, 1914, 60–61. For detailed quarterly reports, "Otchet agenta Russkago Emigrantskago Obshchestva o dieiatel'nosti na Ellis Island za pervuiu tret' 1913 g," *APV*, May 28, 1913, 236–37; and "Otchet Predstavitelia Russkago Emigrantskago Obshchestva o dieiatel'nosti na Ellis Island-ie za vtoruiu tret' 1913 goda," *APV*, September 28, 1913, 395.

33 Nabliudatel' [An Observer], "Novisti s Ellis Ailanda," *Russkii emigrant*, June 26, 1913.

34 "Spravochnyi Otdel," *Russkii emigrant*, May 30, 1912.

35 Arcady Piotrowsky, "Ellis Ailandskie Siluety," *Russkii emigrant*, July 24, 1913.

36 Piotrowsky.

37 Piotrowsky.

38 V. Krugliak, "Sovyety immigrantam," *Russkii emigrant*, November 14, 1912; Tyler Anbinder, *City of Dreams: The 400-Year Epic History of Immigrant New York* (Boston: Houghton Mifflin Harcourt, 2016), 348–49. For immigration practices at Galveston concerning eastern European migrants, see Bernard Marinbach, *Galveston: Ellis Island of the West* (Albany: State University of New York Press, 1983), especially 56–91.

39 Priest Theofan Buketoff, "V dorogye," *APV*, September 28, 1911, 317.

40 Abraham Cahan, *The Rise of David Levinsky* (New York: Harper, 1917), 101.

41 Arcady Piotrowsky, "Ellis Ailandskie siluety," *Russkii emigrant*, September 4, 1913.

42 "Spravochnyi Otdel," *Russkii emigrant*, May 30, 1912.

43 Fr. Alexander Hotovitzky, "Nasha Radost'," *APV*, February 28, 1912, 72–76.

44 "Po Emigrantskomu Voprosu," *APV*, November 4, 1915, 464–65.

45 "Otchet Russkago Emigrantskago Doma za 1913 god," *APV*, February 14, 1914, 60–61.

46 "Otchet agenta Russkago Emigrantskago Obshchestva o dieiatel'nosti na Ellis Island za pervuiu tret' 1913 g.," *APV*, May 28, 1913, 236–37. Ellis Island agents often

subjected unmarried women to intrusive and embarrassing medical examinations, especially if agents suspected a pregnancy. Those claiming to be engaged, perhaps hundreds each year, faced a choice: marry and avoid deportation or be deported for immorality. Details about such weddings are murky, but it is thought that most occurred on Ellis Island as a condition of release. Vincent J. Cannato, *American Passages: The History of Ellis Island* (New York: HarperCollins, 2009), 264–66. Pregnancy could be considered a cause for deportation, even for married women, as it was thought to put a woman at risk of becoming a "public charge." See Eithne Luibheid, *Entry Denied: Controlling Sexuality at the Border* (Minneapolis: University of Minnesota Press, 2002), 9–10. For another aspect of Ellis Island and marriage, see James W. Oberly, "Love at First Sight and an Arrangement for Life: Investigating and Interpreting a 1910 Hungarian Migrant Marriage," *Journal of Austrian-American History* 1 (2017): 69–97.

47 "Malen'kiia zametki—Notes," *APV*, January 14, 1911, 5–8; "Russian Cathedral Here Crowded—Feasting on the East Side," *New York Times*, January 8, 1912; "Sviatoi na Ellis Island'e," *APV*, January 28, 1912, 30.

48 "Liturgiia v shtatnoi n'iu-iorkskoi tiur'mye v Sing-Sing, Ossining, N.Y.," *APV*, May 11, 1916, 206–8.

49 "Arkhipastyrskii prizyv," *APV*, February 27, 1909, 62.

50 Mike Kot, hearing transcript, November 27, 1919, File 54709/552, Box 3495, INS.

51 "Spravachnyi Otdiel," *Russkii emigrant*, February 20, 1912.

52 Jerome P. Davis, *The Russians and Ruthenians in America* (New York: George H. Doran, 1922), 33–35.

53 Davis, 33–35, 42.

54 Katherine Benton-Cohen, *Inventing the Immigrant Problem* (Cambridge, MA: Harvard University Press, 2018), 18.

55 The Dillingham Commission reports most pertinent to major centers of American Orthodox Rus' can be found in volumes 6, 7, 8, and 9. General conditions of Russian and Slavic immigration are described in volume 4. For general observations, see also Davis, *Russians and Ruthenians in America*; and Emily Greene Balch, *Our Slavic Fellow Citizens* (New York: Charities Publication Committee, 1910).

56 Davis, *Russians and Ruthenians in America*, 96.

57 US Immigration Commission, *Reports of the Immigration Commission*, vol. 6, pt. 1, *Bituminous Coal Mining* (Washington, DC: Government Printing Office, 1911), 323.

58 Orthodox Church in America, "St. Mary Church," accessed October 15, 2024, www.oca.org.

59 Orthodox Church in America, "SS. Peter and Paul Church," accessed October 15, 2024, www.oca.org. Susan Tassin, *Pennsylvania Ghost Towns: Uncovering the Hidden Past* (Mechanicsburg, PA: Stackpole Books, 2007), 112–14. For descriptions of a later calamity at Wehrum, see "The Wehrum Mine Explosion," *Mines and Minerals*, September 1909, 118–21.

270 | NOTES

60 "Blagoi pochin," *APV*, August 14, 1902, 306–7.

61 Michael Melancon, *The Lena Goldfields Massacre and the Crisis of the Late Tsarist State* (College Station: Texas A&M University Press, 2006).

62 "Concerning the Labor Question in Russia," *APV*, May 28, 1912, 176–84. Translation is from the Russian text, as a parallel English translation by St. Platon Theological Seminary instructor Charles Johnston contains several variances that slightly alter Archbishop Platon's meaning. The full article is also published as "Rabochiy vopros v Rossii," *Russkii emigrant*, May 30, 1912.

63 Advertisement, "Trebuiutsia rabochie," *Russkii emigrant*, April 3, 1913.

64 James W. Lewis, *At Home in the City: The Protestant Experience in Gary, Indiana, 1906–1975* (Knoxville: University of Tennessee Press, 1992), 25–30.

65 Protopriest Benjamin Kedrovsky, *Na nivye Bozhiei: Istoriia Sv. Pokrovskoi pravoslavnoi russk tserkvi v g. Geri, Indiana, Sev. Amerika* (Southbury, CT: Alatas, 1931), 25–29.

66 Protopriest Benjamin Kedrovsky, "Sv. Pokrovskaia pravoslavnaia russkaia tserkov," IuS II, 178–84; Kedrovsky, *Na nivye Bozhiei*, 18–19, 80–83; Martin E. Carlson, "A Study of the Eastern Orthodox Churches in Gary, Indiana" (MA thesis, University of Chicago, 1942), 15–19; Rev. Theodore Panchak, "A Commentary on the Life and Pastoral Ministry of Fr. Benjamin Kedrovsky of Gary, Indiana" (MDiv thesis, St. Vladimir's Orthodox Theological Seminary, 1984), 35–37.

67 G. Dobrov, "V Geri, Ind.," *Russkii emigrant*, December 4, 1913.

68 Priest I. Fedoronko and family, "Pis'mo v redaktsiiu," *Russkii emigrant*, November 6, 1913.

CHAPTER 2. "MY SADNESS IS BOUNDLESS"

1 Priest Arcady Piotrowsky, "Khoroshii den' v berlinye, sht. n.g.," *APV*, November 25, 1915, 507–10.

2 Alyssa Maldonado-Estrada and Katherine Dugan, "Forum: Studying Masculinities, Catholic Style," *American Catholic Studies* 132 (Summer 2021): 2.

3 Nadieszda Kizenko, *A Prodigal Saint: Father John of Kronstadt and the Russian People* (University Park: Pennsylvania State University Press, 2000), 13.

4 In 1905, Roosevelt welcomed archdiocesan leaders to the White House. The president took pleasure in meeting Bishop Innocent (Pustynsky), announcing that he was "De-light-ed!" to welcome a visitor from Alaska and asking "about the health and living conditions of the natives." See Bishop Innocent (Pustynsky), "Iz otcheta o sostoianii aliaskinskago vikariatstva za 1906 god," IuS I, 199–200. For Roosevelt and masculinity, see Gail Bederman, *Manliness and Civilization* (Chicago: University of Chicago Press, 1993), 170–216.

5 Matthew Frye Jacobson, *Barbarian Virtues* (New York: Hill and Wang, 2000), 139–72; Nell Irvin Painter, *The History of White People* (New York: Norton, 2010), 311–26.

6 Quoted in Erika Lee, *America for Americans: A History of Xenophobia in the United States* (New York: Basic Books, 2019), 120.

7 See Aram G. Sarkisian, "Playing Fair to America: Postwar Americanization as a Religious Project in the English-Speaking Department, 1920–1924," in "The Cross between Hammer and Sickle: Russian Orthodox Christians in the United States, 1908–1928)" (PhD diss., Northwestern University, 2019), 292–348. For the rationale behind the organization of the diocese, see Bishop Tikhon (Bellavin), "Views of Questions to Be Examined by the Local Council of the Russian Church," *APV*, March Supplement, 1906, 65–70.

8 In Russian practice of this period, full deacons were rare in parish settings. The diaconate was considered a perfunctory step before ordination to the priesthood, meaning that the rank often was held for only a matter of days.

9 Archimandrite Timon (Muliar), *Pod shchitom vyery* (Southbury, CT: Alatas, 1934), 43.

10 "Normal'nyi Ustav dlia prikhodov S.-Amerikanskoi Pravoslavnoi Eparkhii," *APV*, March 31, 1909, 102. This quotation comes from the official English translation, published as "The Normal Statute for the Parishes of the American Orthodox Archdiocese," *APV*, November 14, 1911, 373.

11 "The Orthodox Diocese of North America and Canada," *APV*, January 1918, 4–10; continued, February 1918, 26–29.

12 Father Leonid Kishkovsky, "Archbishop Tikhon and the North American Diocese, 1898–1907," in *Orthodox America, 1794–1976*, ed. Constance Tarasar (Syosset, NY: Orthodox Church in America Department of History and Archives, 1975), 86–87; Anatoly Bezkorovainy, "One Hundred Years of Service to God and Man," in *A History of the Holy Trinity Russian Orthodox Cathedral of Chicago, 1892–1992*, ed. Anatoly Bezkorovainy (Chicago: Holy Trinity Orthodox Cathedral, 1992), 3–16. For Bishop Nicholas and the Russian Pavilion, see Prof. Paul Zaichenko, "II. Sviatitel'stvovanie Vladyki Nikolaia (Varshavskago)," IuS I, 144–46.

13 Mitred Archpriest Joseph Dzvonchik, "Reminiscences Concerning His Holiness Patriarch Tikhon," *One Church*, November–December 1965, 226.

14 The fourteen "Vologodians" (*vologodtsev*) included three lay missionaries and eleven priests (two of whom later became bishops). The three Kedrovsky brothers were priests Alexander, Raphael, and Apollinary, all missionaries who served in Alaska. See Fr. Constantine Popoff, "Vologzhane v amerikan. pravoslavnoi missii," IuS I, 203–5.

15 Metropolitan Theophilus (Pashkovsky), "Pravoslavie v Amerikye, IV: Dyeiatel'nost' Episkopa Nikolaia," IuS I, 124. This is a reference to Innocent (Veniaminov) (1797–1879), a priest and bishop and later metropolitan of Moscow known for missionary work in Alaska. The Russian Orthodox Church glorified him as a saint in 1977. For another account of the clergy Nicholas recruited for the US, see Dr. Basil Bensin, "Vazhnyeishie momenty v istorii russkoi pravoslavnoi tserkvi v severnoi amerikye. Sviatitel'stvovanie Episkopa Nikolaia," IuS I, 133–35.

16 Laurie Manchester, *Holy Fathers, Secular Sons: Clergy, Intelligentsia, and the Modern Self in Revolutionary Russia* (DeKalb: Northern Illinois Press, 2008); Jan Plamper, "The Russian Orthodox Episcopate, 1721–1917: A Prosopography,"

Journal of Social History 34 (2000): 5–34; Jennifer Hedda, *His Kingdom Come: Orthodox Pastorship and Social Activism in Revolutionary Russia* (DeKalb: Northern Illinois Press, 2011). For a study of *soslovie*, see Alison K. Smith, *For the Common Good and Their Own Well-Being: Social Estates in Imperial Russia* (Oxford: Oxford University Press, 2014).

17 Ludmilla Buketoff Turkevich, "The Right Reverend Constantin Buketoff, a Biographical Sketch (on His 50th Anniversary as a Priest)," *APV*, July–August 1957, 125–26.

18 F. M. Buketoff, "Rozhestvo na chuzhbinye," in *Amerikanskaia Rus': Sbornik Razskazov* (New York, 1921), 71–72.

19 Buketoff, 77, 79.

20 Rev. Theodore Panchak, "A Commentary on the Life and Pastoral Ministry of Fr. Benjamin Kedrovsky of Gary, Indiana" (MDiv thesis, St. Vladimir's Orthodox Theological Seminary, 1984), 14–17. For the seminary protests after 1905, see Daniel Scarborough, *Russia's Social Gospel: The Orthodox Pastoral Movement in Famine, War, and Revolution* (Madison: University of Wisconsin Press, 2022), 65–82.

21 Metropolitan Evlogy (Georgievsky), *My Life's Journey: The Memoirs of Metropolitan Evlogy, Part I*, trans. Alexander Lisenko (Yonkers, NY: St. Vladimir's Seminary Press, 2014), 200. A *panagia* is a jeweled pectoral icon worn by a bishop. While Platon was an archbishop when Evlogy sent Beskishkin to North America, here Evlogy refers to Platon as a metropolitan, the rank he held from 1917 until his death in 1934.

22 Bureau of the Census, *Religious Bodies 1916*, part 2, *Separate Denominations* (Washington, DC: Government Printing Office, 1919), 261.

23 "Miners Argument in Support of Demand for Increased Wage in Anthracite Field," *Coal Trade Bulletin*, April 3, 1920, 58.

24 National Industrial Conference Board, *Wartime Changes in Wages, September 1914–March 1919* (Boston: National Industrial Conference Board, 1919).

25 Joyce Shaw Peterson, *American Automobile Workers, 1900–1933* (Albany: State University of New York Press, 1987), 47.

26 Holy Trinity Orthodox Church, "History of Holy Trinity Orthodox Church," October 2012, http://htocclayton.org.

27 Archbishop Evdokim (Meschersky), "Report of the State of the Diocese for 1916," trans. Hieromonk Andrew Kostadis, in Kostadis, "Pictures of Missionary Life according to the Russian Clerical Press in America and the Ruling American Bishops about the Life of the American Mission in 1900–1917" (MTh thesis, St. Vladimir's Orthodox Theological Seminary, 1999), 256.

28 *25-letii Iubelei Sv. Ioanno-Bogoslovskaya Tserkov', Vindzor, Ontario, Kanada* (Windsor, ON, St. John the Divine Russian Orthodox Church, 1941), 6; *S.S. Peter & Paul Orthodox Church 90th Anniversary* (Detroit:, Ss. Peter and Paul Orthodox Church, 1997), 10.

29 Buketoff, *Amerikanskaia Rus'*, 39–34; Priest F. Buketoff, "Tainstvennyi zvon," *APV*, November 28, 1907, 428–31.

30 Quoted in Bezkorovainy, "One Hundred Years of Service," 20–21. For Slunin's reassignment from Chicago, see "Dopisi," *Svit*, March 5, 1908.

31 Priest John Sliunin, "Moia poyezdka v doroguiu Rossiiu," *APV*, June 28, 1911, 255.

32 Established in 1722 as part of the Petrine Reforms, the tsar-appointed *ober-prokuror* was both the lay representative to the Most Holy Synod and part of the tsar's cabinet and held significant administrative sway in the Russian Church.

33 Scott M. Kenworthy, *The Heart of Russia: Trinity-Sergius, Monasticism, and Society after 1825* (Oxford: New York University Press, 2010); Robert Greene, *Bodies like Bright Stars: Saints and Relics in Orthodox Russia* (DeKalb: Northern Illinois Press, 2009); Patrick Lally Michelson, *Beyond the Monastery Walls: The Ascetic Revolution in Russian Orthodox Thought, 1814–1914* (Madison: University of Wisconsin Press, 2017).

34 Slunin described his *otpusk* in a series of articles for the *APV*. See Priest John Sliunin, "Moia poyezdka v doroguiu Rossiiu," *APV*, June 28, 1911, 254–55; "Poyezdka moia na rodinu," *APV*, December 14, 1911, 410–11; continued, December 28, 1911, 433–36.

35 Priest John Slunin, "Poyezdka moia na rodinu," *APV*, December 28, 1911, 434.

36 Slunin, 435.

37 Zotikov arrived with priest Evtikhy Balanovich during Holy Week. The first services were held on Good Friday in a parishioner's Lower East Side residence. "Among the Churches," *Christian Work*, April 11, 1895, 577.

38 Deacon Ilia Zotikov to Bishop Nicholas Ziorov, May 19/7, 1895, Box B40/Reel 35, ROGCCA LOC.

39 "Russian Bishop Holds Services," *New York Herald*, May 19, 1895; "Mass by Bishop Nicolas," *New York Herald*, May 20, 1895.

40 "Ryech', skazannaia pri rukopolozhenii sviashchenika A. Khotovitskago, –25-go fevralia, 1896 goda," in *Tridtsat' Ryechei i tri poslaniia preosviashchennago Nikolaia, Episkopa Aleutskago i Aliaskinskago* (New York, 1896), 130.

41 "Pastyrskii iubilei," *APV*, May 28, 1905, 193–95.

42 In a 1909 civil court deposition concerning another New York priest, Hotovitzky said that he paid the parish bills. "In my absence," however, he said, "my assistant, Father Zotikoff does that." Asked who else was authorized to disburse funds, Hotovitzky replied, "None, except Father Zotikoff, who pays for the vestments, and for other things pertaining to the sanctuary." Deposition of Father Alexander Hotovitsky, April 30, 1909, *Kalkhoff Company v. St. Nicholas Church*, 67 Misc. 107 (N.Y. App. Term 1910), 37–38.

43 In this account, Kohanik noted that Hotovitzky had arrived there only a few days before. Peter Kohanik, "Amerikansko-Russkiia vpechatlyeniia iz vremen Vladyki Nikolaia," *IuS I*, 147–49.

44 "The Coronation Mass in This City," *New York Evening Post*, May 27, 1896.

45 Priest Alexander Hotovitzky, "21 Fevralia 1913 goda v N'iu Iorkye," *APV*, March 14, 1913, 92. For other insights into the transnational thought of missionary clergy, see John H. Erickson, "Slavophile Thought and Conceptions of Mission in the

Russian North American Archdiocese, Late 19th–Early 20th Century," *St. Vladimir's Theological Quarterly* 56 (2012): 245–68.

46 Michael Pokrovsky, *St. Nicholas Cathedral of New York: History and Legacy* (New York: St. Nicholas Cathedral Study Group, 1968), 12–15.

47 Pokrovsky, *St. Nicholas Cathedral of New York*, 15–18. Ties between the *Retvizan* and the New York cathedral spanned several years. To this day, the cathedral altar bears an ornate metal cross salvaged from the battleship after its sinking in 1904. See Aram G. Sarkisian, "Blessed Are the Peacemakers: Thinking Historically about Russian Orthodox Soft Diplomacy," *Public Orthodoxy*, March 17, 2022, https://publicorthodoxy.org.

48 Pokrovsky, *St. Nicholas Cathedral of New York*, 78.

49 "Manuscript. Account of the state of the Aleutian Diocese for 1905," translation in Kostadis, "Pictures of Missionary Life," 224. The relocation from San Francisco proved fortuitous. The diocese sold the cathedral there in early 1906, vacating it after Easter Sunday services. Two days later, the building was destroyed in the cataclysmic San Francisco earthquake. See "Bozh'ia groza," *APV*, April 28, 1906, 150–52.

50 "Rechi, proiznesennyia Ego Vysokopreosviashchenstvom, Vysokopreosviash-chenyeishim Tikhonom, Arkhiepiskopom Aleutskim i S.-Amerikanskim, Pri pervom sluzhenii v N'iu-Iorkskom kafedral'nom soborye, 25 Sentiabria 1905 g.," *APV*, October 14, 1905, 372–73.

51 This was a confusing case of mistaken identity in which the Zotikovs faced false accusations of stealing a mail pouch found emptied in their cabin after they disembarked in Germany. The couple was arrested at the hotel where they stopped before continuing on to Russia to allow Maria to recuperate from severe seasickness. Separated and questioned by German police, both were jailed overnight until the situation was resolved. The experiences of detention and police examination, much of it without an interpreter, left both shaken. Fr. Ilia fell into a period of mental anguish, including "fainting fits and hysterics." See Priest Ilia Zotikov to Bishop Nicholas (Ziorov), September 10, 1898, Reel 35, ROGCCA LOC; and "Tyranny in Germany," *Wichita Daily Eagle*, September 11, 1898.

52 "Iubilei, den' Angela i proshchanie," *APV*, June 28, 1910, 182–85. Here Hotovitzky implies that Zotikov served as his father confessor, a spiritual relationship that might have been mutual.

53 Alexander Hotovitzky, "Iz Dnevnika. Otyezd o. Ilii Zotikova," *APV*, August 28, 1910, 250–53.

54 This analysis draws from the 1911 archdiocesan directory, which lists eighty-nine communities and seventy-four priests. "Russian Orthodox Diocese of North America and the Aleutian Islands," *APV*, May 14, 1911, 164–65.

55 Vera Shevzov, *Russian Orthodoxy on the Eve of Revolution* (Oxford: Oxford University Press, 2004), 81.

56 Nicholas Denysenko, "The Joys and Crosses of Clerical Families," in *Married Priests in the Catholic Church*, ed. Adam A. J. DeVille (Notre Dame, IN: University of Notre Dame Press, 2021), 167–68.

NOTES | 275

57 William G. Wagner, "'Orthodox Domesticity': Creating a Social Role for Women," in *Sacred Stories: Religion and Spirituality in Modern Russia*, ed. Mark D. Steinberg and Heather J. Coleman (Bloomington: Indiana University Press, 2007), 120.

58 While *matuskha* can be an endearing term for the wife of either a priest or deacon, in the context of American Orthodox Rus' it was understood to mean the wife of a priest, as the married diaconate was virtually unknown in the Russian Archdiocese of the early twentieth century.

59 For contemporary reflections, see Andrew Jarmus, "'What Did You Expect?': A Reflection on Married Clergy and Pastoral Ministry," in DeVille, *Married Priests in the Catholic Church*, 186–96; and Julian Hayda, "Growing Up in a Rectory: Using *Oikonomia* to Answer the Tough Questions Posed by the Children of Priestly Families," in DeVille, *Married Priests in the Catholic Church*, 146–54. See also Sarah Riccardi-Swartz, *Between Heaven and Russia: Religious Conversion and Political Apostasy in Appalachia* (New York: Fordham University Press, 2022), 62–63.

60 S. V. Bulgakov, *Nastol'naia kniga dlia sviashchenno-tserkovno-sluzhitelei* (Kyiv: Tipografiia Kievo-Pecherskoi Uspenskoi Lavryi, 1913), 1098–1100. See also Irene Galadza, "The Vocation of the *Presbytera*: Icon of the Theotokos in the Midst of the Ministerial Priesthood," in DeVille, *Married Priests in the Catholic Church*, 155–66.

61 In 1918, the Unitarian Society sold the building to a group of eastern European Jews, who reopened it as Beth Israel Synagogue. Today the building is Heritage Baptist Church. Barbara Tetreault, "City Asked to Take over Beth Israel Cemetery," *Berlin (NH) Sun*, December 20, 2017, www.conwaydailysun.com.

62 "Kak Osnovalsia Pravoslavnyi Prikhod v gorodye Berlin, N.H.," *APV*, November 11, 1915, 476–81.

63 Fr. A. P[iotrovsk]y, "K osviashcheniiu sv. khrama v gor. Berlinye, N.H.," *APV*, September 2, 1915, 320–11; "Kak Osnovalsia Pravoslavnyi Prikhod v gorodye Berlin, N.H.," *APV*, November 11, 1915, 476–81.

64 Arcady Piotrowsky, "Radostnoe torzhestvo v Berlinye, N.G.," *APV*, November 18, 1915, 490–94.

65 Almost certainly, this was the *Service Book of the Holy Orthodox-Catholic (Greco-Russian) Church*, translated by Isabel Hapgood and published in 1906. Hapgood was an Episcopalian and committed Russophile with a keen interest in the Orthodox Church. A noted translator of Russian literature, she was acquainted with Leo Tolstoy, who favored her work. In New York City, Hapgood managed the Russian cathedral choir and organized fund-raising efforts for church causes. She died in 1928. See Marina Ledkovsky, "A Linguistic Bridge to Orthodoxy: In Memoriam Isabel Florence Hapgood" (lecture presented at the Twelfth Annual Russian Orthodox Musicians Conference, October 7–11, 1998, Washington, DC); Stuart H. Hoke, "A Generally Obscure Calling: A Character Sketch of Isabel Florence Hapgood," *St. Vladimir's Theological Quarterly* 45 (2001): 55–93.

66 "Eshche russkaia tserkov," *APV*, November 18, 1915, 488–90; "New Hampshire Episcopal Convention," *APV*, March 2, 1916, 100–101.

276 | NOTES

67 "Iz Berlina, N.G.," *APV*, November 4, 1915, 466–67. For another account of the situation in Lincoln and other area towns, see Priest Ioann Zhitinskii, "Na sluzhenii tserkvi," *APV*, August 10, 1916, 471.

68 "Kak Osnovalsia Pravoslavnyi Prikhod v gorodye Berlin, N.H.," *APV*, November 11, 1915, 479.

69 "Church and Saloon," *APV*, March 2, 1916, 102–3.

70 "From the History of the Russian Parish in Berlin, N.H.," *APV*, August 17, 1916, 486–88.

71 "Rasporiazhenie eparkhial'nago nachal'stva," *APV*, February 3, 1916, 48.

CHAPTER 3. "THE HOLY CHURCH IS THEIR MOTHER"

1 US Bureau of the Census, *Religious Bodies 1916*, part 2, *Separate Denominations* (Washington, DC: Government Printing Office, 1919), 262.

2 *St. John's Russian Orthodox Catholic Church Golden Anniversary* (Arnold, PA, 1960), 11, IHRCA.

3 "Fifty Years of Service," in *St. Michael's Orthodox Catholic Church Golden Anniversary* (Philadelphia, 1959), 21, IHRCA.

4 Peter Mock, "Diary of a Parish: Homestead, PA," in *Orthodox America, 1794–1976*, ed. Constance Tarasar (Syosset, NY: Orthodox Church in America Department of History and Archives, 1975), 169.

5 Saint Tikhon of Moscow, *Instructions and Teachings for the American Orthodox Faithful (1898–1907)*, trans and ed. Alex Maximov and David C. Ford (Waymart, PA: St. Tikhon's Monastery Press, 2016), 42.

6 Sebastian Dabovich, "The Education of Children," in *Preaching in the Russian Church* (San Francisco: Cubery, 1899), 78–84.

7 Ann Braude, "The Baptism of a Cheyenne Girl," in *The Study of Children in Religions*, ed. Susan B. Ridgely (New York: New York University Press, 2011), 237.

8 Priest John Nedzelnitsky, "The Fiftieth Anniversary of the Russian Colony in Minneapolis," in *Golden Jubilee Album of the St. Mary's Russian Orthodox Greek Catholic Church* (Minneapolis: St. Mary's Russian Orthodox Greek Catholic Church, 1937), 1–27; and Priest Alexander Kukulevsky, "My Years in Minneapolis," in *Golden Jubilee Album*, 75–77, IHRCA.

9 Rev. Fr. John Dzubay, "Diamond Jubilee: The Triumph of Orthodoxy," in *Diamond Jubilee Album of the St. Mary's Russian Orthodox Greek Catholic Church* (Minneapolis: St. Mary's Russian Orthodox Greek Catholic Church, 1962), 23, IHRCA.

10 Paul Zaichenko, "My Twelve Years of Service in Minneapolis," in *Golden Anniversary Souvenir Album of the St. Mary's Russian Orthodox Church A Capella Choir* (Minneapolis: St. Mary's Russian Orthodox Greek Catholic Church, 1941), 13–18, IHRCA. For a later sociological study of the St. Mary's parish community and the Northeast neighborhood, see Alex Simirenko, *Pilgrims, Colonists, and Frontiersmen: An Ethnic Community in Transition* (Glencoe, NY: Free Press, 1974).

11 The other two missionary schools in this period were both in Alaska: the Innokentii Missionary School in Sitka and the Missionary School in Unalaska.

12 Paul Zaichenko, "For the Fiftieth Anniversary of the Parish in Minneapolis," in *Golden Jubilee Album*, 43, IHRCA.

13 "Sedmoi uchebnyi god v Minneapolisskoi shkolye 1903–4-y.," *APV*, November 14, 1904, 423–25.

14 Bishop Benjamin (Basalyga), "St. Mary's Russian Orthodox Church and Parish of Minneapolis," in *Golden Jubilee Album*, 64–66, IHRCA.

15 Kukulevsky, "My Years in Minneapolis," 75.

16 Clifford Putney, *Muscular Christianity: Manhood and Sport in Protestant America, 1880–1920* (Cambridge, MA: Harvard University Press, 2001), 73–98; see also Timothy B. Neary, *Crossing Parish Boundaries: Race, Sport, and Catholic Youth in Chicago, 1914–1954* (Chicago: University of Chicago Press, 2016), 75–78; Sarah Imhoff, *Masculinity and the Making of American Judaism* (Bloomington: Indiana University Press, 2017), 95.

17 Anatole Kamensky was a missionary priest in Alaska, California, and then in Minneapolis, where he obtained a history degree from the University of Minnesota. He left North America in 1903 to serve as rector of the Odesa Theological Academy. In 1906, he was elevated to the episcopate. In 1922, Kamensky was imprisoned for his opposition to the Bolshevik reclamation of church valuables. Released in 1924, he died a year later in exile in the Siberian city of Omsk. Fr. Viacheslav Sukkhovetskii, "Arkhiepiskop Anatolii (Kamenskii)," *Prikhod v chest' sviatogo prepodobnogo efrema sirina*, accessed October 28, 2024, http://st-efrem.orthodoxy.ru.

18 Kukulevsky, "My Years in Minneapolis," 75.

19 Zaichenko, "For the Fiftieth Anniversary of the Parish in Minneapolis," 47–48.

20 "Religious Educational Institutions," in *Diamond Jubilee Album*, 31. For those who were chosen to study in Russia, see Prot. Peter Kohanik, "Amerikansko-Russkiia vpechatlyeniia iz vremen Vladyki Nikolaia," IuS I, 147–49.

21 Protopriest John Nedzelnitsky, "Po voprosu ob ustroistvye dukh. seminarii v Amerikye," *APV*, November 14, 1903, 372, 373.

22 Nedzelnitsky, 373, 374–75.

23 Priest Constantine Popoff, "Memories of St. Mary's Parish in Minneapolis," in *Golden Jubilee Album*, 70; Nedzelnitsky, "Fiftieth Anniversary of the Russian Colony in Minneapolis," 20–22. For the final annual report of the Missionary School, see "Otchet po Minneapolisskoi Missionerskoi shkolye za 1904–5 uchebnyi god," *APV*, July 28, 1905, 275–77; and Scott M. Kenworthy, "Metropolitan Leonty, Saint Tikhon, and the Establishment of America's First Orthodox Seminary," in *The Life and Works of Metropolitan Leonty, 1876–1965*, ed. David C. Ford (Waymart, PA: St. Tikhon's Monastery Press, 2019), 43. For the Cleveland "Bursa," see Prot. Vasylii Vasyl'ev, "Dukhovnoe uchilishche ili Bursa," IuS II, 230–31; and Archbishop Sylvester [Haruns] of Montreal, "Foundations for Growth, 1870–1898," in Tarasar, *Orthodox America, 1794–1976*, 57.

24 "Offitsial'nyi otdyel," *APV*, July 28, 1905, 285–86.

25 "Kratkii otchet po Minneapolisskoi Pravoslavnoi Dukhovnoi Seminarii za 1907–8 uch. god (3-ii god sushchestvovaniia)," *APV*, June 28, 1908, 229.

278 | NOTES

26 Dr. Basil Bensin, "My Recollections of the North American Ecclesiastical Seminary, 1905 and 1906," in *Golden Jubilee Album*, 83–84; Dr. Basil Bensin, "Memories of Seminary Days in Minneapolis," in *Golden Anniversary Souvenir Album*, 22–23.

27 "Kratkii otchet po Minneapolisskoi Pravoslavnoi Dukhovnoi Seminarii za 1907–8 uch. god (3-ii god sushchestvovaniia)," *APV*, June 28, 1908, 229.

28 *The Catechism of the Orthodox, Catholic, Eastern Church* (San Francisco: Murdock, 1901); *The Service Book of the Holy Orthodox-Catholic Apostolic (Greco-Russian) Church*, trans. Isabel Hapgood (Boston: Houghton, Mifflin, 1906).

29 "Iz Seminarskoi Zhizni," *APV*, June 14, 1907, 198–99.

30 Bishop Benjamin, "St. Mary's Russian Orthodox Church and Parish of Minneapolis," 64–66.

31 Priest L. Turkevich, "Dumy i plany o Minneapolisskoi Dukhovnoi Seminarii," *APV*, December 28, 1906, 472.

32 For Turkevich's role with the seminary, see Kenworthy, "Metropolitan Leonty," 37–50. A third Turkevich brother, Ilarion, briefly served as a missionary in China before his untimely death in 1904.

33 "Chislo kreshchenei, brakov i pogrebenii po pokrovskomu minneapolisskomu prikhodu s 1889 g. po 1937 g.," in *Golden Jubilee Album*, 206–7.

34 Metropolitan Leonty (Turkevich), "Archpastoral Message and Memoirs of the Primate of the Russian Orthodox Greek Catholic Church of America His Beatitude Metropolitan Leonty," in *Diamond Jubilee Album*, n.p. For another account of the parish school, see Reverend Vasily Kolesnikoff, "The Parish of Minneapolis Thirty Years Ago," in *Golden Jubilee Album*, 86.

35 Zaichenko, "For the Fiftieth Anniversary of the Parish of Minneapolis," 48.

36 Benjamin, "St. Mary's Russian Orthodox Church and Parish of Minneapolis," 64–66. For a brief biography, see "Archbishop Benjamin," in Tarasar, *Orthodox America, 1794–1976*, 204.

37 Leonty, "Archpastoral Message and Memoirs," n.p. For the construction of the church and controversies over its cost, see Very Reverend Archpriest Constantine Popoff, "Anniversary Greetings from a Former Pastor," in *Diamond Jubilee Album*, 26–28. For its iconography, see Fr. Constantine Popoff, "Prebyvanie Ego Vysokopreosviashchenstva, Arkhiepiskopa Tikhona, v Minneapolisye 30 Noiabria i 6 Dekabria 1906 g.," *APV*, December 28, 1906, 476.

38 University of Minnesota Department of Music, "Directors," accessed October 28, 2024, https://cla.umn.edu.

39 Leonty, "Archpastoral Message and Memoirs."

40 "Znamenatel'noe sobytie v zhizni nashei Missii," *APV*, October 24, 1911, 327–28.

41 William G. Wagner, "The Transformation of Female Orthodox Monasticism in Nizhnii Novgorod Diocese, 1764–1929, in Comparative Perspective," *Journal of Modern History* 78 (2006): esp. 796, 834. See also Brenda Meehan, *Holy Women of Russia* (San Francisco: HarperSanFrancisco, 1993).

42 "Kratkii otchet o sostoianii Sv. Tikhonovskoi Obiteli i Sirotskago Priiuta s 15-go Iiulia 1905 goda po 15-e Ianvaria 1906 goda," *APV*, February 14, 1906, 41–44. The

monastery site was a farm "bought from an American, Wagner" (41), and portions of it were kept for agricultural purposes.

43 US Bureau of the Census, *Religious Bodies: 1906*, part 2 (Washington, DC: Government Printing Office, 1906), 262.

44 1910 US Census, Wayne County, Pennsylvania, populations schedule, South Canaan Township, Russian Monastery and Orphanage, p. 275, enumeration district 111, sheet no. 3.

45 Tikhon, *Instructions and Teachings*, 242–43.

46 "Svad'ba brachika," *Russkii emigrant*, June 12, 1913. For histories of the orphanage, see "St. Tikhon's Orphanage," in *St. Tikhon's: Center of Orthodoxy for the Russian Orthodox Greek Catholic Church of America, the Metropolia* (South Canaan, PA: St. Tikhon's Theological Seminary, 1968), 10; and "Russian Orphan Home of Brooklyn and Holy Virgin Protection Convent and Orphanage," in Tarasar, *Orthodox America, 1794–1976*, 137–38.

47 "Vecher v sirotskom priiutye" and "Khristos Razhdaetsia!," *Svit*, January 1, 1915.

48 "Vozzvanie," *APV*, April 28, 1915, 115–17.

49 Prot. L. T[urkevi]ch, "Springfild'skii Prazdnik," *APV*, September 23, 1915, 364.

50 "V S.-Amerik. Dukh. Pravlenie postupili sbory i pozhertvovaniia na siroty (dlia Russkago Sirotskago Priiuta v Springfield, Vt.)," *APV*, September 30, 1915, 390; continued, October 7, 1915, 406.

51 Holy Trinity Orthodox Church, "The History of Holy Trinity Parish," accessed October 28, 2024, www.htocvt.org.

52 "Ustav sirotskago priiuta," *APV*, October 14, 1915, 420–21.

53 "Ustav sirotskago priiuta," 421.

54 Prot. Ioann Kozitsky, "Pervyi uchebnyi god v Russkom Zhenskom Kolledzeye," IuS I, 257–58; Father John Matusiak and Vasily Lickwar, "Holy Annunciation Russian Women's College," in Tarasar, *Orthodox America, 1794–1976*, 139–40.

55 Gregory Freeze, *The Parish Clergy in Nineteenth-Century Russia* (Princeton, NJ: Princeton University Press, 1983), 178–79; Laurie Manchester, "Gender and Social Estate as National Identity: The Wives and Daughters of Orthodox Clergymen as Civilizing Agents in Imperial Russia," *Journal of Modern History* 83 (2011): 48–77.

56 William G. Wagner, "'Orthodox Domesticity': Creating a Social Role for Women," in *Sacred Stories: Religion and Spirituality in Modern Russia*, ed. Heather J. Coleman and Mark D. Steinberg (Bloomington: Indiana University Press, 2007), 130.

57 "Missiia i rabota v nei zhenshchiny," *APV*, September 30, 1915, 376.

58 Applications and financial records of the college are collected in St. Mary Women's College subject file, AOCA. Also see Holy Trinity Orthodox Church, "History of Holy Trinity Orthodox Church," October 2012, http://htocclayton.org.

59 "Budnichnaia programma zaniatii v pervom Russkom Zhenskom Kolledzhye v g. Bruklinye," *APV*, November 11, 1911, 484.

60 "Russo-Greek Church Establishes College for Young Women Here," *Brooklyn Daily Eagle*, November 28, 1915.

280 | NOTES

61 E. A. Krilova to Archbishop Evdokim (Meschersky), August 31, 1915, published in *APV*, November 11, 1915, 483.

62 "Pervyi uchebnyi god v russkom zhenskom kolledzhye," *APV*, August 3, 1916, 451–52; "Russo-Greek Church Establishes College for Young Women Here." For the life of Dr. Eugenia Kohanik, see "K konchinye doktora E.D. Kokhanik," *APV*, August 1944, 127–28.

63 "Raspisanie ekzamenov pervago russkago kolledzha v g. Bruklinye," *APV*, May 25, 1916, 292.

64 "Ot sovyeta pervago russkago zhenskago kolledzha v g. Brulkinye," *APV*, September 7, 1916, 536.

65 "Russian Diocese of North America and the Aleutian Islands," in *The American Church Almanac and Year Book for 1917* (New York: Edwin S. Gorham, 1916), 561. All five professors were priests, and only one, priest Nathaniel Irvine, had taught the previous year. The retained female instructors were Sisters Andrea and Mikhaila.

66 Archbishop Evdokim (Meschersky), "Report of the State of the Diocese for 1916," trans. Hieromonk Andrew Kostadis, in Kostadis, "Pictures of Missionary Life," 255.

67 "Lost Kedrovsky Children Lived on Leaves and Grass," *Brooklyn Daily Eagle*, July 21, 1919.

68 Priest Ioann Nedzelnitskii, *Pravoslavnaia Rus' v Syevernnoi Amerikye* (Odesa: Tip. O-va "Russkaia Ryech," 1914), 10–11.

CHAPTER 4. "LET ALL AMERICA SEE"

Epigraph: "List ot nashikh russko-amerikanskikh voiakov," *Svit*, November 1, 1917.

1 "Pis'mo ot russko-amerikanskago voiaka," *Svit*, January 31, 1918.

2 "Pis'mo ot russko-amerikanskago voiaka."

3 "Vnimaniiu dukhovenstva S.-Amerikanskoi pravoslavnoi missii," *Svit*, November 22, 1917.

4 "K delu o sviashchennike dlia obsluzhvaniia dukhovnykh potreb nashikh russkikh voinov v amerikanskoi armii," *Svit*, January 31, 1918.

5 Shailer Mathews, *Patriotism and Religion* (New York: Macmillan, 1918), 25.

6 Cara Lea Burnidge, *A Peaceful Conquest: Woodrow Wilson, Religion, and the New World Order* (Chicago: University of Chicago Press, 2017). For Civil War vocabularies of suffering, duty, and sacrifice, see Drew Gilpin Faust, *This Republic of Suffering: Death and the American Civil War* (New York: Knopf, 2009); and Harry S. Stout, *Upon the Altar of the Nation: A Moral History of the Civil War* (New York: Penguin Books, 2006).

7 "Auto Ambulances Consecrated to Service on Russian Front," *New York Tribune*, April 11, 1916.

8 Melissa Kirschke Stockdale, *Mobilizing the Russian Nation: Patriotism and Citizenship in the First World War* (Cambridge: Cambridge University Press, 2016), 6. For contrasts in war relief efforts between clergy and laity, see Daniel Scarborough, *Russia's Social Gospel: The Orthodox Pastoral Movement in*

Famine, War, and Revolution (Madison: University of Wisconsin Press, 2022), 129–35. Other scholarship has focused on how the war impacted the integrity of the Russian Empire and also its historical memory during the Soviet period as a "Forgotten War." See Joshua A. Sanborn, *Imperial Apocalypse* (Oxford: Oxford University Press, 2014); and Boris Kolonitskii, "Russia and World War I: The Politics of Memory and Historiography," in *Writing the Great War*, ed. Christoph Cornelissen and Arndt Weinrich (New York: Berghahn Books, 2021), 223–62.

9 Stockdale, *Mobilizing the Russian Nation*, 76.

10 Stockdale, 96.

11 "V pol'zu russkago krasnago kresta," *APV*, October 14, 1914, 412.

12 "Ot obshchestva russkago krasnago kresta," *APV*, October 14, 1914, 412.

13 "Vesti i zametki," *APV*, February 28, 1915, 64.

14 "Slova gosudaria imperatora o novoi otechestvennoi voinie," *APV*, September 28, 1914, 381.

15 "Prayers for the Emperor and the People, When at War with the Enemy, Which Are Said during Evening and Morning Services and Also during the Liturgy," *APV*, November 14, 1914, 431.

16 "SLOVO Arkhiepiskopa Kishenevskago PLATONA pred molebnom po sluchaiu ob"iavleniia voiny Germaniei Rossii," *APV*, October 14, 1914, 400–402.

17 Priest A. Philippovsky, "Pravoslavnaia tserkov' i voina," *APV*, April 14, 1915, 101, 104–5.

18 Philippovsky, 102, 103. See also Scott M. Kenworthy, "The Mobilization of Piety: Monasticism and the Great War in Russia, 1914–1916," in "Themenschwerpunkt: Religion und Gesellschaft in Rußland vor der Revolution von 1917," *Jahrbücher für Geschichte Osteuropas*, n.s., 52, no. 3 (2004): 388–401.

19 David M. Kennedy, *Over Here: The First World War and American Society*, 25th anniversary ed. (New York: Oxford University Press, 2004), 41.

20 Christopher Capozzola, *Uncle Sam Wants You: World War I and the Making of the Modern American Citizen* (New York: Oxford University Press, 2008). Also see Paul L. Murphy, *World War I and the Origin of Civil Liberties in the United States* (New York: Norton, 1979); Daniel Kanstroom, *Deportation Nation: Outsiders in American History* (Cambridge, MA: Harvard University Press, 2010). For religious war rhetoric, see Ray H. Abrams, *Preachers Present Arms* (Scottdale, AZ: Herald, 1969); and Jonathan Ebel, *Faith in the Fight: Religion and the American Soldier in the Great War* (Princeton, NJ: Princeton University Press, 2010).

21 "Telegramma na Imia g. Prezidenta ot Vysokopreosviashchenneishago Arkhiepiskopa Evdokima," *APV*, April 12, 1917, 196.

22 "Ryech Preosviashchennago Nikolaia, Episcopa Aleutskago i Aliaskinskago, skazannaia 23 iiunia 1896 g. pred molebnom po sluchaio osvobozhdeniia Syevero-Amerikanskikh Soedinennykh Shtatov ot zavisimosti Anglii," *APV*, June 27, 1897, 408–9.

23 "Amerikanskaia Rus'," *APV*, July 28, 1909, 243–44. It should be distinguished that the author uses the term *Amerikanets*, meaning an American *person*, and not the adjectival *amerikanskii*.

24 "Politicheskaia rol' pravoslavno-russkago dukhovenstvo v S. Amerikie," *APV*, June 14, 1909, 199.

25 "Vy dolzhny vyrazit' osobuiu simpatiiu nashei novoi soiuznitsie amerikie," *APV*, May 31, 1917, 320.

26 "Torzhestvo v russkoi kolonii v Vatervliiet," *Svit*, May 31, 1917.

27 Arnaldo Testi, *Capture the Flag: The Stars and Stripes in American History* (New York: York University Press, 2010), 38. For more on flag culture, see Cecilia Elizabeth O'Leary, *To Die For: The Paradox of American Patriotism* (Princeton, NJ: Princeton University Press, 1999).

28 Testi, *Capture the Flag*, 35.

29 John Higham, *Strangers in the Land: Patterns of American Nativism, 1860–1925*, 2nd ed. (New Brunswick, NJ: Rutgers University Press, 1983), 209.

30 "Iz eparkhial'noi zhizni," *APV*, May 24, 1917, 301.

31 Kennedy, *Over Here*, 148.

32 Nancy Gentile Ford, "'Mindful of the Traditions of His Race': Dual Identity and Foreign-Born Soldiers in the First World War American Army," *Journal of American Ethnic History* 16, no. 2 (Winter 1997): 50.

33 "Skonchalsia Protopresviter Petr Kokhanik," *APV*, June 1969, 82–83.

34 John Loss was one of the two namesakes of Post 1852 of the Veterans of Foreign Wars, which was active in Minneapolis for decades. "St. Mary's Veteran's Association," in *125: St. Mary's Orthodox Cathedral Anniversary Celebration, 1887–2012* (Minneapolis: St. Mary's Orthodox Cathedral, 2012), 50.

35 "List' ot nashikh russko-amerikanskikh voiakov," *Svit*, November 1, 1917.

36 Peter Telep, Registration State: Ohio, Registration County: Cuyahoga, Roll 1831704, Draft Board 05, US, World War I Draft Registration Cards, 1917–1918, Ancestry.com.

37 "List' ot nashikh russko-amerikanskikh voiakov iz' frantsii," *Svit*, March 14, 1918.

38 "Russko-pravoslavnym liudiam, rabotaiushchim v mainakh," *Svit*, August 1, 1918.

39 "Russko-pravoslavnym liudiam, rabotaiushchim v mainakh."

40 Irving Fisher, "How the Public Should Pay for the War," *Annals of the American Academy of Political and Social Science* 78 (July 1918): 112.

41 Advertisement, "Service Stars on Your Pocket Book," *Svit*, October 3, 1918.

42 Advertisement, "Prove That You Are a 100% American," *Svit*, September 12, 1918.

43 Advertisement, "Buy War Savings Stamps?," *Detroit Labor News*, June 7, 1918.

44 Advertisement, "Your Last Chance to Buy," *Detroit Labor News*, March 29, 1918.

45 Advertisement, "This Is a Thrift Card," *Detroit Labor News*, February 1, 1918.

46 Walter Grinewsky, hearing, April 14, 1919, File 54709/565, Box 3496, INS.

47 Sergei Krywonosow, hearing, April 12, 1919, File 54709/562, Box 3495, INS.

48 Alex Bych, hearing, April 17, 1919, File 54709/556, Box 3495, INS.

49 Frank Bondarenko, hearing, April 16, 1919, File 54709/568, Box 3496, INS.

NOTES | 283

50 Woodrow Wilson, "To Various Ethnic Societies," in *Papers of Woodrow Wilson,* vol. 48, ed. Arthur S. Link (Princeton, NJ: Princeton University Press, 1985), 117.

51 "Russkim pravoslavnym liudiam v sievernoi amerikie," *APV,* May 1918, 68–69.

52 "At Home and Abroad Birthday of Liberty Is Being Celebrated," *Washington Evening Star,* July 4, 1918.

53 "Races Welded in Loyalty to Hail the Day," *Chicago Daily Tribune,* July 4, 1918.

54 "Varied Program for 4th of July," *Detroit Free Press,* July 4, 1918.

55 "Celebration Today to Be International," *Baltimore Sun,* July 4, 1918.

56 Woodrow Wilson, "The Four-Point Speech," in *War and Peace: Presidential Messages, Addresses, and Public Papers (1917–1924),* vol. 1., ed. Ray Stannard Baker and William E. Dodd (New York: Harper, 1927), 232.

57 T. C. Wilcox, Report to Bureau, August 27, 1918, File #248775, FBI OGF.

58 Wilcox.

CHAPTER 5. "WAVES OF ANARCHY"

1 Prot. Alexander Schmemann, *Dnevniki 1973–1983* (Moscow: Russkii Put', 2007), 599–600.

2 Vermont Attorney General's Office, *Biennial Report of the Attorney General of the State of Vermont for the Two Years Ending June 30, 1918* (Rutland, VT: Tuttle, 1918), 70–71.

3 "To Aid Russian Orphanage," *New York Evening Post,* March 28, 1918; "Princess Lwoff Hostess at Musicale and Reception," *Brooklyn Daily Eagle,* March 24, 1918; "For Russian Orphanage," *New York Herald,* April 13, 1919; "Spasaite nash sirotskii priot!," *Svit,* November 29, 1917; Springfield, Vermont, *Annual Report of the Town Officers of the Town of Springfield, Vt. for the Year Ending February 1, 1920* (Springfield, VT, 1920), 104–5.

4 Father John Matusiak and Father Leonid Kiskhovsky, "Crisis and Transition, 1917–1922," in *Orthodox America, 1794–1976,* ed. Constance Tarasar (Syosset, NY: Orthodox Church in America Department of History and Archives, 1975), 175; Gregory Afonsky, *A History of the Orthodox Church in America, 1917–1934* (Kodiak, AK: St. Herman Seminary Press, 1994), 25.

5 Sheila Fitzpatrick, *The Russian Revolution,* 3rd ed. (Oxford: Oxford University Press, 2008), 40–57; Laura Engelstein, *Russia in Flames: War, Revolution, Civil War, 1914–1921* (Oxford: Oxford University Press, 2018), 104–30.

6 "Deny Revolution Will Impact Church," *New York Times,* March 18, 1917.

7 "Omits the Czar's Name at Russian Service," *New York Times,* March 19, 1917.

8 Priest Pavel Shadura, "Report to the Most Reverend Phillip, Alaska, August 25, 1917," in *Through Orthodox Eyes: Russian Missionary Narratives of Travels to the Dena'ina and Ahtna, 1850s–1930s,* ed. Andrei A. Znamenski (Fairbanks: University of Alaska Press, 2003), 269–70.

9 Evdokim's report is partially reprinted in Tarasar, *Orthodox America, 1794–1976,* 130. For a full translation, see Archbishop Evdokim (Meschersky), "Report of the State of the Diocese for 1916," trans. Hieromonk Andrew Kostadis, in Kostadis,

"Pictures of Missionary Life according to the Russian Clerical Press in America and the Ruling American Bishops about the Life of the American Mission in 1900–1917" (MTh thesis, St. Vladimir's Orthodox Theological Seminary, 1999), 249–274.

10 Matusiak and Kiskhovsky, "Crisis and Transition," 177–79; Afonsky, *History of the Orthodox Church in America*, 31.

11 "Telegrammy na imia arxiepiskopa," *APV*, August 9, 1917, 468; Scott M. Kenworthy and Alexander S. Agadjanian, *Understanding World Christianity: Russia* (Minneapolis: Fortress, 2021), 127. See also A. I. Mramornov, "Voprosy mezhdunarodnyx I mezhtserkovnyx otnoshenii na Sviashchennom Sobore Pravoslavnoi Rossiiskoi Tserkvi 1917–1918 gg.," *Vestnik MGIMO-Universiteta* 3, no. 66 (2019): 176–201; and Hyacinthe Destivelle, *The Moscow Council (1917–1918): The Creation of Conciliar Institutions of the Russian Orthodox Church* (Notre Dame, IN: University of Notre Dame Press, 2015).

12 Afonsky, *History of the Orthodox Church in America*, 13; Archbishop Evdokim (Meschersky), "Report of the State of the Diocese for 1916," trans. Hieromonk Andrew Kostadis, in Kostadis, "Pictures of Missionary Life according to the Russian Clerical Press in America and the Ruling American Bishops about the Life of the American Mission in 1900–1917" (MTh thesis, St. Vladimir's Orthodox Theological Seminary, 1999), 267–68; "View of Questions to Be Examined by the Local Council of the Russian Orthodox Church," *APV*, March Supplement, 1906, 66.

13 "V pravlenie," *APV*, October–November–December 1918, 127.

14 Cablegram, Archbishop Evdokim to Russian Cathedral, August 31, 1917, published in *APV*, October–November–December 1918, 127. See also Matusiak and Kiskhovsky, "Crisis and Transition," 177–79; Afonsky, *History of the Orthodox Church in America*, 31.

15 *Dokumenty Sviashchennogo Sobora Pravoslavnoi Rossiiskoi Tserkvi 1917–1918 godov, Tom 5: Deianiia Sobora c 1-go po 36-e*, ed. A. I. Mramornov (Moscow: Izdatel'stvo Novospasskogo monastyria, 2015), 548–51.

16 "Serving the Church and Motherland," *APV*, February 1918, 21–24; continued, March 1918, 42–43. This account is corroborated in Metropolitan Evlogy (Georgievsky), *My Life's Journey: The Memoirs of Metropolitan Evlogy*, vol. 1, trans. Alexander Lisenko (Yonkers, NY: St. Vladimir's Seminary Press, 2014), 349–50.

17 These were the more than two hundred pro-Bolshevik soldiers killed during fighting in October, for whom a public funeral was held on November 10, 1917. An account of the gravedigging, burials, and funeral can be found in John Reed, *Ten Days That Shook the World* (New York: International, 1919), 253–59. Reed writes in his concluding summation of the funeral, "I suddenly realized that the devout Russian people no longer needed priests to pray them into heaven. On earth they were building a kingdom more bright than any heaven had to offer, and for which it was a glory to die" (259).

18 "Desiatilyetie sluzheniia na missionerskom poproshchye v sviashchennom sanye o. Ioanna A. Kochurova, nastoiatelia russkoi tserkvi v Chikago," *APV*, September 14, 1905, 346.

19 Bp. Alexander Nemolovsky, "Svyaschennomucheniki Mitropolit Vladimir i Protoierei Ioann Kochurov," *APV*, March 1918, 35–36; Fr. Sergius Snegireff, "O Voztanovlenii na Rusi Patriarshestva," *APV*, March 1918, 36–38. Another account comes from John Reed: "On the evening that Kerensky's troops retreated from Tsarskoye Selo, some priests organised a religious procession through the streets of the town, making speeches to the citizens in which they asked people to support the rightful authority, the Provisional Government. . . . One of the priests, Father Ivan Kutchurov [*sic*], was arrested and shot by the infuriated Red Guards" (*Ten Days That Shook the World*, 352).

20 Mariia Gerasimova, "Moi amerikanskii pradedushka. Zhizn' i smert' sviashchennomuchenika Ioanna Kochurova glazami ego pravnuchki," Pravmir, accessed October 29, 2024, www.pravmir.ru. For the 1905 celebration in Chicago, see "Desiatilyetie sluzheniia na missionerskom poproshchye v sviashchennom sanye o. Ioanna A. Kochurova, nastoiatelia russkoi tserkvi v Chikago," *APV*, September 14, 1905, 346.

21 Bp. Alexander Nemolovsky, "Svyaschennomucheniki Mitropolit Vladimir i Protoierei Ioann Kochurov," *APV*, March 1918, 35–36; Protopresbyter Michael Polsky, "Vladimir, Mitropolit Kievskii i Galitskii," in *Novye Mucheniki Rossiiskie: Pervoe Sobranie Materialov* (Jordanville, NY: Holy Trinity Monastery, 1949), 10–24. The first accounts of Kochurov's death in North America were probably published in *Svit*: Bp. Alexander (Nemolovsky), "Vo khriste vozliublennym pastyriam i pasomym amerikanskoi pravosl. rusi," February 28, 1918; and "Prot. I. Kochurov (Iz pis'ma k prot. F.N.O.)," February 28, 1918.

22 Archbishop Evdokim (Meschersky), "Report of the State of the Diocese for 1916," trans. Hieromonk Andrew Kostadis, in Kostadis, "Pictures of Missionary Life," 267.

23 Evdokim, 251.

24 Evdokim, 262, 267; Tarasar, *Orthodox America, 1794–1976*, 177–78; Afonsky, *History of the Orthodox Church in America*, 26–28.

25 Metropolitan Evlogy (Georgievsky), *My Life's Journey: The Memoirs of Metropolitan Evlogy*, vol. 2, trans. Alexander Lisenko (Yonkers, NY: St. Vladimir's Seminary Press, 2014), 491.

26 Matusiak and Kiskhovsky, "Crisis and Transition," 174–75, 180–81.

27 Quoted in Afonsky, *History of the Orthodox Church in America*, 35.

28 Broadside, "Federatsiia Mirian i Dukhovenstva dlia zashchity Russkoi Narodni Greko-Katolicheskoi Tserkvi v Sievernoi Amerikie," n.d., Archbishop Alexander Nemolovsky Subject File, AOCA.

29 "V spravye sobora," *Svit*, March 21, 1918.

30 The previously biweekly *APV* resumed its print run in January 1918 with six monthly journals, then two quarterly anthologies, before publication ceased again until 1922.

31 "Sobraniia Detroitskago Blagochinnicheskago Okruga," *GTs*, April 11, 1918.

32 "Vo khristye vozliublennym o. o. missioneram," *GTs*, May 23, 1918.

286 | NOTES

33 Prot. Sergii Snegirev, "V otvyet na koshmarnyi son otsa protoiereia P. Kokhanika," *GTs*, August 15, 1918.

34 Protoierei Petr Kokhanik, "Muzhitskaia pravda," *Svit*, August 15, 1918.

35 "Rezoliutsii predsobornago sobraniia dukhovenstva v n'io iorkye," *APV*, July–August–September 1918, 106.

36 Paul Hanebrink, *A Specter Haunting Europe: The Myth of Judeo-Bolshevism* (Cambridge, MA: Harvard University Press, 2018), 13–16; "Bolshevism Unmasked—Its Jewish Origin Revealed to the World," *Svit*, August 21, 1919.

37 Sergei Aleksandrovich Nilus, *The Protocols of World Revolution* (Boston: Small, Maynard, 1920), 3.

38 Nilus, 144.

39 Benjamin Sigel, *A Lie and a Libel: The History of the "Protocols of the Elders of Zion*," ed. and trans. Richard S. Levy (Lincoln: University of Nebraska Press, 1996), xii. Brasol anonymously published the translated *Protocols* as *The Protocols and World Revolution* (Boston: Small, Maynard, 1920). According to a Bureau of Investigation (BI) file on Brasol, in January 1918, he applied to work as a federal intelligence agent to investigate the "American Bolsheviki." Brasol was denied on account of his citizenship status. Even so, BI Chief Alfred Bettman proposed, "we might use him as a confidential informant." Chief to Chas. DeWoody, February 27, 1919, File #8000-147398, Roll #539, FBI OGF. One BI report noted that Brasol was "at present employed by the War Trade Board, [and] who is attached to the Intelligence Bureau of said Board." Report, V. J. Valjavec, In Re: N. Shivotovsky—Bolsheviki Activities, January 8, 1919, File #339512, Roll #764, FBI OGF. By 1921, Brasol was vice president of the *Soiuz' Edinstvo Rusi* (Anglicized as Association Unity of Russia), which published a newspaper, *Pravoe Delo* (*The Right Cause*), and held meetings at the Manhattan cathedral. A Nazi sympathizer in the 1920s and 1930s, Brasol joined the German American Bund and later the nativist, Nazi-appeasing America First Committee, headed by the aviator Charles Lindbergh. During the Second World War, Brasol advanced the Russian émigré belief that acceptance, if not support, of the Hitler regime was necessary in order to topple Soviet Communism. Brasol was also a founding member of the influential Pushkin Society. See Robert Singerman, "The American Career of the 'Protocols of the Elders of Zion,'" *American Jewish History* 71, no. 1 (1981): 48–78; and Eugene Pivovarov, "The Papers of Boris Brasol and the Pushkin Society in America in the Manuscript Division of the Library of Congress," *Journal of Ethnic History* 23, no. 1 (2003): 85–92. The most comprehensive study of Ford's antisemitism is Neil Baldwin, *Henry Ford and the Jews* (New York: PublicAffairs, 2001).

40 "Bogokhranimym vo khristie vozl iublennym pastyriam i pasomym amerikanskoi pravoslavnoi rusi," *APV*, February 1918, 19.

41 "Pravoslavnomu dukhovenstvu i russkomu narodu v Amerikie," *GTs*, July 11, 1918. Alexander retained his strong monarchist and nationalist leanings for decades, though with some complexities therein. Serving in Brussels during the Second World War, Alexander publicly sided with the Soviet Union against

the Nazi regime. The Gestapo arrested Alexander at his cathedral in November 1940, leading to a brief stint in a German prison. By V-Day, Alexander was living in Berlin in a room above a cemetery chapel, surrounded by fading portraits of the Romanovs and living on what little he could earn from grave blessings. Protoierei Sergii Model', *"Vsiakaia chuzhbina dlia niv otechestvo": 150 let prisutsviia Pravoslaviia v Bel'gii (1862–2012 gg.)* (Épinay-sous-Sénart, France: Éditions Sainte-Geneviéve, 2013), 84–85; *Russkoe Pravoslavie v Bel'gii, tom 1: Stat'i i ocherki* (Moscow and Brussels: Conferénce Sainte Trinité du Patriarcat de Moscou ASGL; Ekaterininskii muzhskoi monastyr', 2014), 59.

42 Theodore Kornweibel Jr., *"Investigate Everything": Federal Efforts to Compel Black Loyalty during World War I* (Bloomington: Indiana University Press, 2002), 11.

43 Sylvester A. Johnson and Steven Weitzman, *The FBI and Religion: Faith and National Security before and after 9/11* (Oakland: University of California Press, 2017), 1–11. See also Robert K. Murray, *The First Red Scare: A Study in National Hysteria* (Minneapolis: University of Minnesota Press, 1955); William Preston, *Aliens and Dissenters: Federal Suppression of Radicals, 1903–1933* (New York: Harper Torchbooks, 1966); Christopher M. Sterba, *Good Americans: Italian and Jewish Immigrants during the First World War* (New York: Oxford University Press, 2003); and John Higham, *Strangers in the Land: Patterns of American Nativism, 1860–1925*, 2nd ed. (New Brunswick, NJ: Rutgers University Press, 1983), 234–63.

44 Murray, *First Red Scare*, 34.

45 Kedrovsky to A. V. Darymple, September 3, 1918, File #286305, Roll #703, FBI OGF.

46 Rev. William Chauncey Emhardt, *Religion in Soviet Russia: Anarchy* (Milwaukee: Morehouse, 1929), 219–20.

47 "Ioann (Kedrovskii [Kedrovsky] Ivan Savich) mitropolit," in *Obnovlencheskii raskol v portretakh ego deiatelei*, ed. Protopriest Valerii Lavrinov (Moscow: Obshchestvo liubitelei tserkovnoi istorii, 2016), 276–77; Emhardt, *Religion in Soviet Russia*, 219–20; "Russian Prelate Dies of Stroke," *New York Times*, March 18, 1934.

48 Pamphlet, "How Thinks, How Feels and How Teaches about America Alexander Nemolovsky, Canadian Bishop," File #286305, Roll #703, FBI OGF.

49 Report, W. J. Lazovich, "In re: Russian Ecclesiastical Society, Alleged Bolsheviki Activity," August 3, 1918, File #186860, Roll #590, FBI OGF; Report, A. C. Robeson, "In re: Russian Ecclesiastical Society (Bolsheviki Activities)," July 23, 1918, File #241885, Roll #654, FBI OGF; "Russian Papers Seized at Home of Clergyman," *New York Evening Telegram*, July 21, 1918; "Raid on Russian Church Made by U.S.," *New York Tribune*, July 21, 1918.

50 Robeson, "In re: Russian Ecclesiastical Society."

51 Lazovich, "In re: Russian Ecclesiastical Society (Bolsheviki Activities)."

52 "Rasporiazheniia po missii," *APV*, July–August–September 1918, 103; "Russian Papers Seized at Home of Clergyman," *New York Evening Tribune*, July 21, 1918;

53 A. V. Darymple, "Memorandum for Major Hunt," n.d., File #286305, Roll #703, FBI OGF.

288 | NOTES

54 Bp. Leonty (Turkevich), "V tikhom okeanie," IuS I, 265–66. See also Alexander Schmemann, "Metropolitan Leonty," in Tarasar, *Orthodox America, 1794–1976,* 232–33.

55 These allegations are publicly recorded and corroborated in several places. In a 1923 open letter assailing Evdokim for joining the Soviet-backed "Living Church," Metropolitan Antony (Khrapovitsky) claimed that Evdokim had been drawn to the movement as blackmail for his well-known and numerous "lovers [and] illegitimate children." "Otvietnoe uviedomlenie: Predsieatelia Arkhiereiskago Sinoda Russkoi Pravoslavnoi Tserkvi zagranitsei Vysokopreosviashchennago Mitropolita Antoniia b. Mitropolitu Evdokimu," *Tserkovnye vedemosti,* nos. 19–20 (October 1923): 4–5. The church historian Dimitry Pospielovsky cites these same issues as an explanation for Patriarch Tikhon's wariness of Evdokim when former Living Church clergy approached the patriarch to repent for their schismatic activities. Dimitry Pospielovsky, *The Russian Church under the Soviet Regime, 1917–1982,* vol. 1 (Crestwood, NY: St. Vladimir's Seminary Press, 1984), 53.

56 Darymple, "Memorandum for Major Hunt."

57 Alfred Bettman to A. Bruce Bielaski, n.d., File #286305, Roll #703, FBI OGF.

58 Bishop Leonty (Turkevich), "V tikhom okeanie," IuS I, 265–66. For a contemporaneous account of the council, see Thomas Whittemore, "The Rebirth of Religion in Russia," *National Geographic,* November 1918, 369–401. Turkevich departed from Indonesia on May 15, 1918, and disembarked at San Francisco on June 29, nearly a month before the executions occurred in Yekaterinburg. Manifest, SS *Rembrandt,* May 15, 1918, line 24: "Turkevich, Leonid J.," in *Passenger Lists of Vessels Arriving at San Francisco, California,* NAI: 4498993, Record Group 85, Records of the Immigration and Naturalization Service, 1787–2004, National Archives, Washington, DC.

CHAPTER 6. "UNDER THE CLOAK OF RELIGION"

1 Charles R. Crane, *Memoirs of Charles R. Crane* [manuscript] (2013), Columbia University Libraries Rare Book and Manuscript Library, 301–2, https://archive .org.

2 "O tserkovnyi sobor," *Russkoe slovo,* July 22, 1918.

3 "O tserkovnyi sobor." For other public charges made by Alexandrof, see "Russian Church Reaches Breach in Fight for Control," *New York Herald,* July 18, 1918.

4 Charles McCrary, *Sincerely Held: American Secularism and Its Believers* (Chicago: University of Chicago Press), 2022, 60. See also Paul Christopher Johnson, "Fakecraft," *Journal for the Study of Religion* 31 (2018): 105–37.

5 Patrick W. Carey, *People, Priests, and Prelates: Ecclesiastical Democracy and the Tensions of Trusteeism* (Notre Dame, IN: University of Notre Dame Press, 1987); Patrick Joseph Dignan, *A History of the Legal Incorporation of Catholic Church Property in the United States, 1784–1932* (New York: AMS, 1974); James O'Toole, *The Faithful: A History of Catholics in America* (Cambridge, MA: Harvard University Press, 2008), 53–68; Jay P. Dolan, *In Search of an American Catholicism:*

A History of Religion and Culture in Tension (New York: Oxford University Press, 2002), 29–34; Jay P. Dolan, *The Immigrant Church: New York's Irish and German Catholics, 1815–1865* (Baltimore: Johns Hopkins University Press, 1975), 48–50.

6 Edward Roslof, *Red Priests: Renovationism, Russian Orthodoxy, and Revolution, 1905–1946* (Bloomington: Indiana University Press, 2003), x.

7 Upton Sinclair, *The Jungle* (New York: Doubleday, Page, 1906), 26–27.

8 Anatoly Bezkorovainy, "One Hundred Years of Service to God and Man," in *A History of the Holy Trinity Russian Orthodox Cathedral of Chicago, 1892–1992*, ed. Anatoly Bezkorovainy (Chicago: Holy Trinity Orthodox Cathedral, 1992), 1–20; Charles E. Gregerson, "The Architecture of Holy Trinity Cathedral," in Bezkorovainy, *History of the Holy Trinity Russian Orthodox Cathedral*, 132–40; Archimandrite Timon (Muliar), *Pod Shchitom Vyery* (Southbury, CT: Alatas, 1934), 23–27.

9 Bezkorovainy, "One Hundred Years of Service," 18–24; G. Dobrov, "V Chikago, Ill.," *Russkii emigrant*, November 13, 1913.

10 "Normal'nyi Ustav dlia prikhodov S.-Amerikanskoi Pravoslavnoi Eparkhii," *APV*, March 31, 1909, 101–10. For English translations of sections concerning property, see "The Normal Statute for the Parishes of the American Orthodox Diocese," *APV*, December 14, 1911, 414; continued, December 28, 1911, 436.

11 Polycarp Gulko, "Kratkaia istoriia Sv. Georgievskago Prikhoda," in *Silver Jubilee Book: The Russian Orthodox St. George Parish* (Chicago: St. George Parish, 1940), 12–13, Box 1, Folder 3, RIMAS UIC; "Bol'shevik v riasie," *GTs*, August 15, 1918.

12 T. Peshkov, "The Decennial Jubilee of the First Independent Orthodox Church in America," *Russkii viestnik*, August 15, 1925, CFLPS, https://flps.newberry.org.

13 Gulko, "Kratkaia istoriia Sv. Georgievskago Prikhoda," 12–13.

14 Peshkov, "Decennial Jubilee"; "Krasnow Scrapbooks: The Russian Colony of the Past: Memoirs of an Old Colonist; the Russian Independent Society," *Novoe russkoe slovo*, June 25, 1932, CFLPS, https://flps.newberry.org; K. Ermolik, "Moi vospomininaniia," in *Iubileinyi sbornik 25 letiia russkago nezavisimogo obshchestva vzaimopomoshchi* (Chicago, 1937), 50, Box 1, Folder 5, RIMAS UIC; Gulko, "Kratkaia istoriia Sv. Georgievskago Prikhoda," 12–13; and Ivan Okuntsov, *Russkaia emigratsiia v Severnoi i Iuzhnoi Amerike* (Buenos Aires: Seiatel', 1967), 276–77.

15 G. Dobrov, "V Chikago, Ill.," *Russkii emigrant*, November 13, 1913.

16 "Predsedateli, sekretari i kassiry Sv. Georgievskago prikhoda za 25 let so dnia ego osnovaniia," in *Silver Jubilee Book*, 18–19.

17 "Krasnow Scrapbooks."

18 L. G. Pertsov, "Ot redaktsiia," in *Iubileinyi sbornik 25 letiia russkago nezavisimogo obshchestva vzaimopomoshchi*, 4–5.

19 Okuntsov, *Russkaia emigratsiia v Severnoi i Iuzhnoi Amerike*, 276–78.

20 Nikolai Kozak, "Za dvadtsat' piat' let," in *Iubileinyi sbornik 25 letiia russkago nezavisimogo obshchestva vzaimopomoshchi*, 10.

21 "The Genesis of St. George Russian Orthodox Cathedral," in *St. George Russian Orthodox Cathedral 75th Anniversary, 1914–1989* (Chicago: St. George Russian

Orthodox Cathedral, 1989); Bezkorovainy, "One Hundred Years of Service," 22–23; Gulko, "Kratkaia istoriia Sv. Georgievskago Prikhoda," 12–13.

22 Ivan Okuntsov, "On the 12th Anniversary of the Brotherhood of St. George," *Russkii viestnik*, May 24, 1924, CFLPS, https://flps.newberry.org.

23 "Timothy W. Peshkoff," Naturalization Records, Colorado, 1876–1990, Naturalization Case Files, 1883–1922, Records of the District Courts of the United States, 1685–2009, Record Group 21, National Archives at Denver, Broomfield, Colorado, Ancestry.com; *Valparaiso University Bulletin: Announcement of Department of Engineering for the Year 1913-1914* (Valparaiso, IN: Valparaiso University, 1914), 30.

24 Timothy W. Peshkoff, "The Russian Orthodox Church under the Czars," *Zion's Herald*, August 1, 1923, 978–79.

25 Okuntsov, "On the 12th Anniversary of the Brotherhood of St. George."

26 Okuntsov, *Russkaia emigratsiia v Severnoi i Iuzhnoi Amerike*, 150.

27 Peter F. Anson, *Bishops at Large* (London: Faber and Faber, 1964), 128.

28 Anson, 94. The best synthesis of Vilatte's scattered biography is Julie Byrne, *The Other Catholics: Remaking America's Largest Religion* (New York: Columbia University Press, 2016), 99–124. See also Anson, *Bishops at Large*, 91–129; Karl Pruter, *Bishops Extraordinary* (San Bernardino, CA: Borgo, 1985), 23–38; Karl Pruter, *A History of the Old Catholic Church* (Scottsdale, AZ: St. Willibrord's Press, 1973), 34–39; and Karl Pruter, *The Old Catholic Church: A History and Chronology* (San Bernardino, CA: St. Willibrord's Press, 1996), 43–48. In the early 1890s, Vilatte attempted to enter the Russian Archdiocese but lost patience waiting for a decision to be made. Instead, Vilatte was ordained by a Jacobite bishop of the Syrian Malankara Orthodox Church in what is today Sri Lanka. See Bishop Nicholas (Ziorov) to Joseph René Vilatte, September 28, 1892, Box B40/Reel 34, ROGCCA LOC.

29 "Genesis of St. George Russian Orthodox Cathedral." Vilatte appointed Peshkoff the head of the American Catholic Church's "Byzantine English Rite Apostolate," a post he apparently held for some years. This organization seems unrelated to the St. George parish, and the ties between St. George and Vilatte remain unclear, perhaps not lasting beyond Peshkoff's departure from the parish in 1917. See John Kersey, *Joseph-René Vilatte (1854–1929): Some Aspects of His Life, Work and Succession* (Roseau, Dominica: European-American University Press, 2012), 139–40. The entry for the Old Roman Catholic Church in the 1916 *Census of Religious Bodies* indicates a single Russian parish with one thousand members under its jurisdiction; this may refer to St. George. See US Bureau of the Census, "Old Roman Catholic Church," in *Religious Bodies*, part 2, *Separate Denominations* (Washington, DC: Government Printing Office, 1919), 534.

30 "Eparkhial'naia khronika," *APV*, November 4, 1915, 468.

31 "Pervyi otdel," in *Iubileinyi sbornik 25 letiia russkago nezavisimogo obshchestva vzaimopomoshchi*, 54–55.

32 Kozak, "Za dvadtsat' piat' let," 10.

33 Peshkoff, "Russian Orthodox Church under the Czars," 978–79. Father Kukulevsky was then head of the archdiocesan deanery for Chicago and pastor of the
Holy Trinity parish.

34 "Eparkhial'naia khronika," *APV*, November 4, 1915, 468.

35 "Blagodarnost," *APV*, November 25, 1915, 510–11.

36 Hieromonk Timon (Muliar), "Lzhesviashchennik i samozvanets," *APV*, July–
August–September 1918, 110.

37 "Plant at Argo an Armed Camp," *Chicago Daily Tribune*, March 16, 1916.

38 Okuntsov, "On the 12th Anniversary of the Brotherhood of St. George."

39 "Nastoiateli Sv. Georgievskago Prikhoda," in *Silver Jubilee Book*, 20; Peshkoff,
"Russian Orthodox Church under the Czars," 978–79.

40 Ermolik, "Moi vospomininaniia," 50.

41 "Article Written by Nostor Nikolenko against Constantine Seletzky," affixed to
William Doyas to Bureau, August 13, 1919, File #363727, Roll #799, FBI OGF. For a
history of Orthodoxy in Baltimore, see "Parish History," in *100-Year Jubilee, 1919–
2019* (Baltimore: Holy Trinity Russian Orthodox Church, 2019), 10–15.

42 William Doyas to Bureau, June 25, 1919; William Doyas to Bureau, June 21, 1919,
File #363727, Roll #799, FBI OGF; Harold D. Piper, "Russian Community Loyal to
Churches," *Baltimore Sun*, February 13, 1967.

43 Michael C. Meyer, "The Arms of the Ypiranga," *Hispanic American Historical
Review* 50 (August 1970): 543–56; *Rasst v. Morris*, 135 Md. 243 (1919). For Rasst's
manufacturing concerns, see "Baltimore," *Iron Age*, August 19, 1915, 450; "Baltimore," *Iron Age*, September 23, 1915, 735; "Baltimore," *Iron Age*, August 26, 1915,
497; "Baltimore," *Iron Age*, November 11, 1915, 1160.

44 "Red Tempest Fizzles," *Baltimore Daily Sun*, May 2, 1919; The archdiocese did not
publish a formal notice of Nikolenko's expulsion but did announce in July 1916 the
appointment of a new pastor to Norwich, Connecticut, suggesting Nikolenko was
disciplined sometime around the late spring. See "Naznacheniia i perevody po
eparkhii," *APV*, July 20, 1916, 432.

45 Billups Harris to Bureau, June 13, 1919, File #363727, Roll #799, FBI OGF. The
report notes that "Seletzky . . . has given the information to this office months ago
and it has been reported on."

46 William Doyas to Bureau, May 31, 1919, File #363727, Roll #799, FBI OGF.

47 William E. Allen to Billups Harris, June 5, 1919, File #363727, Roll #799, FBI OGF.
Doyas's report from the next day indicates the letter mailed to the Baltimore
bureau office was initialed by J. Edgar Hoover.

48 Summary report, n.d., attached to William E. Allen to Billups Harris, June 7, 1919,
File #363727, Roll #799, FBI OGF.

49 William Doyas to Bureau, June 14, 1919; William Doyas to Bureau, June 16, 1919,
File #363727, Roll #799, FBI OGF.

50 William Doyas to Bureau, June 25, 1919, File #363727, Roll #799, FBI OGF. *Khleb i
volia* was a communist, though anti-Bolshevik, paper published for nine months

292 | NOTES

in 1919. See Lazar Lipotkin, *The Russian Anarchist Movement in North America* (Edmonton, AB: Black Cat, 2019), 111–12.

51 William Doyas to Bureau, August 25, 1919, for August 5, File #363727, Roll #799, FBI OGF.

52 William Doyas to Bureau, September 4, 1919, for August 11, 1919; William Doyas to Bureau, August 21, 1919, for August 21, 1919; William Doyas to Bureau, September 6, 1919, for August 27, 1919; William Doyas to Bureau, September 10, 1919, for September 5, 1919; William Doyas to Bureau, September 13, 1919, for September 6, 1919; William Doyas to Bureau, September 15, 1919, for September 10, 1919; William Doyas to Bureau, October 6, 1919, for September 24, 1919; William Doyas to Bureau, October 16, 1919, for October 15, 1919; William Doyas to Bureau, November 14, 1919, for October 30, 1919, File #363727, Roll #799, FBI OGF.

53 Report, "Nostor Nikolenko," September 4, 1919, File #363727, Roll #799, FBI OGF.

54 "V gostiakh u g-na Prezidenta," *APV*, February 28, 1914, 67–70; Prot. A. A. Hotovitzky, "Russkaia kafedral'n. Kapella v belom domie," IuS I, 232–34.

55 "Rasporiazhenie eparkhial'noi vlasti," *APV*, May 1918, 69; Notice of Bishop Alexander Nemolovsky, April 18, 1918, *GTs*, May 23, 1918.

56 A. H. Loula to Bureau, March 22, 1919, File #378695, Roll #830, FBI OGF. For another account of BI investigations of Zeltonoga, see Suzanne Orr, "Deporting the Red Menace: Russian Immigrants, Progressive Reformers, and the First Red Scare in Chicago, 1917–1920" (PhD diss., University of Notre Dame, 2010), 139–42.

57 Translation quoted in A. H. Loula to Bureau, August 11, 1919, File #378695, Roll #830, FBI OGF. The original edition of *Daily Free Russia* does not survive. It is likely that "nation" here is a vague translation of *narod*, which more connotes the Russian people as a collective, not a state or government.

58 A. H. Loula to Bureau, August 13, 1919, File #378695, Roll #830, FBI OGF.

59 William Doyas to Bureau, December 3, 1919, File #378695, Roll #830, FBI OGF.

60 William Doyas to Bureau, December 9, 1919, File #378695, Roll #830, FBI OGF.

61 William Doyas to Bureau, December 26, 1919; William Doyas to Bureau, December 30, 1919, File #378695, Roll #830, FBI OGF.

62 William Doyas to Bureau, December 30, 1919, File #378695, Roll #830, FBI OGF.

63 Frank Burke to William Doyas, January 9, 1920, File #378695, Roll #830, FBI OGF. See also Frank Burke to William Doyas, December 23, 1919, File #378695, Roll #830, FBI OGF.

64 "Deportation Move On," *Baltimore Sun*, January 4, 1920. See also Vernon L. Pedersen, *The Communist Party in Maryland, 1919–57* (Urbana: University of Illinois Press, 2001); and Louis Post, *Deportations Delirium of 1920: A Personal Narrative of an Historic Personal Experience* (Chicago: Charles H. Kerr, 1923).

65 Erle S. Parrish to Bureau, January 13, 1920, File #378695, Roll #830, FBI OGF.

66 William Doyas to Bureau, January 14, 1920; William Doyas to Bureau, January 19, 1920; William Doyas to Bureau, January 27, 1920; William Doyas to Bureau, February 5, 1920, File #378695, Roll #830, FBI OGF.

NOTES | 293

67 William Doyas to Bureau, January 27, 1920; William Doyas to Bureau, July 19, 1920; William Doyas to Bureau, October 23, 1920, File #378695, Roll #830, FBI OGF. Pedersen, *Communist Party in Maryland*, 28.

68 "Religiia, Bol'shevizm i Anarkhizm," *Volna*, September 1920, 7.

69 Pedersen, *Communist Party in Maryland*, 34–35. Vernon Pedersen asserts that the Russian-language instructor Prokope Suvarov was an agent planted at Holy Trinity by the Soviet state, which Pedersen claims "made a point of keeping a careful watch on even sympathetic émigré organizations" (35).

70 "Proshloe, nastoiashchee i budushee," in *Golden Anniversary, Russian Orthodox Cathedral of St. George, 1915–1965* (Chicago: St. George Russian Orthodox Cathedral, 1965), 14, Box 1, Folder 3, RIMAS UIC; "Our Father John Diakon," in *St. George Russian Orthodox Cathedral 75th Anniversary*.

71 Jerome P. Davis, *The Russian Immigrant* (New York: Macmillan, 1922), 94–95.

72 Peshkov, "Decennial Jubilee."

73 P. A. Gulko, "Zdravstvuiushchie: Kak my stroili RItsOV," in *Iubileinyi sbornik 25 letiia russkago nezavisimogo obshchestva vzaimopomoshchi*, 13.

CHAPTER 7. "WE GO FEARLESSLY INTO THE MAW OF DEATH"

1 "Poslyednie dni zhizni o. Aleksandra Lupinovicha," *Svit*, November 14, 1918.

2 Nancy Bristow, *American Pandemic: The Lost Worlds of the 1918 Influenza Epidemic* (Oxford: Oxford University Press, 2012), 7.

3 Bristow, 8.

4 Patricia J. Fanning, *Influenza and Inequality: One Town's Tragic Response to the Great Epidemic of 1918* (Amherst: University of Massachusetts Press, 2010), 128.

5 One notable exception is recent interest in the Syrian priest Nicola Yanney, who contracted influenza while visiting afflicted parishioners in Nebraska and who continued to visit them after he showed symptoms himself. Yanney died from influenza on October 28, 1918. Saint Raphael Clergy Brotherhood, *Apostle to the Plains: The Life of Father Nicola Yanney* (Chesterton, IN: Ancient Faith, 2019), 243–52.

6 "Church Institutions," in *Orthodox America, 1794–1976*, ed. Constance Tarasar (Syosset, NY: Orthodox Church in America Department of History and Archives, 1975), 113–18.

7 The Trisagion (or Thrice-Holy) is a common hymn of Eastern Christianity: "Holy God, Holy Mighty, Holy Immortal, have mercy on us."

8 "Poslyednie dni zhizni o. Aleksandra Lupinovicha," *Svit*, November 14, 1918. *Matushka* is an honorific used in Russian practice to refer to the wife of a deacon or priest.

9 "Pamiati O. A. Lupinovicha," *APV*, October–November–December 1918, 125.

10 David M. Morens and Anthony S. Fauci, "The 1918 Influenza Pandemic: Insights for the 21st Century," *Journal of Infectious Diseases* 195 (April 1, 2007): 1022; Alfred W. Crosby, *America's Forgotten Pandemic: The Influenza of 1918*, 2nd ed. (Cambridge: Cambridge University Press, 2003), 17–36.

11 Julia F. Irwin, "An Epidemic without Enmity: Explaining the Missing Ethnic Tensions in New Haven's 1918 Influenza Epidemic," *Urban History Review* 36 (Spring 2008): 5–17; Kyra H. Grantz, Madhura S. Rane, Henrik Salje, Gregory E. Glass, Stephen E. Schachterle, and Derek A. T. Cummings, "Disparities in Influenza Mortality and Transmission Related to Sociodemographic Factors within Chicago in the Pandemic of 1918," *Proceedings of the National Academy of Sciences of the United States of America* 113 (2016): 13839–44; G. Dennis Shanks and John F. Brundage, "Variable Mortality during the 1918 Influenza Pandemic in Chicago," *Proceedings of the National Academy of Sciences of the United States of America* 114 (2017): E3586–E3587.

12 Jerome P. Davis, *The Russian Immigrant* (New York: Macmillan, 1922), 72.

13 "Richter's Anchor Pain Expeller: Nondoctor Analgesia from 'Doctoring' Chili, Black and Guinea Peppers," *Anesthesiology* 126 (January 2017): 15.

14 Advertisement, "Doktor Mendel'son Russkii Doktor," *Svit*, October 31, 1918.

15 Michael M. Davis, *Immigrant Health and the Community* (New York: Harper, 1921), 146.

16 "U kogo shcho bolit?," *Svit*, October 17, 1918; "Leki. chasinoiu predokhraniaiushchii ot influchntsii," *Svit*, October 17, 1918.

17 "Iz minneapolisa," *Svit*, October 24, 1918.

18 The others were priests Maxim Bakunoff, Ioann Komar, and Daniel Yachmenev. See "Missiynaia khronika," *APV*, October–November–December 1918, 121–25.

19 This ideal was outlined, albeit in an earlier influenza epidemic, during a 1900 visit to Alaska by Bishop Tikhon (Bellavin). See Scott Kenworthy, "St. Tikhon Condemns Racism during Epidemic," *Public Orthodoxy*, June 29, 2020. https://publicorthodoxy.org.

20 Ludmilla Buketoff Turkevich, "The Right Reverend Constantin Buketoff, a Biographical Sketch (on His 50th Anniversary as a Priest)," *APV*, November 1957, 125–26.

21 "Iz vitman, v. v-a.," *Svit*, November 7, 1918. For physical effects of influenza, see Crosby, *America's Forgotten Pandemic*, 6–9.

22 "Pogrebenie sviashchennika O.M. Bakuna," *APV*, October–November–December 1918, 122–23.

23 "Ryech' u groba v bozye pochivshago Missionara, Sviashch. o. Maskima Bakuna, proiznesennaia Preosviashchennym Aleksandrom 13/26 oktiabria 1918 g. v Allegenskoi Tserkvi," *APV*, October–November–December 1918, 121–22.

24 "Sumnaia vyest'," *Svit*, January 2, 1919.

25 "Znayte truzhdaiushchikhsia u vas (Vernym chadam Russko-Amerikanskoi Pravoslavnoi Missii—o geroiskikh podvigakh ikh pastyrei)," *GTs*, November 7, 1918.

26 Martin C. J. Bootsma and Neil M. Ferguson, "The Effect of Public Health Measures on the 1918 Influenza Pandemic in U.S. Cities," *Proceedings of the National Academy of Sciences of the United States of America* 104, no. 18 (May 1, 2007): 7591.

27 James E. Higgins, "A Lost History: Writing the Influenza Epidemic in Pennsylvania, 1918–1922," *Pennsylvania History: A Journal of Mid-Atlantic Studies* 85 (Summer 2018): 394–405; Crosby, *America's Forgotten Pandemic*, 70–90.

28 "Vo khristye vozliublennym pastyriam amerikanskoi pravoslavnoi rusi," *GTs*, October 17, 1918.

29 "Bratchikam i parokhianam vilkes–barrskoi spaso-voskresenskoi tserkvi," *Svit*, October 24, 1918.

30 "Iz Kolver, Pa.," *Svit*, December 12, 1918.

31 Aleksandr Pyza, "Pis'ma v redaktsiiu," *Svit*, November 21, 1918.

32 "Isolation Will Be Used in Flu Fight," *Cleveland Plain Dealer*, October 5, 1918; "Wars on Spitting to Help Avoid Flu," *Cleveland Plain Dealer*, October 6, 1918; "How Cleveland Fights Flu," *Cleveland Plain Dealer*, October 14, 1918; "One Service in Churches," *Cleveland Press*, November 4, 1918. See also "Cleveland, Ohio," in *The American Influenza Epidemic of 1918–1919: A Digital Encyclopedia*, accessed October 28, 2024, www.influenzaarchive.org.

33 "Bogokhraminym, vo khristye vozliublennym pastyriam i pasomym amerikanskoi pravoslav. rusi," *GTs* November 7, 1918; "Conventions Postponed," *Cleveland Plain Dealer*, October 30, 1918. In contrast, church historians have long maintained that the decision to postpone the council was driven by finances, given the difficult economic conditions of the archdiocese and local parishes alike. See Gregory Afonsky, *A History of the Orthodox Church in America, 1917–1934* (Kodiak, AK: St. Herman Seminary Press, 1994), 29–32; Father John Matusiak and Father Leonid Kishkovsky, "Crisis and Transition, 1917–1922," in Tarasar, *Orthodox America, 1794–1976*, 178–81; Alexis Liberovsky, "The 2nd All-American Sobor," Orthodox Church in America, accessed October 29, 2024, www.oca.org.

34 Along with Lupinovich's death notice, church newspapers also published a schedule assigning priests across the archdiocese to offer prayers in their churches for the deceased priest until the fortieth day after his passing. "Zhurnal sobraniia chlenov S.-Amerikanskago Dukh. Pravleniia Sent. 24-go 1918 goda," *GTs*, October 10, 1918.

35 "Pamiati missionera," *APV*, October–November–December 1918, 125. For more on the motivations of Orthodox missionary priests, see Aram G. Sarkisian, "The Cross between Hammer and Sickle: Russian Orthodox Christians in the United States, 1908–1928" (PhD diss., Northwestern University, 2019), 92–102.

36 "Otchet o chlenakh po russk. pravoslavnomu kaf. ob-vu vzaimopomoshchi," *Svit*, December 19, 1918.

37 *Russkoe pravoslavnoe kafol. obshchestvo vzaimopomoshchi v syevero-amerikanskikh soedinennykh shtatakhk XX-lyetnemu iubileiu, 1895–1915* (New York: Svit, 1915), 13.

38 For the dynamics of conversion and identity in Carpatho-Rusyn communities, see Joel Brady, "Transnational Conversions: Greek Catholic Migrants and Russky Orthodox Conversion Movements in Austria-Hungary, Russia, and the Americas (1890–1914)" (PhD diss., University of Pittsburgh, 2012), esp. 138–39. As late as the 1960s, ROCMAS publications included virulently anti-Catholic material, as well as material cruelly dismissive of Ukrainian language, identity, and culture.

39 John Bodnar, *The Transplanted: A History of Immigrants in Urban America* (Bloomington: Indiana University Press, 1987), 120–30. For contemporary

296 | NOTES

observations, see Emily Greene Balch, *Our Slavic Fellow Citizens* (New York: Charity Publications Committee, 1910), 378–84; and J. Davis, *Russian Immigrant*, 27–30.

40 Ewa Morawska, *For Bread with Butter: Life-Worlds of East Central Europeans in Johnstown, Pennsylvania, 1890–1940* (Cambridge: Cambridge University Press, 1985), 9.

41 US Immigration Commission, *Reports of the Immigration Commission*, vol. 6, pt. 1, *Bituminous Coal Mining* (Washington, DC: Government Printing Office, 1911), 96.

42 Though *bratstvo* suggests a "brotherhood" for men, this was a colloquial term that referred to chapters that included both men and women. A separate organization, the Russian Orthodox Women's Mutual-Aid Society (Russkoe Pravoslavnoe Zhenskoe Obshchestvo Vzaimopomoshchi), was founded in 1907 and based in Coaldale, Pennsylvania. It offered death benefits policies of $250 or $500 for women aged sixteen through forty-five. Advertisement, "Russkoe Pravoslavnoe Zhenskoe Obshchestvo Vzaimopomoshchi," *Svit*, June 13, 1918.

43 Between 1895 and 1915, ninety-four communities received a total of $33,000 in such grants. "Tserkovnyia zapomogi vydany tserkvam v slyediushchikh gorodakh i seleniiakh," in *70th Anniversary, Russkoe pravoslavnoe obshchestvo vzaimopomoshchi v syev.-amerikanskix soedinennykh shtatakh* (Wilkes-Barre, PA: Tipografiia gazety "Svyet," 1965), 51–54.

44 "Russkoe Pravoslavnoe Obshchestvo Vazimopomoshchi i Ego Vorogi," *Svit*, October 16, 1919.

45 See monthly reports, all titled "Otchet o chlenakh po russk. pravoslavnomu kaf. ob-vu vzaimopomoshchi," *Svit*, February 7, 1918; February 28, 1918; March 27, 1918; May 2, 1918; May 30, 1918; June 27, 1918; August 15, 1918; September 26, 1918; October 24, 1918; and October 31, 1918.

46 *Svit* published four influenza mortality benefits reports: three regular monthly reports for November, December, and January (benefits claims were recorded a month after the member's death) and a fourth, cumulative report published in March. Deaths were listed by the individual member's chapter number. "Otchet o chlenakh po russk. pravoslavnomu kaf. ob-vu vzaimopomoshchi," *Svit*, December 19, 1918; January 9, 1919; and February 6, 1919; and "Spisok umershikh ot 'influentsii' chlenov russk. pravosl. obshchestva vazimopomoshchi," *Svit*, March 13, 1919.

47 These data were compiled by consulting all death certificates filed in Mayfield between October and December 1918. I have counted only those certificates that reported influenza as either the primary or secondary cause of death and also recorded interment in the Mayfield Russian Orthodox Cemetery. Pennsylvania Historic and Museum Commission, *Pennsylvania (State) Death Certificates, 1906–1967*, Certificate Number Ranges 124201–500, 166201–350, and 188851–9000, Ancestry.com.

48 "Michael Serafin," "Still-Born Serafin," "Anna Serafin," in Pennsylvania Historic and Museum Commission, *Pennsylvania (State) Death Certificates, 1906–1967*,

Certificate Numbers 124404, 124405, and 124407, Ancestry.com; "Anna Pawuak Sytch Serafin," Public Family Tree entry, Ancestry.com.

49 Adding to the speculative nature of these statistics, the environmental historian Alfred W. Crosby also points to evidence that influenza cases were remarkably underreported (*America's Forgotten Pandemic*, 203–7).

50 "Iz bozvella," *Svit*, November 7, 1918. As to whether the Kovach children were taken to Springfield, a possible indication is that neither appears in the 1920 US Census schedule for the orphanage, when all would have remained eligible to be in residence there.

51 "Do uvagi pochtennykh bratstv i chlenov obshchestva vzaimopomoshchi," *Svit*, November 7, 1918.

52 "Do uvagi vsekh bra-v i chlenov obshchestva," *Svit*, January 2, 1919; "Nepremyennomu vnimaniiu vsyex chlenov russkogo pravoslavnogo obshchestva vzaimopomoshchi," *Svit*, January 30, 1919. For National Fraternal Congress of America directives, see "Are Extra Assessments Needed Because of Spanish Influenza?," *Fraternal Monitor*, January 1, 1919, 14; and "Meeting of the Presidents' Section of the National Fraternal Congress of America," *Fraternal Monitor*, March 1, 1919, 11. For tensions between private insurance and fraternal organizations over influenza assessments, see "The Epidemic," *Fraternal Monitor*, December 1919, 15–16. See also Lizabeth Cohen, *Making a New Deal: Industrial Workers in Chicago, 1919–1939*, 2nd ed. (Cambridge: Cambridge University Press, 2008), 67. For ROCMAS and Fraternal Congress directives, see "Dolzhnomu vnimaniiu vsyekh chlenov russkogo pravoslavnago ob–va vzaimopomoshchi," *Svit*, May 18, 1919.

53 "Financial Statement," *Svit*, October 16, 1919.

54 A partial list of the dissenting chapters was published as "Ne platiashchii bratstva," *Svit*, May 1, 1919.

55 "Nagliadnaia tablitsa dal'nyeishago rosta chlenstva nashego obshchestva vzaimopomoshchi," in *70th Anniversary*, 32–33.

56 "Obshchestvennyi inventar' k 1 maiu 1915 g.," in *Russkoe pravoslavnoe kafol. obshchestvo vzaimopomoshchi*, 128.

57 R. J. Lucksha to Hon. Thomas B. Donaldson, August 28, 1919, published in *Svit*, October 16, 1919.

58 "Russkoe Pravoslavnoe Obshchestvo Vazimopomoshchi i Ego Vorogi," *Svit*, October 16, 1919. For Kohanik's patriotic activism during the First World War, see Sarkisian, "Cross between Hammer and Sickle," 148–52. For a general biography, see Bogdan Horbal, "Kohanik, Peter / Kokhanik, Petr," in *Encyclopedia of Rusyn History and Culture*, ed. Paul Magocsi (Toronto: University of Toronto Press, 2005), 241; and "Skonchalsia Protopresviter Petr Kokhanik," *APV*, June 1969, 82–83.

59 In response to another extra assessment, the Homestead brotherhood joined the competing Russian Consolidated Mutual-Aid Society (ROOVA) in 1935. See S. Shkoda, "Kratkaia istoria bratstva Sv. Grigoriia Bogoslova v g. gomsted, pensil'vaniia (1912–1943)," IuS II, 252–53.

298 | NOTES

60 "Pro shcho my ne sil'ny finansovo?," *Svit*, June 3, 1920.

61 "O vystupivshikh i iskliuchennykh chlenakh iz obshchestva," *Svit*, June 3, 1920. See also "K iubileinoi konventsii russkogo prav. ob–va vazimopomoshchi," *Svit*, June 17, 1920. "Konets pravoslavnago obshchestva," *GTs*, June 17, 1920; "K spletniam 'golosa tserkvi,'" *Prikarpatskaia Rus'*, June 25, 1920.

62 "Will Meet Next Year at Yonkers," *Wilkes-Barre Evening News*, n.d., reprinted in *Svit*, June 24, 1920.

63 "Nagliadnaia tablitsa dal'nyeishago rosta chlenstva nashego obshchestva vzaimopomoshchi," in *70th Anniversary*, 32–33.

64 *Russian-American Register, 1920* (New York: Russian-American Register, 1920), 134.

65 Peter Mock, "Diary of a Parish: Homestead, PA," in Tarasar, *Orthodox America, 1794–1976*, 169–70.

CHAPTER 8. "THESE RADICALS"

1 Testimony of Fr. Dimitri Darin, September 15, 1921, *All Saints Russian Orthodox Church v. Dimitri Darin, et al.*, 222 Mich. 35, 192 N.W. 697 (1923), Transcript, 181–88, All Saints Subject File, AOCA.

2 Hearing re: Makary Skurko, June 16, 1919, File 54616/170, Box 3331, INS.

3 Makary Lukashov, hearing, October 30, 1919, File 54709/554, Box 3495, INS.

4 Ss. Peter and Paul Russian Orthodox Church, *50th Anniversary of Ss. Peter and Paul Russian Orthodox Church* (Detroit: Ss. Peter and Paul Russian Orthodox Church, 1957).

5 Priest Isidor Salko, Report on the All Saints Parish, 1915, Isidor Salko Subject File, AOCA.

6 Salko helped establish Orthodox parishes elsewhere in Michigan, including Albion and Flint, both founded in 1916. Holy Ascension of Christ Orthodox Church, *65th Anniversary Commemorative Book, Holy Ascension of Christ Orthodox Church* (Albion, MI: Holy Ascension of Christ Orthodox Church, 1981), 19–21. Salko died in a car accident in 1929 while serving a parish in Centralia, Pennsylvania. "Skorbnyi list," *APV*, February 1929, 32.

7 Archpriest John J. Chepeleff, "Brief History of the Founding of the Russian Orthodox All Saints Church of Detroit, Michigan," IuS II, 215.

8 "Dismisses 800 Men," *New York Times*, January 10, 1914; "Crowd at Ford Plant Dwindles," *Detroit News*, January 8, 1914; "Men Flock to City Hoping for Jobs at Ford Factory," *Detroit News*, January 9, 1914; "Greek Santa Claus Comes to Detroit," *Detroit Free Press*, January 8, 1914.

9 Thomas Klug, "Employers' Strategies in the Detroit Labor Market, 1900–1929," in *On the Line: Essays in the History of Auto Work*, ed. Nelson Lichtenstein and Stephen Meyer (Urbana: University of Illinois Press, 1989), 42–72.

10 Testimony of Wasili Rybko, *All Saints v. Darin*, Transcript, 128–30, All Saints Subject File, AOCA.

11 US Bureau of the Census, *Religious Bodies 1916*, part 2, *Separate Denominations* (Washington, DC: Government Printing Office, 1919), 261.

12 "Exhibit 8: By Laws of the All Saints Church of the City of Detroit," August 1, 1918, *All Saints v. Darin*, Transcript, 307–8, All Saints Subject File; AOCA.

13 Agrafena's Children, the Old Families of Ninilchik, Alaska, accessed October 15, 2024, www.geocities.ws.

14 "Mitya Darin," Fort Kenai, Alaska, 1900 United States Census; "Steven Darin," Nenilchik (or Munina), Alaska, 1900 United States Census; Fr. Ioann Bortnovskii to Hieromonk Antonii Dashkevich, September 15, 1902, and Fr. Theophilos Pashkovskii to Hieromonk Antonii Dashkevich, October 29, 1902, Box D271/Reel 185, ROGCCA LOC; Hieromonk Antonii Dashkevich to Bishop Tikhon Bellavin, October 15, 1902, Box D356/Reel 232, ROGCCA LOC; "Po Shtatam i Alyaskye. Iz dorozhik vpechatlyenii sputnika Yego Vysokopreosvyashchenstva," *APV*, June 28, 1911, 214–17.

15 By 1920, the *psalomshchik*, Mike Worobieff, had moved to Pittsburgh. When the priest at Worobieff's new parish there contacted Darin for a reference, the clergyman received a letter stating that Worobieff was "an extreme radical and endeavored to break up the church while in Detroit," with Darin stating that he "could not conscientiously give [Worobieff] any references other than the very poorest." When federal agents searched Worobieff's room in Pittsburgh, they found leftist literature, an image of a church with a caption that agents thought antireligious in character, and "one photo of a semi-nude woman." Report, F. C. Casper, In Re: Mike Worobieff, Pittsburgh, PA, May 25, 1920, File 386474, Roll 844, FBI OGF. See also Report, Michael Yankovich Re: M. Worobieff, Pittsburgh, PA, February 8, 1921, File #202600, Roll 935, FBI BSF.

16 "Protokol Sobraniia Dukhovenstva N'iu-Iorkskago Blagochinnicheskago Okruga, Syevero-Amerikanskoi Pravoslavnoi Russkoi Missii 17 (30) Iiulia, sego goda," *GTs*, August 15, 1918; "Rezoliutsii Predsobornago Sobraniia Dukhovenstva 21–23 avgusta s. g. v Pittsburge," and "Rezoliutsiia Predsoborskago Sobraniia Dukhovenstva v gor. N'iu Iorkye 5-go (18) sentiabria 1918 g.," *APV*, July–September 1918, 104–6.

17 Andrew Cherniawsky, hearing, June 14, 1919, File 54709/566, Box 3495, INS.

18 Christopher H. Johnson, *Maurice Sugar: Law, Labor, and the Left in Detroit, 1912–1950* (Detroit: Wayne State University Press, 1988), 73–74. Also see Steve Babson, *Working Detroit* (Detroit: Wayne State University Press, 1986), 38–40.

19 Broadside, "Proletarskii Bazar prodolzhitsia vosem' dnei v Dome Mass," February 1919, Exhibit File 54616/144B (Nicholas Baikowsky), Box 3329, INS.

20 A number of examples were taken from Baikowsky during the April 1919 Justice Department raid and remain preserved in an "Exhibit File" within the records of the United States Immigration and Naturalization Service. See Exhibit File 54616/144B (Nicholas Baikowsky), Box 3329, INS.

21 Hearing transcript re: Nicholas Baikowsky, June 17, 1919, File 54709/570, Box 3496, INS.

22 Resolution, Russian National Home, January 19, 1919, File 54709/556, Box 3495, INS.

NOTES

23 Hearing transcript re: Nicholas Baikowsky, June 17, 1919.

24 Testimony of Fr. Dimitri Darin, *All Saints v. Darin*, Transcript, 181–88, All Saints Subject File, AOCA.

25 "Detroitskiia Sobytiia," *GTs*, May 15, 1919. Early in the Bolshevik era, many US media outlets recorded Lenin's first name as Nikolai, not Vladimir.

26 Testimony of Makary Skurko, *All Saints v. Darin*, Transcript, 225, All Saints Subject File, AOCA.

27 John Higham, *Strangers in the Land: Patterns of American Nativism, 1860–1925*, 2nd ed. (New Brunswick, NJ: Rutgers University Press, 1983), 234–63; Erica J. Ryan, *Red War on the Family: Sex, Gender and Americanism in the First Red Scare* (Philadelphia: Temple University Press, 2015); Christopher M. Sterba, *Good Americans: Italian and Jewish Immigrants during the First World War* (New York: Oxford University Press, 2003).

28 Apelman corroborated Leontovich's presence in Detroit, writing in a report that Leontovich "is the Minister of the Russian Independent Church at Hamtramck, Mich." The All Saints neighborhood, due to its proximity to Hamtramck (a matter of several blocks), was sometimes referred to as being in Hamtramck, even though it was within the borders of Detroit. Report of J. S. Apelman to Bureau, March 24, 1919, File #330994, Roll #753, FBI OGF. For Leontovich's clerical status, see "Dva Lzhesvidyetelia," *GTs*, July 18, 1918.

29 "Minute No. 1 of meeting held March the 8th, 1919," *All Saints v. Darin*, Transcript, 171–72, All Saints Subject File, AOCA.

30 Minutes for meeting of All Saints "Church-Protecting Committee," March 29, 1919, *All Saints v. Darin*, Transcript, 200–207, All Saints Subject File, AOCA.

31 The deportation cases are described in greater detail in Aram G. Sarkisian, "Their Daily Dread: Russian Orthodox Christians in Red Scare Detroit, 1918–1920," *Journal of American Ethnic History* 41, no. 4 (2022): 37–73. Joseph Apelman emigrated to Detroit from Poland in 1905, then rose through the automotive industry to a management position at the Maxwell Motor Company (a once-major firm later purchased by Chrysler). After serving in the US Army as an intelligence agent, Apelman joined the BI amid the postwar consolidation of federal intelligence agencies. Apelman claimed to speak as many as nine languages, drawing on both this skill set and his Polish origins in his covert surveillance of Slavic immigrant groups. In 1923, he was lauded at "one of the most feared government agents at work against the radicals." "Communists Still at Work for Revolt Here," *Detroit Free Press*, October 28, 1923.

32 These lawyers included Lazarus Davidow and Solomon Paperno, two litigators with long associations and leadership roles within Detroit socialist groups. By one BI estimate, either Davidow or Paperno served as legal counsel for up to 98 percent of Red Scare–related suspects tried in Detroit by May 1919. In addition, at least one All Saints–related case was taken up by Jacob Margolis, an anarchist and IWW-affiliated attorney from Pittsburgh. See A. L. Barkey to W. E. Allen, May 6, 1919, File #8000-362065, Roll #797, FBI OGF; Memorandum for Mr. Hoover

NOTES | 301

In re: Lazarus S. Davidow, January 9, 1920, Roll #792, FBI OGF; J. S. Apelman to Bureau, May 26, 1919, File #355747, Roll #788, FBI OGF.

33 "Church Blamed for 18 Arrests," *Detroit News*, April 16, 1919.

34 Testimony of Fr. Dimitri Darin, *All Saints v. Darin*, Transcript, 187, All Saints Subject File, AOCA.

35 "Minutes No. 8, April 13, 1919," *All Saints v. Darin*, Transcript, 287–88, All Saints Subject File, AOCA.

36 "'Reds' Planned Bar in Church," *Detroit Free Press*, November 4, 1919.

37 Nicholas Baikowsky, deposition re: Makary Skurko, May 10, 1919, File 54709/566, Box 3496, INS.

38 "In the Matter of Nicholas Dukoff Baykovsky and others," File #355747, Roll #788, FBI OGF.

39 "Petition from Russians in Detroit," May 4, 1919, File 54709/566, Box 3496, INS.

40 John Clark to Commissioner, October 25, 1919, File 54709/566, Box 3496, INS.

41 Walter M. Nelson, brief re: Makary Lukashew, n.d., File 54709/554, Box 3495, INS.

42 Patrick W. Carey, *People, Priests, and Prelates: Ecclesiastical Democracy and the Tensions of Trusteeism* (Notre Dame, IN: University of Notre Dame Press, 1987), 39; Patrick Joseph Dignan, *A History of the Legal Incorporation of Catholic Church Property in the United States, 1784–1932* (New York: AMS, 1974).

43 For a general summary of trusteeism, see James O'Toole, *The Faithful: A History of Catholics in America* (Cambridge, MA: Harvard University Press, 2008), 51–64.

44 Boris I. Bittker, Scott C. Idleman, and Frank S. Ravitch, *Religion and the State in American Law* (New York: Cambridge University Press, 2015), 359–93.

45 Archbishop Evdokim (Meschersky), "Report of the State of the Diocese for 1916," trans. Hieromonk Andrew Kostadis, in Kostadis, "Pictures of Missionary Life according to the Russian Clerical Press in America and the Ruling American Bishops about the Life of the American Mission in 1900–1917" (MTh thesis, St. Vladimir's Orthodox Theological Seminary, 1999), 259.

46 Winnifred Fallers Sullivan, *Church State Corporation: Construing Religion in US Law* (Chicago: University of Chicago Press, 2020), 11.

47 Minutes of March 23, 1919, General Parish Meeting, *All Saints v. Darin*, Transcript, 14–16, All Saints Subject File, AOCA.

48 "'Red' Is Banded in Russian Suit," *Detroit Free Press*, January 4, 1921.

49 Prot. Ioann C. Davidov, "Preosviashchennyi Pavel," *IuS* II, 212.

50 Samuel E. Jones to Rev. Isadore Salko, February 11, 1921, All Saints Subject File, AOCA.

51 Michael Rymchanko (or Rimchenko) Anglicized his name to Mike Brink. The home and store on Newton Avenue was located where the General Motors Detroit-Hamtramck Assembly Plant stands today. His killer, Carl Sowka (or Soroka), received a life sentence. "Given Life Term; Thanks the Judge," *Detroit Free Press*, June 13, 1919.

52 Testimony of Makary Skurko, *All Saints v. Darin*, Transcript, 115–16, All Saints Subject File, AOCA.

302 | NOTES

53 The question of state involvement with the late imperial Russian Church has garnered great scholarly debate. From one perspective, Gregory Freeze has asserted that traditional arguments for a "symphonic" relationship between church and state traditionally are greatly overestimated. On the other is the assertion of Richard Pipes that during this period the church "lost its institutional identity and allowed itself to be turned into an ordinary branch of the state bureaucracy." More recently, scholars such as Vera Shevzov have maintained instead that while the state did construct the parameters by which the Russian Church operated, this had little day-to-day impact on church life. It is incontrovertible, however, that the commonly held, often nationalistic view that the tsar was the lay leader of the Russian Church is not accurate. Gregory Freeze, "Handmaiden of the State? The Church in Imperial Russia Reconsidered," *Journal of Ecclesiastical History* 36, no. 1 (1985): 82–102; Richard Pipes, *Russia under the Old Regime* (New York: Charles Scribner and Sons, 1974), 221–45, esp. 221–23. See also Marc Szeftel, "Church and State in Imperial Russia," in *Russian Orthodoxy under the Old Regime*, ed. Robert L. Nichols and Theofanis George Stavrou (Minneapolis: University of Minnesota Press, 1978), 127–41; and Scott M. Kenworthy and Alexander S. Agadjanian, *Understanding World Christianity: Russia* (Minneapolis: Fortress, 2021), 118–28.

54 "Exhibit D: 'How Thinks, How Feels and How Teaches about America Alexander Nemolovsky, Canadian Bishop,'" *All Saints v. Darin*, Transcript, 18–24, All Saints Subject File, AOCA. See also J. Davis, *Russian Immigrant*, 97. The pamphlet was introduced as evidence in at least one BI investigation of the archbishop. See File #286305, Roll #703, FBI OGF.

55 "Exhibit 8: 'By Laws of the All Saints Church of the City of Detroit, August 1, 1918,'" *All Saints v. Darin*, Transcript, 307–9, All Saints Subject File, AOCA.

56 Testimony of Makary Skurko, *All Saints v. Darin*, Transcript, 94, All Saints Subject File, AOCA.

57 Testimony of Fr. Dimitri Darin, *All Saints v. Darin*, Transcript, 179, All Saints Subject File, AOCA. Darin also elucidated these concerns in remarks to the *Detroit Free Press*, speculating that "recalcitrants" intended to remove the cross once they gained the church. "I believe I have enough loyal backers to prevent it," he explained. "The church of Christ is bigger than human selfishness." See "'Reds' Planned Bar in Church," *Detroit Free Press*, November 4, 1919.

58 Building on the strong links between the Episcopal Church and the Russian Archdiocese, Darin fostered close ties with Episcopalians in Detroit, where there was a concerted effort to encourage dialogue and joint worship under the banner of "Christian Americanization." All Saints hosted one such service during the General Convention of the Episcopal Church, which met in Detroit in October 1919. See Thomas Burgess, *Foreign-Born Americans and Their Children* (New York: Department of Missions and Church Extension of the Episcopal Church, 1922), 65–69. Burgess makes special mention of Darin, reporting that he knew Peter Trimble Rowe, the Episcopal bishop of Alaska, from childhood. See "'Revolution Here; We Stand for Industrial Democracy,' Bishop Williams Declares," *Detroit Free*

Press, October 20, 1919; and "Union Service with the Orthodox of Detroit," *Living Church*, January 22, 1921, 401.

59 Opinion of Judge Charles Collingwood, September 29, 1921, *All Saints v. Darin*, Transcript, 29–35; Decree of Judge Charles Collingwood, October 6, 1921, *All Saints v. Darin*, Transcript, 36–39, All Saints Subject File, AOCA.

60 Darin remained a married Byzantine Catholic priest, mostly in the Eparchy of Parma, until his death at the age of sixty-eight. "Rev. Demetrius S. Darin," *Cleveland Plain Dealer*, September 1, 1959.

61 All Saints parishioners (minority faction) to Archbishop Alexander, May 16/June 3, 1922, All Saints Subject File, AOCA.

62 Ernest N. Pappas to Archbishop Alexander, February 21, 1922, All Saints Subject File, AOCA.

63 Andrew Sura and All Saints Parishioners to Archbishop Alexander, n.d. (ca. early June 1922), All Saints Subject File, AOCA; Eparchial Council to Priest A. Sura, May 6/19, 1922, All Saints Subject File, AOCA; Priest Andrew Sura to Archbishop Alexander, June 16, 1922, All Saints Subject File, AOCA.

64 Appeal, June 8, 1922, 8–9, 24, *Russian Orthodox All Saints Church v. Darin*, 222 Mich. 35, All Saints Subject File, AOCA.

65 Decision of Michigan Supreme Court Justice Joseph Steere, March 23, 1923, *Russian Orthodox All Saints Church v. Darin*, 222 Mich. 35, All Saints Subject File, AOCA.

66 Decision of Steere.

67 Decision of Steere.

68 Prot. I. Chepelev, "Kratkaia Istoriia Vsyekhsviatskago Sobora," in *25th Jubilee Book of All Saints Russian Orthodox Cathedral* (Detroit: All Saints Russian Orthodox Cathedral, 1939), 2–8, All Saints Subject File, AOCA.

69 See Aram G. Sarkisian, "From Kedrovsky to Kedroff: The St. Nicholas Cathedral Cases in Their Historical Context," analytical essay, *Teaching Law and Religion Case Study Archive*, August 2019, https://bpb-us-e1.wpmucdn.com.

70 Arcady Piotrowsky to Alexander, May 16, 1918, Fr. Arcady Piotrowsky Subject File, AOCA.

71 Chepelev, "Kratkaia Istoriia Vsyekhsviatskago Sobora," 6–8.

EPILOGUE

1 For the full text of *Ukaz* 362, see "Ukaz nomer 362 sv. Patriarkha Tikhona," Synod of Bishops of the Russian Orthodox Church Abroad, accessed October 15, 2024, www.synod.com.

2 Quoted in Gregory Afonsky, *A History of the Orthodox Church in America, 1917–1934* (Kodiak, AK: St. Herman Seminary Press, 1994), 92.

3 Afonsky, 97.

4 "Telegramma Sobora Prezidentu," *Pravoe Dielo*, April 5, 1924.

5 Fr. Leonid Turkevich, "Hopes for the Orthodox Church of Russia," trans. Vera Johnston, *Constructive Quarterly* 6 (1918): 590–609.

304 | NOTES

6 "Record of Experiences in Moskow Kept by D. A. Lowrie," November 19–27, 1920, and Donald Lowrie to Priest Leonid Turkevich, December 2, 1920, Box 27: Donald A. Lowrie Letters and Diaries, 1917–1921, Folder: International Work in Russia and the Soviet Union and with Russians, Kautz Family YMCA Archives, University of Minnesota Archives and Special Collections. Lowrie references Hotovitzky throughout a book on his travels, though he devotes much of his attention to his Thanksgiving Day visit with Patriarch Tikhon. Donald A. Lowrie, *The Light of Russia: An Introduction to the Russian Church* (Prague: YMCA Press, 1923), 218–24.

7 Sergei Golubtsov, *Moskovskoe dukhovenstvo v preddverii i nachale gonenii 1917–1922 gg.* (Moscow: Izd-vo Pravoslavnogo bratstva Sporuchnitsy greshnykh, 1999), 120–45, 162, 186–87. Sinodal'naia komissia russkoi pravoslavnoi tserkvi po kanonicatsii sviatikh, *Protoierei Ioann Kochurov (1871–1917) Protopresviter Aleksandr Khotovitskii (1872–1937)* (St. Petersburg: Izdatel'stvo "Noakh," 1995), 54–59.

8 Donald Lowrie to Darrell O. Hibbard, April 29, 1923, Box 27: Donald Lowrie Collection, Folder: Donald A. Lowrie Letters and Diaries, 1917–1921, Kautz Family YMCA Archives. This is a copy of a personal letter that Lowrie sent home to his family and that he thought would be of interest to Hibbard, a YMCA missionary to Greece.

9 "A.D. i N.L. Kastal'skie—Ch. R. Kreinu," in *Russkaia dukhovnaia muzyka v dokumentakh i materialakh, tom V: Aleksandr Kastal'skii*, ed. S. G. Svereva (Moscow: Znak, 2006), 769. The letter, from the Russian choral director and folklorist Alexander Kastalsky and his wife, Natalia, is dated Moscow, July 4, 1923.

10 Ethan T. Colton to Charles Crane, April 10, 1924, Box 4: Russia Correspondence and Reports, Folder: Letters and Correspondence—1924, Kautz Family YMCA Archives.

11 Matthew Lee Miller, *The YMCA and Russian Culture: The Preservation and Expansion of Orthodox Christianity, 1900–1940* (Lanham, MD: Lexington Books, 2012), 47–49.

12 "Skorbnyi list," *APV*, July 1930, 167.

13 The others cremated with Hotovitzky were Archbishop Pitirim (Kriylov), Bishop Ioann (Shirokov), Protopriest Alexander Lebedev, and two other priests from the villages of Izmailov and Mordovia. See "Donskoi krematorii," in *Postradavshie za veru i tserkov' khristovu 1917–1937*, ed. Vladimir Vorob'ev (Moscow: Pravoslavnyi Sviato-Tikhonovskii gumanitarnyi universitet, 2012), 616–18.

14 "Vesti iz Rossii," *APV*, January 15, 1923, 1; "Raznyia vesti," *APV*, August 14, 1923, 107; "Vesti iz Rossii," *APV*, April 1924, 26.

15 The declaration denounced Metropolitan Sergius (Stragorodsky)'s 1927 profession of loyalty to the Soviet government, which he hoped would ease state persecution of the Russian Church. This decision garnered great controversy, both inside the Soviet Union and in émigré communities abroad. See Roy Robson, *Solovki: The Story of Russia Told through Its Most Remarkable Islands* (New Haven, CT: Yale University Press, 2004), 249.

16 Details of Zotikov's alleged crimes, filtered through the vocabularies of Soviet state security, were published in the Vladimir newspaper *Prizyv* (*The Call*).

Zotikov was described as "a servant of a religious cult, having been convicted earlier of resisting the selection of church valuables and having served a sentence in a prison camp for counterrevolutionary activities." "GPU raskryta kontrrevoliutsionnaia organizatsiia belykh ofitserov i dvorian," *Pryzyv* (Vladimir), October 28, 1930. See also "Lebedev Mikhail Petrovich," *Obrazovanie i Pravoslavie*, March 2, 2023, http://orthedu.ru.

17 A. Ch. Kozarzevskii, "Tserkovnoprikhodskaia zhizn' moskvy 1920–1930-kh godov. Vospominaniia prikhozhanina," *Zhurnal Moskovskoi Patriarkhii*, nos. 11–12 (1992): 22. Also see Andrei Leonidovich Ershov, "Sud'ba trekh sviashchennikov (k voprosu o gonenii na tserkov' vo Vladimirskom krae v 1930-e gody)," *Komissiia po kanonizatsii sviatykh Vladimirskaia eparkhiia*, accessed October 30, 2024, www .vladkan.ru; and "Il'ia Ivanovich Zotikov," *Liubov bezuslovnaia*, accessed October 30, 2024, http://lubovbezusl.ru.

18 Mikhail Polsky, *Novye mucheniki rossiiskie: Pervoe sobranie materialov* (Jordanville, NY: Holy Trinity Monastery, 1949), 215; Mikhail Polsky, *Novye mucheniki rossiiskie: Vtoroi tom sobraniia materialov* (Jordanville, NY: Holy Trinity Monastery, 1957), 225. A 1944 list of deceased priests who had served in the North American Archdiocese recorded Hotovitzky's death as having occurred in 1930. Zotikov was not listed. See "Iubileinyi pomiannik," IuS I, 307–9.

19 For the full list of glorified New Martyrs and Confessors, see "Spisok novomuchennikov I Ispovyednikov Rossiiskikh (utverzhden Arkhiereiskim Soborom RPTsZ v 1981 g.)," in *Troitskii Pravoslavnyi Russkii Kalendar na 1999 god* (Jordanville, NY: Holy Trinity Monastery, 1998), 305–13. I thank the ROCOR deacon and church historian Andrei Psarev for his helpful clarification that Hotovitzky apparently was one of many potential candidates excluded from the 1981 ROCOR glorifications. This was a result of Hotovitzky's continued service under then-Metropolitan (later Patriarch) Sergius (Stragorodsky) after the bishop's 1927 declaration of loyalty to the Soviet government, an act that ROCOR denounced as heretical. See Fr. Andrei Psarev, "Poriadok proslavleniia sviatykh v Russkoi Pravoslavnoi Tserkvi Zagranitsei (1920–2007 gg.)," *ROCOR Studies: Historical Studies of the Russian Church Abroad*, August 9, 2019, www .rocorstudies.org.

20 "Zotikov Il'ia Ivanovich—protoierei," *Komissiia po kanonizatsii sviatykh Vladimirskaia eparkhiia,* accessed October 30, 2024, www.vladkan.ru.

21 Yuri Sergeevich Alyakrinskii to Afanasii (Sakharov), July 1, 1959, in *Pis'ma raznykh lits k sviatiteliu Afanasiiu (Sakharovu): V dvukh knigakh, Kniga 1, A-N* (Moscow: Izadatel'stvo PSTGU, 2013), 42–43.

22 Quoted in Sinodal'naia Komissia Russkoi Pravoslavnoi Tserkvi po Kanonizatsii Sviatykh, *Protoierei Ioann Kochurov (1871–1917) Protopresviter Aleksandr Khotovitskii (1872–1937)* (St. Petersburg: Izdatel'stvo "Noakh," 1995), 61.

23 Andrei Kozarzhevsky, "Avtobiografiia Andreia Cheslavovicha Kozarzhevskago," Andrei Cheslavovich Kozarzhevsii website, accessed October 30, 2024, www .kozarzewski.org.

24 "Ne prishlos' mne idti v khristianstvo," *Tat'ianin Den'*, January 29, 2003, http://old
.taday.ru. At the time, Zotikov was rector of the Church of the Holy Spirit at the
Prichistinsky Gates.

25 Kozarzevskii, "Tserkovnoprikhodskaia zhizn' moskvy," 25. See also Andrei Kozarzhevsky, *Moskovskii pravoslavnyi mesiatseslov* (Moscow: Moskovskii rabochii,
1995), 121. For Hotovitzky's original description of that same day, which omits the
poem for reasons of both emotion and column inches, see Prot. A. Hotovitzky,
"Iz dnevnika. Ot"yezd o. Ilii Zotikova," *APV*, August 28, 1910, 250–53.

INDEX

Page numbers in italics indicate Figures.

Adamiak, Olga, 106

Alaska, 72, 140, 148, 156, 180, 271nn14–15, 302n58; autonomy of clergy in, 8, 56; Bishop Nicholas work in, 58–59; Darin from, 220–21; mission established in, 7, 8; parish numbers in, 57; sale of, 120

Alexander (Nemolovsky) (priest and bishop), 67, 77–78, 146, 150, 173, 180, 220–21, 240–41; Bakunoff death and, 196–97; BI file on, 159; on Bolshevism, 131, 154; character and reputation, 148–49, 158, 162, 233–34; clerical suspensions by, 151–52, 157, 181; Darin and, 233–36; First World War and, 112, 127–28, 156–57; in German prison, 286n41; influenza epidemic of 1918 response from, 197–99; Orphan Home and, 101, 102; Red Scare and, 139; as *Svit* editor, 28

Alexandrof, Vladimir (priest), 161–62, 168–69, 174–75, 222

All-American Church Council (*sobor*): of 1919 in Cleveland, 149, 200–201, 295n33; of 1924 in Detroit, 244–46

All-Russian Church Council (*sobor*) of 1917–1918, 8, 141–46, 149, 158, 160, 165

All Saints Russian Orthodox Church, Detroit, Michigan, 132, 213–15, 216–29, 231–40, 244

Americanization Committee of Detroit, 218

American Orthodox Rus': defined, 4, 9–11, 16, 18; education and, 85, 105; immigration and, 29; influenza epidemic of 1918 and, 192–95, 206–10; missionary expansion and, 58; patriotism and, 121; relationship to transnational Russian identity, 70–71; role as protector, 193, 246–47

Anastasia, Sister, 98, 100

Andrea, Sister, 98, 100

Andronoff, Vsevolod (deacon), 122

antisemitism, 28–29, 153–54

Apelman, Joseph S., 213, 226–27, 300n31

architecture. *See* church architecture and design

Argo, Illinois, 174, 182

automotive industry, 130, 216, 219, 223, 232, 244

Baikowsky, Nicholas, 217, 222, 227, 228, 240

Bakhmeteff, Boris, 148

Bakhmeteff, George, 101

Bakunoff, Maxim (priest), 196–97, 211

Balanovich, Evtikhy (priest), 67–68, 68, 273n37

Baltimore, Maryland, 164; Holy Resurrection parish, 175, 178; Holy Trinity parish, 175–80, 185–87

Basalyga, Basil (Benjamin) (priest and bishop), 89, 95–96, 98

battleship, Russian, 71, 274n47

308 | INDEX

Bellavin, Tikhon (bishop and patriarch). *See* Tikhon

Bensin, Basil, 93, 95, 96, 98

Bergesen, John, 101

Berlin, New Hampshire, Holy Resurrection parish in, 52, 76–82, 103

Beskishkin, Pavel (Paul) (priest), 62, 234

BI. *See* Bureau of Investigation

Black Hundreds (*chornaia sotnia*), 8, 29, 153

Bolshevism, 146, 176, 246, 248; age of, 16, 134, 216; All Saints Russian Orthodox Church and, 213–14, 222–23, 225–26, 235–40; BI investigation into, 133, 159, 164, 177, 178–83, 185–86, 213, 226, 227, 228; Bishop Alexander on, 131, 154; Church-Protecting Society and, 226, 235–36; domestic intelligence on, 133; Kamensky, A., imprisonment and, 277n17; responses against, 152–54, 155–56, 177, 277n17; *Svit* and, 152; Zeltonoga on, 186–87. *See also* Russian Revolution

Brasol, Boris, 153, 286n39

Bread and Freedom (*Khleb i Volia*) (newspaper), 179

Brooklyn, New York: Holy Trinity parish in, 101; Orphan Home in, 101; St. Mary Women's College in, 85, 104–9, *105*, 120. *See also* Holy Virgin Protection Convent

Brown, Orton, 77–82

Buketoff, Constantin (*psalomshchik* and priest), 60

Buketoff, Theofan (priest), 38, 60–62, 64, 152

Bureau of Investigation (BI): Apelman as agent with, 213, 226–27, 300n31; Bishop Alexander and, 159; Bolshevism investigation of, 133, 159, 164, 177, 178–83, 185–86, 213, 226, 227, 228; Darin and, 227–28

Cahan, Abraham, 39

Canada, 57, 148, 218

Carpatho-Rusyns, 9; Russification and, 89, 201–2, 247; *Svit* and, 149–50, 194

Catskill Aqueduct, 21–22

celibacy, 12

Cherepnin, Gabriel (*psalomshchik*), 107

Chernobaeva, Z. I., 107

Chicago, 132, 164; Holy Trinity parish, 49, 57, 65, 145, 166–69, *167*, 174; St. George parish, 168–75, 181, 188–89, 238; World's Columbian Exposition in, 58, 166

children. *See* Orphan Home

chornaia sotnia (Black Hundreds), 8, 29, 153

Chubik, Martha, 169

church architecture and design, 57, 61, 79; Greek Catholicism influence in, 87–88; of Holy Trinity in Chicago, 166–68, *167*; iconostasis, 49–50, 75, 78

churchness (*tserkovnost'*), 13

Church-Protecting Society, 224–26, 235–36, 241

Clayton, Wisconsin, 23, 63, 106

clergy: in Alaska, 8, 56, 58–59; anti-semitism of, 28; appearance of, 53–54; assimilation of, 54–55, 65; celibacy and, 12; clerical writing of, 14, 60–61, 67; homesickness of, 61, 64; kinship, 59, 60, 95; marriage and, 73–74; masculinity and, 55; ranks and ecclesiastical structures, 56; Russian clerical caste and, 59; wages of, 62, 158–59; working conditions of, 13, 54, 63–64, 81, 195–98, 218–20, 221, 227, 234–35

clergy wife (*matushka*), 75–76, *105*, 106, 108, 197, 250, 275n58, 293n8

clerical family, 60, 74–76

Cleveland, Ohio, 78, 91; All-American Church Council of 1919 in, 149, 200–201, 295n33; "Bursa" in, 92; St. Theodosius parish, 58, 77, 92

coal industry, 46–48, 127–28, 194, 205–6

Collingwood, Charles (judge), 236, 239

Colton, Ethan, 251
Committee on Public Information (CPI), 130
conciliarity (*sobornost*), 8, 141, 161–62, 164
consistory. *See* ecclesiastical consistory
Coolidge, Calvin (president), 245
CPI. *See* Committee on Public Information
Crane, Charles, 166, 169, 250–51

Dabovich, Sebastian (priest), 84, 152
Daily Free Russia (*Svobodnaia Rossiya*) (newspaper), 181, 182
Darin, Dimitri (priest), 222, 229, 231; Alaskan origins of, 220–21; BI and, 227–28; Bolshevism response from, 213–14, 223, 240; Church-Protecting Society support of, 224–26, 235–36, 241; court case against, 215, 232–38; Episcopal Church and, 302n58
Davidow, Lazarus, 226–27, 228, 300n32
Davis, Jerome P., 44–45
Debs, Eugene V., 166, 213, 222
Detroit, Michigan, 130, 243, 247; All-American Church Council of 1924 in, 244–46; All Saints Russian Orthodox Church and parish in, 132, 213–15, 216–29, 231–40, 244; House of the Masses, 222–24; Orthodox mutual-aid society brotherhoods in, *202*; RNH in, 132, 214–15, 217, 218, 226, 227, 228, 231, 235, 236, 241; Russian Consultation Bureau, 218, 226, 227; Ss. Peter and Paul parish, 1, 64, 216, 218, 246, 248; St. Michael's parish, 246, 248
Dillingham Commission, 45, 269n55
Dobrov, Gabriel, 101
Doyas, William, 177–79, 183–85

ecclesiastical awards (*tserkovnye nagrady*): *otpusk* (sabbatical), 14, 65, 73, 161; types of, 13–14
ecclesiastical consistory (*pravlenie*), 87, 103, 107, 116, 131, 140, 141, 148, 149, 150, 151, 156, 162, 169, 173, 243; BI investigation of, 159; ecclesiastical structures and, 56–57; reform efforts, 143–44; relocations of, 7, 56, 72
Ellis Island Immigration Station, 40, 52, 78; experiences at, 37–38, 51; opening of, 33; "special representatives" at, 33–34; women treatment at, 43, 268n46
emblems, of mutual-aid society brotherhoods, 11, *202*
Episcopal Church, 80–81, 200, 302n58
eugenics, 25, 33, 45, 55
Evdokim (Meschersky) (archbishop), 63, 140, 141, 173, 230, 233; arrival in Berlin, New Hampshire, 76, 79; character and reputation, 159, 288n55; delegation to Moscow led by, 142–43, 146; material struggles and, 146–48; patriotism during First World War of, 120, 122, 123; St. Mary Women's College leadership of, 106, 107
Evlogy (Georgievsky) (bishop), 62, 148

First World War: Bishop Alexander and, 112, 127–28, 156–57; federal surveillance during, 155–56, 163–64; patriotism and, 120–23, 130–32, 209; Russian war effort, 116–19, 131; United States home front, 113, 127–34; United States war effort, 111–12, 119–20, 123–24; war bonds, 128–30, 198, 226
Ford, Henry, 1, 3, 63, 153, 217, 221, 243, 244

Gary, Indiana, 62, 246; St. Mary's parish in, 49–50
Gavriloff, Paul (priest), 241
Georgievsky. *See* Evlogy
Germany, 274n51, 286n41
Goldman, Emma, 166
Golos tserkvi (*Voice of the Church*) (newspaper), 149, 151, 154, 236
Great Canon of St. Andrew of Crete, 193

310 | INDEX

Greek Catholicism: church architecture and design influenced by, 87–88; conversions to Orthodoxy, 57–58, 72, 86–87, 98–99, 201–2, 247; Orthodox Christianity differences from, 9, 99; Orthodox tensions with, 26, 91, 99, 168, 216

Gress, Katherine, 106

Gress, Nikita (priest), 63, 106

Grigorieff, Dimitry (priest), 15

Hapgood, Isabel, 94, 275n65

Haywood, "Big Bill," 166

Holy Resurrection parish: in Baltimore, Maryland, 175, 178; in Berlin, New Hampshire, 52, 76–82, 103

Holy Trinity parish: in Baltimore, Maryland, 175–80, 185–87; in Brooklyn, New York, 101; in Chicago, 49, 57, 65, 145, 166–69, *167*, 174; in Springfield, Vermont, 100, 101–2, 137–38

Holy Virgin Protection Convent (Brooklyn, New York and Springfield, Vermont), 98–100, 102, *102*, 104, 107, 137–38

Homestead, Pennsylvania, 210, 211, 221

Hoover, J. Edgar, 177, 184

Hopko, Frank, 111–12

Hotovitzky, Alexander (*psalomshchik* and priest), *68*, 180, 243, 248–49, 273n42, 305n19; arrest and imprisonment, 250–51; execution of, 252; fundraising trip to Russia, 71; immigrant labor and, 22–23, 27, 32; legacy of, 252–55; Russian Immigrant Home and, 40, 42; at St. Nicholas parish, 68–72

Hotovitzky, Maria (clergy wife), 249–51

House of the Masses, Detroit, Michigan, 222–24

icons, 32–33, 120, 267n26

Illinois, 174, 182. *See also* Chicago

immigrants: assimilation of, 25, 33, 37–39, 45, 52–53, 54–55, 119, 121, 128–29, 223–24; Hotovitzky on labor of, 22–23, 27, 32; living conditions of, 21–22, 38–39, 45–46, 50, 193–94; Roman Catholic Church outreach to, 26; United States attitudes towards, 52–53, 55; working conditions of, 26, 44–45, 47, 48. *See also* Russian Immigrant Home

immigration: Dillingham Commission and, 45, 269n55; documentation and, 31, 223; patterns of, 23–24, 29, 31–32, 42; Russian imperial policy and, 30–31, 35; United States policy and, 33, 34–36, 38, 44, 45, 119, 240, 268n46. *See also* Ellis Island Immigration Station; Russian Orthodox Immigration Society

Indiana. *See* Gary, Indiana

Industrial Workers of the World (IWW), 133, 166, 184

influenza epidemic of 1918: American Orthodox Rus' and, 192–95, 206–10; beginning and scope of, 190–91; deaths, 190–91, 296nn46–47; end of, 210–12; missionary work and, 195–98; Orthodox mutual aid and, 201–6; Orthodox practice and public health during, 198–201; ROCMAS and, 192, 201–11; *Svit* and, 182, 194–95, 296n46

Innocent (Veniaminov) (priest and bishop), 271n15

Ireland, John (archbishop), 86–87

Irvine, Ingram Nathaniel (priest), 107

IWW. *See* Industrial Workers of the World

John of Kronstadt (Ioann Sergieff) (priest), 7, 71

Judaism: Orthodox Christianity confusion with, 230; Russian Orthodox prejudices against, 28–29, 66, 152–54

Kamensky, Anatole (priest), 68, *68*, 90, 277n17
Kamensky, Joseph, 178–79, 186
Kappanadze, Jason (priest), 68, *68*
Kazansky, Paul, *68*
Kedrovsky, Benjamin (*psalomshchik* and priest), 62, 271n14
Kedrovsky, John (priest), 109, 151, 156–58
Khleb i Volia (Bread and Freedom) (newspaper), 179
Kochurov, John (priest), 65, 68, *68*, 145–46, 152, 168, 253, 285n21
Kohanik, Eugenia (clergy wife), 107
Kohanik, Peter (priest), 67, 69, 99, 207–8; background, 124; mortality policy of, *204*; as *Svit* editor, 101, 107, 124–26, 149–50
Kozarzhevsky, Andrei, 254–55
Kozitzky, John (priest), 158
Krilova, Evgenia, 107
Kropotkin, Peter, 166
Kukulevsky, Alexander (priest), 89–90, 142, 173
Kurdiumoff, Vasily (priest), 175
Kursk Root Icon, 32, 267n26

labor: actions and strikes, 47, 48, 217; Hotovitzky, A., and immigrant, 22–23, 27, 32; IWW and, 133, 166, 184; migration for, 30, 48; wages, 44, 217; working conditions, 26, 44–45, 47–48, 77, 194
Laskowski, Charles, 178
Lenin, Vladimir Ilych, 16, 213, 222, 223, 233
Leontovich, Constantin, 224–25
The Light (newspaper). See *Svit*
liturgical language, 8, 70, 83, 95
liturgical music, 87–88
lived religion, 12, 53
local church council. See *sobor*
Loss, John, 125
Lowrie, Donald, 249–51

Lupinovich, Alexander (priest), 190–91, 192–93, 201
Lupinovich, Natalia (clergy wife), 190, 192, 193, 201, 208

marriage, 13, 35, 59, 163, 243–44, 268n46; clergy and, 73–74; clergy wives and, 75–76, *105*, 106, 108, 197, 250, 275n58, 293n8
Martens, Ludwig, 181
Masculinity, 55, 90
Massachusetts, 190, 193, 201, 208–9
matuskha (clergy wife), 75–76, *105*, 106, 108, 197, 250, 275n58, 293n8. *See also specific individuals*
Mayfield, Pennsylvania, 46, 205–6, 211, 246, 296n47
Maynard, Massachusetts, 190, 193, 201, 208–9
Mescherskaia, Anna (clergy wife), *105*, 107
Meschersky, Evdokim. *See* Evdokim
Michigan. *See* Detroit
Mikhaila, Sister, 98, 100, *102*, 107
Miniewsky, Andrew, 224, 226, 241
Minneapolis, Minnesota, 57, 195; Russian Missionary School in, 88–92, 97–98; Russian Theological Seminary in, 91–98, 221; St. Mary's church buildings in, 87–88, 96–97; St. Mary's parish in, 85, 86–91, 95, 97–98, 124, 221; St. Mary's Russian Band in, *98*
Mirnoff, Thomas, 183–86
Mock, Peter, 83–84, 211
monasticism, 66, 99
mortality policies, 201, 203–5, *204*, 207–8
Moscow Patriarchate, 188, 253; restoration of, 142, 144–45; in United States, 247–48
Most Holy Synod of the Russian Orthodox Church, 7, 55, 64, 141, 142, 273n32; state involvement in, 302n53
MPUSA (Moscow Patriarchal Exarchate in USA), 247–48

312 | INDEX

Muliar, Timon (priestmonk), 174
music: Bensin and, 93; ensembles, 74, 97, 98; liturgical music, 65, 87–88
mutual-aid societies: defined, 202–3; influenza epidemic of 1918 and, 201–6; membership ribbons, 11, 202; RIMAS, 170, 174, 181; for women, 101, 296n42. *See also* Russian Orthodox Catholic Mutual Aid Society

National Fraternal Congress of America, 208
Nazis, 154, 286n39, 286n41
Nedzelnitsky, John (priest), 109
Nemolovsky, Alexander (priest and bishop). *See* Alexander
New Hampshire, Holy Resurrection parish in, 52, 76–82, 103
New Jersey, 97, 108
newspapers, 14, 28, 163
New York, tunnel building in, 21–23, 50
New York City. *See* Brooklyn, New York; St. Nicholas Cathedral and parish, New York
Nicholas (Ziorov) (bishop), 58–59, 62, 88, 91, 93, 120, 166
Nicholas II (tsar), 4, 70, 71, 79, 114, 138, 166; abdication of, 139–40, 233, 244; execution of, 160
Nikolenko, Nestor (priest), 175–79, 182
North American Ecclesiastical Consistory. *See* Russian Orthodox Greek Catholic Archdiocese of North America

Obshchestvo Russkikh Bratstv (Russian Brotherhood Organization), 202
OCA. *See* Orthodox Church in America
Ohio. *See* Cleveland, Ohio
Old Roman Catholic Church, 172, 180
Orphan Home: in Brooklyn, New York, 101; education at, 103–4; establishment of, 100; financial crisis for, 137–38; financial support of, 101, 102–3, 137–38,

141; monks role in, 100–101; in South Canaan, Pennsylvania, 100–101; in Springfield, Vermont, 85, 101–4, *102*, 137–38, 207, 297n50
Orthodox Church in America (OCA), 188, 247, 253
otpusk (sabbatical), 14, 65, 73, 161

Palmer Raids (of 1920), 185, 186, 187, 213, 232
Pashkovsky, Theophilus (bishop), 244
patriotism: American Orthodox Rus' and, 121; First World War, 120–23, 130–32, 209
Paulina, Mother (abbess), 98–100, 102, *102*, 104, 107, 137–38
Pennsylvania: Homestead, 210, 211, 221; Mayfield, 46, 205–6, 211, 246, 296n47; Wehrum, 46–47, 50; Wilkes-Barre, 191, 194, 199, 201, 203, 205. *See also* South Canaan, Pennsylvania
Peshkoff, Timothy (priest), 171–72, 174, 181, 188, 290n29
Peter I (Peter the Great) (tsar), 7
Petrine Reforms, 59, 273n32
Philippovsky, Adam (priest), 118–19
Piotrowsky, Arcady, (lay church worker and priest): as priest, 52, 76–82, 103, 112, 150, 219, 240–41; as Russian Orthodox Immigration Society representative, 34–38, 39–40, 51
Piotrowsky, Mary (clergy wife), 76
Platon (Rozhdestvensky) (archbishop), 46, 62, 66–67, 117, 144, 147, 151, 221; on Bishop Alexander, 148–49; immigrant labor and, 44; on labor and violence, 48; Russian Immigrant Home and, 40, 42
Popoff, Peter (priest), 43
pravlenie. See ecclesiastical consistory
Protestants, attitudes towards the Orthodox, 79–80
Protocols of the Elders of Zion, 153–54

psalomshchik (psalm-singer), 11, 56, 57, 59, 62, 180, 198, 221, 234. *See also specific individuals*

public health. *See* influenza epidemic

Putin, Vladimir, 247

Rasst, Leon, 176

Red Scare, 133, 138–39, 164, 176, 213, 221, 229, 232, 236, 239, 240, 300n32

Repella, Basil (priest), 106

Repella, Martha (clergy wife), 106

Retvizan (Russian battleship), 71, 274n47

ribbons, of mutual-aid society brotherhoods, 11, *202*

RIMAS. *See* Russian Independent Mutual Aid Society

The Rise of David Levinsky (Cahan), 39

RNH. *See* Russian National Home

Rockwood, H. L., 200–201

ROCMAS. *See* Russian Orthodox Catholic Mutual Aid Society

ROCOR. *See* Russian Orthodox Church Outside of Russia

Roman, Baron Rosen, 27

Roman Catholic Church: immigrant outreach of, 26; Orthodox Church differences from, 10–11, 12–13, 80, 99, 109; Russian Orthodox attitudes towards, 66; trusteeism and, 164, 229–30

Romani, 90–91

Rozhdestvensky. *See* Platon

Russian Archdiocese. *See* Russian Orthodox Greek Catholic Archdiocese of North America

Russian Brotherhood Organization (Obshchestvo Russkikh Bratstv), *202*

Russian Consultation Bureau, Detroit, Michigan, 218, 226, 227

The Russian Immigrant (newspaper). *See Russkii emigrant*

Russian Immigrant Home, 24, 43, 147, 156; advertisement for, *41*; Archbishop Platon and, 40, 42

Russian Independent Mutual Aid Society (RIMAS), 170, 174, 181

Russian Land (Russkaia zemlia) (newspaper), 43, 148, 234

Russian Metropolia, 246–47; OCA and, 188, 247, 253. *See also* Russian Orthodox Greek Catholic Archdiocese of North America

Russian Missionary School, Minneapolis, Minnesota, 88–92, 97–98

Russian National Home (RNH), 132, 214–15, 217, 218, 226, 227, 228, 231, 235, 236, 241

Russian Orphanage. *See* Orphan Home

Russian Orthodox All Saints Brotherhood, *202*

Russian Orthodox American Messenger (periodical), 6, *6*, 24, 48, 67, 102, 107, 148, 149, 251, 252; founding, 69

Russian Orthodox Catholic Mutual Aid Society (ROCMAS), 49, 50, 100, 101, 124, 169, 170, 191, 198, 200, 220; founding and mission, 201–3; influenza epidemic of 1918 and, 192, 201–11; mortality policies, 201, 203–5, *204*, 207–8. See also *Svit*

Russian Orthodox Catholic Women's Mutual Aid Society, 101, 296n42

Russian Orthodox Church Outside of Russia (ROCOR), 188, 247, 248, 253

Russian Orthodox Greek Catholic Archdiocese of North America (Russian Archdiocese): ecclesiastical consistory (*pravlenie*) of, 7, 56, 57, 72, 87, 103, 107, 116, 131, 140, 141, 143, 148, 149, 150, 151, 156, 159, 162, 169, 173, 243; ecclesiastical structures of, 55–57, 64, 142, 215, 225, 233–34; financial situation of, 137–38, 140–43, 147–48; governing statute of, 57, 164, 236, 238; self-autonomous status of, 245–46

314 | INDEX

Russian Orthodox Immigration Society, 22, 24, 27, 33, 42, 43, 158; Piotrowsky, A., as representative of, 34–38, 39–40, 51

Russian Revolution: of February 1905, 4, 10, 30, 171; of February 1917, 138, 139–40, 152, 165; of October 1917, 138, 152, 159, 180, 181, 189, 223, 236, 284n17

Russian Theological Seminary, Minneapolis, Minnesota, 91–98, 221

Russification, 89, 201–2, 247

Russkaia zemlia (*Russian Land*) (newspaper), 43, 148, 234

Russkii emigrant (*The Russian Immigrant*) (newspaper), 27, 35, 44, 48, 50, 51, 148; antisemitic content, 28–29, 153; circulation of, 29

sabbatical (*otpusk*), 14, 65, 73, 161

sacramental donations (*trebi*), 63, 175, 218–19, 220, 221, 227, 232–33

Ss. Peter and Paul parish, Detroit, Michigan, 1, 64, 216, 218, 246, 248

St. George parish, Chicago, 168–75, 181, 188–89, 238

St. Mary's Russian Orthodox Greek Catholic Church: in Gary, Indiana, 49–50; in Minneapolis, Minnesota, 85, 86–91, 95–98, *98*, 124, 221

St. Mary Women's College, Brooklyn, New York, 85, 104–9, *105*, 120

St. Michael's parish, Detroit, Michigan, 246, 248

St. Nicholas Cathedral and parish, New York, 43, 55, 57, 65, 115, 140, 243, 244, 255; construction of, 71–72, 180; Hotovitzky at, 68–72; Turkevich, L., as dean of, 107; Zotikov, at, 67–73

St. Platon Russian Theological Seminary, Tenafly, New Jersey, 97, 108

St. Theodosius parish, Cleveland, Ohio, 58, 77, 92

St. Tikhon of Zadonsk monastery, South Canaan, Pennsylvania, 99, 100, 193

Salko, Isidor (priest), 216, 218

Schmemann, Alexander (priest), 137

Second World War, 29, 247, 286n39, 286n41

Seletzky, Constantine (priest), 175–80

Semanitsky, John (priest), 123

Sergieff, Ioann (John of Kronstadt) (priest), 7, 71

Sinclair, Upton, 166

Sirotyak, Olga, 106

Skurko, Makary, 225, 233, 241

Slunin, John (priest), 32, 65–67, 243

Snegireff, Sergei (priest), 8, 116, 150–51, 157, 158

sobor (local church council): All-Russian Church Council of 1917–1918, 8, 141–46, 149, 158, 160, 165; first since seventeenth century, 141. *See also* All-American Church Council

sobornost (conciliarity), 8, 141, 161–62, 164

social estates. See *soslovie*

socialism, 222; clerical attitudes towards, 47–48; lay attitudes towards, 162

Sokolovsky-Avtomonov, Vladimir (bishop), 87

Solanka, Andrew (priest), 197

Solanka, Anna (clergy wife), 197

soslovie (social estates), clerical caste of, 59, 85, 95; defined, 8

South Canaan, Pennsylvania: Orphan Home in, 100–101; St. Tikhon of Zadonsk monastery in, 99, 100, 193

Springfield, Vermont: Holy Trinity parish in, 100, 101–2, 137–38; Orphan Home in, 85, 101–4, *102*, 137–38, 207, 297n50. *See also* Holy Virgin Protection Convent

Sullivan, Louis, 57, 145, 166–68, *167*

Sviridov, Ioann (priest), 242, 246, 247–48

Svit (The Light) (newspaper), 111, 127, 149, 151, 191, 205, 209; Bishop Alexander as editor of, 28; Bolshevism and, 152; Carpatho-Rusyns readership of, 149–50, 194; clerical writing in, 67; influenza epidemic of 1918 and, 182, 194–95, 296n46; Kohanik, P., as editor of, 101, 107, 124–26, 149–50; war bonds advertised in, 128–29

Svobodnaia Rossiya (Daily Free Russia) (newspaper), 181, 182

Swirid, Mokryna, 241–42

Syro-Arab Vicariate, 8, 57

Telep, Peter, 126

Tenafly, New Jersey, 97, 108

Theophilus (Pashkovsky) (bishop), 244

Tikhon (Bellavin) (bishop and patriarch), 27, 47, 69, 72, 84, 93, 95, 142; Bolshevism and, 152, 159; death of, 251; glorification of, 253; Orphan Home and, 100–101; patriarchal election of, 144–45; Zotikov on, 254

Timon (Muliar) (priestmonk), 174

Toth, Alexis (priest), 9, 86, 100

trebi (sacramental donations), 63, 175, 218–19, 220, 221, 227, 232–33

trusteeism, 164, 229–30

tserkovnost' (churchness), 13

tserkovnye nagrady. See ecclesiastical awards

Turkevich, Anna (women's college instructor and clergy wife), *105*, 107

Turkevich, Benedict (priest), 67, 95

Turkevich, Leonid (Leonty) (priest and bishop), 67, 94, 102, 105, 142, 144, 158–60, 243, 288n58; background, 95; blessing war ambulances, *114*, *115*; as dean of St. Nicholas Cathedral, 107; Orphan Home and, 102–3; at St. Mary's parish in Minneapolis, 95–97

United States: immigrants in, attitudes towards, 52–53, 55; immigration policy, 33, 34–36, 38, 44, 45, 119, 240, 268n46; MPUSA in, 247–48

United States, First World War and: federal surveillance and, 155–56, 163–64; home front, 113, 127–34; patriotism and, 120–23, 130–32, 209; war effort and, 111–12, 119–20, 123–24

Valhalla, New York, 21–23, 50

Veniaminov, Innocent (priest and bishop), 271n15

Vermont. *See* Springfield, Vermont

Vilatte, René (archbishop), 172, 180, 290nn28–29

Vladimir (Sokolovsky-Avtomonov) (bishop), 87

Voice of the Church (Golos tserkvi) (newspaper), 149, 151, 154, 236

Volna (The Wave) (journal), 187

Vsevolod (Andronoff) (deacon), 122

The Wave (Volna) (journal), 187

Wehrum, Pennsylvania, 46–47, 50

Whitman, West Virginia, 196–97, 211

Wilcox, T. C., 132

Wilkes-Barre, Pennsylvania, 191, 194, 199, 201, 203, 205

Wilson, Woodrow (president), 114–15, 119, 120, 130–31, 132, 157, 180

Wisconsin, 23, 63, 106

Witte, Count Sergei, 100

Wolf, Robert, 77–82

women: church service and, 10, 54, 74–75, 104; as clerical wives, 75–76, *105*, 106, 108, 197, 250, 275n58, 293n8; education of, 92, 104–10; at Ellis Island Immigration Station, 43, 268n46; at Holy Virgin Protection Convent, 98–100, 102, *102*, 104, 107, 137–38; monasticism, 98–100, 104; mutual-aid society for, 101, 296n42;

316 | INDEX

women (*cont.*)
  St. Mary Women's College for, 85,
    104–9, *105*, 120
World's Columbian Exposition (of 1893),
  Chicago, 58, 166
World War I. *See* First World War
World War II, 29, 247, 286n39, 286n41
Wright, Frank Lloyd, 168

Zaichenko, Paul, 87–88, 89, 90, 95
Zeltonoga, John (*psalomshchik* and
  priest), 180–88

Zhuk, Fyodor, 39–40
Ziorov, Nicholas (bishop), 58, 62, 88, 91,
  93, 120, 166
Zotikov, Ilia (*psalomshchik*, deacon,
  and priest), *68*, 244, 248–50, 273n37,
  273n42; arrest and imprisonment, 251,
  252, 274n51; crimes of, alleged, 304n16;
  execution of, 254; glorification of, 253;
  memorials and legacy of, 254–55; ordination of, 67–68; on Patriarch Tikhon,
  254; at St. Nicholas parish, 67–73
Zotikova, Maria (clergy wife), 67, 68, 73

ABOUT THE AUTHOR

ARAM G. SARKISIAN received his PhD in history from Northwestern University, where his dissertation was awarded the Harold Perkin Prize. A historian of religion, immigration, and labor, he has also taught at National Louis University and Washington University in St. Louis. He lives in southeastern Michigan.